INTERMEDIATE ECONOMIC ANALYSIS FOR MANAGEMENT AND ENGINEERING

PRENTICE-HALL INTERNATIONAL, INC., *London*
PRENTICE-HALL OF AUSTRALIA, PTY. LTD., *Sydney*
PRENTICE-HALL OF CANADA, LTD., *Toronto*
PRENTICE-HALL OF INDIA PRIVATE LIMITED, *New Delhi*
PRENTICE-HALL OF JAPAN, INC., *Tokyo*

INTERMEDIATE ECONOMIC ANALYSIS FOR MANAGEMENT AND ENGINEERING

John R. Canada

North Carolina State University
Raleigh, North Carolina

Prentice-Hall, Inc., Englewood Cliffs, N. J.

ISBN: 0-13-469916-5

Library of Congress Catalog Card Number 73-157658

Printed in the United States of America

To the Canada girls:

Pearle, Wanda,
Beth, Anne, and Cathy

Preface

This book has developed through long-expressed needs for a text and reference on capital project economic evaluation which is more concise and yet more advanced than the traditional applied works and which contains abundant example problems and solutions.

Besides concisely covering the basic principles of interest computations and basic analysis methods, the book extensively treats techniques for the quantitative analysis of investment problems involving risk and uncertainty. Most of these techniques are candidates for straightforward and widespread application in practice, while some are presented in the belief that they will prove valuable as progressive analysts and management personnel work to develop their usefulness.

This book is intended primarily for advanced undergraduate or graduate study and for students of all disciplines, particularly business and engineering. The concise explanatory features also make the book suitable as a reference in industry. It contains a rather succinct summary of basic capital project evaluation techniques (Part I), and emphasizes more advanced techniques, concepts, and analysis procedures (Part II).

For the use of Part I, only a knowledge of first year algebra is required, while for much of Part II, it is assumed that the student understands the basic analysis procedures of Part I and has a fair knowledge of elementary probability. Some fundamental probability concepts are explained in Appendix 10-A. However, for those with an insufficient knowledge of fundamental probability, the first half of most basic probability and statistics texts will serve as a very adequate review.

For an abbreviated first course on the fundamentals of engineering or project economy, Part I can serve as an applications-oriented text which contains essentially the same breadth of coverage as traditional undergraduate texts. The integration of project economic analysis into the larger picture of capital budgeting within the firm is accomplished in Chapter 9, which contains two excellent appendices on procedures and forms used in practice.

For a course in economic evaluation of alternative projects at the advanced undergraduate or initial graduate level, Part I can be used for review purposes as needed, with Part II providing the primary study material. The chapters in Part II are largely independent of one another, so one can include or delete chapters according to the needs of individual classes. A major exception is that the latter part of Chapter 15 on the use of Bayesian statistics draws upon foundation information in Chapter 14.

Chapter 10 introduces risk and uncertainty concepts in the context of estimating, while Chapters 11 and 12 illustrate a wide range of techniques or procedures for quantifying evaluations in the face of risk and uncertainty. Chapter 13 shows the use of Monte Carlo simulation as a computational tool, and Chapter 14 provides a rather detailed explanation of decision techniques utilizing Bayesian statistics. Chapter 15 focuses on the use of decision tree concepts as a means of taking into account future outcomes, alternatives, and decisions in determining the best initial decision. Chapter 16 explains some special analytical tools which provide power and yet ease in quantifying continuous outcome variability of one project or of multiple projects under comparison. Finally, Chapter 17 illustrates quantitative means for weighting objectives and nonmonetary factors.

Innumerable persons—friends, colleagues, and helpers—have contributed to the development of this work, so complete acknowledgement is not possible. I would particularly like to thank two former mentors, Professor H. L. Manning of Virginia Polytechnic Institute and Professor F. F. Groseclose of Georgia Institute of Technology, for the guidance, counsel, and opportunities they so capably provided during my early years of teaching and graduate study. The preparation of this work was made much more tolerable than would have otherwise been possible by the extremely competent secretarial services of Mrs. Martha Jackson and Mrs. Elaine Myers. My wife, Wanda, helped by providing encouragement and (usually) good working conditions. Mr. Matt Fox and Mr. David Ungerer of Prentice-Hall have provided an excellent professional working relationship. Dr. James R. Buck of Purdue University made highly conscientious and helpful observations. Dr. Jack Turvaville of the University of Florida and Mr. Nathan Wolf of the International Business Machines Corporation supplied valuable additions to the book. To all these, as well as to the authors and publishers providing reprint permissions, and to many others unnamed, I wish to express my gratitude.

JOHN R. CANADA

Contents

three   **Annual Worth Method**   **36**

four   **Present Worth Method**   **48**

five   **Rate of Return Method**   **60**

six   Depreciation   77

seven   Consideration of Taxes   86

eight   Replacement Analyses   99

xiv

part I

BASIC CAPITAL PROJECT EVALUATION TECHNIQUES

one

Introduction and
Cost Concepts

Project economic analysis involves techniques for comparing and deciding between alternatives on the basis of monetary or economic desirability. With the increasing complexity of our industrial technology, economic decision-making is becoming more difficult and at the same time more critical. Economic analyses serve to quantify differences between alternatives and reduce them to bases which provide for ease of project comparison. The importance of use of these methods varies with alternatives under consideration. In general, the use of these techniques is vitally important, for there is much to be saved or lost by virtue of the particular alternative chosen in usual project investment decisions. Indeed, project investment decisions are the single most important factor in determining the success or failure of a firm.

Importance of Estimates in Economic Analyses

Since economic analyses are concerned with which alternative or alternatives are best for future use, they are, by nature, based on estimates of what is to happen in the future. The most difficult part of an economic analysis is the estimating of relevant quantities for the future, for the analysis is no better than the estimates comprising it. Most estimates are based on past results, and the usual best source of information on past results is the accounting

3

records of the enterprise. Chapter 10 focuses on the vital subject of estimation in some detail.

Cost Concepts

The word *cost* has many meanings in many different settings. The kind of cost concept which should be used depends upon the business decision to be made. Financial records resulting from the firm's accounting function aim at describing what has happened in the past, whereas useful decision-making concepts of cost aim at projecting what is expected to happen in the future as a result of alternative courses of action. Indeed, different combinations of cost ingredients are appropriate for various kinds of management problems. But it should always be remembered that the viewpoints of the accountant and of the economic analyst are generally quite opposite—one is historian and the other is fortune-teller. The following sections contain descriptions of some cost concepts which are most important in the making of economic analyses.

Usual accounting classification of production costs

The accounting function of an enterprise keeps records of happenings affecting the finances of the enterprise. Accounting records of production costs normally are separated into three main categories:

1. Direct labor
2. Direct material
3. Overhead

Direct labor costs or *direct materials costs* are those labor or materials costs which can be conveniently and economically charged to products or jobs on which the costs are incurred. Examples are, respectively, the cost of a turret lathe operator and the cost of the bar stock required to produce a large number of a given part.

By contrast, indirect labor cost and indirect materials cost are those costs which cannot be conveniently and economically charged to particular products or jobs on which the costs are incurred. Examples are, respectively, the cost of a janitor serving several departments or products and the cost of tool bits used on different products. Indirect labor and indirect material costs are part of the third category, *overhead costs*, which includes all production costs other than the costs of direct labor and direct material. Examples of other types of overhead costs are power, maintenance, depreciation, insurance, etc. Overhead costs are often referred to as "indirect costs" or "burden." Ways in which overhead costs are allocated and should be taken into account in economic analyses are discussed in the Chapter 10 section on "Use of Accounting Data for Estimates."

Appendix 1-A contains a very brief exposition of accounting fundamentals for those who have had no previous exposure to the subject. While understanding of accounting fundamentals is not essential to progress in understanding the content of this book, this appendix should be useful to students with no previous exposure, at least to help provide the framework of the economic setting within which business decisions are made.

Opportunity cost

An *opportunity cost* is a cost which, though hidden or implied, is incurred because of the use of limited resources in such a manner that the chance or opportunity to use those resources to monetary advantage in some alternative use is foregone. As an example, suppose a project involves the use of firm-owned warehouse space which is presently vacant. The cost for that space which should be charged to the project in question should be the income or savings which other possible alternative uses of the space may bring to the firm. In other words, the cost for the space for purposes of an economy study should be the *opportunity cost* of the space. This may be more than or less than the average cost of that space which might be obtained from accounting records.

As another example, consider a student who could earn $5,000 for working during a year and who chooses instead to go to school and spend $2,000 to do so. The total cost of going to school for that year is $7,000: $2,000 cash outlay and $5,000 for income foregone. (*Note*: This neglects the influence of taxes, and assumes that the student has no earning capability while in school.)

Opportunity cost in determination of interest rates for economic analyses. A very important use of the opportunity cost principle is in the determination of the interest cost chargeable to a proposed capital investment project. The proper interest cost is not just the amount which would be paid for the use of borrowed money, but is rather the opportunity cost, i.e. , the return foregone or expense incurred because the money is invested in this project rather than in other possible alternative projects. Even when internally owned funds rather than borrowed funds are used for investing, the interest cost chargeable is determined by the same opportunity cost principle.

As an example, suppose a firm always has available certain investment opportunities such as expansion or bonds purchases which will earn a minimum of, say, $X\%$. This being the case, the firm would be unwise to invest in other alternative projects earning less than $X\%$. Thus, in computing the cost of various alternatives, the analyst may simply add in $X\%$ of the amount invested for each. Such a cost may be thought of as the opportunity cost of not investing in the readily available alternatives.

In economy studies, it is necessary to recognize the time value of money irrespective of how the money is obtained, whether it be through debt financing, through owners' capital supplied, or through reinvestment of earnings generated by the firm. Interest on project investments is a cost in the sense of an opportunity foregone, an economic sacrifice of a possible income that might have been obtained by investment of that same money elsewhere.

Opportunity cost in replacement analyses. As another illustration of the opportunity cost principle, suppose a firm is considering replacing an existing piece of equipment which originally cost $50,000, presently has an accounting book value of $20,000, and can be salvaged now for $5,000. For purposes of an economic analysis of whether or not to replace the existing piece of equipment, the investment in that equipment should be considered as $5,000; for by keeping the equipment, the firm is giving up the *opportunity* to obtain $5,000 from its disposal. This principle is elaborated upon in Chapter 8.

Sunk costs

Sunk costs are costs resulting from past decisions and which are therefore irrelevant to the consideration of alternative courses of action. Thus, sunk costs should *not* be considered directly in economic analyses.

As an example, suppose Joe Student finds a car he likes on a Saturday and pays $50 "down payment" which will be applied toward the $1,000 purchase price but which will be forfeited if he decides not to take the car. Over the weekend, Joe finds another car which he considers equally desirable for a purchase price of $910. For purposes of deciding which car to purchase, the $50 is a sunk cost and thus such should not enter into the decision. The decision then boils down to paying $1,000 minus $50, or $950, for the first car versus $910 for the second car.

A classical example of a sunk cost occurs in the replacement of assets. Suppose that the piece of equipment in the last section, which originally cost $50,000, presently has an accounting book value of $20,000 and can be salvaged now for $5,000. For purposes of an economic analysis, the $50,000 is actually a sunk cost. However, the viewpoint is often taken that the sunk cost should be considered to be the difference between the accounting book value and the present realizable salvage value, which is called "book loss" or "capital loss." According to this viewpoint, the sunk cost is $20,000 minus $5,000, or $15,000. Neither the $50,000 nor the $15,000 should be considered in an economic analysis, except for the manner in which the $15,000 affects income taxes, as discussed in Chapter 8.

Postponable cost

A *postponable cost* is a cost which can be avoided or delayed for some period of time. As an example, the costs of certain types of maintenance or of personnel for certain planning functions may be postponable, while the cost of direct labor is unavoidable or not postponable if production is to continue.

Replacement cost

Replacement cost is, as the name implies, the cost of replacing an item. It is important to economic analyses because replacement cost rather than historical original cost is the relevant cost factor for most economic decisions. For example, if a storekeeper has been stocking an item costing him $8 and selling that item for $12, and the price to the storekeeper for replacing the item is suddenly increased to $14, then the selling price should be raised to at least $14 before he buys any additional units of that item.

Fixed costs vs. incremental costs

In most any change which is subject to an economic analysis (like buying a new machine, changing volume of production, etc.), some costs are affected and other costs are not affected. Those costs which are not affected by the change (i.e., remain constant) are often referred to as *fixed costs* while those costs which are affected by the change are referred to as *incremental costs*. These terms are often used to describe costs for different volumes of production. When it is desired to describe changes in costs for a small change in volume of production, the terms "differential" and "marginal" are often used in place of "incremental."

If one is making an economic analysis of a proposed change, it can be remembered that only the incremental costs need be considered, since only prospective differences between alternatives need be taken into account.

Cash costs vs. book costs

Costs which involve payments of cash or increases in liability are called *cash costs* to distinguish them from noncash (*book*) costs. Other common terms for cash costs are "out-of-pocket costs" or costs which are "cash flows." Book costs are costs which do not involve cash payments, but rather represent the amortization of past expenditures for items of lengthy durability. The most common examples of book costs are depreciation and depletion charges for the use of assets such as plant and equipment. In economic analyses, only those costs need be considered which are cash flows or potential cash flows. Depreciation, for example, is not a cash flow and is important only in the way it affects income taxes, which are cash flows.

Cost Factors

In an economic analysis, a listing of main factors which may be relevant for each project under consideration is as follows:

Investment (all nonrecurring costs of purchase, shipment, and installation)

Economic life

Salvage value (net after costs of dismantling)

Annual revenue or savings

Annual expenditures:

   Direct labor

   Direct material

   Indirect labor

   Indirect material

   Taxes

   Insurance

   Maintenance

   Power

   Supplies

   Space

Other opportunities foregone

A more complete listing of cost factors, as well as nonmonetary factors, is given in Table 17-A-1 (in Appendix 17-A).

Objectives of Firm and Nonmonetary Factors

While the primary concern of this book is techniques for considering economic or monetary desirability, it should be recognized that the usual decision between alternatives involves many factors other than those which can be reasonably reduced to monetary terms. For example, a limited listing of objectives other than profit maximization or cost minimization which may be important to a firm are

Minimization of risk of loss

Maximization of safety

Maximization of sales

Maximization of service quality

Minimization of cyclic fluctuation of firm

Minimization of cyclic fluctuation of economy

Maximization of well-being of employees

Creation or maintenance of a desired public image

Economic analyses provide only for the consideration of those objectives or factors which can be reduced to monetary terms. The results of these analyses should be weighed together with other nonmonetary (irreducible) objectives or factors before a final decision can be made. Techniques for weighting objectives and nonmonetary as well as monetary factors are given in Chapter 17.

The Role of the Engineer and Manager
in Economic Decision-making

Economic analyses and decisions between alternatives can be made by the engineer considering alternatives in his design of equipment, facilities, or man-machine systems. However, the decisions are more commonly made by a manager acting upon a number of investment opportunities and alternatives within each opportunity. Whenever the alternatives involve technical considerations, the engineer serves to provide estimates and judgment for the analyses upon which the final managerial decision can be made.

Scope and Importance

All analysis procedures covered in Chapters 2 through 8 are based on single estimates or amounts for each of the variable quantities considered. That is, if an analysis involves estimates of project investment, life, salvage value, operating expenses, etc., only single estimates for each are made even though it is recognized that each of the estimates may be subject to considerable variation or error. Analyses under these conditions are often called "assumed certainty" analyses. Part II, beginning with Chapter 10, will show methods which explicitly consider the variation in estimated quantities and incorporate many refinements for rational economic analyses.

Regardless of who performs economic analyses or who makes the final investment decisions, the proper performance of these functions is critical to the economic progress of our country and of the world, as well as to the economic health or even survival of the individual firm. Business decisions frequently involve investments which must be planned and executed many years before the expected returns will be realized. Moreover, the scale of the investments in research and capital assets which are required for our expanding economy grows increasingly larger as new technologies develop. Hence, knowledge of the principles and techniques underlying economic analyses is extremely important.

PROBLEMS

1-1. A supplier purchased an Ajax charger five years ago for $5,000, intending to sell it at its usual markup for $5,800.

Before they were able to obtain delivery, a competitor brought out a radically new charger for the same type of service, better in every way, but selling at a retail price of only $3,000. As a result, the Ajax charger has been a white elephant in the supplier's hands—it is a large piece of obsolete equipment that has been occupying valuable floor space which is now vitally needed.

In discussing what to do, two members of the firm find themselves in disagreement. The president feels that the charger should be kept unless the $5,000 purchase price is realized on the sale. The accountant feels that the equipment should not be sold unless both the $5,000 cost and $500 cost of storage to date can be realized.

Which course of action would you recommend? Why?

1-2. Smith purchased his house several years ago for $20,000, and was just offered $25,000 cash for it. Smith and his family had not been planning to sell and move, even though they are willing to do so. A neighborhood economist has correctly computed that the pretax annual rate of profit on the cash Smith has invested in the house would be 45%, and on this basis he recommends that Smith sell the house. What additional information does Smith need to make a decision? What irrelevant information was given?

1-3. A merchant has been attempting to maintain his stock of goods at a constant physical volume even though prices have been rising. His stock of one item was originally purchased for $10 per unit. He sold these goods at $16 per unit (applying his usual markup) and immediately replaced them by identical ones purchased at the new wholesale price of $18 per unit. What do you think of the profitableness of this transaction?

1-4. Certain factory space cost $10.00 per square foot to build and is estimated to have an economic life of 25 years and 0 salvage value. The minimum attractive rate of return on invested capital is 10%. The annual out-of-pocket cost of property taxes, heat, lights, and maintenance is $0.50 per square foot whether or not the space is being used. What should be the cost per square foot considered in an economic analysis of a certain new project A which entails proposed use of that space under each of the following conditions?

  a. The space is now being used for another project B which will have to be moved to new quarters costing $2.00 per square foot per year.
  b. The space is idle and there is no alternative use of it expected for the entire period in which the project under consideration would exist.
  c. The space is part of a large area which is used normally; hence, it is thought reasonable to charge only long-run average costs.

APPENDIX 1-A

Accounting Fundamentals

This section contains an extremely brief and simplified exposition of the elements of accounting in recording and summarizing transactions affecting the finances of the enterprise. These fundamentals apply to any entity (such as an individual, corporation, governmental unit, etc.), called here just a "firm."

All accounting is based on the so-called *fundamental accounting equation*, which is

$$\text{Assets} = \text{Liabilities} + \text{Ownership} \qquad \text{(1-A-1)}$$

where "Assets" are those things of monetary value which the firm *possesses*, "Liabilities" are those things of monetary value which the firm *owes*, and "Ownership" is the worth of what the firm *owns* (also referred to as "equity," "net worth," etc.).

The fundamental accounting equation defines the format of the *balance sheet*, which is one of the two most common accounting statements, and which shows the financial position of the firm *at any given point in time.*

Another important, and rather obvious, accounting relationship is

$$\text{Revenue} - \text{Expenses} = \text{Profit (or Loss).} \qquad \text{(1-A-2)}$$

This relationship defines the format of the *income statement* (also commonly known as "profit-and-loss statement"), which summarizes the revenue and expense results of operations *over a period of time.*

It is useful to note that a revenue serves to increase the ownership amount for a firm, while an expense serves to decrease the ownership amount for a firm.

To illustrate the workings of accounts in reflecting the decisions and actions of a firm, suppose you decide to undertake an investment opportunity and that the following sequence of events occurs over a period of a year.

1. Organize a firm and invest $3,000 cash as capital.
2. Purchase equipment for a total cost of $2,000 by paying cash.
3. Borrow $1,500 through note to bank.
4. Manufacture year's supply of inventory through the following:
   a. Pay $1,200 cash for labor.
   b. Incur $400 account payable for material.
   c. Recognize the partial loss in value (depreciation) of the equipment amounting to $500.
5. Sell on credit all goods produced for year, 1,000 units at $3.00 each. Recognize that the accounting value of these goods is $2,100, resulting in an increase in equity (through profits) of $900.
6. Collect $2,200 of account receivable.
7. Pay $400 account payable and $1,000 of bank note.

A simplified version of the accounting entries recording the same information in a format that reflects the effects on the fundamental accounting equation (with a "+" denoting an increase and a "−" denoting a decrease) is shown in Table 1-A-1.

Table 1-A-1

ACCOUNTING EFFECTS OF TRANSACTIONS

	Account	Transaction 1	2	3	4	5	6	7	Balances at end of year
ASSETS {	Cash	+$3,000	−$2,000	+$1,500	−$1,200		+$2,200	−$1,400	+$2,100
	Account receivable					+$3,000	−$2,200		+$ 800
	Inventory				+$2,100	−$2,100			0
	Equipment		+$2,000		−$ 500				+$1,500
equals LIABILITIES {	Account payable				+$ 400			−$ 400	
plus	Bank note			+$1,500				−$1,000	+$ 500
OWNERSHIP {	Equity	+$3,000				+$ 900			+$3,900

A balance sheet at the end of the year of enterprise operation would appear as follows:

Your Firm
Balance sheet as of end of year _____

Assets		*Liabilities and Ownership*	
Cash:	$2,100	Bank note:	$ 500
Accounts receivable:	800		
Equipment:	1,500	Equity:	3,900
Total:	$4,400	Total:	$4,400

An income statement is not so directly determinable from the above simplified format as was the balance sheet. In this case, the statement for the year would appear as follows:

Your Firm
Income statement for year ending _____

Operating revenues (Sales):		$3,000
Operating costs (Inventory depleted):		
Labor:	$1,200	
Material:	400	
Depreciation:	500	
		$2,100
Net income (Profits):		$ 900

It should be noted that the profit for a period serves to increase the value of the ownership in the firm by that amount. Also, it is worth noting that the net cash flow of $1,400 (= $3,000 — $1,200 — $400) is not all profit. This was recognized in transaction 4c, in which a capital consumption for equipment of $500 was declared. Thus, the profit was $900, or $500 less than the net cash flow.

two

Computations
Involving Interest

Introduction

Just as the spacing of forces is a primary consideration in mechanics, the spacing of cash flows (receipts and disbursements) is important in economic analyses. The timing of cash flows influences what is termed "the time value of money." Because of the opportunities for investing money and increasing its value, a sum of money today is worth more than the same amount at some time in the future. Failure to consider the effect of timing of money involved in investment alternatives may yield poor investment decisions.

Equivalence

An item of money (single sum or uniform series) has an infinite range of equivalent and potential values over time, although it can have actual existence at only one point in time. Thus, to have precise meaning, an item of money must be identified in terms of timing as well as of amount. For purposes of definition, two amounts of money or series of monies at different

14

points in time are said to be equivalent if they are equal to each other at some point in time at a given interest rate. This chapter deals with the use of interest formulas for equivalence conversions.

Interest Calculations

Interest calculations may be based on interest rates which are either *simple* or *compound*.

Simple interest

Whenever the interest charge for any period is based on the principal amount only and not also on any accumulated interest charges, the interest is said to be *simple*. Calculations involving simple interest may be performed utilizing the following formula:

$$I = P \times s \times N$$

where P = Amount borrowed (invested)
   s = Simple interest rate
   N = Number of periods before repayment (withdrawal)

Example:
   A man borrows $1,000 at a simple interest rate of 6% per yr and wishes to repay the principal and interest at the end of 3 years. How much does he repay?
Solution:

$$I = P \times s \times N$$
$$I = (\$1,000)(0.06)(3)$$
$$I = \$180$$

Therefore, he repays $1,000 + $180 = $1,180 in 3 years.

Compound interest

Whenever the interest charge for any interest period is based on the remaining principal amount plus any accumulated interest charges up to the beginning of that period, the interest is said to be *compound*. To illustrate the effect of compounding, the following example is given.

Example:
   A man borrows $1,000 at a compound interest rate of 6% per yr and wishes to repay the principal and interest in 3 years. How much does he repay?

Solution:

Year	Amount owed at beginning of year	Interest charge for year	Amount owed at end of year
1	$1,000.00	$1,000.00 × 0.06 = $60.00	$1,060.00
2	1,060.00	1,060.00 × 0.06 = 63.60	1,123.60
3	1,123.60	1,123.60 × 0.06 = 67.42	1,191.02

Thus, $1,192.02 is repaid. The difference between this and the $1,180 answer in the previous example utilizing simple interest is due to the effect of compounding of interest over the 3 years.

Compound Interest Formulas

Compound interest is much more often encountered in practice than is simple interest. Hence, compound interest will be used throughout this book unless otherwise stated. Basic compound interest formulas and tables assuming discrete (lump sum) payments and discrete interest periods are discussed below.

Notation and cash flow diagram

The following notation is used throughout this book for compound interest calculations:

i = Effective interest rate per interest period

N = Number of compounding periods

P = Present sum of money
   (the equivalent worth of one or more cash flows at a relative point in time called the present)

F = Future sum of money
   (the equivalent worth of one or more cash flows at a relative point in time called the future)

A = End-of-period cash flows (or equivalent end-of-period values) in a uniform series continuing for a specified number of periods

and

G = Uniform period-by-period increase or decrease in cash flows or amounts (the arithmetic gradient)

The use of cash flow diagrams is strongly recommended for most problems, at least whenever the analyst desires to visualize the cash flow situation. Whenever some distinction between types of cash flows seems desirable, it is recommended to use an upward arrow for a cash inflow and a downward arrow for a cash outflow.

Interest Formulas Relating Present and Future Sums

Figure 2-1 shows a time diagram involving a present single sum P and a future single sum F separated by N periods with interest at $i\%$ per period. Two formulas relative to those sums are presented below.

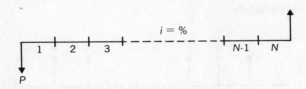

Figure 2-1. Time diagram for single sums.

Find F when given P

If P dollars are deposited now in an account earning $i\%$ per period, the account will grow to $P(1 + i)$ by the end of one period; by the end of two periods, the account will be $P(1 + i)(1 + i) = P(1 + i)^2$; and by the end of N periods, the account will have grown to a future sum F, as given by

$$F = P(1 + i)^N \tag{2-1}$$

where the quantity $(1 + i)^N$, designated (F/P), is tabled in Appendix A-A for numerous values of i and N. Symbolically, we shall use the notation

$$F = P(F/P, i\%, N) \tag{2-2}$$

where the factor in parentheses denotes the unknown and known, the interest rate, and the number of periods, respectively.

Find P when given F

The reciprocal of the relationship between P and F, from above, is given mathematically as

$$P = F\left(\frac{1}{1 + i}\right)^N \tag{2-3}$$

where the quantity $1/[(1 + i)]^N$ is tabled in Appendix A-A. Symbolically,

$$P = F(P/F, i\%, N) \tag{2-4}$$

Interest Formulas Relating Uniform Series of Payments to Their Present Worth and Future Worth

Figure 2-2 shows a time diagram involving a series of uniform cash flows of amount A occurring at the end of each period for N periods with interest at $i\%$ per period. As depicted in Fig. 2-2, the formulas and tables below are derived such that

※ 1. P occurs one interest period before the first A; and
2. F occurs at the same point in time as the last A, and
   N periods after P.

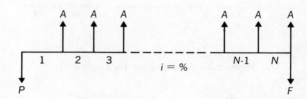

Figure 2-2. Time diagram for uniform series.

Four formulas relating A to F and P are given below.

Find F when given A

If A dollars is deposited at the end of each period for N periods in an account earning $i\%$ per period, the future sum F accrued at the end of the Nth period is

$$F = A[1 + (1 + i) + (1 + i)^2 + \cdots + (1 + i)^{N-1}]$$

It can be shown that this reduces to

$$F = A\left[\frac{(1 + i)^N - 1}{i}\right] \tag{2-5}$$

where the quantity $\{[(1 + i)^N - 1]/i\}$ is tabled in Appendix A-A. Symbolically,

$$F = A(F/A, i\%, N) \tag{2-6}$$

Find A when given F

The reciprocal of the relationship between A and F, from above, is given mathematically as

$$A = F\left[\frac{i}{(1+i)^N - 1}\right] \qquad (2\text{-}7)$$

where the quantity $\{i/[(1+i)^N - 1]\}$ is tabled in Appendix A-A. Symbolically,

$$A = F(A/F, i\%, N) \qquad (2\text{-}8)$$

Find *P* when given *A*

If we take the relation

$$F = A\left[\frac{(1+i)^N - 1}{i}\right]$$

and substitute

$$F = P(1+i)^N$$

then we find that

$$P = A\left[\frac{(1+i)^N - 1}{i}\right]\left[\frac{1}{1+i}\right]^N$$

which simplifies to

$$P = A\left[\frac{(1+i)^N - 1}{i(1+i)^N}\right] \qquad (2\text{-}9)$$

The factor in the brackets is tabled in Appendix A-A. Symbolically,

$$P = A(P/A, i\%, N) \qquad (2\text{-}10)$$

Find *A* when given *P*

The reciprocal of the relationship between *A* and *P*, from above, is given mathematically as

$$A = P\left[\frac{i(1+i)^N}{(1+i)^N - 1}\right] \qquad (2\text{-}11)$$

Again, the factor in brackets is tabled in Appendix A-A. Symbolically,

$$A = P(A/P, i\%, N) \qquad (2\text{-}12)$$

A summary of the formulas and their symbols, together with example problems, is given in Table 2-1. The two symbol systems shown, functional and mnemonic, are those officially recommended by the Engineering Economy Division of the American Society for Engineering Education. The functional-symbol system will be used throughout this book.

It should be noted that for all problems in this book involving uniform series, end-of-year payments are assumed unless stated otherwise.

Table 2-1

SUMMARIZATION OF DISCRETE COMPOUND INTEREST FACTORS AND SYMBOLS

To find	Given	Multiply "Given" by factor below	Factor name	Factor functional symbol	Factor mnemonic symbol	Example (answer for $i = 5\%$) (Note: All uniform series problems assume end of period payments.)
F	P	$(1+i)^N$	Single sum compound amount	F/P	CA	A firm borrows $1,000 for 5 years. How much must it repay in a lump sum at the end of the fifth year? Ans.: $1,276
P	F	$\dfrac{1}{(1+i)^N}$	Single sum present worth	P/F	PW	A company desires to have $1,000 8 years from now. What amount is needed now to provide for it? Ans.: $676.84
P	A	$\dfrac{(1+i)^N - 1}{i(1+i)^N}$	Uniform series present worth	P/A	SPW	How much should be deposited in a fund to provide for 5 annual withdrawals at $100? Ans.: $432.95
A	P	$\dfrac{i(1+i)^N}{(1+i)^N - 1}$	Capital recovery	A/P	CR	What is the size of 10 equal annual payments to repay a loan of $1,000? First payment 1 year after receiving loan. Ans. $129.50
F	A	$\dfrac{(1+i)^N - 1}{i}$	Uniform series compound amount	F/A	SCA	If 4 annual deposits of $2,000 each are placed in an account, how much money has accumulated immediately after the last deposit? Ans.: $8,620
A	F	$\dfrac{i}{(1+i)^N - 1}$	Sinking fund	A/F	SF	How much should be deposited each year in an account in order to accumulate $10,000 at the time of the fifth annual deposit? Ans.: $1,809.70

Key: i = Interest rate per interest period
N = Number of interest periods

A = Uniform series amount
F = Future worth

P = Present worth

Interest Factor Relationships

The following relationships exist among the six basic interest factors:

$$(P/F,i\%,N) = \frac{1}{(F/P,i\%,N)} \tag{2-13}$$

$$(A/P,i\%,N) = \frac{1}{(P/A,i\%,N)} \tag{2-14}$$

$$(A/F,i\%,N) = \frac{1}{(F/A,i\%,N)} \tag{2-15}$$

$$(A/P,i\%,N) = i\% + (A/F,i\%,N) \tag{2-16}$$

$$(F/A,i\%,N) = (P/A,i\%,N)(F/P,i\%,N) \tag{2-17}$$

$$(P/A,i\%,N) = \sum_{j=1}^{N} (P/F,i\%,j) \tag{2-18}$$

$$(F/A,i\%,N) = \sum_{j=0}^{N-1} (F/P,i\%,j) \tag{2-19}$$

Interest Formulas for Uniform Gradient Series

Some economic analysis problems involve receipts or disbursements that are projected to increase by a constant amount each period. For example, maintenance and repair expenses on specific equipment may increase by a relatively constant amount of change, G, each period.

Figure 2-3 is a cash flow diagram of a series of end-of-period disbursements increasing at the constant amount of change, G dollars per period. For convenience in derivation of the formulas it is assumed that a series of uniform payments of amount G is started at the end of the second period, another series of amount G is started at the end of the third period, and so on. Each of these series terminates at the same time, the end of the Nth period. The future sum (at the end of the Nth period) equivalent to the gradient series shown in Fig. 2-3 is

$$F = G[(F/A,i,N-1) + (F/A,i,N-2) + \cdots + (F/A,i,2) + (F/A,i,1)]$$

$$= \frac{G}{i}[(1+i)^{N-1} + (1+i)^{N-2} + \cdots + (1+i)^2 + (1+i) - (N-1)]$$

$$= \frac{G}{i}[(1+i)^{N-1} + (1+i)^{N-2} + \cdots + (1+i)^2 + (1+i) + 1] - \frac{NG}{i}$$

The expression in the brackets reduces to

$$\frac{(1+i)^N - 1}{i} = (F/A,i,N)$$

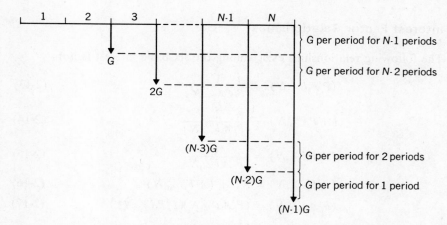

Figure 2-3. Cash flow diagram for uniform gradient of G dollars per period.

Hence,

$$F = \frac{G}{i}\left[\frac{(1+i)^N - 1}{i} - N\right] \qquad (2\text{-}20)$$

The equivalent uniform annual worth of the gradient series may be found by multiplying the above sum of compound amounts by $(A/F,i,N)$. Hence,

$$A = F(A/F,i,N)$$
$$= \frac{G}{i}\left[\frac{(1+i)^N - 1}{i} - N\right]\left[\frac{i}{(1+i)^N - 1}\right]$$
$$= \frac{G}{i} - \frac{NG}{i}\left[\frac{i}{(1+i)^N - 1}\right]$$
$$= G\left\{\frac{1}{i} - \left[\frac{N}{(1+i)^N - 1}\right]\right\} \qquad (2\text{-}21)$$

The factor in the braces is given in Table A-A-17 for a wide range of i and N. Symbolically, the relationship to find the uniform series equivalent to the gradient series is

$$A = G(A/G, i,N) \qquad (2\text{-}22)$$

SOLVED PROBLEMS

1. Mr. Smith loans Mr. Brown \$5,000 with an interest rate of 5% compounded annually. How much will Mr. Brown pay Mr. Smith if he repays at the end of 5 years?

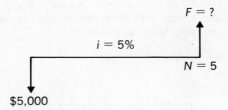

Since the problem is of the form "Find F when given P," the formula to use is

$$F = P(F/P,5\%,5)$$
$$= \$5,000(1.276) = \$6,380$$

2. Mr. Thomas wishes to accumulate \$10,000 in a savings account in 10 years. If the bank pays 5% compounded annually on deposits of this size, how much should Mr. Thomas deposit in the account?

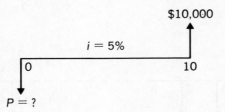

This problem is of the form "Find P when given F," and the formula to use is

$$P = F(P/F,5\%,10)$$
$$= \$10,000(0.6139) = \$6,139$$

3. A man deposits a sum of money in an account which earns interest at a rate of 4% compounded annually. He plans to withdraw \$2,000 a year from the account for 4 years, with the first withdrawal occurring 1 year after the deposit. How much should he deposit so that his fourth withdrawal just depletes the account?

$$P = A(P/A,4\%,4)$$
$$= \$2,000(3.630) = \$7,260$$

4. A man borrows $10,000 at 6% compounded annually. If he repays the loan in ten annual payments, what will be the size of the payments if the first payment is made 1 year after borrowing the money?

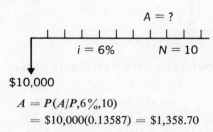

$$A = P(A/P,6\%,10)$$
$$= \$10,000(0.13587) = \$1,358.70$$

5. Depositing $400 per year in an account for 15 years, when the account pays 5% compounded annually, provides an accumulation of how much money at the time of the fifteenth deposit?

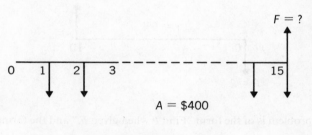

$$F = A(F/A,5\%,15)$$
$$= \$400(21.579) = \$8,631.60$$

6. How much must be deposited annually in an account which pays 4% compounded annually to accumulate $5,000 at the time of the tenth deposit?

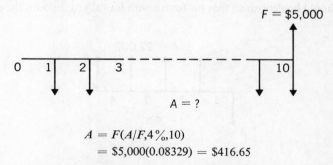

$$A = F(A/F,4\%,10)$$
$$= \$5,000(0.08329) = \$416.65$$

7. It is expected that a machine will incur operating costs of $4,000 the first year and that these costs will increase $500 each year thereafter for the 10-year life

of the machine. If money is worth 15% per year to the firm, what is the equivalent annual worth of the operating costs?

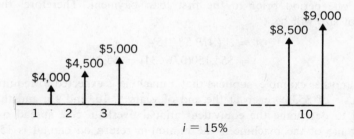

The problem reduces to a constant $4,000 per year plus the $500 gradient:

$$A = \$4,000 + G(A/G,i,N)$$
$$= 4,000 + \$500(A/G,15\%,10)$$
$$= 4,000 + \$500(3.38) = \$5,690$$

Deferred Uniform Payments

Frequently, uniform payments occur at points in time such that more than one interest formula must be applied in order to obtain the desired answer. For example, suppose a man borrows $50,000 to purchase a small business, and he does not wish to begin repaying the loan until the end of the third year after he purchases the business. With an interest rate of 5% compounded annually, it is desired to determine the amount of his annual payment if he makes 15 payments.

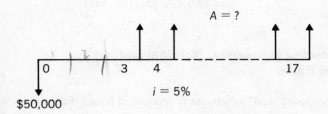

From the cash flow diagram it is apparent that direct use of the formula "Find A when given P" is not possible, since P does not occur one period prior to the first A. However, the problem can be logically solved in two steps. First, the amount of the loan, plus interest, after 2 years is

$$F_2 = P(F/P,5\%,2)$$
$$= \$50,000(1.103) = \$55,150$$

Note the use of the subscript to denote the point in time. The direct use of $A = P(A/P,i\%,N)$ is now possible, since the amount to be repaid ($55,150) occurs one period prior to the first loan payment. Therefore, the loan payment size will be

$$A = P_2(A/P,5\%,15)$$
$$= \$55,150(0.09634) = \$5,313$$

As another example, suppose that a machine is expected to require overhaul costs of $5,000 each at the end of years 5, 10, and 15, and that it is desired to determine the equivalent annual overhaul cost spread over the 25-year life of the machine if the minimum return on capital is 15% per year.

While the three payments of $5,000 each constitute a uniform series, it should be recognized that interest is compounded annually, while the payments are less often. One way to adjust for this is to find the equivalent annual worth of $5,000 at the end of each 5-year period as

$$A = F(A/F,15\%,5)$$
$$= \$5,000(0.14832) = \$742$$

Thus, $742 at the end of each year for 15 years is equivalent to the $5,000 payments at the end of each fifth year. The present worth of the $742 payments is

$$P = A(P/A,15\%,15)$$
$$= \$742(5.847) = \$4,338$$

and the equivalent annual worth over the 25-year life is

$$A = P(A/P,15\%,25)$$
$$= \$4,338(0.1547) = \$671$$

Compounding Frequency; Nominal and Effective Rates

In most economy studies, interest is accounted for as if compounding occurs once a year. In practice, the interest accumulation may take place more frequently, so it is important to note the effects of compounding frequency and to treat properly those problems where the assumption of annual compounding is not appropriate.

As an example, an interest rate may be stated as 12% compounded quarterly. In this case, the 12% is understood to be an annual rate, and is called the nominal interest rate. The number of compounding periods in a year is four. Hence, the interest rate per interest period is $12\%/4 = 3\%$ per quarter. The effective interest rate is the exact annual rate which takes into account the compounding which occurs within the year. The following formula may be used to calculate the effective interest rate:

$$\text{Effective rate} = (1 + r/M)^M - 1 \qquad (2\text{-}23)$$

where M = Number of interest periods per year
r = Nominal interest rate

Recalling that $(1 + r/M)^M$ is the single sum compound amount factor, the effective interest rate may be determined directly from the interest tables using the relation

$$\text{Effective rate} = (F/P, r/M, M) - 1 \qquad (2\text{-}24)$$

Hence, for our example, the effective rate is $(F/P, 3\%, 4) - 1 = 12.6\%$.

The effective interest rate under continuous compounding can be determined from Eq. (2-23) by letting M, the number of interest periods per year, become infinitely large. Thus, the effective rate of interest when it is compounded continuously is $e^r - 1$, where e is the base of the Naperian or natural logarithms and equals 2.7183. As an example, the effective rate of 12% compounded continuously is $e^{0.12} - 1 = 12.7 + \%$.

The effect of compounding frequency on the effective interest rate for a nominal rate of 12% is given in Table 2-2.

Table 2-2

IMPACT OF COMPOUNDING FREQUENCY UPON EFFECTIVE INTEREST RATE

Frequency of compounding	No. of compounding periods per year	For a nominal rate of 12%	
		Interest rate per period	Effective rate
Annual	1	12%	12.0%
Semiannual	2	6	12.4
Quarterly	4	3	12.6
Monthly	12	1	12.7
Continuously	$\longrightarrow \infty$	$\longrightarrow 0$	12.7+

Continuous Compounding Interest Formulas

In some instances, particularly when payments are flowing rather frequently within periods rather than at the beginning or end of periods, the additional theoretical accuracy of continuous compounding may be significant. Continuous compounding means that the interest or profit growth is proportional to the amount of total principal and interest at each instant.

To find the future worth of a present single sum under continuous compounding, one need only substitute r/M for i in the corresponding discrete compounding Eq. (2-1). Thus,

$$F = P(1 + r/M)^{MN} = P\left[\left(1 + \frac{1}{M/r}\right)^{M/r}\right]^{rN} \tag{2-25}$$

Letting M approach infinity, the relationship reduces to

$$F = Pe^{rN} \tag{2-26}$$

To find the present worth of a single sum under continuous compounding, the above equation can be transposed to

$$P = Fe^{-rN} \tag{2-27}$$

As an example, the future worth of a present amount of \$10,000 at 20% nominal interest compounded continuously for 5 years is $\$10,000e^{0.20(5)} = \$27,183$.

The effective rate of interest in this case can be calculated as $e^r - 1 = e^{0.20} - 1 = 22.2\%$.

We can find that the future worth of the same \$10,000 at effective interest of 22.2% compounded at the end of each year for 5 years is

$$F = P(F/P,22.2\%,5) = \$10,000(1 + 0.222)^5 = \$27,183$$

 This illustrates the general principle that continuous compounding at a given nominal interest rate is equivalent to discrete annual compounding at the corresponding effective rate for continuous compounding.

Continuous Payments Throughout the Year

If \$1.00 is received or disbursed continuously throughout the year at the nominal rate r or effective rate i, it can be shown that the present worth of that \$1.00 is

$$P = \frac{e^r - 1}{re^r} = \frac{i(1 + i)^{-1}}{\ln(1 + i)} \tag{2-28}$$

This is commonly known as the continuous compounding present worth factor. Symbolically,

$$P = \bar{F}(P/\bar{F},i\%,1) \tag{2-29}$$

where $\bar{F}$ is the annual amount spread uniformly over a year. Table 2-3 provides a tabulation of these factors for a wide range of effective interest rates.

To illustrate the use of Eq. (2-29), the present worth of an annual continuous flow income of \$20,000 with interest at a nominal rate of 15%, which is an effective rate of 16.2% under continuous compounding, is

$$P = \$20,000(P/\bar{F},16.2\%,1)$$
$$= \$20,000(0.9284) = \$18,568$$

Table 2-3

CONTINUOUS COMPOUNDING PRESENT WORTH FACTOR (PRESENT WORTH AT BEGINNING OF YEAR OF UNIFORM CONTINUOUS PAYMENT AT RATE OF $1.00 PER YEAR THROUGHOUT YEAR)

$$(P/\bar{F}, i\%, 1) = \frac{i(1 + i)^{-1}}{\ln (1 + i)}$$

Effective annual interest rate i	*Factor*	*Effective annual interest rate* i	*Factor*
$\frac{1}{2}\%$	0.9957	10%	0.9538
1	0.9950	12	0.9454
2	0.9902	15	0.9333
3	0.9854	20	0.9141
4	0.9806	25	0.8963
5	0.9760	30	0.8796
6	0.9714	40	0.8491
8	0.9625	50	0.8221

If it were desired to determine the present worth or future worth of annual payments flowing continuously over a period of years, one need only to convert the continuous flows to discrete annual flows using the relation above and then use the appropriate discrete compounding formula for the corresponding effective interest rate. For example, suppose it were desired to find the present worth of $20,000 per yr flowing continuously over a period of 10 years with interest at 15% nominal compounded continuously. From the example above, the $20,000 per yr flowing continuously for 10 years is the same as $18,568 at the beginning of each year for 10 years. The effective rate of 15% nominal compounded continuously is 16.2%. Thus, the total present worth of the $20,000 flowing continuously for 10 years is

$$P = \$18,568 + \$18,568(P/A, 16.2\%, 9)$$
$$= \$18,568 + \$18,568(4.95) = \$110,400$$

SOLVED PROBLEMS

1. Mr. Gould makes six end-of-year deposits of $1,000 in an account which pays 5% compounded annually. If he withdraws the accumulated fund 4 years after the last deposit, how much money will be withdrawn?

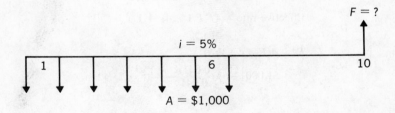

Since F does not occur at the time of the last A, it is necessary that the solution proceed in two steps. The amount of money in the account at the time of the last deposit may be computed as

$$F_6 = A(F/A,5\%,6)$$
$$= \$1,000(6.802) = \$6,802$$

The problem now is to find F_{10}, given $F_6 = P_6 = \$6,802$

$$F_{10} = P_6(F/P,5\%,4)$$
$$= \$6,802(1.216) = \$8,270$$

2. What is the effective interest rate for 4.75% compounded annually and 4.60% compounded quarterly?

$$\text{Effective rate} = (1 + r/M)^M - 1$$
$$= (1 + 0.0475)^1 - 1$$
$$= 4.75\%$$

$$\text{Effective rate} = (1 + r/M)^M - 1$$
$$= \left[1 + \frac{0.046}{4}\right]^4 - 1$$
$$= 4.68\%$$

3. A loan company advertises that it will loan \$1,000 to be repaid in 30 monthly installments of \$47.78. What is the effective interest rate?

$$A = P(A/P,i\%,30)$$

$$\frac{\$47.78}{\$1,000.00} = (A/P,i\%,30)$$

By inspection (with interpolation in tables), $i = 2\frac{1}{2}\%$, and

$$\text{Effective rate} = (F/P,2\tfrac{1}{2}\%,12) - 1 = 0.345 = 34.5\%$$

4. Mr. Wilson makes annual deposits of \$1,000 in an account which pays 4% compounded quarterly. How much money should be in the account immediately after the fifth deposit?

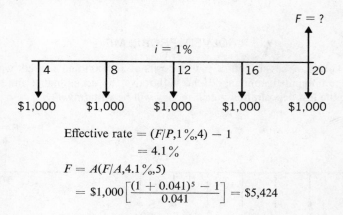

$$\text{Effective rate} = (F/P,1\%,4) - 1$$
$$= 4.1\%$$

$$F = A(F/A,4.1\%,5)$$
$$= \$1,000\left[\frac{(1 + 0.041)^5 - 1}{0.041}\right] = \$5,424$$

An alternate solution method is to treat the five annual deposits as single sums of money. Therefore,

$$F = \$1,000[(F/P,1\%,16) + (F/P,1\%,12) + (F/P,1\%,8) + (F/P,1\%,4) + 1]$$
$$= \$1,000[1.173 + 1.127 + 1.083 + 1.041 + 1.000] = \$5,424$$

5. Given the payments shown in the cash flow diagram, what is the equivalent worth at 1969 with interest at 6%?

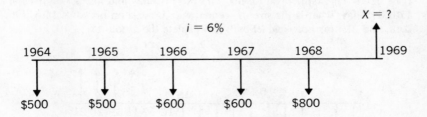

$$X = [\$500(F/A,6\%,5) + \$100(F/A,6\%,3) + \$200](F/P,6\%,1)$$
$$= [\$500(5.637) + \$100(3.184) + \$200](1.060) = \$3,537$$

6. With interest at 5% compounded annually, how long does it take for a certain amount to double in magnitude?

$$2 = 1(F/P,5\%,N)$$
$$(F/P,5\%,N) = 2.00$$

By inspection of 5% interest tables, 14 years $< N <$ 15 years.

7. Joe Doaks approaches the Loan Shark Agency for $1,000 which he wishes to repay in 24 monthly installments. The agency advertises interest at $1\frac{1}{2}\%$ per month. They proceed to calculate the size of his payment in the following manner:

Amount requested:	$1,000
Credit investigation:	25
Credit risk insurance:	5
Total:	$1,030

Interest:	$(1030)(24)(0.015) = \$371$
Total owed:	$\$1,030 + \$371 = \$1,401$
Payment:	$\dfrac{\$1,401}{24} = \$58.50$

What effective interest rate is Mr. Doaks paying?

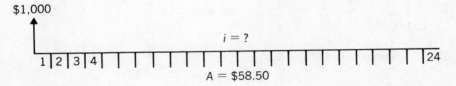

$$A = P(A/P,i\%,24)$$
$$\$58.50 = \$1,000(A/P,i\%,24)$$

By interpolation in tables, $i = 2.9\%$ per month, and

Effective rate $= (F/P,2.9\%,12) - 1 = 1.41 - 1 = 41\%$

8. A man wishes to set aside money for his son's college expenses. He makes annual deposits of \$1,000 in a fund which pays 5% compounded annually. If he makes his first deposit on his son's 5th birthday and his last on his son's 15th birthday, what is the size of 4 equal withdrawals on his son's 18th, 19th, 20th, and 21st birthdays which will just deplete the account?

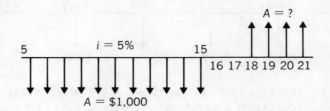

Amount in fund at $t = 15$:

$$F_{15} = A(F/A,5\%,11)$$
$$= \$1,000(14.207) = \$14,207$$

Amount in fund at $t = 17$:

$$F_{17} = P_{15}(F/P,5\%,2)$$
$$= \$14,207(1.103) = \$15,650$$

Amount of withdrawals:

$$A = P_{17}(A/P,5\%,4)$$
$$= \$15,650(0.28201) = \$4,410$$

9. A college student borrows money in his senior year to buy a car. He defers payments for 6 months and makes 36 beginning-of-month payments thereafter. If the original note is for \$3,000 and interest is $\frac{1}{2}\%$ per month on the unpaid balance, how much will his payments be?

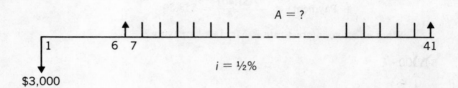

Amount owed at $t = 5$:

$$F_5 = P_0(F/P,\tfrac{1}{2}\%,5)$$
$$= \$3,000(1.025) = \$3,075$$

Amount of monthly payments:

$$A = P_5(A/P, \tfrac{1}{2}\%, 36)$$
$$= \$3,075 \left[\frac{i(1 + i)^N}{(1 + i)^N - 1} \right]$$
$$= \$3,075 \left[\frac{(0.005)(1.005)^{36}}{(1.005)^{36} - 1} \right] = \$93.50$$

10. What is the present worth of $100,000 ten years hence if interest is (a) 15% compounded annually? (b) 15% compounded continuously?
    a. $P = F(P/A, 15\%, 10) = \$100,000(0.2472) = \$24,720$
    b. $P = Fe^{-rN} = \$100,000 e^{-0.15(10)} = \$22,300$

11. What is the worth at the end of 10 years of $10,000 per year deposited continuously over the first 7 years with an effective annual interest rate of 20%?

$$P = \bar{F}(P/\bar{F}, 20\%, 1)$$
$$= \$10,000(0.9141) = \$9,141$$

at the beginning of each year for 7 years.

$$F_{10} = A(F/A, 20\%, 7)(F/P, 20\%, 4)$$
$$= \$9,141(12.916)(2.074) = \$245,000.$$

PROBLEMS

2-1. Mrs. Rudolph purchased a refrigerator which cost $500. She decided to use the store's revolving charge account to pay for the refrigerator. The store charges 2% on the unpaid monthly balance. If Mrs. Rudolph agrees to pay for the refrigerator in 30 months, what will be the size of her monthly payments?

2-2. How much money today is equivalent to $1,000 in 5 years, with interest of 4% compounded annually?

2-3. One thousand dollars today is worth $1,967 in 10 years at what annual interest rate?

2-4. How much money today is equivalent to $5,000 in 10 years, with an interest rate of 6% compounded semiannually?

2-5. How much money should be placed in a fund today and every year thereafter to accumulate $3,500 in 5 years? (Assume an interest rate of 5% compounded annually and the $3,500 includes the deposit made at the end of the fifth year.)

2-6. Borrowing $1,000 today at 8% compounded quarterly necessitates repaying how much in 3 years?

2-7. How many monthly payments are necessary to repay a loan of $5,000 with an interest rate of 1% per month and payments of $235.35? (The first payment is made 1 month after receipt of the $5,000.)

2-8. What interest rate makes an investment of $1,000 today equivalent to five annual withdrawals of $400 each with the first $400 occurring 6 years from now?

2-9. What is the effective interest rate for 6% compounded (a) annually? (b) semiannually? (c) monthly? (d) continuously?

2-10. A man borrows $6,000 at 6% compounded annually. He plans to pay off the loan in annual installments over a 5-year period. If he makes three annual payments and elects to pay off the balance of the loan at the end of the fourth year, how much should he repay at that time?

2-11. A man borrows $3,000 to pay for an automobile. He wishes to pay for the car with 36 equal monthly payments. The loan agency advertises that they charge "$\frac{1}{2}$% per month" and compute the interest charge using the simple interest formula:

$$I = P \times s \times N$$

$$= (\$3,000)(0.005)(36) = \$540$$

The interest is added to the principal and the sum is divided by 36 to determine the monthly payment amount of $98.33. What will be the effective interest rate for this method of financing?

2-12. Mr. Jefferson borrows $5,000 for 3 years. The interest rate was given as 6% compounded annually. The amount of interest was computed as follows:

$$\text{Interest} = F - P$$

$$= P(F/P,6\%,3) - P$$

$$= \$5,000(1.191 - 1.000)$$

$$= \$955$$

The interest was deducted from the principal and Mr. Jefferson was given $4,045 with the instruction to repay $5,000 in 3 years. What was the effective interest rate?

2-13. A company purchased a machine tool for $5,000, kept it for 6 years, and sold it for $500. The company spent $400 a year in maintenance and operating expenses for the machine. What annual cost for the 6-year period would be equivalent to the expenditures with an interest rate of 5% compounded annually?

2-14. A person deposits $1,000 in an account each year for 5 years; at the end of 5 years, one-half of the account balance is withdrawn; $2,000 is deposited annually for 5 more years, with the total balance withdrawn at the end of the fifteenth year. If the account earns interest at a rate of 5%, how much is withdrawn (a) at the end of 5 years? (b) at the end of 15 years?

2-15. A man purchases a piece of equipment for $5,000 and uses it for 5 years, at which time he sells it for $400. With an interest rate of 6%, convert the cash flows to an equivalent uniform annual cost. Designating the purchase price P and the salvage (resale) value F, show that the equivalent uniform annual cost may be determined using either

$$(P - F)(A/P,i\%,N) + F(i)$$

or

$$(P - F)(A/F,i\%,N) + P(i)$$

2-16. Given the cash flow diagram shown below and an interest rate of 8% per period, solve for the value of an equivalent amount at (a) $t = 5$, (b) $t = 12$, (c) $t = 15$. (*Note:* Upward arrows represent cash inflows and downward arrows represent cash outflows.)

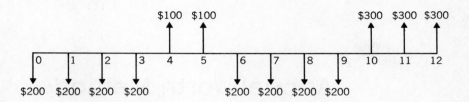

2-17. A firm borrows $80,000 at 6% compounded monthly. If they repay the loan in monthly installments over a 10-year period, what should be the size of their monthly payment?

2-18. Mr. Jones receives an annual bonus from his employer which he wishes to deposit in a fund which pays interest at a rate of 4% compounded annually. His first bonus is $1,000. The size of the bonus is expected to increase at a rate of $50 each year thereafter. Suppose Mr. Jones follows his initial plan and makes 10 deposits. (a) What will be the size of his last deposit? (b) How much money will be in the fund after making the tenth deposit?

2-19. Revenues from a certain project are expected to be $20,000 at the end of the first year and to decrease at the rate of $1,000 per year through the 15-year life of the project. If interest is 20%, (a) what is the equivalent annual worth of those revenues? (b) what is the equivalent present worth?

2-20. What is the equivalent worth at the end of 6 years of a present expenditure of $5,000 if interest is 25% nominal compounded continuously?

2-21. What is the present worth of operating expenditures of $100,000 per yr which are assumed to be incurred continuously throughout an 8-year period if the effective annual rate of interest is 12%?

2-22. What is the equivalent present worth of $1,000 obligations at the beginning of each year for 5 years if interest is 9.53% nominal, compounded continuously; i.e., the effective rate is 10%?

three

Annual Worth Method

This chapter and the two following explain three common methods for studying the economic desirability of a project or for comparing the relative economic desirabilities of two or more projects. These methods are as follows.

1. Annual worth
2. Present worth
3. Rate of return

The first two of these methods involve calculations using the minimum attractive rate of return as an interest rate. The last method involves calculating a rate of return and comparing this with the minimum attractive rate of return.

The term *annual worth* (A.W.) means a uniform annual series of money for a certain period of time which is equivalent in amount to a particular schedule of receipts and/or disbursements under consideration. If disbursements only are considered, the term is usually expressed as annual cost (A.C.)

Calculation of Capital Recovery Cost

The *capital recovery cost* (C.R.) for a project is the equivalent uniform annual cost of the capital invested. It is an annual amount which covers the following two items:

36

1. Depreciation (loss in value of the asset)
2. Interest (minimum attractive rate of return) on invested capital

As an example, consider a machine or other asset which will cost $10,000, last 5 years, and then have a salvage value of $2,000. Further, the interest on invested capital, i, is 8%.

It can be shown that no matter which method of calculating depreciation is used, the equivalent annual cost of the capital recovery is the same. For example, if straight line depreciation is used, the equivalent annual cost of interest is calculated to be $563 as shown in Table 3-1. The annual depreciation cost by the straight line method is ($10,000 − $2,000)/5 = $1,600. The $563 added to $1,600 results in a calculated capital recovery cost of $2,163.

Table 3-1

CALCULATION OF EQUIVALENT ANNUAL COST OF INTEREST
ASSUMING STRAIGHT LINE DEPRECIATION

Year	Investment at beginning of year	Interest on beginning-of-year investment @8%	Present worth of interest @8%	
1	$10,000	$800	$800(P/F,8%,1) =	$745
2	8,400	672	672(P/F,8%,2) =	576
3	6,800	544	544(P/F,8%,3) =	432
4	5,200	416	416(P/F,8%,4) =	306
5	3,600	288	288(P/F,8%,5) =	196
			Total:	$2,255

Annual equivalent of interest = $2,255(A/P,8%,5) = $563

There are several convenient formulas by which capital recovery cost may be calculated in order to obtain the same answer as above. The most apparent formula is (using the same figures as for the machine above)

$$\text{C.R.} = P(A/P,i\%,N) - F(A/F,i\%,N)$$
$$= \$10,000(A/P,8\%,5) - \$2,000(A/F,8\%,5)$$
$$= \$10,000(0.250) - \$2,000(0.170) = \$2,163$$

Two other convenient formulas for calculating the capital recovery cost are

$$\text{C.R.} = P(i\%) + (P - F)(A/F,i\%,N)$$
$$= P(0.08) + (P - F)(A/F,8\%,5)$$
$$= \$10,000(0.08) + \$8,000(0.17) = \$2,163$$

and

$$\text{C.R.} = (P - F)(A/P,i\%,N) + F(i\%)$$
$$= (P - F)(A/P,8\%,5) + F(8\%)$$
$$= \$8,000(0.250) + \$2,000(8\%) = \$2,163$$

The last of the above formulas will be used for the calculation of capital recovery cost throughout the rest of this book.

Net Annual Worth (Net A.W.) for Single Project

Example:

Suppose that the project for which capital recovery cost was calculated above is expected to involve total cash receipts of $5,000 per yr and cash disbursements of $2,200 per yr for the 5-year life and it is desired to determine if the project seems justified by the net annual worth method. (Keep in mind that the interest on invested capital was 8%.)

Solution:

Annual receipts:		$5,000
Annual disbursements:	−$2,200	
C.R. Cost = ($10,000 − $2,000)(A/P,8%,5) + $2,000(8%):	−$2,170	
		−4,370
Net A.W.:		$ 630

Since the net annual worth is greater than 0, this means that the project can be expected to earn more than the interest rate used, 8%. The $630 can be regarded as an annual amount over and above the 8% on invested capital that the project is expected to earn.

Comparing Projects When Receipts and Disbursements are Known

When receipts as well as disbursements figures for more than one mutually exclusive project are known, that project should be chosen which has the highest net annual worth, as long as that net annual worth is greater than zero.

As an example, consider the following two alternative lathes, only one of which should be selected, if any.

Example:

	Lathe	
	A	*B*
First cost:	$10,000	$15,000
Life:	5 yr	10 yr
Salvage value:	$2,000	0
Annual receipts:	$5,000	$7,000
Annual disbursements:	$2,200	$4,300
Minimum attractive rate of return = 8%		

Solution:

	Project	
	A	B
Annual receipts:	$5,000	$7,000
Annual disbursements:	−$2,200	−$4,300
C.R. Cost = $8,000($A/P$,8%,5)		
+ $2,000(8%):	−$2,170	$15,000($A/P$,8%,10): −$2,220
Net A.W.:	$ 630	$ 480

Thus project A, having the higher net annual worth, is the better economic choice.

Comparing Projects When Receipts are Constant or Not Known

Very often alternative projects are expected to perform almost identical functions and thus each results in the same receipts, savings, or benefits. Sometimes these savings or benefits are intangible or cannot be estimated, and hence the alternatives are judged on the basis of negative net annual worth, which can be more easily described as annual cost. As an example, consider the following alternative compressors, each of which will do the desired job but which differ as shown.

Example:

	Compressor	
	I	II
First cost:	$3,000	$4,000
Life:	6 yr	9 yr
Salvage value:	$500	0
Annual operating disbursements:	$2,000	$1,600
Minimum return on investment = 15%		

Solution:

	Compressor	
	I	II
C.R. Cost = ($3,000 − $500)($A/P$,15%,6) + $500(15%):	−$ 735	
C.R. Cost = $4,000($A/P$,15%,9):		−$ 840
Annual operating disbursements:	−$2,000	−$1,600
Net A.W.:	−$2,735	−$2,440

Thus, compressor II, having the lower annual cost (least negative annual worth), is apparently the more economic choice. It should be noted that this analysis of competing alternatives with different lives makes certain assumptions which will be discussed later in this chapter.

Annual Worth Comparisons for More Than Two Alternatives

If more than two alternatives are to be compared by this method, the procedure for calculation for each project and also the criteria for choice are the same as illustrated above for two projects.

Calculating Annual Worths When Annual Receipts and/or Disbursements are Irregular

The above examples each involved annual receipts and disbursements which were constant throughout the respective project lives. If either or both were irregular rather than a uniform series, they could be converted into equivalent uniform annual amounts by ordinary interest computations. The most common means of computing is to find the equivalent worth at some base time (such as present worth) and then convert this directly into the annual amount.

Example:

A project will have receipts of $5,000, $7,000, and $3,000 at the end of the first, second, and third years, respectively. If interest is 20%, what is the equivalent uniform annual worth of the receipts?

Solution:

Present worth $= \$5,000(P/F,20\%,1) + \$7,000(P/F,20\%,2) + \$3,000(P/F,20\%,3)$

$\qquad\qquad\quad = \$5,000(0.8333) + \$7,000(0.6944) + \$3,000(0.5787) = \$10,770$

A.W. $= \$10,770(A/P,20\%,3) = \$10,770(0.4747) = \$5,100$

Assumptions in Comparisons of Alternatives With Different Lives

In the comparison of projects A and B and also the comparison of compressors I and II, the alternatives compared had different expected lives. The solutions as shown are fully valid only if the following conditions are reasonable:

1. The period of needed service for which the alternatives are being compared is either indefinite or a length of time equal to a common multiple of the lives of the alternatives.

2. What is estimated to happen in the first life cycle will happen in all succeeding life cycles, if any.

These assumptions are usually made in economic analyses by default; i.e., they are made because there is no good basis for estimates to the contrary. They are implicitly contained in all examples and problems illustrating all methods of economic evaluations herein unless there is a statement to the contrary.

Applied to the earlier example in which the compressors were compared, these conditions mean the following:

1. The services of a compressor will be needed either 18 years, 36 years, 54 years, etc., or indefinitely.
2. When either compressor I or II is replaced at the end of a life cycle, it will be replaced with a compressor having characteristics affecting cost (i.e., first cost, life, salvage value, and annual operating disbursements) which are identical to the estimates used for the first life cycle.

Whenever alternatives to be compared have different lives and one or both of the conditions is not appropriate, then it is necessary to enumerate what receipts and what disbursements are expected to happen at what points in time for each alternative for as long as service will be needed or the irregularity is expected to exist. This enumerated information can then be converted into an equivalent annual worth by ordinary money–interest computations.

Example:

Suppose that for the compressor illustration above, it is expected that the standard assumptions are not met as follows: (a) a compressor is needed for only 12 years; (b) the replacement for compressor II is expected to cost $7,000 rather than $4,000, and its salvage value after 3 years' service (end of the twelfth year of study) is expected to be $200. Compare the two compressors by the annual cost method.

Solution:

The annual cost (A.C.) for compressor I remains the same at $2,735. For compressor II, the cash flow diagram and solution are

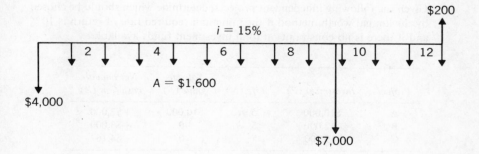

$i = 15\%$

$A = \$1,600$

$\$200$

$\$4,000$

$\$7,000$

A.C. = [$4,000 + $7,000(P/F,15\%,9) - $200(P/F,15\%,12)](A/P,15\%,12) + $1,600
     = [$4,000 + $7,000(0.2843) - $200(0.1869)](0.18448) + $1,600 = $2,650

Thus, under the changed conditions, compressor II is still the least costly, but by less margin.

Capital Recovery Cost for Investment With Perpetual Life

Sometimes projects involve investments which are expected to provide useful service for an indefinitely long period, or perpetually. Examples might be a roadbed or a concrete dam. If the annual cost of capital recovery (i.e., depreciation and interest) is desired for such a project, all that has to be done is to multiply the investment amount by the annual interest rate, since the annual depreciation cost is nil when the life is infinite.

Example:
A dam costing $10,000,000 is expected to last perpetually. If interest on this money is 5%, what is the annual cost of capital recovery?
Solution:

$$\text{C.R.} = \$10,000,000(A/P,5\%,\infty) = \$10,000,000(5\%) = \$500,000$$

Non-Mutually Exclusive (Independent) Alternatives

All previous examples of the comparison of projects in this chapter assume that the alternatives are mutually exclusive, i.e., that the choice of one project excludes the choice of any other project so that at most one project under consideration will be chosen. The annual worth method can also be used for the comparison of non-mutually exclusive (independent) alternatives, in which any number of projects may be chosen so long as sufficient capital is available.

Example:
Given the following independent projects, determine which should be chosen by the annual worth method if the minimum required rate of return is 10% and if there is no constraint on total investment funds available:

Project	Investment (P)	Life (N)	Salvage value (F)	Net annual cash flow (A)
A	$10,000	5 yr	$10,000	+$2,000
B	12,000	5	0	+$3,000
C	15,000	5	0	+$4,167

Solution:

Project	Net annual cash flow (A)	Annual cost of capital recovery $(P - F)(A/P,10\%,5) + F(10\%)$	Net annual worth (Net A.W.)
A	+$2,000	$1,000	+$1,000
B	+$3,000	$3,170	-$170
C	+$4,167	$3,950	+$217

Thus, projects A and C, having positive net annual worths, would be satisfactory for investment, but project B would not be satisfactory.

PROBLEMS

3-1. Two manufacturing methods have been proposed for a new production requirement. One method involves two general-purpose machines that cost $15,000 each, installed, each of which will produce 10 pieces per hr and will require a man costing $3.00 per hr during operation. The other method requires a special-purpose machine costing $45,000 which will produce 20 pieces per hr and will require a man costing $2.50 per hr during operation. Both types of machines are expected to last 10 years and have 0 salvage value. Other relevant data is:

	General-purpose machine (each)	Special-purpose machine
Power cost per hr:	$0.25	$0.40
Fixed maintenance per yr:	$350.00	$500.00
Variable maintenance per hr:	$0.15	$0.10
Insurance and floor space per yr:	$1,800.00	$2,200.00

a. If the expected output is 20,000 pieces per yr and the minimum before-tax rate of return is 20%, which method has the lower total annual cost?

b. At what annual output rate would one be indifferent between the two methods?

3-2. A large firm employing 20,000 workers is considering the use of a comprehensive aptitude test to help fit new employees into the proper jobs. It is estimated that these tests will reduce annual turnover from 30% (6,000 replacements) to 25% (5,000 replacements). The proposed new test will cost $10,500 annually to administer plus $5.00 in services foregone for each new employee who takes the test. The cost of hiring and training each new employee is estimated at $55.00. Assume that turnover is reduced to 5,000 replacements as soon as the testing is initiated. Compare the annual costs of testing vs. not testing.

3-3. For the past 10 years a city has spent an average of $2,500 per yr to maintain a certain section of pavement on one of its main streets. A politician claimed that the city could have had a new pavement for less than was paid for repairs on the old one. A conservative estimate indicated that the new paving could have been installed 10 years ago for a total cost of $20,000, which could have been financed by equal annual amortization payments over 10 years at 5% interest. The annual cost of maintenance of the new paving would have been $400. By comparison of total annual costs, determine if the politician's claim is a correct statement.

3-4. A certain electric motor-driven pumping plant has a capacity of 2,500 gal per min operating against a 132-ft head. The plant operates full load 4,000 hr per yr at 80% overall efficiency, i.e., from electric input to water delivered to the pond. It also operates at half-load 3,760 hr per yr at 60% efficiency. Water weighs 8.34 lb/gal and 44,254 foot-pounds/minute = 1 kilowatt. Relevant cost data is as follows:

First cost installed:	$5,500
Annual fixed charges for depreciation, interest, and maintenance (% of first cost):	15%
Average cost for electricity:	1.4¢/kwhr

Determine (a) the total annual cost of operating the plant; (b) the average cost per 1,000 gal pumped.

3-5. It is desired to determine the most economic thickness of insulation for a large cold-storage room. Insulation is expected to cost $150 per 1,000 sq ft of wall area per in. of thickness installed and to require annual property taxes and insurance of 5% of first cost. It is expected to have 0 net salvage value after a 20-year life. The following are estimates of the heat loss per 1,000 sq ft of wall area for several thicknesses:

Insulation, in.	Heat loss, Btu per hr
3	4,400
4	3,400
5	2,800
6	2,400
7	2,000
8	1,800

The cost of heat removal is estimated at $0.01 per 1,000 Btu per hr. The minimum required yield on investment is 20%. Assuming continuous operation throughout the year, which thickness is the most economic?

3-6. Alternative methods I and II are proposed for a plant operation. The following is comparative information:

	Method I	*Method II*
Initial investment:	$10,000	$40,000
Life:	5 yr	10 yr
Salvage value:	$1,000	$5,000
Annual disbursements		
Labor:	$12,000	$4,000
Power:	$250	$300
Rent:	$1,000	$500
Maintenance:	$500	$200
Property taxes and insurance:	$400	$2,000

All other expenses are equal for the two methods and the income from the operation is not affected by the choice. If the minimum attractive rate of return is 20%, which is the better choice using the annual worth method?

3-7. Compare the total annual costs of two temporary structures that will be retired at the end of 10 years. One has a negative net salvage value. Assume the minimum attractive rate of return $= 8\%$, and that estimates are as follows:

	Structure A	*Structure B*
First cost:	$14,000	$20,000
Net salvage value:	3,000	−1,000
Annual maintenance and property taxes:	1,500	700

3-8. A proposed material for covering the roof of a building will have an estimated life of 10 years and will cost $5,000. A heavier grade of this roofing material will cost $800 more but will have estimated life of 15 years. Installation costs for either material will be $1,300. Compare the annual costs using a minimum attractive return of 10%.

3-9. A small tractor is required for snow removal. It can be purchased for $3,000 and is expected to have a $500 salvage value at the end of its economic life of 5 years. Its annual operating cost is $1,000 and maintenance will be $300 the first year and increase by $100 per yr. If the minimum attractive rate of return is 10%, and if a contractor will provide this service for $2,000 per yr, which alternative has lower total annual costs?

3-10. Compare the annual costs of pumps A and B for a 15-year service life using an interest rate of 10%.

	Pump A	Pump B
First cost:	$3,500	$5,000
Estimated salvage value:	0	2,000
Annual pumping cost:	450	300
Annual repair cost:	150	80

3-11. It is desired to determine the optimal height for a proposed building which is expected to last 40 years and then be demolished at zero salvage. The following is pertinent data:

	\			
	2	3	4	5
Building first cost:	$200,000	$250,000	$320,000	$400,000
Annual revenue:	40,000	60,000	85,000	100,000
Annual cash disbursements:	15,000	25,000	25,000	45,000

Number of floors

In addition to the building first cost, the land requires an investment of $50,000 and is expected to retain that value throughout the life period. If the minimum required rate of return is 15%, show which height, if any, should be built based on annual worth comparisons.

3-12. A company requires automobiles for its salesmen. As a matter of prestige the president has decided that salesmen should not drive automobiles more than 3 years old. Automobiles can be purchased for $2,400 and will have a salvage value of $800 at the end of 3 years. The annual operating cost is estimated at $600 including maintenance, servicing, and insurance. The same automobile can be rented for $1,200 per year also including maintenance, servicing, and insurance. If the company's minimum acceptable return is 15%, which alternative should be selected using the annual worth method?

3-13. Two alternative machines will produce the same product, but one will produce higher-quality items which can be expected to return greater revenue. Given the following data, determine which machine is better using the annual worth method and a minimum required rate of return of 15%.

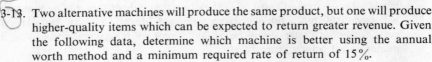

	Machine A	Machine B
First cost:	$20,000	$25,000
Life:	10 yr	8 yr
Salvage value:	$2,000	0
Annual receipts:	$150,000	$180,000
Annual disbursements:	$138,000	$170,000

3-14. A manufacturing process can be designed for varying degrees of automation. The minimum required rate of return is 20%. Which degree should be selected if the economic life is 5 years and the salvage value is 0? Use the annual cost method.

Degree	First cost	Annual labor cost	Annual power and maint. cost
A	$10,000	$7,000	$ 500
B	17,500	5,500	650
C	30,000	3,500	870
D	50,000	2,000	1,100

3-15. The Ajax Taxi Company desires to determine the best type of car to use as taxis. They find that a higher-priced car attracts more customers and is less expensive to maintain than a lower-priced car. The following is estimated data based on an economic life of 3 years.

Car	First cost	Salvage value	Annual oper. & maint. cost	Annual revenue
A	$2,000	$ 800	$1,030	$ 8,400
B	2,600	1,000	950	8,700
C	3,100	1,200	940	9,400
D	4,200	1,350	860	10,500
E	6,000	2,000	700	11,400

If the minimum required rate of return is 20%, which car is most desirable based on an annual worth analysis?

four

Present Worth Method

The *present worth* (P.W.) method is the second common method for comparing alternative projects. The term *present worth* means an amount at some beginning or base time which is equivalent to a particular schedule of receipts and/or disbursements under consideration. If disbursements only are considered, the term can be best expressed as *present worth–cost*.

Determining the Economic Desirability of an Individual Project

As long as annual cash inflow figures are known, the question of whether a given individual project is economically satisfactory can be determined by the present worth method. The decision criterion is that a project is desirable as long as its net present worth is greater than zero. As an example, consider the same single project illustrated in the last chapter.

Example:

First cost:	$10,000
Project life:	5 yr
Salvage value:	$2,000
Annual receipts:	$5,000
Annual disbursements:	$2,200
Minimum rate of return:	8%

48

Solution:

	Present worth
Annual receipts = $5,000(P/A,8%,5)$:	$19,950
Salvage value = $2,000(P/F,8%,5)$:	1,340
Total P.W. of cash inflow:	$21,290
Annual disbursements = $2,200(P/A,8%,5)$:	− 8,750
First cost:	− 10,000
Total P.W. of cash outflow:	−$18,750
Net P.W. (Inflow − Outflow):	$ 2,540

Thus, the project is shown to be favorable by the present worth method.

Study Period in Comparisons of Alternative Projects

In comparing alternatives by the present worth method, it is essential that all alternatives be considered over the same length of time. If the alternatives each have the same expected life, there is no problem, for that life can be used. When the alternatives have different expected lives, it is common to use a study period equal to the lowest common multiple of the lives, or the length of time during which the services of the chosen alternative will be needed, whichever is less. For example, if two alternatives have expected lives of 3 and 4 years respectively, then the lowest common multiple of the lives to use as a study period is 12 years. However, if the service for which the alternatives are being compared is expected to be needed for only 9 years, then 9 years should be the study period used.

Comparing Projects When Receipts and Disbursements are Known

When receipts (cash inflow) as well as disbursements (cash outflow) figures for more than one mutually exclusive project are known, that project should be chosen which has the highest net present worth, as long as that present worth is greater than zero. As an example, consider the same two alternative lathes A and B that were compared in the last chapter:

Example:

	Lathe	
	A	*B*
First cost:	$10,000	$15,000
Life:	5 yr	10 yr
Salvage value:	$2,000	0
Annual receipts:	$5,000	$7,000
Annual disbursements:	$2,200	$4,300
Minimum attractive rate of return $= 8\%$		

Solution:

The lowest common multiple of the lives is 10 years. Making the usual assumptions that the service will be needed for at least that long and that what is estimated to happen in the first 5 years for project A will be repeated in the second 5 years, the solution is

	Lathe	
	A	*B*
Annual receipts $= \$5,000(P/A,8\%,10)$:	$33,600	
$7,000(P/A,8\%,10)$:		$47,000
Salvage value at year $10 = \$2,000(P/F,8\%,10)$:	925	
Total P.W. of cash inflow:	$34,525	$47,000
Annual disbursements $= \$2,200(P/A,8\%,10)$:	$-$14,800	
$4,300(P/A,8\%,10)$:		$-$28,900
First cost:	$-$ 10,000	$-$ 15,000
Replacement $= (\$10,000 - \$2,000)(P/F,8\%,5)$:	$-$ 5,440	
Total P.W. of cash outflow:	$-$30,240	$-$43,900
Net P.W.:	$ 4,285	$ 3,100

Thus, project A, having the highest net present worth which is greater than zero, is the better economic choice.

Comparing Projects When Receipts are Constant or Not Known

When alternatives which perform essentially identical services involve only known cash outflows, it is possible to compare the alternatives on the basis of present worth–cost. The method of study is the same as illustrated for the example above except, of course, the choice criterion is that the alternative with the lowest present worth–cost is best. As an example, consider the same two compressors that were compared in the last chapter.

Example:

	Compressor	
	I	II
First cost:	$3,000	$4,000
Life:	6 yr	9 yr
Salvage value:	$500	0
Annual operating disbursements:	$2,000	$1,600
Minimum return on investment = 15%		

Solution:

(Lowest common multiple of lives is 18 years):

	Present worth–cost Compressor	
	I	II
First cost:	$ 3,000	$ 4,000
First replacement = ($3,000 − $500)($P/F$,15%,6):	1,080	
$4,000($P/F$,15%,9):		1,138
Second replacement = ($3,000 − $500)($P/F$,15%,12):	468	
Operating disbursements = $2,000($P/A$,15%,18):	12,225	
$1,600($P/A$,15%,18):		9,800
Less Salvage value @18 = $500($P/F$,15%18):	− 41	
Net P.W.–cost:	$ 16,732	$ 14,938

Capitalized Worth Method

One special variation of the present worth method is to find the worth of all receipts and/or disbursements for a perpetual length of time. This is known as the *capitalized worth* (C. W.) method. If disbursements only are considered, results obtained by this method can be more appropriately expressed as *capitalized cost*. This is a convenient basis for comparison when the period of needed service is indefinite or when the common multiple of the lives is very long and the cash inflows and outflows follow a uniform pattern so that they can be easily considered.

The capitalized worth of a perpetual series of end-of-period uniform payments A with interest at i% per period is A/i. The capitalized worth of a perpetual series of payments X at the end of every kth period with interest at $i\%$ per period is $X(A/F, i\%, k)/i$. Below is shown a comparison by this method of the same compressors in the example problem just above.

Example:

	Compressor	
	I	II
First cost:	$3,000	$4,000
Life:	6 yr	9 yr
Salvage value:	$500	0
Annual operating disbursements:	$2,000	$1,600
Minimum return on investment $= 15\%$		

Solution:

	Capitalized cost compressor	
	I	II
Initial investment:	$ 3,000	$ 4,000
Replacements		
($3,000 $-$ $500)(A/F,15\%,6)/0.15	1,905	
$4,000(A/F,15\%,9)/0.15:		1,585
Annual disbursements		
$2,000/0.15:	13,300	
$1,500/0.15:		10,650
Total capitalized cost:	$18,205	$16,235

Thus, compressor II, having the lower total capitalized cost, would be the choice.

Valuation of Prospective Receipts

The concept of present worth applies conveniently to the computation of the value of property based on the expected receipts or savings from that property. The computation involves merely discounting the expected receipts or savings at the rate of interest which the prospective investor wants to receive from the property.

Example:
>An engineer believes that a certain building will result in net cash savings of $2,000 a year for 5 years and then a lump savings of $5,000 in the sixth

year. If the minimum attractive rate of return is 20%, what is the value of the building now?

Solution:

$$\text{P.W.} = \$2,000(P/A,20\%,5) + \$5,000(P/F,20\%,6) = \$7,657$$

Valuation of the Purchase Price of Financing Bonds

Financing bonds are a common media for long-term borrowing by corporations and governmental agencies. A bond is a certificate of indebtedness given to the lender by the borrower stipulating the terms of repayment to the lender. The repayments normally consist of periodic interest payments and then payment of the principal at the end of the life of the bond.

The bond certificate contains the information which determines the repayment terms. The minimum information shown would be the borrower's name and address, the face value of the bond, the bond interest rate, the timing of the bond interest payments, and the timing of the repayment of the principal. The amount of the principal repayment is usually equal to the face value of the bond, although there can be terms stated on the bond which allow for repayment of some amount other than the face value if the repayment occurs at some time other than at the end of the normal life of the bond. A description of what happens during the life cycle of a bond can be illustrated by the diagram and three-step explanation of Fig. 4-1.

The amount that a lender can afford to pay for a bond in order to obtain a certain yield (overall rate of return) on his investment can be easily calculated, as shown in the following example.

Example:

A bond has a face value of $1,000. Bond interest payments are to be made semiannually using a bond interest rate of 4% nominal. The life of the bond is 20 years. How much can an investor afford to pay for the bond in order to receive a yield or overall rate of return of 5% compounded semiannually on his investment?

Solution:

Find the present worth of all the expected cash inflows due to the investment using the yield rate as the interest rate. The cash flow diagram for this problem is shown in Fig. 4-2.

$$\text{Bond interest payments} = \$1,000(4\%/2) = \$20$$

$$\text{Redemption value after 20 years} = \$1,000$$

$$\text{Yield rate} = 5\%/2 = 2\tfrac{1}{2}\%$$

$$\text{P.W.} = \$20(P/A,2\tfrac{1}{2}\%,40) + \$1,000(P/F,2\tfrac{1}{2}\%,40) = \$502 + \$372 = \$874$$

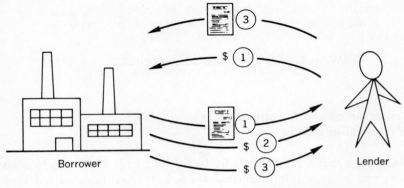

Description of Step	Supplementary Comments
① Bond sold by borrower to lender. Lender gets bond certificate.	Bonds are issued in even denominations (face values) like $250, $1,000, $10,000, etc., but amount paid by lender is determined by market supply and demand. The transaction is usually done through a broker.
② Periodic bond interest payments are made to lender.	The amount of each bond interest payment is computed as face value times bond interest rate.
③ Borrower "redeems" bond by paying principal and getting bond certificate back.	Usually done at end of the stated bond life and the amount paid back is usually the face value.

Figure 4-1. Illustration of life cycle of financing bond.

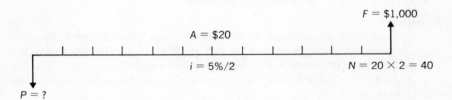

Figure 4-2. Cash flow diagram for example problem on evaluation of financing bonds.

Relationship of Various Analysis Methods

All methods of economic evaluation shown up to this point have the reassuring property of providing consistent results regarding the economic desirability or relative ranking of projects compared. In fact, it can be shown that the annual worths, present worths, and capitalized worths for any projects under comparison are linearly proportional to each other.

Example:

Show the consistency of economic comparison results for compressors I and II by the various methods given in this and the last chapter.

Solution:

$$\frac{A.W._I}{A.W._{II}} = \frac{P.W._I}{P.W._{II}} = \frac{C.W._I}{C.W._{II}}; \quad \frac{\$2,735}{\$2,440} = \frac{\$16,732}{\$14,938} = \frac{\$18,205}{\$16,235} = 1.12$$

Which Economic Analysis Method To Use

Since the annual worth and the present worth methods yield consistent results for a given condition of study, it is reasonable to discuss which method should generally be used. Basically this answer should be weighted most heavily by personal preference, particularly that of the decision-makers considering the results of the studies. Figure 4-3 illustrates several project comparison study conditions together with the recommended study method. Parts (a), (b), and (c) of Fig. 4-3 are described verbally below:

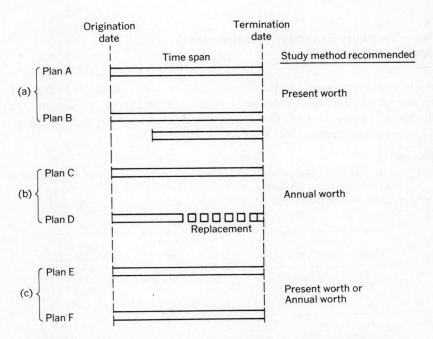

Figure 4-3. Illustration of conditions and study methods recommended.

a. If all alternatives compared are assumed to originate (be placed) at different points in time and to be retired at some common later point in time, the present worth method is easiest to use.

b. If all alternatives being compared are assumed to originate at the same point in time and to be retired at different later points in time, the annual worth method is easiest to use, provided that annual cash flows for each alternative follow some constant pattern for easy conversion into equivalent annual worths.

c. If the alternatives being compared are assumed to originate at the same point in time and to be retired at some later common point in time, the methods are equally easy to use. An exception to this is that if annual cash flows for each alternative do not follow some pattern for easy conversion to equivalent annual worths, then the present worth method is somewhat easier.

The rate-of-return method (to be discussed next chapter) can be best used whenever it is desired to know not just "Which alternative is best?" but rather "What is the rate of profitability?" While generally more difficult to compute than the present worth or annual worth, it has the advantage of results expressed in terms desired and most easily understood by many decision-makers—the profitability as a percentage of invested capital.

Non-Mutually Exclusive (Independent) Alternatives

As in the annual worth method chapter, all previous examples of the comparison of projects in this chapter assume that the alternatives are mutually exclusive. The present worth method can also be used for the comparison of non-mutually exclusive (independent) alternatives.

Example:
Given the same independent projects as in the last section of the chapter on the annual worth method, show which project should be chosen by the present worth method if the minimum required rate of return is 10%.

Project	Investment (P)	Life (N)	Salvage value (F)	Net annual cash flow (A)
A	$10,000	5 yr	$10,000	+ $2,000
B	12,000	5	0	+ 3,000
C	15,000	5	0	+ 4,167

Solution:

Project	Investment	P.W. of net annual cash flow A(P/A,10%,5)	P.W. of salvage F(P/F,10%,5)	Net present worth (Net P.W.)
A	−$10,000	+$ 7,580	+$6,210	+$3,790
B	− 12,000	+ 11,370	0	− 630
C	− 15,000	+ 15,850	0	+ 850

Thus projects A and C, having positive net present worths, would be satisfactory for investment, but project B would not be. This result is, of course, completely consistent with results using the annual worth method.

PROBLEMS

4-1. What is the maximum you would be willing to pay now for each of the alternatives A, B, and C, if your minimum expected return is 8% and the alternatives yield receipts as below?

	Alternative		
	A	B	C
Receipts 1 yr hence	$ 100	$ 500	$ 300
Receipts 2 yr hence	200	400	300
Receipts 3 yr hence	300	300	300
Receipts 4 yr hence	400	200	300
Receipts 5 yr hence	500	100	300
Totals:	$1500	$1500	$1500

4-2. What is the maximum amount an investor can afford to pay for a $10,000 face value bond with a bond rate of 5% payable quarterly and a life of 10 years if he desires to receive a yield (overall rate of return) of 8% compounded quarterly?

4-3. A promissory note has ten end-of-year payments of $500 each remaining. What should be the market price of the note to yield the investor 8% nominal compounded quarterly?

4-4. A machine can be repaired today for $2,500. If repairs are not made, operating expenses are expected to increase by $400 each year for the next 5 years. The minimum acceptable rate of return is 12%. Compare the present worths of the costs of repairing versus not repairing, assuming that the machine will have no value at the end of the 5-year period.

4-5. The following alternatives are available to fill a given need which is expected to exist indefinitely. Each is expected to have 0 salvage value at the end of each life cycle.

	Plan A	*Plan B*	*Plan C*
First cost:	$2,000	$6,000	$12,000
Life cycle:	6 yr	3 yr	4 yr
Annual disbursements:	$3,500	$1,000	$400

If the minimum attractive rate of return is 10%, compare the alternatives using the following methods:
   a. Present worth method
   b. Annual worth method
   c. Capitalized worth method

4-6. A processing firm entered into a contract for raw materials by agreeing to pay $50,000 immediately and $10,000 per yr for 5 years beginning at the end of 7 years from the date of the contract. At the end of the fourth year, the firm requested that it be allowed to make a lump sum payment in advance for the rest of the contract. What was the amount of the lump sum if interest at the settlement was agreed to be 8%?

4-7. Work Prob. 3-6 using the P.W. method.

4-8. Work Prob. 3-7 using the P.W. method.

4-9. Work Prob. 3-8 using the P.W. method.

4-10. Work Prob. 3-9 using the P.W. method.

4-11. Work Prob. 3-10 using the P.W. method.

4-12. Work Prob. 3-11 using the P.W. method.

4-13. Work Prob. 3-12 using the P.W. method.

4-14. Work Prob. 3-13 using the P.W. method.

4-15. Work Prob. 3-14 using the P.W. method.

4-16. Work Prob. 3-15 using the P.W. method.

4-17. A couple is considering constructing a single-level house costing $15,000, which they feel would be adequate to meet their needs for the next 5 years, at which time they could add a wing costing $10,000. An alternative plan is to construct a house for $20,000 now which will be adequate for all their future needs. They estimate that the eventual salvage values of both houses would be equal when they plan to sell upon retirement 30 years hence. If the couple can invest its money at 10%, which house is the best buy? Use the present worth method.

4-18. The contract of a manager of a baseball team has 4 years to run and calls for an irrevocable annual salary of $30,000. The owners of the team want to hire a new manager whom they believe will increase annual attendance by a minimum of 25,000 people or at most by 200,000. Further, they believe the man they want will take the job under a 4-year contract at $42,000 a year. The club clears an average of $2 net from each admission. The owners' minimum required rate of return is 10%. Without losing money, what amount could they reasonably offer the present manager to buy up his contract? How much might the manager reasonably want?

five

Rate of Return Method

The *rate of return* (R.R.) method of economic comparison involves the calculation of a rate or rates of return and comparison against a minimum standard of desirability (i.e., the minimum required rate of return).

There are two common techniques for calculating rates of return which can be said to be theoretically sound because they directly take into account the effects of any particular timing of cash flows throughout the study period considered. These methods, which can lead to slightly different calculated results, will be referred to as follows:

1. Rate of return method (using discounted cash flow)
2. Explicit reinvestment rate of return method

The first of the above is most commonly advocated in the literature and hence will be used in the discussion to follow. It is the only technique which leads to what will be called here simply *rate of return*.

The calculation of the rate of return for a single project involves merely finding the interest rate at which the present worth of the cash inflow (receipts or cash savings) equals the present worth of the cash outflow (disbursements or cash savings foregone). That is, one finds the interest rate at which P.W. of cash inflow equals P.W. of cash outflow; or, at which P.W. of cash inflow minus P.W. of net cash outflow equals 0; or at which P.W. of net cash flow equals 0.

The method of solving normally involves trial and error until the rate is found or can be interpolated. This procedure will be described for several situations below. (When both cash inflows and outflows are involved, the convention of using a "+" sign for inflows and a "−" sign for outflows in the solution will be followed.)

Computation of Rate of Return
for a Single Project

Example:

First cost:	$10,000
Project life:	5 yr
Salvage value:	$2,000
Annual receipts:	$5,000
Annual disbursements:	$2,200

Solution:

Expressing P.W. of net cash flow:

$-\$10,000 + (\$5,000 - \$2,200)(P/A,i\%,5) + \$2,000(P/F,i\%,5) = 0$

$@i = 15\%: \; -\$10,000 + \$2,800(P/A,15\%,5) + \$2,000(P/F,15\%,5) \stackrel{?}{=} 0$

$$\$365 \neq 0$$

$@i = 20\%: \; -\$10,000 + \$2,800(P/A,20\%,5) + \$2,000(P/F,20\%,5) \stackrel{?}{=} 0$

$$-\$598 \neq 0$$

Since we have both a positive and a negative P.W. of net cash flow, the answer is bracketed. Linear interpolation for the answer can be set up as follows:

i	*P.W. of net cash flow*
15%	$365
$x\%$	0
20%	−$598

The answer $x\%$ can be found by solving either

$$\frac{15\% - x\%}{15\% - 20\%} = \frac{\$365 - 0}{\$365 - (-\$598)}$$

or

$$x\% = 15\% + \frac{\$365}{\$365 + \$598}(20\% - 15\%)$$

The latter form is probably easier to use. Solving, $x\% = 16.9\%$.

Principles in Comparing Projects by the Rate of Return Method

When comparing projects by the R.R. method when at most one project will be chosen, there are two main principles to keep in mind. These are as follows:

1. Each increment of investment capital must justify itself (by sufficient R.R. on that increment).
2. Compare a higher investment project against a lower investment project only if that lower investment project is justified.

The usual criterion for choice when using this method is: "Choose the project which requires the highest investment for which each increment of investment capital is justified."

This choice criterion assumes that the firm wants to invest any capital needed as long as that capital is justified by earning a sufficient R.R. on each increment of capital. In general, a sufficient R.R. is any R.R. which is greater than the "minimum required R.R."

Alternate Ways to Find the Rate of Return on Incremental Investment

The rate of return on the incremental investment for any two alternatives can also be found by

1. finding the rate at which the present worth of the net cash flow for the difference between the two alternatives is equal to zero; or
2. finding the rate at which the present worths of the two alternatives are equal; or
3. finding the rate at which the annual worths of the two alternatives are equal.

Comparing Projects When Receipts and Disbursements are Known

Consider the same two alternative lathes A and B that were compared in the last two chapters, and let us determine which is better by the rate of return method, using the first alternative way outlined above.

Example:

	Lathe	
	A	B
First cost:	$10,000	$15,000
Life:	5 yr	10 yr
Salvage value:	$ 2,000	0
Annual receipts:	$5,000	$7,000
Annual disbursements:	$2,000	$4,300
Minimum attractive rate of return = 8%		

Solution:

The first increment of investment to be studied is the $10,000 for lathe A. This project is the same as illustrated in the "single project" solution shown earlier in this chapter. The rate of return for the lathe, and hence the first increment of investment, was shown to be approximately 16.9%. Since 16.9% is greater than the minimum required rate of return of 8%, the increment of investment in lathe A is justified.

The next step is to determine if the next increment of investment (i.e., increasing the investment from $10,000 in lathe A to $15,000 in lathe B) is justified. The clearest way to show the solution is to calculate the year-by-year difference in net cash flow for the two projects and then to find the rate of return on this difference. In order for this year-by-year difference in net cash flow to be computed, the cash flows for each project must be shown for the same number of years (length of study period). This length of study period should be a common multiple of the lives of the projects under consideration, or the length of time during which the services of the chosen alternatives will be needed, whichever is less. For the example lathes, a study period of 10 years will be used.

Year	Lathe A	Lathe B	Difference Lathe B − Lathe A
0	− $10,000	− $15,000	− $5,000
1	+ 2,800	+ 2,700	− 100
2	+ 2,800	+ 2,700	− 100
3			
4			
5	− $8,000		+ $8,000
6			
7			
8			
9			
10	+ 2,800 + $2,000	+ 2,700	− 100 − $2,000

The equation expressing the present worth of the net cash flow for the difference between the two lathes is

$$-\$5,000 - \$100(P/A,i\%,10) + \$8,000(P/F,i\%,5) - \$2,000(P/F,i\%,10) = 0$$

$$@0\%: \quad -\$5,000 - \$100(10.0) + \$8,000(1.0) - \$2,000(1.0) = 0$$

Thus, the rate of return on the incremental investment is 0%. Since the minimum rate of return is 8%, this means the extra investment in lathe B is not justified, and lathe A would be choice.

In this particular problem, one could have calculated the rate of return for lathe B alone. This can be found by solving the following equation:

$$-\$15,000 + \$2,700(P/A,i\%,10) = 0$$

Since there is only one unknown factor in the equation, we can solve directly to find $(P/A,i\%,10) = \$15,000/\$2,700 = 5.55$. We can then observe in the tables that $(P/A,12\%,10) = 5.019$, and $(P/A,15\%,10) = 5.650$, and interpolate to find that the $(P/A,i\%,10) = 5.55$ at $i\% \approx 12.7\%$. Thus, the rate of return for lathe B alone is greater than 8%. However, this is irrelevant to this decision and certainly not grounds to choose lathe B rather than lathe A, as it was previously shown that the incremental investment required for lathe B was not justified. It should be noted that, of course, the indicated decision is the same using the rate of return method as when using either the annual worth method or present worth method.

The rate of return on the incremental investment can also be calculated by the second alternative way outlined in the last section, i.e., finding the rate at which the present worths of the two alternatives are equal. The equation for the two lathes is

$$-\$10,000 + \$2,800(P/A,i\%,10) - \$8,000(P/F,i\%,5) + \$2,000(P/F,i\%,10)$$
$$= -\$15,000 - \$2,700(P/A,i\%,10)$$

This can be solved to find that $i = 0\%$.

To find the rate of return on the incremental investment by the third alternative way outlined in the last section, one needs only to find the interest rate at which annual worths of the two alternatives are equal. This equation for the two lathes is

$$(-\$10,000 + \$2,000)(A/P,i\%,5) - \$2,000(i) + \$2,800$$
$$= -\$15,000(A/P,i\%,10) + \$2,700.$$

This too can be solved to find that $i = 0\%$, again indicating that the incremental investment is not justified.

Comparing Numerous Mutually Exclusive Alternatives

The following example is given to further illustrate the principle that the return on each increment of investment capital should be justified. To make the computations easier, the projects in this example each have a salvage value equal to the investment. In such cases, the rate of return can be calculated directly by dividing the annual net cash inflow or savings by the investment amount. In the tabulated solution shown, the symbol Δ is used to mean "incremental" or "change in." The letters on each end of the arrows designate the projects for which the increment is considered.

Example:

	Alternative project					
	A	B	C	D	E	F
Investment:	$1,000	$1,500	$2,500	$4,000	$5,000	$7,000
Annual savings in cash disbursements:	150	375	500	925	1,125	1,425
Salvage value:	1,000	1,500	2,500	4,000	5,000	7,000

If the company is willing to invest any capital which will earn at least 18%, find which alternative, if any, should be chosen using the rate-of-return method.

Solution:

It should be noted that the alternatives are arranged in order of increasing investment amount and that calculations regarding an increment must be completed before one knows which increment to consider next. The symbol ΔR.R. means R.R. on incremental investment.

Increment considered	A	B	B → C	B → D	D → E	E → F
ΔInvestment:	$1,000	$1,500	$1,000	$2,500	$1,000	$2,000
ΔAnnual savings:	$150	$375	$125	$550	$200	$300
ΔR.R.:	15%	25%	12.5%	22%	20%	15%
Is increment justified?	No	Yes	No	Yes	Yes	No

By the above analysis, alternative E would be chosen because it is the alternative requiring the highest investment for which each increment of investment capital is justified. Note that this analysis was performed without even considering the rate of return on the total investment for each of the alternatives.

In choosing alternative E, what was done was to justify several increments of investment as shown below:

Increment	Investment	Rate of return on increment ($\Delta R.R.$)
B	$1,500	25%
B $\longrightarrow$ D	2,500	22
D $\longrightarrow$ E	1,000	20
Total:	$5,000	

As a side note, the rate of return on the total investment for each alternative is as follows

	Alternative project					
Rate of return:	*A*	*B*	*C*	*D*	*E*	*F*
	15%	25%	20%	23%	22.5%	20%

Note that alternative B has the highest overall rate of return and that alternative F has an overall rate of return which is greater than the minimum of 18%. Nevertheless, alternative E would be chosen on the rationale that the company wants to invest any increment of capital when and only when that increment will earn at least the minimum return.

Comparing Projects When Disbursements Only are Known

When disbursements only are known, rates of return can be calculated for incremental investments only and not for the investment in any one project. Thus, the lowest investment has to be assumed to be justified (or necessary) without being able to calculate the rate of return on that project. As an example, consider the same alternative compressors that were compared in the last two chapters, and determine which is the better alternative.

Example:

	Compressor	
	I	*II*
First cost:	$3,000	$4,000
Life:	6 yr	9 yr
Salvage value:	$500	0
Annual operating disbursements:	$2,000	$1,600
Minimum rate of return $= 15\%$		

Solution:

Listing the cash flows for the lowest common multiple of the lives:

Year	Compressor I	Compressor II	Difference (Compr. II − Compr. I)
0	− $3,000	− $4,000	− $1,000
1	− 2,000	− 1,600	+ 400
2			
3			
4			
5			
6	− $2,500		+ $2,500
7			
8			
9		− $4,000	− $4,000
10			
11			
12	− $2,500		+ $2,500
13			
14			
15			
16			
17			
18	− 2,000 + $500	− 1,600	+ 400 − $500

The rate of return for the difference between the compressors (i.e., on the incremental investment) can be obtained by solving the following equation for the difference in the net cash flows:

$$-\$1,000 - \$4,000(P/F,i\%,9) - \$500(P/F,i\%,18) + \$400(P/A,i\%,18)$$
$$+ \$2,500(P/F,i\%,6) + \$2,500(P/F,i\%,12) = 0$$

The rate of return can be found to be approximately 47%. Since this return on the increment is greater than the minimum required, 15%, compressor II is justified.

The third alternative way of finding the rate of return on incremental investment provides a convenient shortcut for problems where the two main assumptions stated in Chapter 3 (regarding the period of needed service and the repeatability of cost factors) hold true. For the compressor problem above, the rate of return may be found by solving the following:

$$(\$3,000 - \$500)(A/P,i\%,6) + \$500(1\%) + 2,000$$
$$= \$4,000(A/P,i\%,9) + \$1,600.$$

The equation is satisfied for an interest rate of approximately 47%, which is the same answer as obtained by the solution based on the differences in cash flows.

Comparing Numerous Mutually Exclusive Alternatives for Which Disbursements Only are Known

Example:

	Incinerator			
	A	B	C	D
First cost:	$3,000	$3,800	$4,500	$5,000
Life:	10 yr	10 yr	10 yr	10 yr
Salvage value:	0	0	0	0
Annual operating disbursements:	$1,800	$1,770	$1,470	$1,320

If the minimum required rate of return = 10%, show which alternative is best by the rate-of-return method.

Solution:

Increment considered	$A \rightarrow B$	$A \rightarrow C$	$C \rightarrow D$
ΔInvestment:	$800	$1,500	$500
ΔAnn. oper. disb. (Sav.):	$30	$330	$150
ΔR.R.:	negative	17.3%	15.0%
Is increment justified?	No	Yes	Yes

Thus, from the above analysis, incinerator D would be chosen because it is the highest investment alternative which will return at least the minimum rate, 10%, on each increment of investment.

As an example of how the above rate of return figures are calculated, the present worth relation for increment A $\rightarrow$ C is

$$-\$1,500 + \$330(P/A, i\%, 10) = 0$$

Therefore,

$$(P/A, i\%, 10) = 4.545.$$

Interpolating in the interest tables, the rate which solves this relation is 17.3%.

Finding Rate of Return for Financing Bonds

Example:

An investor paid $874 for a $1,000 face value bond which provides for bond payments at 4% nominal. The bond payments are to be made semiannually for 20 years. What yield (overall rate of return) will the investor make on his investment? (*Note:* This is the same bond problem as in the last part of Chapter 4 except with a different unknown.)

Solution:

$$\text{Bond interest payments} = \$1,000(4\%/2) = \$20$$

$$-\$874 + \$20(P/A,i\%,40) + \$1,000(P/F,i\%,40) = 0$$

By trial and error, equation is satisfied at $i = 2\frac{1}{2}\%$. Therefore,

$$\text{Yield} = 5\% \text{ compounded semiannually}$$

Aid for Calculation of Rate of Return

The computations to determine the rate of return by the discounted cash flow method can be rather laborious, particularly if the annual cash flows do

	TIMING		TRIAL #1 0% INT. RATE	TRIAL #2 10% INT. RATE		TRIAL #3 25% INT. RATE		TRIAL #4 40% INT. RATE		TRIAL #5 80% INT. RATE	
	Cal. Year	Period	Disbursement	Factor	Present Worth	Factor	Present Worth	Factor	Present Worth	Factor	Present Worth
BEFORE		5TH YR.		1.46		2.44		3.84		6.56	
		4TH		1.33		1.95		2.74		4.10	
		3RD		1.21		1.56		1.96		2.56	
	1969	2ND	20,000	1.10	22,000	1.25	25,000	1.40		1.60	
	70	1ST	30,000	1.00	30,000	1.00	30,000	1.00		1.00	
	TOTALS (A)		50,000		52,000		55,000				
	Cal. Year	Period	Annual Return	Factor	Present Worth	Factor	Present Worth	Factor	Present Worth	Factor	Present Worth
AFTER ZERO TIME	70	1ST YR.	21,000	.91	19,100	.80	16,800	.71		.63	
	71	2ND	19,000	.83	15,700	.64	12,200	.51		.39	
	72	3RD	17,000	.75	12,800	.51	8,700	.36		.24	
	73	4TH	15,000	.68	10,700	.41	6,100	.26		.15	
	74	5TH	18,000	.62	11,200	.33	5,900	.19		.10	
		6TH		.56		.26		.13		.06	
		7TH		.51		.21		.09		.04	
		8TH		.47		.17		.07		.02	
		9TH		.42		.13		.05		.01	
		10TH		.39		.11		.03		.01	
		11TH		.35		.09		.02			
		12TH		.32		.07		.02			
		13TH		.29		.06		.01			
		14TH		.26		.04		.01			
		15TH		.24		.04					
		16TH		.22		.03					
		17TH		.20		.02					
		18TH		.18		.02					
		19TH		.16		.01					
		20TH		.15		.01					
		21ST		.14							
		22ND		.12							
		23RD		.11							
		24TH		.10							
		25TH		.09							
	TOTALS (B)		90,000		69,000		49,700				
	RATIO A/B		.55		.75		1.12				

Figure 5-1. Rate of return calculation form with entries for example project.

not follow some pattern to which tabled interest factors can be readily applied.

Figure 5-1 is a form which can be used to simplify the calculations. Cash flows for each year are entered in the column headed "Trial #1 − 0% int. rate." These are the present worths at 0%. Each of these numbers is then multiplied by the factor in the adjacent subcolumn labeled "Factor" and the result entered in the next subcolumn headed "Present worth." These are the present worths at 10% trial interest rate. The calculations are repeated for the 25%, 40%, and 60% interest rates as needed and the columns added to obtain the total present worth of disbursements (A) and the total present worth of receipts (B) for each trial interest rate. At each interest rate the total present worth of expenditures is divided by the total present worth of receipts, and the result entered in the space "Ratio A/B."

The rate of return answer sought is the interest rate at which A equals B, or at which the "Ratio A/B" equals unity. If one of the interest rates we have tried does not result in the unity ratio, hopefully the unity ratio will be bracketed so the answer can be interpolated. To provide for ease of interpolation, a chart is provided in Fig. 5-2.

To illustrate the use of these aids, a sample problem and the associated computations are shown. Note in Fig. 5-1 that the sample problem involves investments of $20,000 one year before the base, or present time and $30,000 at the base time, and then annual returns (net cash flows) of $21,000, $19,000,

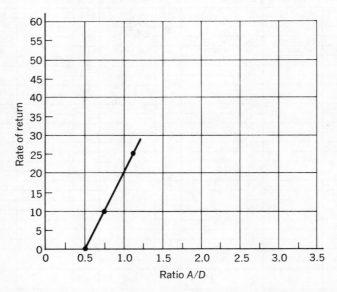

Figure 5-2. Rate of return interpolation chart with entries for example project of Fig. 5-1.

$17,000, $15,000, $18,000, respectively, each year thereafter. Figure 5-2 shows the interpolation resulting in the answer rate of return of 20% at the "Ratio *A/B*" of 1.0.

This form can be used to calculate the rate of return on incremental investments as well as for individual investment projects.

Non-Mutually Exclusive (Independent) Alternatives

Following the pattern of the two preceding chapters, all examples to this point in this chapter assume that the alternatives are mutually exclusive. Of course, the rate of return method can also be used to determine the relative desirability of non-mutually exclusive (independent) alternatives.

Example:
Given the same independent projects as in the last sections of the chapters on the annual worth method and the present worth method, show which project should be chosen by the rate of return method if the minimum required rate of return is 10%.

Project	Investment	Life	Salvage value	Net annual cash flow
A	$10,000	5 yr	$10,000	+ $2,000
B	12,000	5	0	+ 3,000
C	15,000	5	0	+ 4,167

Solution:
Finding the interest rate at which the present worth of receipts equals the present worth of disbursements yields the following results:

Project	Rate of return
A	20%
B	8
C	12

Thus, projects A and C, having rates of return greater than 10%, would be satisfactory for investment, but project B would not be. This result is, of course, completely consistent with results using the annual worth and present worth methods.

Differences in Ranking of Independent Projects

It was pointed out in the last section that the rate of return method will always give results which are completely consistent with results using the present worth and annual worth methods. However, the rate-of-return method can give a different *ranking* of the order of desirability of independent projects than the annual worth or present worth methods. As an example, consider Fig. 5-3 depicting the relation of rate of return to net present worth for two non-mutually exclusive projects X and Y.

The rate of return for each project is the point at which the net present worth for that project is zero. The net present worth for each project is shown for a typical interest rate of return. For the hypothetical but quite feasible relationship shown, project Y has the higher rate of return, while project X has the higher net present worth for all rates of return less than the rate at which the net present worths are equal. This illustrates a case in which the rate-of-return method does result in a different *ranking* of alternatives as compared to the present worth (or annual worth) method. However, since both projects had a net present worth greater than zero, and the rate of return for both projects is greater than the minimum rate of return, the determination of acceptance of both projects is consistently shown by either method.

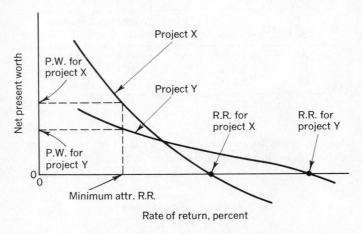

Figure 5-3. Illustration of differences in ranking of non-mutually exclusive projects.

Problems in Which Either No Solution or Several Solutions for Rate of Return Exist

It is possible, but not commonly experienced in practice, to have situations in which there is no single rate of return solution by the discounted cash flow method. This can occur whenever the cumulative cash flow reverses sign (from net outflow to net inflow or the opposite) more than once over the period of study. As an example, consider the following project for which the rate of return is desired.

Example:

Year	Net cash flow
−1	+$ 500
0	− 1,000
1	0
2	+ 250
3	+ 250
4	+ 250

Solution:

Year	Net cash flow	P.W. @35% Factor	P.W. @35% Amount	P.W. @63% Factor	P.W. @63% Amount
−1	+$ 500	1.35	+$ 676	1.63	+$ 813
0	− 1,000	1.00	− 1,000	1.00	− 1,000
1	0				
2	+ 250	0.55	+ 137	0.38	95
3	+ 250	0.41	+ 102	0.23	57
4	+ 250	0.30	+ 75	0.14	35
		Net P.W.:	Σ = 0		Σ = 0

Thus, the present worth of the net cash flows equals 0 for interest rates of 35% and 63%. Whenever multiple answers such as this exist, it is likely that neither is correct.

An effective way to overcome this difficulty and obtain a "correct" answer is to manipulate cash flows as little as necessary so that there is only one reversal of the cumulative net cash flow. This can be done by using the minimum attractive rate of return to manipulate the funds, and then solving by the discounted cash flow method. For the above example, if the minimum attractive rate of return is 10%, the +$500 at year −1 can be compounded to year 0 to be $500 $(F/P,10\%,1) = +\$550$. This, added to the −$1,000 at year 0, equals −$450. The −$450, together with the remaining cash flow, which is all positive, now fits the condition that there be only one reversal in the cumulative net cash flow. The interest rate at which the present worth of the net cash flows equals 0 can now be shown to be 19% per the following table:

Timing	Net cash flow	P.W. @19%	
		Factor	Amount
0	− $450	1.00	− $450
2	+ 250	0.70	+ 177
3	+ 250	0.59	+ 150
4	+ 250	0.48	+ 123
	Net P.W.:		$\Sigma = 0$

It should be noted that whenever a manipulation of net cash flows such as the above is done, the calculated rate of return will vary according to what cash flows are manipulated and at what interest rate. The less the manipulation and the closer the minimum rate of return to the calculated rate of return, the less the variation in the final calculated rate of return.

Explicit Reinvestment Rate of Return Method

The explicit reinvestment rate of return method involves dividing a "net profit" amount by the initial investment, where the net profit is calculated using a depreciation charge based on the sinking fund method of depreciation. As will be explained in Chapter 6, the sinking fund depreciation charge is obtained by multiplying the depreciable investment by the sinking fund factor, A/F. The interest rate used is the explicit rate at which recovered depreciation monies are assumed to be reinvested. To illustrate, consider the same single project for which the rate of return was calculated at the beginning of the chapter.

Example:

First cost:	$10,000
Project life:	5 yr
Salvage value:	$ 2,000
Annual receipts:	$ 5,000
Annual disbursements:	$ 2,200

Solution:

The following solution by the explicit reinvestment rate-of-return method uses a reinvestment rate of 10%.

Annual receipts:		$5,000
Annual expenses:		
Disbursements:	$2,200	
Depreciation = ($10,000 − $2,000)($A/F$,10%,5):	1,310	
		3,510
Net annual profit:		$1,490

$$\text{Explicit reinvestment rate of return} = \frac{\$1,490}{\$10,000} = 14.9\%$$

If a reinvestment rate of, say, 20% were used for the sinking fund in the above example, the explicit reinvestment rate of return could be calculated to be 17.3%. If a reinvestment rate of 16.9% had been used, then the explicit reinvestment rate of return would have been 16.9%, which is the same as the rate of return by the usual discounted cash flow procedure. From this, it can be inferred that the rate of return calculated by the discounted cash flow method involves the assumption that monies recovered for depreciation purposes can be reinvested at the same rate as the calculated rate.

In general, it can be said that calculated rate-of-return results using the explicit reinvestment method do not differ significantly from the discounted cash flow method. Even though the explicit reinvestment method is not used commonly, it does have the great advantage of computational ease when there is a single beginning investment and constant receipts and disbursements each year.

PROBLEMS

5-1. A construction firm is considering leasing a crane needed on a project for 4 years for $200,000 payable now. The alternative is to buy a crane for $250,000 and sell it at the end of 4 years for $100,000. Annual maintenance costs for ownership only are expected to be $10,000 per yr for the first 2 years and $15,000 per yr for the last two years. At what interest rate are the two alternatives equivalent?

5-2. An industrial machine costing $1,000 will produce net savings of $400 per year. The machine has a 5-year economic life but must be returned to the factory for major repairs after 3 years of operation. These repairs cost $500. The company's cost of capital is approximately 10%. What rate of return will be earned on purchase of this machine?

5-3. An improved facility costing $50,000 has been proposed. Construction time will be 2 years with expenditures of $20,000 the first year and $30,000 the second year. Savings beginning the first year after construction completion are as follows:

Year	Savings
1	$10,000
2	14,000
3	18,000
4	22,000
5	26,000

The facility will not be required after 5 years and will have a salvage value of $5,000. Determine the rate of return on this project.

5-4. A distillery is considering the erection of a bottle-making plant. The number of bottles needed annually is estimated at 600,000. The initial cost of the facility would be $50,000 with estimated life of 20 years. Annual operation and maintenance costs are expected to be $7,500, and annual taxes and insurance $2,500. Should the distillery erect the bottle-producing facility or buy the bottles from another company at $0.03 each? Use the rate of return method with a minimum attractive rate of 12%.

5-5. What is the rate of return on an investment of $1,000 which will yield $325 per year for 5 years?

5-6. Work Prob. 3-6 using the R.R. method.

5-7. Work Prob. 3-7 using the R.R. method.

5-8. Work Prob. 3-8 using the R.R. method.

5-9. Work Prob. 3-9 using the R.R. method.

5-10. Work Prob. 3-10 using the R.R. method.

5-11. Work Prob. 3-11 using the R.R. method.

5-12. Work Prob. 3-12 using the R.R. method.

5-13. Work Prob. 3-13 using the R.R. method.

5-14. Work Prob. 3-14 using the R.R. method.

5-15. Work Prob. 3-15 using the R.R. method.

5-16. A promissory note calls for 20 payments of $1,500 to be made semiannually beginning 6 months from today. If the note can be purchased for $22,000, what is the nominal rate of return on the investment? What is the effective rate?

5-17. A $2,000 face value bond with interest payments at 4% nominal on the face value is for sale for $1,586. Interest is payable semiannually beginning 6 months from now. What is the nominal interest rate that a purchaser will receive? The bond life is 20 years.

5-18. Work Prob. 5-4 using the explicit reinvestment rate-of-return method for the following reinvestment rates: (a) 8%, (b) 12%, (c) 20%. Compare these answers with the answer to Prob. 5-4.

5-19. There are five alternative machines to do a given job. Each is expected to have a salvage value of 100% of the investment amount at the end of its life of 4 years. If the firm's minimum attractive rate of return is 12%, which machine is the best choice based on the following data?

		Machine			
	A	B	C	D	E
Investment:	$1,000	$1,400	$2,100	$2,700	$3,400
Net cash flow per yr:	110	180	280	340	445

six

Depreciation

Introduction

The primary purpose of depreciation accounting is to provide for the recovery of capital invested in property which is expected to decline in value as a result of time and/or use. This is done through the mechanism of *depreciation charges*, which are allocations or noncash charges made periodically. Depreciation accounting also provides a systematic means for placing a declared or unamortized value, commonly called *book value*, on property.

Only cash flows or charges need be considered in determining the economic desirability of an alternative in an economic analysis. As will be discussed in Chapter 7, income taxes are relevant cash flows and should be considered whenever their omission may cause the selection of an uneconomical alternative. Although depreciation write-offs are not, in themselves, cash flows, they do affect income taxes, and hence affect cash flows.

The purpose of this chapter is primarily to acquaint the student with the computational mechanics of the following three common depreciation plans or methods so that he can apply these appropriately in the computation of after-tax cash flows:

1. Straight line
2. Delining balance
3. Sum-of-years-digits

Straight line depreciation

The *straight line depreciation plan* provides for uniform periodic depreciation charges over the write-off period.

Letting $P =$ Cost of asset,

$F =$ Salvage value, and

$W =$ Write-off period (in years),

the depreciation charge, denoted by D, may be given as $D = (P - F)/W$, where $(P - F)$ is known as the *depreciable investment*.

The value of the asset on the books of account at the end of year x is termed the *book value*, denoted B.V.$._x$, and is given as

$$\text{B.V.}_{\cdot x} = P - \left[\frac{P - F}{W}\right] \times x \qquad (6\text{-}1)$$

Example:

A machine costs $15,000 installed. The allowable write-off period is 12 years, at which time the salvage value is assumed to be $1,500. What will be the annual depreciation charge and what will be the book value at the end of the third year?

Solution:

$$D = \frac{P - F}{W} = \frac{\$15,000 - \$1,500}{12} = \$1,125$$

$$\text{B.V.}_{\cdot 3} = P - \left[\frac{P - F}{W}\right] \times 3 = \$15,000 - \left[\frac{\$15,000 - \$1,500}{12}\right] \times 3$$

$$= \$11,625$$

Declining balance depreciation

The *declining balance method* of depreciation provides for an accelerated write-off (depreciation) during the early years of the life of an asset, with progressively smaller depreciation charges with increasing years. For this method, the depreciation charge for the xth year, D_x, is equal to a fixed percentage d_r of the book value at the beginning of the xth year [end of $(x - 1)$th year]. Thus,

$$D_x = \text{B.V.}_{\cdot x - 1}(d_r) \qquad (6\text{-}2)$$

It can be shown that the book value at the end of the $(x - 1)$th year is given by

$$\text{B.V.}_{\cdot x - 1} = P(1 - d_r)^{x - 1} \qquad (6\text{-}3)$$

Thus,

$$D_x = P(1 - d_r)^{(x-1)}(d_r) \tag{6-4}$$

In order for the book value to equal the estimated salvage value at the end of the write-off period, W years, d_r should be calculated as

$$d_r = 1 - \sqrt[W]{\frac{F}{P}} \tag{6-5}$$

Example:

For the previous example using straight line depreciation, determine the book value at the end of the third year and the depreciation charge for the fourth year using the declining balance method of depreciation.

Solution:

$$d_r = 1 - \sqrt[W]{\frac{F}{P}} = 1 - \sqrt[12]{\frac{1,500}{15,000}} = 1 - 0.826 = 0.174$$

$$\text{B.V.}_3 = \$15,000(1 - 0.174)^3 = \$8,460$$

$$D_4 = \$8,460(0.174) = \$1,470$$

A special version of the declining balance depreciation method is called the *double declining balance method*. For this method d_r is calculated as $200\%/W$ and all other computations are comparable. Using this version of the method, the book value at the end of the write-off period, W years, will not normally equal the salvage value. Because of this, the taxpayer is generally permitted to switch later to straight line depreciation for the remaining years.

Example:

Work the same problem as above except using the double declining balance method. Also, assume that it is desired to switch to the straight line method after the fourth year. What is the depreciation charge for all remaining years?

Solution:

$$d_r = \frac{200\%}{12} = 0.167$$

$$\text{B.V.}_3 = \$15,000(1 - 0.167)^3 = \$8,700$$

$$D_4 = 8,700(0.167) = \$1,450$$

$$\text{B.V.}_4 = \$8,700 - \$1,450 = \$7,250$$

$$D = \frac{\$7,250 - \$1,500}{12 - 4} = \$720 \text{ per yr after the fourth year}$$

Sum-of-years-digits depreciation

The *sum-of-years-digits method* is an alternative depreciation method for achieving accelerated write-off during the early years of life of an asset.

To use this method, the digits corresponding to the number of years of estimated life are added together. This sum can also be conveniently obtained by use of the formula S.Y.D. $= (W)(W+1)/2$. The depreciation charge for the first year is $(W/\text{S.Y.D.})(P-F)$; for the second year is $[(W-1)/\text{S.Y.D.}]$ $\cdot(P-F)$; for the third year $[(W-2)/\text{S.Y.D.}]/(P-F)$; and so forth until the Wth year it is $(1/\text{S.Y.D.})(P-F)$.

Example:
    Work the same problem as above except using the S.Y.D. method.
Solution:

$$\text{S.Y.D.} = 1 + 2 + \cdots + 12 = \frac{12(13)}{2} = 78$$

$$\text{B.V.}_3 = \$15{,}000 - \left[\frac{12}{78}(\$13{,}500) + \frac{11}{78}(\$13{,}500) + \frac{10}{78}(\$13{,}500)\right]$$

$$= \$15{,}000 - \$5{,}700 = \$9{,}300$$

$$D_4 = \frac{9}{78}(\$13{,}500) = \$1{,}580$$

Additional First-Year Depreciation

In addition to the ordinary first-year depreciation deduction, taxpayers can elect to take an initial deduction equal to 20% of the cost of tangible personal property having a useful life of at least 6 years. The full cost or a fractional part of the cost of an item may be selected for the extra write-off but only up to an aggregate amount for all items of $10,000 per individual per yr.

Example:
    Work the same problem as above using the straight line method of depreciation and assuming that full advantage of the extra first-year depreciation is taken.
Solution:

$$\text{Extra first-year depreciation} = \$15{,}000(20\%) = \$3{,}000$$

$$D = \frac{P - \$3{,}000 - F}{W} = \frac{\$15{,}000 - \$3{,}000 - \$1{,}500}{12} = \$875$$

$$\text{B.V.}_3 = P - \$3{,}000 - (\$875)(3) = \$9{,}375$$

Comparison of Depreciation Methods

To provide a common basis for comparison of the foregoing three methods of depreciation, the following year-by-year amounts are given for a typical asset.

Example:
    A new machine, which costs $16,000, is expected to last 5 years and then be sold for a net of $1,000. It is desired to show the depreciation charge, the

accrued depreciation charge, and the book value at the end of each year for the straight line, double declining balance, and sum-of-years-digits methods respectively.

Solution:

For straight line depreciation:

Age (yr)	Depreciation charge	Accrued depreciation charge	Book value
0	——	——	$16,000
1	$3,000	$ 3,000	13,000
2	3,000	6,000	10,000
3	3,000	9,000	7,000
4	3,000	12,000	4,000
5	3,000	15,000	1,000

For double declining balance depreciation:

Age (yr)	Depreciation charge	Accrued depreciation charge	Book value
0	——	0	$16,000
1	$6,400	$ 6,400	9,600
2	3,840	10,240	5,760
3	2,304	12,544	3,456
4	1,382	13,926	2,074
5	1,734*	15,000	1,000

*Based on exercising option of switching to straight line depreciation to adjust to final salvage value. In this example, the change in method occurs at the beginning of the fifth year.

For sum-of-years-digits depreciation:

Age (yr)	Depreciation charge	Accrued depreciation charge	Book value
0	——	0	$16,000
1	$5,000	$ 5,000	11,000
2	4,000	9,000	7,000
3	3,000	12,000	4,000
4	2,000	14,000	2,000
5	1,000	15,000	1,000

Figure 6-1 provides a graphical comparison of the year-by-year book values for the above example machine using each of the three depreciation methods.

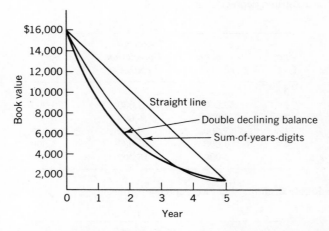

Figure 6-1. Comparison of effect of depreciation method on book value.

Units-of-Production Depreciation

All the depreciation methods discussed to this point are based on elapsed time on the theory that the decrease in value of property is mainly a function of time. When the decrease in value is mostly a function of use, depreciation may be based on the *units-of-production method.*

This method results in the total depreciable investment being allocated equally over the units produced, and requires an estimate of the total lifetime of productive use. The depreciation rate is calculated as

$$\text{Depreciation per unit of production} = \frac{P - F}{\text{Estimated lifetime production}}$$

$$(6\text{-}6)$$

Example:

An auto has a first cost of $5,000 and is expected to have $1,000 salvage value when traded after 100,000 miles of use. It is desired to find its depreciation rate based on functional use, and its book value after 20,000 miles of use.

Solution:

$$\text{Depreciation per unit of production} = \frac{\$5,000 - \$1,000}{100,000 \text{ miles}} = \$0.04 \text{ per mile}$$

$$\text{B.V.} = \$5,000 - \$0.04(20,000 \text{ miles}) = \$4,200$$

Choosing a Depreciation Method

There are many factors to be considered in the choice of a method of depreciation. Generally the most important factor is the effect of the method on the timing of income taxes paid.

If income tax rates are constant and the firm has taxable income over the depreciable life, then the total income taxes paid is identical regardless of the depreciation method employed. However, given the choice of paying a dollar of income tax now versus a dollar of income tax later, the time-value-of-money effect encourages one to choose the postponement. Indeed, this postponement is achieved by depreciation methods which result in higher depreciation charges (and thus lower taxable incomes and taxes) in the early years of an asset, as in the sum-of-years-digits and declining balance methods.

The choice between depreciation methods for income tax purposes can be quite important to the firm. Among the factors which should be considered in this decision are (a) the expected trend of income tax rates as the result of legislation and variability of firm earnings, (b) whether or not the firm has losses to be carried forward to future years, and (c) the effects on future after-tax earnings reported to the stockholders or owners.

Group Accounting vs. Item Accounting

In its determination of depreciation policy for accounting and tax purposes, a firm generally has the option of either accounting for each item of property separately or accounting for groups of items. The possible groupings may vary according to one or more characteristics, such as similarity of items, date of installation, mortality characteristics, or geographic location. In this chapter we have limited our discussion to item accounting. While the idea of depreciation charges and accruals to reflect remaining book values is the same for group accounting as for item accounting, there are important differences, particularly in the treatments of retirements, which involve tax law provisions beyond the scope of this book.

Items Not Depreciable for Tax Purposes

It should be recognized that all items constituting a one-time-only first cost or capital expenditure are not necessarily depreciable for income tax purposes. These include the following:

1. Items which supposedly do not diminish in value over time, such as working capital and land;

2. Items which are charged as expenses in year of incurrence, such as advertising, training, and research;
3. Items which are only an implied or opportunity cost;
4. Moves and rearrangements of facilities.

Depreciation Guidelines and Rules

The depreciable life which is used for tax reporting purposes is of great interest to taxpayers and taxing governments. Guidelines for useful lines of depreciable assets were issued by the U.S. Internal Revenue Service in 1962,* superseding the guidelines under the old *Bulletin F*, published in 1942. The guidelines are divided into approximately 75 broad classes of assets. The guideline lives provide auditing rules and procedures designed to treat depreciation by a grouping of assets instead of considering individual assets. Essentially, these procedures involve a "reserve ratio test," which is a method for proving that the accrued depreciation for assets in a guideline class bears a reasonable relationship to the basis (first cost minus present salvage value) of those assets. Where the test is not met, the question of whether the taxpayer's retirement and replacement values are consistent with the class life being used must be determined on the basis of the facts and circumstances.

PROBLEMS

6-1. A machine tool costs $40,000. Its life for depreciation purposes is estimated at 10 years, and its salvage value is assumed to be $4,000. Determine (1) the depreciation charge for the fifth year, and (2) the book value at the end of the fifth year using each of the following methods:
   a. Straight line
   b. Sum-of-years-digits
   c. Double declining balance

6-2. A new machine has just been purchased by a manufacturer for $25,000. Freight and trucking charges were $500, and the installation cost was $300. The machine has an estimated useful life of 8 years, at which time it is expected that $1,000 dismantling costs will have to be paid in order to sell it for $5,000. Compute (1) the depreciation charge for the first year, and (2) the book value at the end of the first year using each of the following methods:
   a. Straight line
   b. Sum-of-years-digits
   c. Declining balance

---

*Internal Revenue Service Publication No. 456, *Depreciation—Guidelines and Rules*, Government Printing Office, Washington, D.C.

6-3. An asset costs $10,000 and is expected to have $1,000 salvage value at the end of 5 years. Graph its book value as a function of year using each of the following methods:

    a. Straight line

    b. Sum-of-years-digits

    c. Double declining balance

6-4. Compute the depreciation on an automobile—your own car or one in which you are interested. Obtain from a dealer the cost of the new car and the "Blue Book" values of this car, or its equivalent, at the ages of 1, 2, 3, 4, and 5 years. Note that these are average market values based on average mileage and maintenance. From the values obtained, compute the year-by-year depreciation costs. Compare the results with depreciation costs computed by the depreciation method in this chapter that most nearly approximates the above values.

6-5. Work Prob. 6-1 assuming that the 20% additional first-year depreciation is taken.

6-6. A special-purpose machine is to be depreciated as a linear function of use. It costs $25,000 and is expected to produce 100,000 units and then be salvaged for $5,000. Up to the end of the third year it had produced 60,000 units and during the fourth year it produced 10,000 units. What is the depreciation charge for the fourth year and the book value at the end of the fourth year?

seven

Consideration of Taxes

This chapter provides a brief overview of main tax considerations and a general technique for including the effect of income taxes in economy studies.

Main Types of Taxes

Below are described the main types of taxes important to economic analyses.

1. *Property taxes* are based on the valuation of property owned, such as land, equipment, buildings, inventory, etc., and the established tax rates. They do not vary with income, and are usually much lower in amount than income taxes.
2. *Sales taxes* are taxes imposed on product sales, usually at the retail level. They are not normally relevant in economy studies.
3. *Excise taxes* are taxes imposed upon the manufacture of certain products, such as alcohol and tobacco. They are not normally significant in economy studies.
4. *Income taxes* are taxes on profits or income in the course of regular business as well as on gains on the disposal of capital property. They

are the most significant type of tax to consider in usual economic analyses and are the subject of the remainder of this chapter

When Income Taxes Should Be Considered

In the preceding chapters we have treated income taxes either as if they are not applicable or only implicitly, i.e., by using a before-tax rate of return which is larger than the after-tax rate of return, with the intention that the resulting cash flows will be sufficient to provide for both the after-tax rate of return and the income tax.

An approximation of the before-tax rate of return requirement to include the effect of income taxes in studies using before-tax cash flows can be determined from the following relationship:

[Before-tax R.R.][1 — {Effective income tax rate}] = [After-tax R.R.]

Thus,

$$[\text{Before-tax R.R.}] = \frac{[\text{After-tax R.R}]}{[1 - \{\text{Effective income tax rate}\}]} \qquad (7\text{-}1)$$

If the property is nondepreciable and the financing is entirely by equity capital, then the above relationship is exact, not an approximation. If, however, some debt financing (as with bonds) is involved, the effect of the interest deduction on taxable income should be reflected in the before-tax rate of return. If salvage value is less than 100% of first cost and if life of the property is finite, then the depreciation method selected for income tax purposes affects the timing of income tax payments and, therefore, error can be introduced by use of the relationship in Eq. 7-1. In practice, it is usually desirable to make after-tax analyses for any income-tax-paying enterprise unless one knows that income taxes would have no effect on the alternatives being considered.

After-tax analyses can be performed by exactly the same methods as before-tax analyses. The only difference is that after-tax cash flows should be used in place of before-tax cash flows by mere adjustment for tax effects, and the calculation made using an after-tax minimum attractive rate of return. Tax effects can result from many causes, such as ordinary income or losses, gains or losses on the disposal of assets, depreciation write-offs, and investment credits. The federal and state provisions for these tax effects can be quite complex and are subject to change; hence, attempt will be made herein only to describe briefly some main provisions of the tax law as of the late 1960's and then to illustrate the general procedure for computing after-tax cash flows and making after-tax analyses. While some tax rates are provided as examples, it should be recognized that the rates are quite subject to change.

Indeed, most economic analyses should be concerned with the rates and provisions expected in the future rather than just those existing in the present.

Type of Income Tax Effects

Ordinary income

Ordinary income is that which results from the regular business operations (such as sale of products or services) performed by a corporation or individual. Federal taxes are imposed on ordinary taxable income according to a graduated scale with provision for higher rates with higher income. Ordinary taxable income includes all business income minus all allowable business expenses including depreciation and certain contributions and exemptions. For corporations in 1970, the federal rates were 22% for the first $25,000 of taxable income and 48% for taxable income above $25,000 per year. For individuals, the federal rates increase progressively from approximately 14 to 70%. Most states also levy taxes on the ordinary income of individuals and corporations.

Gains and losses on disposal of property

When an asset other than those sold as part of normal business operations is disposed for more or less than its book value, that gain or loss usually affects taxes. The amount of effect depends upon the amount of gain or loss (selling price minus book value), the type of gain or loss, and the applicable

Table 7-1

TYPES OF GAINS AND LOSSES ON SALE OR EXCHANGE OF PROPERTY
FOR FEDERAL TAX PURPOSES

If property sold was held for	*Such as*	*The gain is*	*The loss is*
Sale to customers	Merchandise inventory	Ordinary income	Ordinary income
Investment	Stocks, bonds, land	Capital	Capital
Personal use	Home, car, jewelry	Capital	Nondeductible
Use in business	Buildings, trucks, equipment	Capital or ordinary income*	Capital or ordinary income*

*Depreciable assets used in a trade or business are not capital assets as defined by law. However, under certain complex restrictions a part or all of a gain on the sale of certain depreciable assets can be taxed as capital gain rates, with the remainder of the gain, if any, taxed at the higher rates applicable to ordinary income.

tax rate or rates. Table 7-1 summarizes in very condensed form the types of gains and losses on sale or exchange of property.

Tables 7-2 and 7-3 summarize the federal tax effects (including some rates) for various types of gains and losses for individuals and corporations respectively. A key point is that total gains of a type must be used to offset total losses of a type in a given tax period, and the tax payment or tax saving must be computed on the difference (subject to restrictions).

Table 7-2

FEDERAL TAX EFFECTS OF GAIN AND LOSS TYPES FOR INDIVIDUALS
(AS OF 1968)

Type of gain or loss	*Tax effect*
Ordinary income gain	At ordinary income rates (progressive scale from 14 to 70%)
Capital gain (long-term—held more than 6 months)	At $\frac{1}{2}$ of ordinary income rates up to 50%, but never more than 25% on the full gain
(short-term—held less than 6 months)	At ordinary income rates
Ordinary income loss	Reduce other income by full amount of the loss
Capital loss (long-term or short-term)	Reduce capital gains; loss in excess of capital gains can be deducted from ordinary income up to $1,000; any remaining excess loss can be applied for up to 5 later tax years against capital gains and up to $1,000 of other income
Nondeductible loss	Cannot be deducted

Table 7-3

FEDERAL TAX EFFECTS OF GAIN AND LOSS TYPES FOR CORPORATIONS
(AS OF 1968)

Type of gain or loss	*Tax effect*
Ordinary income gain	At ordinary income rates (22% for first $25,000 and 48% for all over $25,000)
Capital gain	At ordinary income rate in most cases; under some circumstances, no more than 25% of the full gain
Ordinary income loss	Reduce other income by the full amount of the loss; a net operating loss may be carried back to each of the 3 preceding years, and carried over to each of the 5 following years
Capital loss	Reduce capital gains; any remaining excess loss can be applied as a short-term capital loss for up to 5 succeeding years
Nondeductible loss	Cannot be deducted

Investment Tax Credit

A special provision of the federal tax law which, when in force*, may have direct bearing on economic analyses is the investment tax credit. This allows businesses to subtract from their tax liability as much as 7% of what they invest in equipment and certain other business property, not including buildings. This is subject to limitations according to the expected life of the eligible asset and the total tax credit claimed. The limitation according to expected life per 1968 federal tax law is summarized below:

If the expected life is	*The maximum possible investment credit (as a percentage of investment) is*
8 yr or more	7%
6 to 8 yr	$\frac{2}{3}$ of 7%
4 to 6 yr	$\frac{1}{3}$ of 7%
less than 4 yr	0%

Example:

A firm invested $500,000 in property expected to last for 10 years, and $1,000,000 in property expected to last 5 years. What is the maximum possible tax credit?

Solution:

$$\$500,000 \times 7\% \qquad\quad = \$35,000$$
$$\$1,000,000 \times \tfrac{1}{3} \times 7\% = \underline{23,333}$$
$$\text{Total:} \quad \$58,333$$

The allowable investment tax credit in any year cannot exceed the tax liability. If the tax liability is more than $25,000, the tax credit cannot exceed $25,000 plus 25% of the tax liability above that amount. However, the investment tax credit can be carried back as many as 3 years and forward as many as 5 years.

Example:

Suppose that a firm in a given year has a tax liability of $105,000 before consideration of credits and a maximum possible investment credit of $58,333 (such as calculated in the last example). What is the firm's tax liability for that year?

Solution:

Allowable investment credit:
$25,000 + 25%($105,000 − $25,000) = $45,000

---

*During the 1960's, the investment tax credit was made law and then later cancelled at least two times. Provisions of the law as of 1968 are presented herein in the belief that the credit may well become law again in the 1970's, though the rates and exact provisions may differ upon reenactment.

Tax liability for year:
$105,000 − $45,000 = $60,000

It should be noted that, for the above two examples, the difference between the maximum possible tax credit and the allowable investment credit for the year is $13,333($58,333 − $45,000) and can be carried backward or forward to reduce taxes paid or payable in other years.

As an additional side note, even though the investment tax credit results in a cash savings and, therefore, in a reduction in the net investment, 1968 federal tax law provides that the credit does not reduce the investment to be depreciated.

Example:
Given a $10,000 investment which is expected to have a life of 10 years and a $1,000 salvage value, what is the net investment assuming that the full investment tax credit can be used? What is the depreciable investment?

Solution:
Investment tax credit:
$10,000 × 7% = $700
Net effective investment:
$10,000 − $700 = $9,300
Depreciable investment:
$10,000 − $1,000 = $9,000

The above discussion of income taxes is a minimal description of some main provisions of the federal income tax law which are important to economic analyses. It is by no means complete, but is intended to provide a basis for illustrating after-tax (i.e., after income tax) economic analyses. In general, the analyst should either know how to determine the specific provisions of the state and federal income tax law affecting projects being studied or seek the information from persons qualified in tax laws.

The remainder of the chapter will illustrate various after-tax economy studies using a suggested tabular form for computing after-tax cash flows.

Tabular Procedure for Computing After-tax Cash Flow

Below is a suggested table to facilitate the computation of after-tax cash flows.

(1)	(2)	(3)	(4) = (2) + (3)	(5) = −(4) × Rate	(6) = (2) + (5)
Year	Before-tax cash flow	Depreciation for tax purposes	Taxable income	Cash flow for income taxes	After-tax cash flow

Column (2) contains the same information used in "before-tax" analyses. Column (3) is for the write-off of asset value which can be declared as an expense for tax purposes. Column (4) is the income or amount subject to taxes. Column (5) is the taxes paid or saved. Column (6) contains the "after-tax" cash flows to be used directly in after-tax economic analyses just the same as the cash flows in column (2) are used in before-tax economic analyses. The column headings indicate the arithmetic operations for computing columns (4), (5), and (6). It is intended that the table be used with the conventions of "+" for cash inflow or savings and "−" for cash outflow or opportunity foregone. A slight deviation from this is the convention of assigning a "−" to a depreciation charge even though it is not a cash expense item.

Illustration of Computations of After-tax Cash Flows for Various Common Situations

The following series of example problems illustrates the computation of after-tax cash flows as well as various common situations affected by taxes. All problems herein include the common assumption that any tax disbursement or savings occurs at the same time (year) as the income or expense which affects the taxes. For purposes of comparison of the effect of various situations, the after-tax rate of return will be shown for each example. One can observe from the results of Examples 1 through 5 below that the faster (sooner) the depreciation write-off, the higher the after-tax rate of return.

Example 1:
Certain new machinery is estimated to cost $120,000 installed. It is expected to reduce net annual operating disbursements by $24,000 per yr for 10 years and to have $20,000 salvage value at the end of the tenth year. (a) What is the before-tax rate of return? (b) Show the cash flow tabulation and the after-tax rate of return if straight line depreciation is used and the ordinary income tax rate is 48%.

Solution:
a. Before-tax rate of return:

$-\$120,000 + \$24,000(P/A,i\%,10) + \$20,000(P/F,i\%,10) = 0$

@15%: $-\$120,000 + \$24,000(5.019) + \$20,000(0.2472) = +\$5,050$

@20%: $-\$120,000 + \$24,000(4.192) + \$20,000(0.1615) = -\$16,300$

$i = 15\% + \left(\dfrac{5,050}{5,050 + 16,300}\right)(20\% - 15\%) = 16.2\%$

b.

(1)	(2)	(3)	(4) = (2) + (3)	(5) = −(4) × *Rate*	(6) = (2) + (5)
Year	Before-tax cash flow	Depreciation for tax purposes	Taxable income	Cash flow for income taxes	After-tax cash flow
0	− $120,000				− $120,000
1–10	+ 24,000	− $10,000	+$14,000	− $6,720	+ 17,280
10	+ 20,000				+ 20,000

$$-\$120,000 + \$17,280(P/A,i\%,10) + \$20,000(P/F,i\%,10) = 0$$

By trial and error, $i = 8.9\%$.

Example 2:

Same problem as Example 1(b) above except that sum-of-years-digits depreciation is used.

Solution:

$$\text{S.Y.D.} = \frac{N(N+1)}{2} = \frac{10(11)}{2} = 55$$

First year depreciation: $\frac{10}{55}(\$120,000 - \$20,000) = \$18,200$

Decrease in depreciation each year thereafter:

$$\frac{1}{55}(\$120,000 - \$20,000) = \$1,820$$

(1) Year	(2) Before-tax cash flow	(3) Depreciation for tax purposes	(4) = (2) + (3) Taxable income	(5) = −(4) × Rate Cash flow for income taxes	(6) = (2) + (5) After-tax cash flow
0	− $120,000				− $120,000
1	+ 24,000	− $18,200	+ $5,800	− $2,780	+ 21,220
Each Year 2–10	+ 24,000	Decreases $1,820	Increases $1,820	$875 more negative	Decreases $875
10	+ 20,000				+ 20,000

$$-\$120,000 + \$21,220(P/A,i\%,10) - \$875(A/G,i\%,10)(P/A,i\%,10)$$
$$+ \$20,000(P/F,i\%,10) = 0$$

By trial and error, $i = 12.9\%$.

Example 3:

Same problem as Example 1(b) above except assume that the full investment tax credit can be taken at the same time the investment is made.

Solution:

(1) Year	(2) Before-tax cash flow	(3) Depreciation for tax purposes	(4) = (2) + (3) Taxable income	(5) = −(4) × Rate Cash flow for income taxes	(6) = (2) + (5) After-tax cash flow
0	− $120,000			+ $8,400*	− $111,600
1–10	+ 24,000	− $10,000	+ $14,000	− 6,720	+ 17,280
10	+ 20,000				+ 20,000

*$120,000 × 7% = $8,400.

$$-\$111,600 + \$17,280(P/A,i\%,10) + \$20,000(P/F,i\%,10) = 0$$

By trial and error, $i = 10.5\%$.

Example 4:

Same problem as Example 1(b) above regarding the cash flows expected to happen. However, tax regulations will permit the equipment to be depreciated over a 4-yr period using straight line depreciation and zero salvage value. Assume that any annual loss reduces taxable ordinary income and that any capital gain is taxable at 25%.

Solution:

Annual depreciation: $\dfrac{\$120,000 - \$0}{4} = \$30,000$

(1)	(2)	(3)	(4) = (2) + (3)	(5) = -(4) × Rate	(6) = (2) + (5)
Year	*Before-tax cash flow*	*Depreciation for tax purposes*	*Taxable income*	*Cash flow for income taxes*	*After-tax cash flow*
0	- $120,000				- $120,000
1–4	+ 24,000	- $30,000	- $ 6,000	+ $ 2,880	+ 26,880
5–10	+ 24,000	0	+ 24,000	- 11,500	+ 12,500
0	+ 20,000		+ 20,000*	- 5,000*	+ 15,000

*Tax on capital gain: $20,000 × 25% = $5,000.

$$-\$120,000 + \$26,880(P/A,i\%,4) + \$12,500(P/A,i\%,6)(P/F,i\%,4)$$
$$+ \$15,000(P/F,i\%,10) = 0$$

By trial and error, $i = 12.5\%$.

Example 5:

Same problem as Example 1(b) above regarding expected cash flows except that the equipment is expected to have no salvage value after 10 years. Even though the equipment is serviceable for only 10 years, assume that tax regulations now require that the equipment be amortized over a 15-yr period using straight line depreciation. As in Example 4, assume that any annual loss reduces taxable ordinary income and that any capital gain is taxable at 25%.

Solution:

Annual depreciation: $\dfrac{\$120,000}{15} = \$8,000$

(1)	(2)	(3)	(4) = (2) + (3)	(5) = -(4) × Rate	(6) = (1) + (5)
Year	*Before-tax cash flow*	*Depreciation for tax purposes*	*Taxable income*	*Cash flow for income taxes*	*After-tax cash flow*
0	- $120,000				- $120,000
1–10	+ 24,000	- $8,000	+ $16,000	- $7,700	+ 16,300
11–15		- 8,000		+ 3,840	+ 3,840

$$-\$120,000 + \$16,300(P/A,i\%,10) + \$3,840(P/A,i\%,5)(P/F,i\%,10) = 0$$

By trial and error, $i = 7.5\%$.

The after-tax rate-of-return results from Examples 1(b) through 5 above are summarized in Table 7-4. Note the marked increase in this return with increased rates of depreciation.

Table 7-4

SUMMARIZATION OF AFTER-TAX RATES OF RETURN
FOR EXAMPLES 1(b) THROUGH 5

Example	Method of depreciation (with special treatment)	After-tax rate of return
1(b)	Straight line	8.9%
2	Sum-of-years-digits	12.9
3	Straight line (investment tax credit taken)	10.5
4	Straight line (over 4 years)	12.5
5	Straight line (over 15 years)	7.5

Illustration of After-tax Analyses Using Different Economic Analysis Methods

Example:

It is desired to compare the economics of wooden vs. brick construction for a certain building. Below is given the pertinent data.

	Wood	Brick
First cost:	$40,000	$100,000
Life:	20 yr	40 yr
Salvage value:	$10,000	$20,000
Annual before-tax cash disbursement:	$9,000	$3,000

Use a table to compute the after-tax cash flows based on straight line depreciation and a 30% tax rate to cover both state and federal income taxes. Assuming a 6% minimum attractive after-tax rate of return, show which alternative is best by the (a) annual worth method, (b) present worth method, and (c) rate of return method.

Solution:

Annual depreciation for wood: $\dfrac{\$40,000 - \$10,000}{20} = \$1,500$

Annual depreciation for brick: $\dfrac{\$100,000 - \$20,000}{40} = \$2,000$

(1)	(2)	(3)	(4) = (2) + (3)	(5) = −(4) × Rate	(6) = (2) + (5)
Year	Before-tax cash flow	Depreciation for tax purposes	Taxable income	Cash flow for income taxes @30%	After-tax cash flow
Wood { 0	−$ 40,000				− $40,000
1–20	− 9,000	−$1,500	−$10,500	+$3,150	− 5,850
20	+ 10,000				+ 10,000
Brick { 0	− 100,000				− 100,000
1–40	− 3,000	− 2,000	− 5,000	+ 1,500	− 1,500
40	+ 20,000				+ 20,000

a. Annual worth comparison:

Wood:

$$-\$40,000(A/P,i\%,20) + \$10,000(A/F,i\%,20) - \$5,850$$
$$= -\$40,000(0.087) \qquad + \$10,000(0.027) \qquad - \$5,850 = -\$9,060$$

Brick:

$$-\$100,000(A/P,i\%,40) + \$20,000(A/F,i\%,40) - \$1,500$$
$$= -\$100,000(0.0664) \qquad + \$20,000(0.0064) \qquad - \$1,500 = -\$8,012$$

Thus, the brick is more economical.

b. Present worth comparison:

	Wood	Brick
First cost:	− $ 40,000	−$100,000
Annual disbursement: −$ 5,850(P/A,i%,40) =	− 88,000 − $1,500(P/A,i%,40) =	− 22,600
Replacement: −$30,000(P/F,i%,20) =	− 9,350	
Salvage value: +$10,000(P/F,i%,40) =	+ 970 + $20,000(P/F,i%,40) =	+ 1,930
Net P.W.: =	−$136,380	−$120,670

Thus, the brick again is shown to be more economical.

c. Rate-of-return comparison:

Equating the annual costs to obtain the return on the extra investment:

$$-\$40,000(A/P,i\%,20) + \$10,000(A/F,i\%,20) - \$5,850$$
$$= -\$100,000(A/P,i\%,40) + \$20,000(A/F,i\%,40) - \$1,500$$

By trial and error, $i \approx 8\%$, which means that the extra investment for the brick, having an after-tax return of more than 6%, is justified and thus, the brick is again shown to be the better alternative.

Note: The signs (positive and negative) could have been reversed in the computations for each of the above three methods. This is commonly done when it is understood that one is dealing with costs rather than savings or incomes.

PROBLEMS

7-1. Determine the more economical means of acquiring a business machine if you may either (1) purchase the machine for $5,000 with a probable resale value of $2,000 at the end of 5 years, or (2) rent the machine at an annual rate of $900 per yr for 5 years with an initial deposit of $500 refundable upon returning the machine in good condition. If you own the machine, you will depreciate it for tax purposes at the annual rate of $600. Of course, all leasing rental charges are deductible from taxable income. As either owner or lessee you will assume liability for all expenses associated with the operation of the machine. Compare the alternatives using the annual cost method. The after-tax minimum attractive rate of return is 10% and the income tax rate is 40%.

7-2. Work Prob. 3-13 by an after-tax analysis based on straight line depreciation, an income tax rate of 33%, and a minimum attractive after-tax rate of return of 10% using the following methods:
   a. Annual worth method
   b. Present worth method
   c. Rate of return method

7-3. Work Prob. 3-6 by an after-tax analysis assuming straight line depreciation is used, the income tax rate is 40%, and the minimum attractive rate of return after taxes is 12%.

7-4. Work Prob. 3-14 by an after-tax analysis based on straight line depreciation, an income tax rate of 50%, and a minimum attractive after-tax rate of return of 8% using the following methods:
   a. Annual worth method
   b. Present worth method
   c. Rate of return method

7-5. A certain machine which can be installed at a cost of $15,000 will bring annual savings of $4,000 and zero salvage at the end of a 5-yr economic life. The firm's income tax rate is 50%. Determine the after-tax rate of return for this investment using the following methods of depreciation:
   a. Straight line
   b. Sum-of-years-digits
   c. Double rate declining balance

7-6. Work Prob. 7-5a with the following changes:
   a. The whole investment amount can be declared as an expense at the end of the first year of project life without resorting to straight line depreciation.
   b. Straight line depreciation is used and the investment tax credit is allowed per the limitations according to expected life.

7-7. A $50,000 investment is expected to cause a reduction in net annual out-of-pocket costs of $11,000 a year for 10 years and then have zero salvage value. The investment will be depreciated for income tax purposes using the sum-of-years-digits method with a life of 10 years and zero salvage value. If the tax rate is 50%, find the after-tax rate of return. Use the gradient formula in the solution.

7-8. Jim Crooner has such a high income that he is in the 70% tax bracket on ordinary income. He buys a farm as a side business for $50,000. He figures that, because of his tax bracket, it would be a good idea to fix up the farm and sell it for a capital gain which is taxed at 25%. He keeps the farm for 5 years, and the annual out-of-pocket costs are $10,000 more than the annual cash revenues. Each year he is able to deduct that loss and also $4,000 depreciable expense from his taxable income. At the end of the fifth year he sells the farm for $100,000. Find the following:

a. The before-tax rate of return
b. The after-tax rate of return

eight

Replacement Analyses

Replacement studies are of two general types. The first type involves studies on whether to keep an old asset (sometimes called *defender*) or to replace the old with a new asset (sometimes called *challenger*) at a given point in time. The second general type involves determining, in advance, the economic service life of an asset. Examples of the latter type of replacement study, which is often included in the first type, will be given later in the chapter.

The economics of replacement can generally be studied by any of the methods used for usual economic analyses of alternatives; e.g., rate of return, annual cost, or present worth.

Importance of Replacement Studies

The formulation of a replacement policy plays a major part in the determination of the basic technological and economic progress of a firm. Undue or hasty replacement can leave a firm pressed for capital which may be needed for other beneficial uses. A more important problem in practice is that if replacement is postponed beyond a reasonable time, the firm may find that its production costs are rising, whereas the costs of its competitors who are using more modern equipment are declining. This can result in the firm's loss of ability to meet price competition and a consequent technological and economic trap of drastic consequences.

Causes of Retirement

Property retirement for economic study purposes is said to occur whenever the asset is physically removed, abandoned, or reassigned to a secondary service function. The following are common causes of retirement:

1. unsatisfactory functional characteristics, such as deterioration or inadequacy to meet requirements for safety, capacity, style or quality;
2. end of need for output capability of asset; and
3. existence of improved assets which have reduced operating costs to the extent that the old asset is uneconomical.

Replacement Considerations and Assumptions

Below are discussed several important classes of considerations and assumptions inherent in replacement analyses (as well as in most analyses of non-replacement alternatives) together with some of the alternatives within these classes.

1. The *planning horizon* is the furthest time in the future which is considered in the analysis. Often, an infinite planning horizon is used when it is difficult or impossible to predict when the activity under consideration will be terminated. Whenever it is clear that the project will have a definite and predictable duration, it is more realistic to base the study on a finite planning horizon.
2. The *technology* is important with respect to the characteristics of machines which are candidates to replace those under analysis. If it is assumed that all future assets will be the same as those presently in service, this implies that there will be no technological progress for that type of asset. It is probably more realistic to expect some obsolescence of old assets with respect to available new assets.
3. *Cost and return patterns over asset life* can take an infinite variety of forms. It is fairly common to assume that these are uniform (constant) for lack of ability or willingness to try to estimate more closely. Common alternatives to this are to assume an increasing or decreasing pattern according to some function of time (usually linear).
4. The *availability of capital* can be quite important to any replacement analysis, for the alternatives usually involve keeping the old asset and thereby needing little or no additional capital as opposed to investing in some replacement asset with a marked capital outlay. Many studies are made assuming infinite capital available at some specified minimum rate of return. On the other hand, it may be desirable to consider some

limitation on capital available, at least in the choice between alternative projects in a given time period.

Determination of Investment Amounts for Replacement Alternatives

A key principle in replacement analyses is that sunk costs in the old asset should be disregarded in the determination of the investment in each alternative. (See Chapter 1, section on "Sunk Costs.") Thus, rules for determining the investment in each alternative are

1. Investment in old asset = Present realizable (salvage) value + Any capital expenditure necessary to make it perform the needed function during the expected future life
2. Investment in new asset = Total money to be tied up in new asset if acquired

Example:
Given the following information on an old lathe and a prospective new lathe, show what would be the total investment in each (neglecting the effect of income taxes).

	Old lathe (Defender)	New lathe (Challenger)
Investment when bought 6 years ago:	$10,000	Investment if acquired now: $18,000
Book value now:	4,500	
Net salvage value if sold now:	1,500	
Present overhaul cost if kept:	1,000	

Solution:
The before-tax investment in the old asset would be the $1,500 present net salvage value plus the $1,000 overhaul cost, or a total of $2,500. The investment in the new asset would be $18,000, not $15,500 ($18,000 minus $2,500), which is the net extra (incremental) investment required to switch from the old to the new asset.

Salvage Value of Old Asset in Trade-in

When a piece of equipment replaces another piece of equipment, the old piece of equipment is often accepted as partial payment for its replacement. If the vendor offers an allowance of, say, $3,000 on an older truck when traded for a newer model listed at, say, $5,000, the exchange price ($2,000) is then known, but the true salvage value of the older truck is not necessarily known. It is only by knowing the cash price of the newer model, say $4,200, that we can have a true estimate of the actual salvage value of the old truck ($4,200 − $2,000 = $2,200). Thus, the difference between the "apparent" salvage value based on trade-in quotation and the true salvage value is $3,000 − $2,200 = $800. The erroneous overstatement of challenger and defender costs by this $800 does not result in compensating errors whenever the expected life of the challenger differs from that for the defender, for the added stated investment for the challenger then is spread over a different number of years than for the defender.

Consideration of Differing Lives of Replacement Alternatives

In replacement analyses, it is very common for the expected remaining life of the old asset to be different from (usually less than) the expected life of the new asset. The usual assumptions in comparisons of alternatives with different lives are covered in Chapter 3. These are not entirely valid for replacement analyses, for if the old asset is chosen based on a certain life, it is usually not reasonable to expect that same asset to be capable of the same performance during second, third, etc. assumed repetitions of this life. Hence, for replacement analyses it is usually assumed that, if an old asset is chosen, then after its remaining life has expired it will be replaced with a new asset comparable to the one for which economic comparison was formerly made; and it is further assumed that the period of needed service is of a length to take full advantage of the new replacement or any reasonably anticipated successor of that replacement. If such a replacement is to occur far enough in the future and the interest rate is sufficiently high, then violations of this assumption would have little effect on the indicated choice based on the present economic analysis.

Example:

Suppose that for the two lathes in the above example, the old lathe has an expected remaining life of 3 years and the new lathe has a life of 15 years and that neither has an anticipated salvage value at the end of that time. Further, the annual cash disbursements are $3,100 for the old and $2,000 for the new. Show which alternative is better by an annual cost analysis using a minimum rate of return of 10%, and explain the implications of the different lives for the alternatives.

Solution:

	Old lathe	New lathe
C.R. = $2,500($A/P$,10%,3):	$1,010	
C.R. = $18,000($A/P$,10%,15):		$2,360
Cash disbursements:	3,100	2,000
Total annual costs:	$4,110	$4,360

Thus, the old lathe is the more economical and would, on the face of the situation, be kept for 3 years. It is assumed in this analysis that the old lathe will be replaced with the new lathe and that the new lathe will be needed for an additional 15 years. Of course, at the end of the 3 years or before, a new analysis should actually be made to determine if, in light of the updated information, it appears that the old lathe should still be retained or replaced with any new alternative.

Consideration of Differing Capacities of Alternatives

An economy study of alternatives (replacement or otherwise) is usually based on the assumption that each of the alternatives is of comparable capacity—that is, each is capable of providing the needed function or functions. If one or more of the alternatives has excess capacity and this excess capacity is expected to be of value to the owner, then this added value is treated as an intangible or is included in the economy study to the extent that a dollar figure can be reasonably assigned to it.

Example:
Suppose that for the old vs. new lathes compared above, it is thought that the new lathe has usable extra capacity compared to the old lathe. Close study indicates that the extra capacity should result in gross additional business of $2,000 per yr, of which 25% should be cash profit. A comparison of the two lathes by the annual cost method under these conditions is as follows:

	Old		*New*
Total annual cost (from above):	$4,110		$4,360
Annual worth of extra capacity:		$-$2,000 \times 25%$:	$-$ 500
Net annual cost:	$4,110		$3,860

Thus, under these conditions, the new lathe is better. The same relative result could have been obtained by adding the $500 to the old lathe as an annual opportunity cost.

Types of Asset Accounting and Effect on Federal Taxes Upon Disposal

There are two ways of accounting for assets on the company's books. The way used for a particular asset has a bearing on the tax treatment when that asset is disposed.

1. *Group accounting* is used for items similar in nature and numerous enough to be lumped together (such as a company's fleet of cars or bank of automatic lathes). Under some circumstances, especially when group accounting is used, federal tax laws will not allow a loss upon disposal to be declared when it occurs, but rather will require that the loss be spread over future years—i.e., be depreciated over the future.
2. *Item accounting* is used for items of which there is only one or a few (like a building or a very costly machine). Under certain circumstances, especially when item accounting is used, federal tax laws will allow a loss on disposal to be declared at the time of occurrence.

Whenever a gain or loss on disposal of an asset is illustrated in this book, it will be assumed that the gain or loss is declared for tax purposes at the time of the occurrence.

Tax Rates on Gains or Losses on Disposal of Old Assets

Tables 7-2 and 7-3 summarize in gross form the tax rates involved in both capital gains and ordinary income gains and losses for individuals and for corporations, respectively. These will be illustrated for various situations by the next two example problems.

Example:

An individual taxpayer for whom applicable incremental ordinary income is taxed at 40% has an asset with a book value of $4,500 which is disposed of for $1,500. Show the net after-tax cash flow of this transaction if the loss is treated as:

   a. ordinary income loss;
   b. capital loss—and the individual has $4,000 in net long-term capital gains from disposal of other assets; and
   c. capital loss—and the individual has no capital gains from other sources.

Solution:

Using Table 7-2 for the applicable tax notes:

	(2) *Before-tax cash flow*	(3) *Depreciation for tax purposes*	(4) = (2) + (3) *Taxable income*	(5) = −(4) × *Rate* *Cash flow for income taxes*	(6) = (2) + (5) *After-tax cash flow*
(a)	+$1,500		− $3,000	+$1,200*	+$2,700
(b)	+ 1,500		− 3,000	+ 600†	+ 2,100
(c)	+ 1,500		− 3,000	+ 1,000‡	+ 2,500

*$3,000 book loss × 40% = $1,200 tax reduction.
†3,000 reduction in capital gains × 40%/2 = $600 tax reduction.
‡$3,000 book loss × 40% = $1,200 possible tax reduction; however, this is limited to a maximum of $1,000 in the year. The remaining $2,000 can be carried back as many as 3 years or forward up to 5 years.

Example:

A corporation paying taxes in the 48% bracket owns an old asset with a book value of $500 which is disposed for $1,500. Show the net after-tax cash flow for this transaction if the gain is treated as

a. ordinary income;
b. long-term capital with a rate of 25%; and
c. short-term capital.

Solution:

	(2) *Before-tax cash flow*	(3) *Depreciation for tax purposes*	(4) = (2) + (3) *Taxable income*	(5) = −(4) × *Rate* *Cash flow for income taxes*	(6) = (2) + (5) *After-tax cash flow*
(a)	+$1,500		+$1,000	−$480*	+$1,020
(b)	+ 1,500		+ 1,000	− 250†	+ 1,250
(c)	+ 1,500		+ 1,000	− 480‡	+ 1,020

$*-\$1,000(0.48) = -\$480.$
$†-\$1,000(0.25) = -\$250.$
$‡-\$1,000(0.48) = -\$480.$

Asset Life Types

Economic studies, since they deal with the future, involve estimated rather than observed lives of properties. The term *life* can have a number of meanings; hence, the following defining distinctions are given:

1. *Economic life (service life)* is the period of time from the date of installation to date of retirement from the primary intended service of the asset. An estimate of the economic life of an asset may be based on the period which maximizes the annual worth of the proposed asset, assuming that the asset's service will be needed for that long and that no superior alternatives become available during that period. Retirement, however, is signaled by a future economy study when the annual worth of a prospective new asset becomes greater than the annual worth of retaining the present asset for 1 or more years. Retirement may constitute either disposal or demotion of the asset to a lower, less useful, grade of service than was originally intended (such as for standby service).

2. *Ownership life* is the period of time from the date of installation to the date of actual disposal by a specific owner. The ownership life of an asset may well consist of one or more periods of secondary (downgraded) service in addition to the period of primary service, which constitutes its economic life.

3. *Physical life* is the period of time from the date of installation by the original owner until the asset is ultimately disposed of by its final owner.

There are several reasons underlying the difference between physical life and economic life. The first reason is the technological improvements in reliability or uniformity, the increased output capacities, and the reduced operating costs of successive new models. Secondly, the old equipment may show a pattern of increasing maintenance and operating costs as well as a deterioration in the quality of the goods or services produced. While the above reasons underlie the need for replacement in general, they also should dictate the pattern, if any, of physical life in addition to economic life. It should be kept in mind that we are generally concerned with economic lives in replacement studies.

Calculation of Economic Life

The second general type of replacement study mentioned at the beginning of this chapter is the determination, in advance, of how many years an asset should be kept for most economical service. In determining the economic life of a prospective new asset, there are three main types of costs to be taken into account: (1) costs of capital recovery, (2) costs inherent to the asset, and (3) costs relative to available improved models. Generally, the longer an asset is kept, the lower will be its annual cost of capital recovery and the higher will be its inherent and relative operating costs. An explanation of the meaning and calculation of each of these three types of costs is given in the following sections.

Costs of capital recovery

A realistic year-by-year cost of capital recovery can be determined only by estimating the net salvage (resale) value at the end of each year. The capital recovery cost for any year can be calculated as the decline in salvage

Table 8-1

YEARLY CAPITAL RECOVERY COST DATA FOR ASSET X

Year	Salvage value at end of year	Decrease in salvage value during year	Interest on investment at beginning of year (@10%)	Capital recovery cost for year
1	$15,000	$8,000	$2,300	$10,300
2	8,500	6,500	1,500	8,000
3	3,000	5,500	850	6,350
4	1,000	2,000	300	2,300
5	1,000	0	100	100

value plus the interest on the asset value for that year. For example, the expected year-by-year salvage values of an asset X costing \$23,000 and the calculation of yearly capital recovery costs, assuming interest at 10%, are shown in Table 8-1.

Costs inherent to the asset

Asset inherent costs include the cost of operation and maintenance, the cost of capacity decreasing compared to when the asset was new, and the cost of quality declining compared to when the asset was new. Decreasing-capacity cost is the loss in output due to downtime and reduced operating rate. Declining-quality cost is the cost of lost sales, and reduced sales price or scrap rework due to the reduced-quality capability of the asset. It should be kept in mind that the costs of decreasing capacity and declining quality are costs compared to the asset when it was new and not compared to possible improved models of the asset. Consideration of the effect of improved models is included in the next section.

For example, the inherent costs of the asset X for which capital recovery data was given in the preceding section is shown in Table 8-2.

Table 8-2

YEARLY INHERENT COST DATA FOR ASSET X

Year	Cost of operation and maintenance	Cost of decreasing capacity	Cost of declining quality	Total inherent costs for year
1	\$ 6,000	\$ 0	\$ 0	\$ 6,000
2	6,000	0	0	6,000
3	6,000	500	500	7,000
4	8,000	1,000	4,000	13,000
5	10,000	2,000	5,000	17,000

Costs relative to improved models

It is common that improved models of an asset will produce at lower operating costs and/or will produce a higher-quality product than the original models of that asset. There is thus an increase in operating costs and an increase in the cost of declining quality in the old asset relative to the new improved model of the asset. These increases in costs are alternative or opportunity costs. Another relative cost is the decreasing net income caused by obsolescence affecting the demand for the asset's products or services.

For example, the relative costs for the same asset X as in the preceding two sections are shown in Table 8-3.

Table 8-3
YEARLY RELATIVE COST DATA FOR ASSET X

Year	Operating cost inferiority	Quality inferiority	Obsolescence	Total relative costs for year
1	$ 0	$ 0	$ 0	$ 0
2	500	0	0	500
3	800	850	0	1,650
4	2,000	3,000	0	5,000
5	2,500	3,500	1,000	7,000

Table 8-4 summarizes the data of Tables 8-1, 8-2, and 8-3 to provide for the calculation of total costs for each year and total equivalent annual costs for purposes of determining the most economical life for the asset X.

Thus, from Table 8-4, it can be seen that the equivalent annual cost is at a minimum if asset X is retired at the end of 3 years. It can also be observed that the total marginal cost (shown in the fifth column as "Total cost for year") exceeds the equivalent annual cost after the third year. This illustrates the general principle for the determination of economic life, which may be stated as follows:

Replace at the end of any period for which the total cost in the next period exceeds the average cost up to that period. Do not replace as long as the total cost in a period does not exceed the average cost to the end of that period.

Example:

As an additional example of calculation of economic life without consideration of income taxes, suppose a certain machine has an installed price of $10,000 and the projected year-by-year operating costs and salvage values shown in the table below.

Year	Total annual inherent and relative operating cost	Salvage value
1	$3,000	$6,000
2	3,500	3,000
3	8,000	1,000

Neglecting income taxes and assuming an interest rate of 0%, below are shown calculations for determination of the most economic replacement interval.

A.C. (for 1-yr interval):
$$(\$10,000 - \$6,000)(A/P,0\%,1) + \$6,000(0\%) + \$3,000 = \$7,000$$

Table 8-4

ECONOMIC LIFE CALCULATION FOR ASSET X

Year	Capital recovery cost for year	Total inherent cost for year	Total relative cost for year	Total cost for year	$(P/F,10\%,N)$	P.W. of cost for year [Total cost × $(P/F,10\%,N)$]	Cumulative P.W. of cost since placed in service ($\sum P.W.$)	$(A/P,10\%,N)$	Equivalent (average) annual cost if retired at end of year [$\sum P.W.$ × $(A/P,10\%,N)$]
1	$10,300	$ 6,000	$ 0	$16,300	0.909	$14,790	$14,790	1.100	$16,300
2	8,000	6,000	500	14,500	0.826	12,700	27,400	0.576	15,800
3	6,350	7,000	1,650	15,000	0.751	11,300	38,700	0.402	15,570 (minimum)
4	2,300	13,000	5,000	20,300	0.683	13,900	52,600	0.315	17,800
5	100	17,000	7,000	24,100	0.621	15,000	67,600	0.264	17,850

A.C. (for 2-yr interval):

$$(\$10,000 - \$3,000)(A/P,0\%,2) + \$3,000(0\%)$$
$$+ [\$3,000 + \$3,500(P/F,0\%,1)](A/P,0\%,2) = \$6,750$$

A.C. (for 3-yr interval):

$$(\$10,000 - \$1,000)(A/P,0\%,3) + (\$1,000)(0\%) + [\$3,000$$
$$+ \$3,500(P/F,0\%,1) + \$8,000(P/F,0\%,2)](A/P,0\%,3) = \$7,830$$

Thus, replacement at 2-yr intervals is apparently slightly more economical than 1-yr or 3-yr intervals.

Example:

As an example of replacement analysis involving determination of optimal remaining life of old asset and including effect of income taxes, suppose the replacement of a spray system is being considered by the Hokie Metal Stamping Company. The new improved system will cost $60,000 installed, and will have an estimated economic life of 12 years and $6,000 salvage value. Further, it is estimated that annual operating and maintenance costs will average $32,000 per yr for the new system, and that straight line depreciation will be used. The present system has a book value of $12,000 and a present realizable salvage value of $8,000. Its estimated costs and book values for the next 3 years are as follows:

Year	Salvage value at end of year	Book value at end of year	Inherent and relative operating costs during year
1	$6,000	$9,000	$40,000
2	5,000	6,000	50,000
3	4,000	3,000	60,000

Table 8-5 shows calculations to determine relevant after-tax cash flows for this problem. It is assumed that the ordinary income tax rate is 50% and that any gain or loss on disposal of the old asset affects taxes at the full ordinary rate.

After-tax annual cost calculations for each alternative utilizing the results in column (6) of Table 8-5 (with the signs reversed) and a 15% minimum after-tax rate of return are:

New system,

$$(\$60,000 - \$6,000)(A/P,15\%,12) + \$6,000(15\%)$$
$$+ \$13,750 = \$24,600$$

Old system,
keep 1 yr:

$$(\$10,000 - \$7,500)(A/P,15\%,1) + \$7,500(15\%)$$
$$+ \$18,500 = \$22,500$$

Table 8-5

CALCULATION OF AFTER-TAX CASH FLOWS FOR EXAMPLE REPLACEMENT ANALYSIS

(1) Year	(2) Before-tax cash flow	(3) Depreciation for tax purposes	(4) = (2) + (3) Taxable income	(5) = −(4) × Rate Cash flow for income taxes −(4) × 50%	(6) = (2) + (5) After-tax cash flow
New system					
0	− $60,000				− $60,000
1–12	− 32,000	− $4,500	− $36,500	+ $18,250	− 13,750
12	+ 6,000				+ 6,000
Old system, keep 1 yr					
0	(−)$ 8,000		(−)($ 8,000 − 12,000)	(−)$ 2,000	(−)$10,000
1	− 40,000	− $3,000	− 43,000	+ 21,500	− 18,500
1	+ 6,000		+ 6,000 − 9,000	+ 1,500	+ 7,500
Old system, keep 2 yr					
0	(−)$ 8,000		(−)($ 8,000 − 12,000)	(−)$ 2,000	(−)$10,000
1	− 40,000	− $3,000	− 43,000	+ 21,500	− 18,500
2	− 50,000	− 3,000	− 53,000	+ 26,500	− 23,500
2	+ 5,000		+ 5,000 − 6,000	+ 500	+ 5,500
Old system, keep 3 yr					
0	(−)$ 8,000		(−)($ 8,000 − 12,000)	(−)$ 2,000	(−)$10,000
1	− 40,000	− $3,000	− 43,000	+ 21,500	− 18,500
2	− 50,000	− 3,000	− 53,000	+ 26,500	− 23,500
3	− 60,000	− 3,000	− 63,000	+ 31,500	− 28,500
3	+ 4,000		+ 4,000 − 3,000	− 500	+ 3,500

Note: Negative signs in parentheses represent the result of "opportunity foregone"—i.e., if the old system were sold, a certain cash flow would result, but by keeping it the opportunity for the cash flow is foregone; hence, the reversal of cash flow sign.

Old system,
keep 2 yr:

$$(\$10,000 - \$5,500)(A/P,15\%,2) + \$5,500(15\%)$$
$$+ [\$18,500(P/F,15\%,1)$$
$$+ \$23,500(P/F,15\%,2)](A/P,15\%,2) = \$24,400$$

Old system,
keep 3 yr:

$$(\$10,000 - \$3,500)(A/P,15,3) + \$3,500(15\%)$$
$$+ [\$18,500(P/F,15\%,1) + \$23,500(P/F,15\%,2)$$
$$+ \$28,500(P/F,15\%,3)](A/P,15\%,3) = \$26,475$$

On the basis of the above analysis, one would tend to say that the old system should be replaced at the end of the second year. But the above analysis procedure is deceiving, for it is not generally correct. Instead, one should examine marginal costs. The valid economic criterion is to keep the old system as long as the marginal cost of an additional year of service is less than the equivalent annual cost of the new system. The marginal cost of keeping the old system for the first year is the \$22,500 previously computed. This \$22,500 is less than the \$24,550 average annual cost of the new system, thus justifying keeping the old system for the first year.

The marginal cost of keeping the old system for the second year is (\$7,500 − \$5,500) + 7,500(15\%) + \$23,000 = \$26,125. This is greater than the \$24,550 average annual cost of the new system, thus indicating that the old

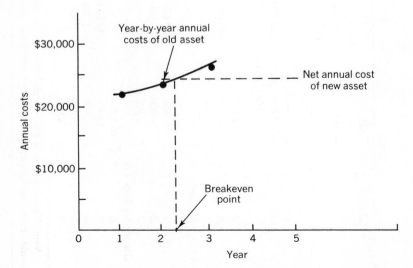

Figure 8-1. Old versus new asset costs.

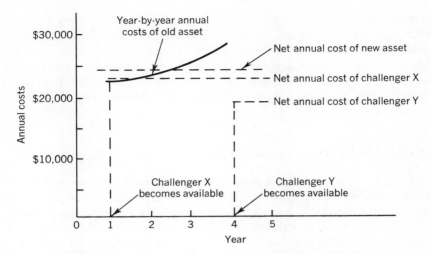

Figure 8-2. Old versus new asset costs with improved challengers becoming available in future.

system should not be kept the second year, but rather that it be replaced at the end of the first year.

The above example assumes that there is only one new asset (challenger) alternative available. It shows the general relationship that if the old asset (defender) is retained beyond the break-even point, its costs continue to grow and replacement becomes more urgent as illustrated in Fig. 8-1.

Figure 8-2 illustrates the effect of improved new challengers in the future. If an improved challenger X becomes available before replacement with the new asset of Fig. 8-1, then a new replacement study probably should take place to consider that improved challenger. If there is a possibility of a further-improved challenger Y as of, say, 4 years later, it may be still better to postpone replacement until that challenger becomes available. Thus, retention of the old asset beyond the break-even point has a cost which may well grow with time, but this cost of waiting can, in some instances, be worthwhile if it permits purchase of an improved asset having economies that offset the cost of waiting. Of course, a decision to postpone a replacement may "buy time and information" also. Because technological change tends to be sudden and dramatic rather than uniform and gradual, new challengers with significantly improved features can arise sporadically and can change replacement plans substantially.

Intangibles in Replacement Problems

As in other management decisions, replacement problems have intangible aspects that may have sufficient weight to control the decision. Intangibles in replacement analysis may include competing needs for capital, future uncertainties in market and costs, possibilities of product change, financial condition of the business, attitudes and limitations of personnel, labor shortage or surplus, ethical and social problems, etc. Intangibles are notably reflected in two of the quantitative factors or elements used in the illustrations above, namely the study period and the minimum required rate of return on investment.

Models for Replacement Analysis

There is an infinite variety of possible mathematical models for analysis of replacement situations. These models vary even in calculated results because of varying assumptions and degrees of complexity. In developing models to determine optimum replacement policy (e.g., economic life or when to replace in advance), it is common to differentiate between two main categories of assets: those not subject to failure, and those which can suddenly fail. We shall examine each of these separately.

Replacement of Assets Not Subject to Sudden Failure

The following sections show replacement analysis models for assets which do not suddenly fail in service, but rather which are probably subject to some inherent deterioration or at least to decreases in relative desirability over time. The replacement problems illustrated up to now in this chapter are limited to this type. The following four illustrative models* are based on common, noncomplex assumptions and serve to indicate the variety of models of this type which can be utilized.

One life cycle of asset

The present worth of an investment in one life cycle of an asset, as a function of N, can be expressed as†

$$\text{P.W.}(N) = P + \sum_{n=1}^{N} \frac{D_n}{(1 + i)^n} + \frac{F_N}{(1 + i)^N} \tag{8-1}$$

where P.W.(N) = Present worth for a life of N years
P = Initial investment (at same time as P.W.)

*Adapted with permission from William T. Morris, *The Analysis of Management Decisions* (Homewood, Ill.: R. D. Irwin, Inc., 1964), pp. 199–207.
†*Note:* The equivalent expression for the continuous compounding case is

$$\text{P.W.}(N) + P + \int_{0}^{N} D_n e^{-in}\, dn + F_N e^{-iN}$$

D_n = Net annual receipt or disbursement amount at end of year n (= annual receipts minus annual disbursements).

F_N = Salvage or resale value (at end of life, N years)

i = Annual interest rate

N = Life of asset in years

In general, it is desired to find the value of N at which the asset has greatest economic advantage. If it is desired to compare alternative assets on the basis of annual worth, A.W.(N), it is easy to convert by the relation

$$\text{A.W.}(N) = \text{P.W.}(N) \times (A/P, i, N) \tag{8-2}$$

Infinite chain of identical assets

If an asset is assumed to be replaced by an infinite series of identical assets, the present worth (capitalized worth) of that type of asset, as a function of N, may be expressed as

$$\text{P.W.}(N) = \left[P + \sum_{n=1}^{N} \frac{D_n}{(1+i)^n} + \frac{F_N}{(1+i)^N} \right]\left[1 + \frac{1}{(1+i)^N} \right.$$
$$\left. + \frac{1}{(1+i)^{2N}} + \cdots \right] \tag{8-3}$$

This can be reduced to

$$\text{P.W.}(N) = \left[P + \sum_{n=1}^{N} \frac{D_n}{(1+i)^n} + \frac{F_N}{(1+i)^N} \right]\left[\frac{(1+i)^N}{(1+i)^N - 1} \right] \tag{8-4}$$

Improved replacement asset; infinite planning horizon

It is common that a present asset can prospectively be replaced by an improved asset; the improvement may be in the investment required, prospective salvage value function, and/or net annual receipts or disbursements. This type of situation results in two key variables for decision: the best time to replace the present asset and the economic life of the new asset once it has been placed in service. If it is assumed that there is an infinite series of identical replacement assets, the present worth may be written as

$$\text{P.W.}(N) = P_0 + \sum_{n=1}^{N} \frac{D_{0n}}{(1+i)^n} + \frac{F_{0N}}{(1+i)^N} + \frac{\text{A.W.}_1(N_1)}{i(1+i)^N} \tag{8-5}$$

where $\text{A.W.}_1(N_1) = \left[P_1 + \sum_{n=1}^{N_1} \frac{D_{1n}}{(1+i)^n} + \frac{F_{1N_1}}{(1+i)^{N_1}} \right]\left[\frac{i(1+i)^{N_1}}{(1+i)^{N_1} - 1)} \right]$

P_0 = Investment in present asset

P_1 = Investment in replacement asset

D_{0n} = Net annual receipts or disbursement at end of year n for present asset

D_{1n} = Net annual receipts or disbursement at end of year n for replacement asset

F_{0N} = Salvage value for present asset at end of N years

F_{1N_1} = Salvage value for replacement asset at end of N_1 years

N_0 = Life of present asset in years

N_1 = Life of replacement asset in years

i = Annual interest rate

Deterioration and obsolescence of asset; indefinite planning horizon

Obsolescence can occur in the form of gradual regular as well as dramatic infrequent increases in operating expenses for existing assets and/or operating improvements for prospective new assets. Since dramatic infrequent changes are quite difficult to predict in terms of timing and monetary effect, it is common to approximate the effect of obsolescence in terms of linear trends. For example, if it is assumed that net annual receipts or disbursements D_m for a given asset decrease linearly with age at rate a per year, this can be reflected as

Year of use	Net annual receipts or disbursements
1	First-year net
2	First-year net $-a$
3	First-year net $-2a$
.	.
.	.
.	.
n	First-year net $-(n-1)a$

If it is expected that future replacing assets will result in first-year net annual receipts or disbursements which increase linearly at a rate b for each elapsing year, this can be reflected as

Time of purchase or installation of asset	First-year net receipts or disbursements
1	C
2	$C + b$
3	$C + 2b$
.	.
.	.
.	.
k	$C + (k-1)b$

In general, the relative net annual receipts for the nth year of use of an asset which was purchased new at the beginning of year k is $C + (k - 1)b - (n - 1)a$.

The present worth (capitalized worth) of a chain of assets characterizing the effects of obsolescence as described above, and for which replacement is made at the end of each Nth year, is

$$\text{P.W.}(N) = P + \sum_{n=1}^{N} \frac{C - (n - 1)a}{(1 + i)^n} + \frac{P}{(1 + i)^N}$$
$$+ \sum_{n=1}^{N} \frac{C - (n - 1)a + Nb}{(1 + i)^{N+n}} + \frac{P}{(1 + i)^{2N}}$$
$$+ \sum_{n=1}^{N} \frac{C - (n - 1)a + 2Nb}{(1 + i)^{2N+n}} + \frac{P}{(1 + i)^{3N}} + \cdots \quad (8\text{-}6)$$

Equation (8-6) can be reduced to

$$\text{P.W.}(N) = \left[P + \sum_{n=1}^{N} \frac{C - (n - 1)a}{(1 + i)^n} \right] \left[\frac{(1 + i)^N}{(1 + i)^N - 1} \right]$$
$$+ \sum_{k=1}^{\infty} \sum_{n=1}^{N} \frac{kNb}{(1 + i)^{kN+n}} \quad (8\text{-}7)$$

It can be shown that the above analysis is equivalent to

$$\text{P.W.}(N) = \left[P + \sum_{n=1}^{N} \frac{C - (n - 1)(a - b)}{(1 + i)^n} \right] \left[\frac{(1 + i)^N}{(1 + i)^N - 1} \right] \quad (8\text{-}8)$$

Equations (8-7) and (8-8) can be expressed as net annual worths through multiplying by i and the replacement problem reduces to finding the value of N at which the net present worth or net annual worth is maximized.

Economic replacement point and MAPI method

Because the decision to retire and replace an asset is made at a time subsequent to installation, the accumulation of better information upon which to estimate the most economic life is possible. Then, as an old asset (defender) is compared to a proposed new asset (challenger), the problem may be one of comparing the cost of keeping the defender one more year vs. the annual equivalent cost of the challenger. This is essentially what is done using the MAPI method developed by the Machinery and Allied Products Institute (see Appendix 8-A).

Replacement of Assets Subject to Sudden Failure

Some assets, as light bulbs, electronic parts, and missiles, do not exhibit significant deterioration in capabilities over time as such, but are usually subject to increasing opportunities for failure as cumulative usage or age increases. The usual objective in this type of problem is to determine the amount and timing of replacement (or maintenance) of such assets. Three main types of problems are as follows:

1. Should a group of such assets be replaced in entirety, or should they be individually replaced upon failure?
2. If group replacement is the best policy, what is the optimum group-replacement interval?
3. How much and how often should preventive maintenance be performed?

To solve the first type of problem the cost of group replacement can be compared with that of individual replacement upon failure. Whenever group replacement can lead to reduced costs (through labor savings, materials discounts, etc.), the optimum group-replacement interval can be computed using calculus or arithmetic approximation methods. The same methods may be used to solve preventive-maintenance problems. Group-replacement and preventive-maintenance interval problems can also be solved by dynamic programming.

An illustrative model

Let us assume that failures occur only at the end of a period. Thus, replacements of failures which occur at the end of, say, the third period will be age zero at the beginning of the fourth period. During the first $(t - 1)$ time intervals, all failures are replaced as indicated in the foregoing. At the end of the tth time interval, all units are replaced regardless of their ages. The problem is to find that value of t which will minimize total cost per period. If it is assumed that the entire replacement interval in question is of short duration such that the timing of money can be neglected, then the total cost from time of group installation until the end of t periods can be given by

$$K(t) = NC_1 + C_2 \sum_{X=1}^{t-1} f(t) \qquad (8\text{-}9)$$

where $K(t)$ = Total cost for t periods
C_1 = Unit cost of replacement in a group
C_2 = Unit cost of individual replacement after failure
$f(t)$ = Number of failures in the tth period
N = Number of units in the group

Then, the objective is to find the value of t which minimizes $K(t)/t$. The relationship of the various costs is shown in Fig. 8-3.

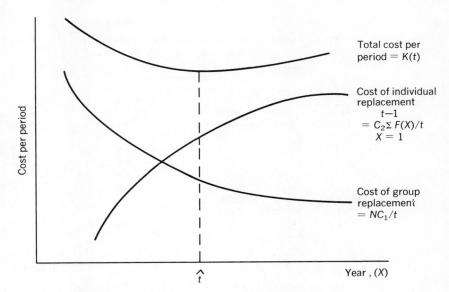

Figure 8-3. Illustration of replacement costs for assets that fail as a function of group-replacement interval.

Costs are minimized for a policy of group replacing after $\hat{t}$ periods if

$$\frac{K(\hat{t})}{\hat{t}} < \frac{K(\hat{t} + 1)}{\hat{t} + 1} \quad \text{and if} \quad \frac{K(\hat{t})}{\hat{t}} < \frac{K(\hat{t} - 1)}{\hat{t} + 1}. \tag{8-10}$$

It can be shown* that one should group-replace at the end of the tth period if and only if the cost of individual replacements for the tth period is greater than the average per period cost of a group-replacement policy through the end of t periods.

Example:

To illustrate calculations of the optimal group-replacement interval for a situation which fits the model represented by Eq. (8-9), suppose that for a group of 10,000 electronic parts subject to sudden failure the net cost of group replacement is $0.50 per unit, while the unit cost of individual replacement is $2.00. Further, the expected failure amounts each period are as shown in Table 8-6. Table 8-7 shows the calculations which indicate that the lowest cost is obtained if group replacement is performed after each third period. It should be noted that this answer is not very sensitive to increases in the group-replacement interval up to 4 or 5 years.

*See Churchman, Ackoff, and Arnoff, *Introduction to Operations Research* (New York: John Wiley & Sons, 1957), pp. 505–507.

Table 8-6

TOTAL FAILURES (REPLACEMENT) IN EACH PERIOD *t*
FOR 10,000 ELECTRONIC PARTS.

Period	Replacements	
	Current $[f(t)]$	Cumulative $[\sum f(t)]$
1	100	100
2	400	500
3	1,100	1,600
4	1,200	2,800
5	2,500	5,300
6	2,300	7,600
7	2,600	10,400
8	2,500	12,900

Table 8-7

CALCULATION OF MOST ECONOMICAL GROUP-REPLACEMENT INTERVAL
FOR 10,000 ELECTRONIC PARTS OF TABLE 8-6

Period	Cumulative replacements $[\sum f(t)]$	Total cost $\left[K(t) = 10,000(\$0.50) + \$2.00 \sum_{1}^{t-1} f(t) \right]$	Average cost per period $[K(t)/t]$
1	100	\$ 5,000	\$5,000
2	500	5,200	2,600
3	1,600	6,000	2,000 (minimum)
4	2,800	8,200	2,050
5	5,300	10,600	2,120
6	7,600	15,600	2,600
7	10,400	20,200	2,890
8	12,900	25,800	3,220

Summary

The early part of this chapter illustrated replacement analyses concerned with whether and when to replace existing equipment for commonly assumed constant conditions. The latter part of the chapter provides only a brief sampling of types of models for determination, in advance, of economical replacement intervals under various circumstances. Models such as these should be used only when the inherent assumptions mesh sufficiently closely with the estimated situation under study. In general, the closer such models approach reality, the more complex the construction and use of those models. The greatest strength in using models such as the above is that they tend to force the analyst to examine objectively the nature of the estimates and assumptions which must be made in the process of analysis for decision-making.

PROBLEMS

8-1. The initial installed cost of a compressor is $6,000. Operation and repair costs are $1,000 for the first year and increase by $300 each year thereafter. The expected salvage value is $3,600 after 1 year, and decreases by $400 each year thereafter until the compressor reaches a maximum life of 8 years. If the minimum required rate of return is 15% before taxes, determine, by a before-tax annual cost analysis, the most economical year in which to replace the compressor.

8-2. A new machine is expected to cost $25,000. Its salvage value is expected to be $15,000 at the end of the first year and to decrease by $1,500 each year thereafter for as long as the machine is kept. The operation and maintenance costs are expected to be $8,000 the first year and to increase by $4,000 each year thereafter. If interest on invested capital is 20% before taxes and a machine of this type is expected to be needed indefinitely, determine the most economical replacement interval by a before-tax annual cost analysis.

8-3. An old bridge must either be strengthened or replaced. The estimated outlay to strengthen the bridge is $12,000, while a new bridge will cost $55,000. The old bridge has a present estimated net salvage value of $14,000. It is estimated that the reinforcement will be sufficient for 10 years, after which time question of reinforcement vs. replacement would again need to be considered. The net salvage value of the reinforced bridge is estimated to be $18,000 at the end of 10 years, while the salvage value of the new bridge is estimated as $22,000 after 30 years. The additional annual cost of maintenance and inspection on the old structure is expected to be $300. If the cost of money is 5% for this government project, determine which alternative has the lower equivalent annual cost. Assume that a bridge will be needed indefinitely.

8-4. The butt of a telephone pole has decayed to the point where it is necessary either to replace the pole or to reinforce the butt. A new pole will cost $70.00 installed and have a life of 20 years, whereas if the old pole is reinforced at a cost of $10.00, it can be expected to last for 10 more years. The old pole has a salvage value of only $8.00, now, and if it is reinforced it would be expected to have no salvage value at the end of 5 years. The terminal salvage value of the new pole after 20 years is $24.00. If the minimum before-tax rate of return is 10%, which is the better alternative?

8-5. A recent flood indicates the need for a larger drainage structure. Three possibilities are considered:

    A. Leave the existing 2-ft pipe in place (it is undamaged) and install another of equal size alongside.

B. Remove the existing 2-ft pipe and replace it with a single 3-ft pipe.

C. Remove the existing 2-ft pipe and replace it with a concrete box culvert. If the present 2-ft pipe is removed, it will have a salvage value of $400. Estimates regarding the new installations are as follows:

	A	B	C
Cost installed:	$1,500	$2,700	$2,800
Estimated life:	15 yr	15 yr	30 yr

Comparing annual costs with interest at 6% before taxes, which alternative is recommended? Assume that the existing pipe will have the same life as the one proposed for installation under alternative A and that a drainage system is needed indefinitely.

8-6. A man owns a side business which he purchased 10 years ago for $46,000. Straight line depreciation has been charged assuming a 25-year life and $6,000 salvage value. He now has an offer to sell the business for $50,000. He estimates that if he does not sell now, he will hold the property for another 7 years and sell it at that time for $45,000. If he keeps the business, he estimates he will pay taxes at the rate of 60% on an annual net taxable income of $5,000 due to this side business. (Any capital gain or capital loss will affect taxes at the rate of 25%. The business will have an annual net cash flow of $6,600, from which $1,600 depreciation is deducted.) (a) Compute the before-tax rate of return from continued ownership of the side business. (b) If he can get 4% after taxes from the use of his capital in some other venture of comparable risk, should he sell now, or wait 7 years? Compute the after-tax rate of return on continued ownership.

8-7. Jones owns his home for which he paid $15,000 8 years ago. This property is free of debt. He has been transferred to another city where he has decided to rent an apartment. He has the opportunity to sell his house now for $18,850 net before taxes. He also has the opportunity to rent his house on a 5-year lease for $2,400 per yr. If he rents the property, he estimates his annual disbursements for property taxes, insurance, and upkeep as $600. He anticipates that if he rents the property now, he will sell it at the end of 5 years for $16,950 before taxes.

If he sells the property now, he will be taxed on a long-term capital gain $3,850. (No depreciation on the house was allowable on tax returns during the years it was his personal residence.) If he rents the house, he can deduct $300 per yr depreciation on his tax return in addition to his cash disbursements.

His effective tax rate on ordinary income from rental would be 30% and on capital gains would be 15%. What would be his after-tax rate of return if he elects to rent the property now?

8-8. An individual owns a rental property in an industrial district of a city. This is rented to a single tenant at an annual rate of $10,000. The present lease is about to expire. The tenant is willing to renew the lease for a long term at the present figure but not at a higher one. A manufacturing company adjoining the building site has made an offer of $120,000 for this property.

Because of the particular needs of this manufacturer for an area to expand, the property owner believes that this is a better offer than can be secured from any other buyer. If the offer is not accepted at once, it is considered likely that the manufacturer will make other plans for plant expansion and that the offer will therefore not be renewed at a later date. A decision must therefore be made at once whether or not to accept this offer.

It is believed that if the property is not sold at once, ownership will be continued for a fairly long time. For purposes of the economy study to guide the decision, assume that ownership will continue for 20 years and that the net resale value before income taxes at the end of that period will be $50,000. The original cost of the property 5 years ago was $80,000, divided for accounting and tax purposes into $20,000 for land and $60,000 for the building. Since purchase, the building has been depreciated for accounting and tax purposes at $1,500 per yr on the basis of an estimated remaining life of 40 years from the purchase date and a terminal salvage value of zero.

If ownership is continued, it is estimated that receipts from rental will continue at $10,000 per yr. Annual disbursements are estimated to be $1,500 for upkeep, $2,100 for property taxes, and $400 for insurance.

    a. Compute a rate of return before income taxes that provides a basis for comparison between the alternatives of continued ownership and immediate sale.

    b. Compute a rate of return after income taxes that provides a basis for comparison between these two alternatives. Consider the income taxes both on any capital gain and on annual taxable income. Assume a 55% tax rate on ordinary income and a 25% tax rate on capital gains.

8-9. A diesel engine was installed 10 years ago at a cost of $70,000. It presently has a salvage value of $14,000. If kept, it can be expected to last 5 more years, have operating disbursements of $14,000 per yr, and have a salvage value of $8,000 at the end of the fifth year from now. This engine is being depreciated by the straight line method using a 15-year life and an estimated salvage value of $10,000.

The old engine can be replaced with an improved version which will cost $65,000, have operating disbursements of $9,000, and an ultimate salvage value of $15,000 at the end of a 20-year life. If the replacement is made, this improved version will be depreciated by the straight line method using the life and salvage value estimated for economy study purposes. Annual disbursements will affect taxes at 50%, and any gain or loss on disposal of old assets will affect taxes at 25%. It is thought that an engine will be needed indefinitely.

    a. Set up table for computation of after-tax cash flows, and determine if replacement now is economical using the annual cost method. (Minimum after-tax R.R. = 10%.)

    b. Write an equation which will result in determining the rate of return on the incremental investment. Will this R.R. be greater than or less than 10%?

8-10. The replacement of a group of routing machines is being considered by the

Finer Furniture Co. The new model would cost $40,000 installed, and would have an estimated economic life of 10 years with annual operating and maintenance costs of $16,000 and a salvage value of $6,000.

The existing model has a present salvage value of $4,000. Estimated cost data for the next 3 years are as follows:

Year	Salvage value at end of year	Operating and maintenance costs for year
1	$3,000	$25,000
2	2,500	30,000
3	2,000	37,000

Assume that income taxes do not affect your analysis significantly and make a before-tax annual cost comparison with a minimum rate of return of 15% to determine when it is economical to make the replacement.

8-11. A 3-year-old machine has the following cost history:

	Disbursements	
Year	For operation and repairs	For delays due to breakdowns
1	$ 700	$ 0
2	900	200
3	1,100	400

If the machine is continued in service for the fourth year, it is estimated that the operation and repair costs will be $1,300 and breakdowns will cost $800. The corresponding estimates for the fifth year of service are $1,700 and $1,000. The machine has a present net realizable cash value of $1,500, and this will probably reduce to $1,200 in another year and to $900 in 2 years. It has a present book value of $2,000, and depreciation will be charged at $500 for each additional year it is kept.

It is suggested that the old machine be replaced by a new machine of improved design costing $7,000. It is believed that this will completely eliminate any breakdowns and the resulting cost of delays, and that it will reduce operation and repair costs to $200 per yr less at each age than the corresponding costs with the old machine. The new machine would be depreciated by the straight line method over the estimated economic life of 6 years based on $1,000 salvage value. If the minimum attractive rate of return is 12% after taxes, what is the best time to replace the old machine? Assume an income tax rate of 50% applied to any operating result or gain or loss on disposal.

8-12. The Hi-Arc Department is currently fabricating tanks using a series of jigs that cost $50,000 5 years ago. They were depreciated using the straight line method; their book value is therefore $25,000. Using these jigs, an average of two man-days (8-hour day) are required to fabricate a tank. The labor rate is $2.00 per hr, and the variable overhead (fringe benefits, payroll cost, etc.) is about 50% of the labor cost.

A semiautomatic tank fabricator has come on the market. This machine will cost $18,000, will eliminate the need for the jigs now used, will require two men (at $2.50 per hr) to operate it, but will produce an average of 10 tanks per day. It will be necessary to keep a scrap lumber pile outside in the future to free a 50-sq-ft floor area to provide the additional space required by the new fabricator. The average annual cost per sq ft of plant is estimated at $3.00 including interest, depreciation, and maintenance. Additional power cost is estimated at $5.00 per day; maintenance costs are $300 for the first year and increase by $500 per yr thereafter. The new machine will eliminate one inspection. This will save a total of $5.00 per tank.

If purchased, the fabricator will be required for 8 years. Since only 200 tanks per yr are required, it will be used only 20 days per yr. The jigs have no realizable salvage value if terminated now, and the fabricator is expected to have no salvage value after 8 years' use. What before-tax rate of return would be earned on the purchase of this machine?

8-13. A firm is presently using a specialized machine which has a market value of $8,000. The requirement for the specialized operation is expected to last only 6 more years. The predicted costs and salvage values for the present machine are as follows:

	Year					
	1	2	3	4	5	6
Operating cost:	$2,000	$2,500	$3,800	$4,500	$4,700	$5,000
Salvage value:	7,000	6,000	5,000	4,000	3,000	2,000

A new machine has been developed which can be purchased for $12,000 and which has the following predicted cost performance:

	Year					
	1	2	3	4	5	6
Operating cost:	$ 1,000	$ 1,200	$ 1,600	$ 1,700	$ 2,000	$ 2,200
Salvage value:	11,600	11,200	11,000	10,500	10,000	10,000

If interest is 0% per yr, when, if at all, should the new machine be purchased?

8-14. Find the optimal replacement policy for machines having an initial cost of $20,000, no salvage value, and annual operating costs of $1,500 + $(n - 1)(\$400)$, where n is the age of the machine in years. Interest is 10% per yr and an indefinite planning horizon is assumed.

8-15. Work Prob. 8-14 except assume that the salvage value varies according to the function $8,000 − $300($n$).

8-16. Suppose there are 1,000 identical independent electronic components, the failure rate of which as a function of days of use, t, is $f(t) = 50 + 60t$. The unit cost of replacement of the entire group is $0.30, while the unit cost of individual replacement after failure is $2.00. Find the most economical replacement interval.

8-17. The probability that a certain critical machine component will last t hours is given by

		t		
	20	40	60	80
$P(t)$	0.90	0.70	0.45	0.15

If the component fails during production, the machine is stopped and a cost of $400 is incurred for downtime and repairs. Preventive replacement of the component costs approximately $50. Find the replacement policy which will minimize total expected costs.

8-18. Show mathematically how you would develop a replacement policy based upon the assumptions of infinite planning horizon, technological progress reflected in linearly declining net annual disbursements, constant replacement investment costs, no salvage values, and a nonzero interest rate.

8-19. Show mathematically how you would develop a replacement policy based upon the assumptions of infinite planning horizon, technological progress reflected in linearly declining replacement investment costs over time, constant net annual disbursements, and a nonzero interest rate.

APPENDIX 8-A

The MAPI Method for Replacement and General Investment Analyses*

This appendix is intended to provide a brief summarization of the main provisions, strengths, and weaknesses of the current (third) version of the

*By Dr. Jack Turvaville, Associate Professor of Industrial Engineering, University of Florida. Based largely on pp. 149–158 of George Terborgh's *Business Investment Manage-*

MAPI method and to illustrate its use for a typical project analysis. The MAPI method or system for investment analysis has evolved over the past 20 years through several major works by George Terborgh, Research Director of the Machinery and Allied Products Institute. The first version, which applied only to replacement problems, was described in *Dynamic Equipment Policy* and the *MAPI Replacement Manual*, both published in 1950. The second and more general-purpose MAPI system was published in *Business Investment Policy* in 1958. The current (third) version was summarized in 1967 in *Business Investment Management*. All the above works were published by the Machinery and Allied Products Institute, Washington, D.C.

Basically, the MAPI method provides a series of charts and forms to facilitate ease in investment analysis computation. One of its main strengths is the inclusion of provision for consideration of obsolescence and deterioration which affect operating results as a linear function of time. The MAPI charts provide for ease in determining the percentage retention value. These charts are computed for various service lives, salvage values, and tax write-off methods. They are available for straight line, double declining balance, sum-of-years-digits and current expensing depreciation methods for either a 1-year or longer-than-1-year comparison period—a total of eight charts. Figures 8-A-1 and 8-A-2 illustrate two such charts as given for a wide range of service lives and salvage value ratios. Assumptions on which the charts are based include 50% income tax rate, a 25–75% debt-to-equity-capital ratio, an average debt capital interest rate of 3%, and an after-tax equity return of 10%.

It should be recognized that allowance for deterioration and obsolescence is built into the chart retention values. According to Terborgh, the function of computation for the retention values

> ... is to project a stream of pretax earnings over the estimated service life that conforms in shape to the projection pattern, and in size to the following requirements: (1) it must include the income tax, payable at the specified rate, on the excess of the earnings over the deductions provided by tax depreciation and interest; (2) the remainder of the earnings after tax (with terminal salvage, if any) must suffice to permit a full recovery of the investment over the service life, and to provide a return throughout on the unrecovered balance of equity at the prescribed after-tax return rate and on the unrecovered balance of debt at the prescribed interest rate.

The use of the MAPI method is consummated through a standard form as shown in Figs. 8-A-3 and 8-A-4 with example amounts entered therein. The example amounts are based upon the following example project taken from page 156 of Terborgh's *Business Investment Management* (op. cit.):

ment (Machinery and Allied Products Institute, 1967). Reproduced by permission of the publisher.

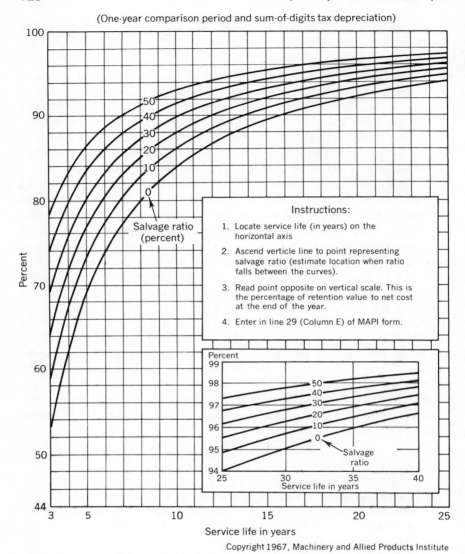

(One-year comparison period and sum-of-digits tax depreciation)

Copyright 1967, Machinery and Allied Products Institute

Figure 8-A-1. Example MAPI Chart.

An analyst desires to investigate whether it would be more economical for the company to make its own corrugated containers. He finds that to do this the company will have to purchase a large box machine and a boxstitcher at a combined cost of $29,800.

It is estimated that direct labor cost will be increased by $900 per yr, indirect labor (supervision) by $50, and fringe benefits by $190. Maintenance will be higher by $200, tool costs by $80, power consump-

(Longer than one-year comparison periods
and sum-of-digits tax depreciation)

Instructions:

1. Locate on horizontal axis percentage which
   comparison period is of service life.

2. Ascend verticle line to point representing salvage ratio
   (estimate location when ratio falls between the curves).

3. Read point opposite on vertical scale. This is the percentage
   of retention value to net cost at end of comparison period.

4. Enter in line 29 (Column E) of MAPI form.

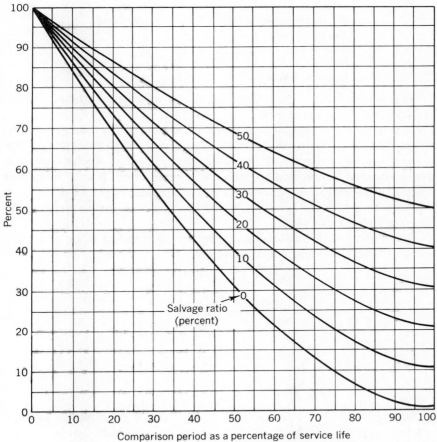

Copyright 1967, Machinery and Allied Products Institute

Figure 8-A-2. Example MAPI Chart.

tion by $40, and property taxes and insurance by $320. On the other hand, there will be a saving of $16,800 in the cost of purchased materials, $1,100 in inventory carrying costs (other than floor space), and $1,000 in floor space. The net cost reduction is therefore $17,020.

In addition to this operating advantage, the equipment will permit a reduction of $4,000 in inventory investment. After consulting with operating officials and others, the analyst comes up with the following stipulations:

Comparison period:	1 yr
Project operating rate:	1,200 hr
Service life:	13 yr
Terminal salvage ratio:	10% of net cost
Tax depreciation method:	sum-of-years-digits
Tax rate:	50%
Debt ratio:	30%
Debt interest rate:	5%
Investment credit:	7%

The results shown on line 40 of Fig. 8-A-4 indicate an after-tax return of 34.5% for the above project.

In reviewing the application of the MAPI method to the example project, it should be observed that all of the considerations given to the determination of the operating advantage would be necessary regardless of what technique were to be used in developing a measure of comparison. It must be further noted that line 29 of Fig. 8-A-4 states that an estimate of the retention value does not have to come from the MAPI charts. If the analyst has a better estimate, then he can use it.

An after-tax cash flow diagram using the information from the MAPI forms in Figs. 8-A-3 and 8-A-4 would be

$$\left.\begin{array}{l}(\text{line 38}) \rightarrow \$10,605 \\ \qquad\qquad + \\ (\text{line 31}) \rightarrow \$20,760\end{array}\right\} = \$31,365$$

$$\$23,700 \leftarrow (\text{Line 28})$$

Solving, $-\$23,700 + \$31,365(P/F,i\%,1) = 0$, and from interest tables, i can be interpolated to be 32.4%. This is close to the 34.5% return by the MAPI method. Generally, if the MAPI assumptions are not violated substantially, the return calculated by the MAPI method is a good approximation of the rate of return calculated by the discounted cash flow method.

The MAPI method can be applied to problems involving a comparison period of more than one year in a manner very similar to the above example.

PROJECT NO. _____
MAPI SUMMARY FORM
(AVERAGING SHORTCUT)

PROJECT   Box Machine and Stitcher

ALTERNATIVE   Continuing as is

COMPARISON PERIOD (YEARS)   (P)   1

ASSUMED OPERATING RATE OF PROJECT (HOURS PER YEAR)   1.200

I. OPERATING ADVANTAGE

(NEXT-YEAR FOR A 1-YEAR COMPARISON PERIOD,° ANNUAL AVERAGES FOR LONGER PERIODS)

A. EFFECT OF PROJECT ON REVENUE

	INCREASE	DECREASE	
1. FROM CHANGE IN QUALITY OF PRODUCTS	$	$	1
2. FROM CHANGE IN VOLUME OF OUTPUT			2
3. TOTAL	$ X	$ Y	3

B. EFFECT ON OPERATING COSTS

	INCREASE	DECREASE	
4. DIRECT LABOR	$ 900	$	4
5. INDIRECT LABOR	150		5
6. FRINGE BENEFITS	190		6
7. MAINTENANCE	200		7
8. TOOLING	80		8
9. MATERIALS AND SUPPLIES		16.800	9
10. INSPECTION			10
11. ASSEMBLY			11
12. SCRAP AND REWORK			12
13. DOWN TIME			13
14. POWER	40		14
15. FLOOR SPACE		1.000	15
16. PROPERTY TAXES AND INSURANCE	320		16
17. SUBCONTRACTING			17
18. INVENTORY		1.100	18
19. SAFETY			19
20. FLEXIBILITY			20
21. OTHER	$		21
22. TOTAL	1.880 Y	$ 18.900 X	22

C. COMBINED EFFECT

23. NET INCREASE IN REVENUE (3X—3Y)	$	23
24. DECREASE IN OPERATING COSTS (22X—22Y)	$ 17.020	24
25. ANNUAL OPERATING ADVANTAGE (23 + 24)	$ 17.020	25

*Next year means the first year of project operation. For projects with a significant break-in period, use performance after break-in.

Figure 8-A-3. MAPI Summary Form, Page 1 (with entries for example project).

To most people trained in engineering economy principles, the use of a formula approach such as the MAPI method is too rigid. The assumptions built into the method can be significantly inappropriate and cause error in the analysis result. Furthermore, the development of the MAPI charts is complicated to understand. However, the MAPI method does provide for obsolescence and deterioration, offers an excellent checklist, will provide consistent results, and is relatively easy to use.

II. INVESTMENT AND RETURN
A. INITIAL INVESTMENT

26. INSTALLED COST OF PROJECT	$ 29,800			
MINUS INITIAL TAX BENEFIT OF	$ 2,100	(Net Cost)	$ 27,700	26
27. INVESTMENT IN ALTERNATIVE				
CAPITAL ADDITIONS MINUS INITIAL TAX BENEFIT	$			
PLUS: DISPOSAL VALUE OF ASSETS RETIRED				
BY PROJECT*	$ 4,000		$ 4,000	27
28. INITIAL NET INVESTMENT (26—27)			$ 23,700	28

B. TERMINAL INVESTMENT

29. RETENTION VALUE OF PROJECT AT END OF COMPARISON PERIOD

(ESTIMATE FOR ASSETS, IF ANY, THAT CANNOT BE DEPRECIATED OR EXPENSED. FOR OTHERS, ESTIMATE OR USE MAPI CHARTS.)

Item or Group	Installed Cost, Minus Initial Tax Benefit (Net Cost) A	Service Life (Years) B	Disposal Value, End of Life (Percent of Net Cost) C	MAPI Chart Number D	Chart Percentage E	Retention Value $\frac{A \times E}{100}$ F
Box Machine and Stitcher	$ 27,700	13	10	1A	89.4	$ 24,760

ESTIMATED FROM CHARTS (TOTAL OF COL. F)	$		
PLUS: OTHERWISE ESTIMATED	$	$ 20,760	29
30. DISPOSAL VALUE OF ALTERNATIVE AT END OF PERIOD*		$ 4,000	30
31. TERMINAL NET INVESTMENT (29—30)		$ 20,760	31

C. RETURN

32. AVERAGE NET CAPITAL CONSUMPTION $\left(\frac{28-31}{P}\right)$		$ 2,940	32
33. AVERAGE NET INVESTMENT $\left(\frac{28+31}{2}\right)$		$ 22,230	33
34. BEFORE-TAX RETURN $\left(\frac{25-32}{33} \times 100\right)$		% 63.3	34
35. INCREASE IN DEPRECIATION AND INTEREST DEDUCTIONS		$ 4,190	35
36. TAXABLE OPERATING ADVANTAGE (25—35)		$ 12,830	36
37. INCREASE IN INCOME TAX (36 × TAX RATE)		$ 6,415	37
38. AFTER-TAX OPERATING ADVANTAGE (25—37)		$ 10,605	38
39. AVAILABLE FOR RETURN ON INVESTMENT (38—22)		$ 7,665	39
40. AFTER-TAX RETURN $\left(\frac{39}{33} \times 100\right)$		% 34.5	40

*After terminal tax adjustments.

Figure 8-A-4. MAPI Summary Form, Page 2 (with entries for example project).

nine

Capital Planning
and Budgeting

Proper capital planning, budgeting, and management represent the basic top management function of an enterprise and are crucial to its welfare.

Capital budgeting is commonly understood to be a function which takes place at the highest levels of management, such as office of the controller or corporate executive committee, but it should be recognized that decisions made at the lower levels in the management hierarchy directly affect those proposals which are ultimately considered as contenders in the overall capital budget. For example, before a major project is considered in top management's capital budget, usually many subalternatives of design and specification will have been considered and the related decisions virtually made as part of the recommended project package. Appropriate procedures for evaluation of these subalternatives should be available and uniformly applied to insure that economic consequences are considered at all levels.

Capital budgeting may be defined as the series of decisions by individual economic units as to how much and where resources will be obtained and expended for future use, particularly in the production of future goods and services. The scope of capital budgeting encompasses

  a. how the money is acquired and from what sources;
  b. how individual capital project alternatives (and combinations of alternatives) are identified and evaluated;

    c. how minimum requirements of acceptability are set;

    d. how final project selections are made; and

    e. how postmortem reviews are conducted.

The above facets of capital budgeting are highly interrelated and will be discussed in turn below.

Sources of Funds

The determination of how much capital and from what sources should be applied toward project investments is a function of the individual project investment amount requirement; prospective profitability, type, and risk; the amount, conditions, and prices of funds to be obtained from internal or external sources, and the firm's financial policies and condition.

Most investment funds are obtained from internal sources: retained earnings and reinvested depreciation reserves. When outside sources are used, it can be to the disadvantage of the present owners to the extent that present ownership control is diluted, as in the case of new equity stock issuance; or to the extent that the company is burdened with new fixed monetary obligations and operating restrictions, as in the case of long-term borrowing. However, outside sources are often used when it is judged to be in the best interests of the existing stockholders.

In general, the more attractive the investment proposals available, the more the company will be willing to go to outside sources to obtain capital so as to be able to take advantage of more investments. However, this has to be balanced against the cost of obtaining outside capital. The more outside capital the company obtains by borrowing, the higher the cost—in terms of both interest and risk—is likely to be.

Identification and Evaluation of Alternatives

Identification

All levels of the organization—operating, staff, supervisory, and engineering, as well as top management—should be encouraged to develop proposals for capital investment projects. For example, the research section may discover new products and processes. The engineering section may create improved designs in product, packaging, or methods. The manufacturing section may propose the installation of more efficient facilities. The marketing section may propose programs of advertising, sales, or inventory expansion for the development of new markets or expansion of existing ones. Finally, top management may, for example, develop plans for major acquisitions leading to integration or diversification.

A dearth of good investment proposals within a firm indicates that the firm lacks a healthy climate for encouraging the search for investment opportunities. This climate should exist in order for the firm to create the best economic opportunities for itself. Indeed, the development of good investment proposals can even become a question of firm survival.

Evaluation

Evaluation of alternatives is undertaken to determine which of the alternatives is (are) best and, sometimes, also to determine whether the "best" is (are) good enough. This book has been concerned primarily with methods of evaluation on the basis of monetary criteria, supposedly leading to profit maximization or cost minimization. But it must be recognized again that the objectives of a firm are not necessarily solely, or even dominantly, based on monetary criteria. Some examples of firm objectives other than profit maximization or cost minimization are given in the first part of Chapter 17.

Minimum Requirements of Acceptability

The determination of the *minimum acceptable rate of return*, sometimes called *cost of capital* or *cut-off rate*, for the project proposals of a firm is generally controversial and difficult. From a purely monetary viewpoint this minimum rate of return should be selected so as to maximize the economic well-being of present owners. The outward manifestation of this viewpoint is that an investment should be undertaken as long as the present value of the existing owners' equity in the firm is enhanced. Even with agreement on this, there are many viewpoints on just how the minimum rate of return should be determined. Several of these viewpoints will be discussed below.

An easy-to-compute method for determining what is alleged to be a "minimum rate of return" is to determine the rate of cost of each source of funds and to weight these by the proportion that each source constitutes of the total. For example, if one-third of a firm's capital is borrowed at 6% and the remainder of its capital is equity earning 12%, then the alleged minimum rate of return is $\frac{1}{3} \times 6\% + \frac{2}{3} \times 12\% = 10\%$.

Another school of thought maintains that if particular projects are to be undertaken using borrowed funds, then the minimum rate of return should be based on the rate of cost of those borrowed funds alone. Yet another school of thought, as exemplified by Solomon*, maintains that the mini-

---

*Ezra Solomon, *The Management of Corporate Capital* (New York: The Free Press, 1959), p. 136.

mum rate of return should be based on the cost of equity funds alone, on the grounds that firms tend to adjust their capitalization structure to the point at which the real costs of new debt and new equity capital are equal.

Great stimulation to thinking on the determination of the minimum rate of return or cost of capital was caused by Modigliani and Miller.* They developed a theory which essentially asserts that the average cost of capital to any firm is completely independent of its capital structure and is strictly the capitalization rate of future equity earnings. Since Modigliani and Miller's article, there have been many articles criticizing their contention on the grounds of oversimplification and unfounded postulation.† There has been no clearcut settlement of this issue, and the problem of determining the cost of capital is still one of open controversy in both theory and practice.

Another viewpoint on the determination of the minimum rate of return which is commonly overlooked and which this writer feels is most sound is the *opportunity cost* viewpoint, which comes as a direct result of the phenomenon of "capital rationing."

Capital rationing describes what is necessary when there is a limitation of funds relative to prospective proposals to use the funds. This limitation may be either internally or externally imposed. Its parameter is often expressed as a fixed sum of capital; but when the prospective returns from investment proposals together with the fixed sum of capital available to invest are known, then the parameter can be expressed as a minimum acceptable rate of return, or cut-off rate.

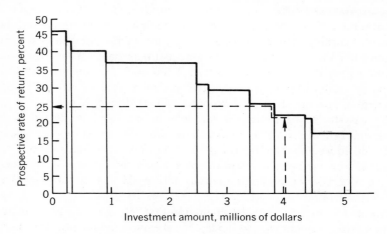

Figure 9-1. Schedule of prospective returns and investment amounts.

*Franco Modigliani and Menton H. Miller, "The Cost of Capital, Corporation Finance, and the Theory of Investment," *American Economic Review* (June 1958), 261–297.

†See principally D. Durand, "The Cost of Capital in an Imperfect Market: A Reply to Modigliani and Miller," *American Economic Review* (September 1959), 639–655.

Ideally, the cost of capital by the opportunity cost principle can be determined by ranking prospective projects according to a ladder of profitability and then establishing a cut-off point where the capital is used on the better projects. The rate of return which the last project before the cut-off point earns is the cost of capital or minimum rate of return by the opportunity cost principle.

To illustrate the above, Fig. 9-1 ranks projects according to prospective rate of return and the cumulative investment required. For purposes of illustration, the amount of capital shown available is $4 million. By connecting up (to the next whole project within the $4 million) and across, one can read the minimum rate of return under the conditions, which turns out to be 25%.

Risk and Uncertainty Effects on Minimum Requirements of Acceptability

The above-suggested procedure for the setting of minimum requirements of acceptability does not directly consider allowance for varying degrees of risk and uncertainty. To do this, one might categorize proposals into several groups according to the risk and uncertainty of realizing their indicated profitabilities. Then the minimum rate of return as determined above might be adjusted higher for those categories which involve the greater risk and uncertainty. This method for allowing for risk and uncertainty (discussed as the "risk discounting method" in Chapter 11) is weak because it suppresses the information regarding the risk of individual projects and because the specification of what interest rate is appropriate for what degree of risk is difficult and subjective.

Project Selection

To the extent that project proposals can be justified through profitability measures, the most common basis of selection is to choose those proposals which offer the highest prospective profitability subject to allowances for intangibles or nonmonetary considerations, risk considerations, and limitations on the availability of capital. If the minimum acceptable rate of return has been determined correctly, one can choose proposals according to the rate of return method, annual worth method, or present worth method.

For certain types of project proposals, monetary justification is not feasible—or at least any monetary return is of minor importance compared to intangible or nonmonetary considerations. These types of projects should require careful judgment and analysis, including how they fit in with long-range policies and plans. Factor weighting methods such as those in Chapter 17 are particularly suited to projects for which monetary justification is not feasible.

The capital budgeting concepts discussed in this chapter are based on the presumption that the projects under consideration are *not* mutually exclusive (i.e., the adoption of one does not preclude the adoption of others, except with regard to the availability of funds). Whenever projects are mutually exclusive, the alternative chosen should be based on justification through the incremental return on any incremental investment(s) as well as proper consideration of nonmonetary factors.

Classifying Investment Proposals

For purposes of study of investment proposals, there should be some system or systems of classification into logical, meaningful categories. Investment proposals have so many facets of objective, form, and competitive design that no one classification plan is adequate for all purposes. Several possible classification plans are given below:

1. according to the kinds and amounts of scarce resources used, such as equity capital, borrowed capital, available plant space, the time required of key personnel, etc.;
2. according to whether the investment is tactical or strategic: a *tactical investment* does not constitute a major departure from what the firm has been doing in the past and generally involves a relatively small amount of funds; *strategic investment* decisions, on the other hand, may result in a major departure from what a firm has done in the past and involve large sums of money;
3. according to the business activity involved, such as marketing, production, product line, warehousing, etc.;
4. according to priority, such as absolutely essential, necessary, economically desirable, or general improvement;
5. according to type of benefits expected to be received, such as increased profitability, reduced risk, community relations, employee benefits, etc.;
6. according to whether the investment involves facility replacement, facility expansion, or product improvement; or
7. according to the way benefits from the proposed project are affected by other proposed projects; this is generally a most important classification consideration, for there quite often exist interrelationships or dependencies between pairs or groups of investment projects.

Degrees of dependency between projects

Several main categories of dependency between projects are briefly defined in Table 9-1. Actually, the possible degress of dependency between projects

Table 9-1
DEGREES OF DEPENDENCE BETWEEN PAIRS OF PROJECTS

"If the results of the first project would _____ by acceptance of second project . . .	. . . then the second project is said to be _____ the first project."	Example
be technically possible or would result in benefits only	a prerequisite of	Car radio purchase feasible only with purchase of car
have increased benefits	a complement of	Additional hauling trucks more beneficial if automatic loader purchased
not be affected	independent of	A new engine lathe and a fence around the warehouse
have decreased benefits	a substitute for	A screw machine which would do part of work of a new lathe
be impossible or would result in no benefits	mutually exclusive with	A brick building or a wooden building for a given need

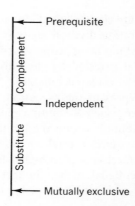

Figure 9-2. Continuum of degrees of dependence between pairs of projects.

can be expressed as a continuum from "prerequisite" to "mutually exclusive," with the degrees "complement," independent," and "substitute" between these extremes, as shown in Fig. 9-2.

In developing a project proposal to be submitted for review and approval, the sponsor should include whatever complementary projects seem desirable as part of a single package. Also, if a proposed project will be a partial substitute for any projects to which the firm is already committed or which are under consideration, this fact should be noted in the proposal.

In cases where choices involved in planning a proposed project are considered sufficiently important so that the final decision should be made by higher levels of management, the project proposal should be submitted in the form of a set of mutually exclusive alternatives. For example, if it is to be decided whether to move a plant to a new location and several alternative sites are possible, then separate proposals should be made for each site so as to facilitate the choice of which site, if any, should be chosen.

Organization for Capital Planning and Budgeting

In most large organizations project selections are accomplished by sequential review through various levels of the organization. The levels required for approval should depend upon the nature and importance of the individual project, as well as the particular organizational makeup of the firm. In general, a mix of central control and coordination together with authority to make project commitments delegated to operating divisions is considered desirable. Three typical basic plans for delegating investment decisions are listed below.

1. Whenever proposals are clearly "good" in terms of economic desirability according to operating division analysis, the division is given the power to commit as long as appropriate controls can be maintained over the total amount invested by each division and as long as the division analyses are considered reliable.
2. Whenever projects represent the execution of policies already established by headquarters, such as routine replacements, the division is given the power to commit within the limits of appropriate controls.
3. Whenever a project requires a total commitment of more than a certain amount, this request is sent to higher levels within the organization. This is often coupled with a budget limitation regarding the maximum total investment which a division may undertake in a budget period.

To illustrate the concept of larger investments requiring higher administrative approval, the limitations for a particular firm might be as follows:

| *If the total investment is . . .* | | *then approval is required through* |
more than	*but less than*	
$ 50	$ 1,000	Plant manager
1,000	10,000	Division vice-president
10,000	25,000	President
25,000	——	Board of directors

Communication

If project proposals are to be transmitted from one organizational unit to another for review and approval, there must be effective means for communication. The means can vary from standard forms to personal appearances. In communicating proposals to higher levels, it is desirable to use a format which is as standardized as possible to help assure uniformity and completeness of evaluation efforts. In general, the technical and marketing aspects of each proposal should be completely described in a format which is most appropriate to each individual case. However, the financial implications of all proposals should be summarized in a standardized manner so that they may be uniformly evaluated. Examples of formats used in practice are given in Appendices 9-A and 9-B.

Postmortem review

The provision of a system for periodic postmortem reviews of the performance of consequential projects previously authorized is an important aspect of a capital budgeting system. That is, the earnings or costs actually realized on each project undertaken should be compared with the corresponding quantities estimated at the time the project investment was committed. This kind of feedback review serves two main purposes. First and primarily, knowledge of past estimating errors should provide bases for adjustments and more reliable estimates on future projects. Secondly, estimating responsibilities may be taken more seriously when the estimators know the results will be checked. This latter purpose of the feedback review should not be overexercised, for there is a human tendency to become overly conservative in estimating when one fears severe accountability for unfavorable deviations.

An additional benefit of postmortem reviews is that they should tend to reduce biases in favor of what individual divisions or project proposal preparing units see as their own interests. When divisions of a firm have to compete with each other for available capital funds, this tends to produce optimistic evaluations of the proposals which they generate. Postmortems, properly administered within a reasonable time after project commitment, should help correct this tendency, as should independent checks or evaluations by management before project commitment.

It should be noted that a postmortem audit is inherently incomplete. That is, if only one of several alternative projects is selected, it can never be known exactly what would have happened if one of the other alternatives had been chosen. "What might have been if..." is at best conjecture, and all postmortem audits should be made with this reservation in proper perspective.

Budget periods

The usual approved capital budget is limited to a 1 or 2-year period or less, but this should be supplemented by a long-range capital plan with provision for continual review and change as new developments occur. This long-range plan (or plans) can be for a duration of from 2 years to 20 years, depending on the nature of the business and the desire of management to force preplanning.

Even when the technological and market factors in the business are so changeable that plans are no more than guesses which must be continually revised, it is valuable to plan and budget as far ahead as possible. This planning should encourage the search for investment opportunities, provide a basis for adjusting other aspects of management of the firm as needed, and sharpen management's forecasting abilities. Long-range budget plans also provide a better basis for establishing minimum rate-of-return figures which properly take into account future investment opportunities.

Timing of Capital Investments

An aspect of capital budgeting which is difficult and often important is that of deciding how much to invest now as opposed to later. If returns are expected to increase for future projects, it may be profitable to withhold funds from investment for some time. The loss of immediate return, of course, must be balanced against the anticipation of higher future returns.

In a similar vein, it may be advantageous to supplement funds available for present projects whenever returns for future projects are expected to become less than those for present projects. Funds for present investment can be supplemented by the reduction of liquid assets, the sale of other assets, and the use of borrowed funds.

Examples of Project Analysis and Control Procedures

Appendices 9-A and 9-B are reprints of excellent works which describe rather detailed project analysis and control procedures used by two different firms. While these examples at least partially reflect well-considered analysis and control programs by the firms involved, they should not be interpreted as necessarily the best programs available or as programs which should be emulated without modification by any other firm. Indeed a firm's capital budgeting analysis and control procedures should be built around its own set of business objectives and needs.

Appendix 9-A, by J. R. Frost, explains the capital expenditure control and analysis procedures used by the California and Hawaiian Sugar Company. It does not, however, illustrate the use of a form for calculation of project rate of return by the discounted cash flow method. Such a form and an accompanying interpolation chart are shown in Figs. 5-1 and 5-2, as well as in Appendix 9-B.

Appendix 9-B is an illustrative segment of the excellent *Instruction*

Manual—DCF Plan by Giddings & Lewis, Inc. Reprinted is primarily an example using their "Shortcut Method" forms. Their "Shortcut Method" differs from their "Long-Form Method" only by assuming an approximately constant "Income From Operations" each year throughout the comparison period. Page 3-S of the forms references certain charts in the *Manual* which contain various discount factors, but which are not shown herein. The full *Manual* also contains comprehensive instructions concerning what to consider and how to complete the forms line-by-line as needed.

PROBLEMS

9-1. Discuss the scope of capital budgeting with particular emphasis on how the various main considerations in capital budgeting are interrelated.

9-2. In your opinion, what is the most valid philosophy on how the minimum acceptable rate of return should be determined?

9-3. Under what circumstances is it reasonable to have more than one minimum acceptable rate of return for a given firm?

9-4. Select the classification systems for investment proposals which you think would be most useful for the typical small (say, fewer than 200 employees) enterprise. Do the same for the typical large (say, more than 2,000 employees) enterprise. Explain the reasonableness of any differences in your selections for the two size groups.

9-5. What is the purpose of a postmortem review? Can it be a means of correcting unwise commitments made as a result of past project analyses?

9-6. Explain the various degrees of dependency between two or more projects. If there are one or more projects which seem desirable and are complementary to a given project, should those complementary projects be included in a proposal package or kept separate for review by management?

APPENDIX 9-A

The Industrial Engineer's Responsibility in the Control and Analysis of Capital Expenditure*

Cost reduction probably accounts for the major portion of our time and efforts as Industrial Engineers—and, for that matter, constitutes the principal justification for Industrial Engineering as a profession. A great deal of the

*By J. R. Frost. Reprinted from *The Journal of Industrial Engineering*, Vol. 19, No. 5 (May 1968), by permission of the publisher.

responsibility for the economic success and growth of business has been placed squarely in the hands of professionals who have been trained to recognize, evaluate, and implement ideas which have as their objective the assurance of continuity in business.

In this day of mechanization and automation, however, the implementation of ideas usually costs money—sometimes lots of money—and the spending of money within the business enterprise has to proceed within rigid restrictions, both as to the availability of funds and the scope of alternatives for use of these funds.

One writer has said that "Management's ability to operate effectively within these restrictions (both in the short and the long run) will determine to a large measure whether or not the *firm* will be operating in the future" (1).

An explanation of the financial planning and its interrelation with company objectives which enters into any capital expenditure program is outside the scope of this discussion. What the article does attempt to point up is how we, as Industrial Engineers at the California and Hawaiian Sugar Company, assist within the broad framework of the capital appropriation policy to achieve program objectives at the intermediate management level.

As the title of the discussion indicates, emphasis will be on control rather than implementation. The implementation of cost reduction ideas involves the utilization of many tools and skills, which took several years of college followed by other years of experience for most of us to acquire.

What some of us are guilty of is that we become too enamored with these tools, or the "means," rather than with the "ends." We tend to place too much emphasis upon the sophistication of our techinques rather than upon what will be accomplished. Once we have wrapped up our proposal in the sophistry of equations, break-even point analyses, therbligs, learning curves, behavior models, and the many other marks of our profession, there is a tendency to sit back and consider our "mission accomplished."

I am not implying that we at C&H are faultless in this respect nor that our system of handling "money matters" is above reproach. Everyone likes to bathe in the glory of his own works. The greatest satisfaction comes to the artist not when he has sold his masterpiece but when he has created it. The peak of our satisfaction may come when we have completed the feasibility study and laid it on the boss's desk. And being human, we tend to rationalize away the many uncertainties which may, without proper audit and screening, result in less than anticipated benefits—or even failure at the performance level.

No one bats 1.000. But when the proper methods of costing are followed and adequate screening devices are instituted, the chances of failure are minimized.

One other point before launching into a description of our program. Nothing about C&H's methods can be claimed as unique. Everything I am going to talk about has been talked about before by numerous practitioners in the field. But our system does, I believe, constitute an effective assembly and utilization of recognized components which may be of interest to you.

In order to orient our discussion properly, let us see how the Industrial Engineering function fits into the capital appropriation program. Figure 9-A-1 provides a broad overview of this program.

The flow of program components progresses through six main phases:

1. Creative search for investment opportunities.
2. Preselection.
3. Screening and establishing of priorities.
4. Final approval.
5. Implementation.
6. Control and postcompletion review.

We are chiefly concerned with phases 1, 2, 5, and 6, with emphasis on the second and last phases.

Creative Search for Investment Opportunities

The search for investment opportunities is carried out at all levels and in all departments at C&H. A suggestion program provides employees below the professional level with the opportunity and incentive to submit cost reduction ideas for management's consideration. A climate which stimulates communication among the various departments is generated by staff meetings and the delegating of project assignments across departmental lines.

Most ideas start because of a need for an improved or expanded process or for improving an expensive or inefficient method of operation. If the idea has potential or merit, it is given a project number and formally assigned for study by the General Manager.

The assignment (Fig. 9-A-2) delegates the principal and support responsibility for the assignment, indicates the type of priority, establishes an estimated completion date, assigns a project number, and briefly delineates the scope of the study.

In most instances, principal responsibility for the assignment is vested in the department whose major responsibility is related to the nature of the project. A project dealing with product quality or process development will be assigned to the Technical Department. If it deals with methods it is assigned to the Methods and Standards (Industrial Engineering) Department. Or if it deals with equipment development or selection it is assigned to the Engineering Department. Other departments concerned to a lesser degree are given support responsibility.

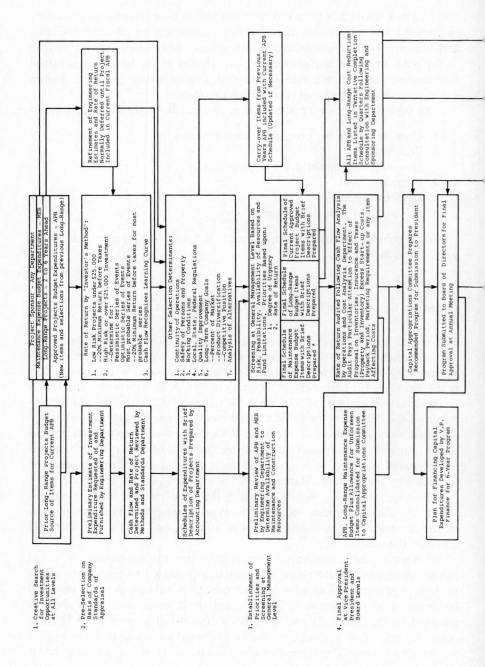

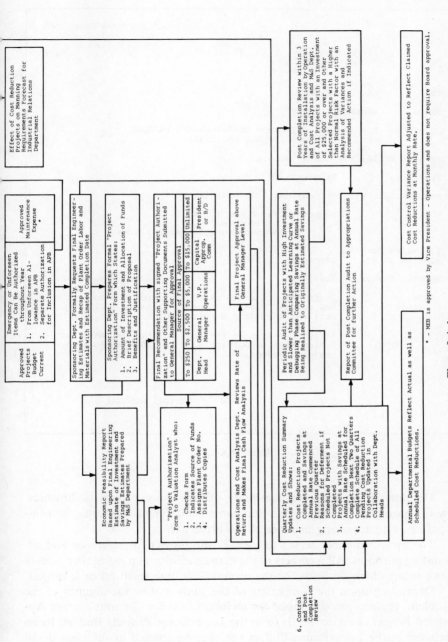

Figure 9-A-1.

* – MEB is approved by Vice President – Operations and does not require Board approval.

147

```
                                         CC'S:    Those Concerned

                                                           DATE



TO:        ALL CONCERNED

FROM:      GENERAL MANAGER

SUBJECT:   NEW PROJECT - IMPROVE CONTAINER AND REFINED
                          SUGAR STORAGE FACILITIES

Project Title:    Same as above.

Priority:         Important.

Responsibility:   Methods and Standards (A. B. C.)

                  Support:  Warehouse (D. E. F.)
                            Engineering (G. H. I.)
                            Accounting & Stores (K. L. M.)

Estimated Com-
pletion Date:     September 1, 1967

Project Number:   226-9

Scope:            Study need  for improving and expanding container
                  and refined sugar storage facilities, including
                  rail car unloading and loading.

                  A firm estimate of the cost to improve these faci-
                  lities will be submitted in the 1968 Authorized
                  Projects Budget.



                                         GENERAL MANAGER
```

Figure 9-A-2.

Developing the economic feasibility of any major project is, however, the function of the Methods and Standards Department—either as the principal or as a supporting member of the project team.

The project number serves to identify the project for reference and accounting purposes. All members of the management group maintain a weekly work recap which accounts for the professional time spent on each project.

Depending upon the complexity of the study and/or the urgency of the problem, projects are developed for inclusion in either the next current Approved Projects Budget (APB) or in the Long-Range Projects Budget. Items included in the Long-Range Budget can then be studied in sufficient detail for inclusion in subsequent Approved Projects Budgets. The Long-Range Budget is used principally as a vehicle to collect ideas for future expansion or improvement and for planning the company's financial requirements ahead.

Preselection on Basis of Company Standards of Appraisal

The initial evaluation of a project to determine whether it should be included in the pending APB or Long-Range Budget—or excluded from further consideration—occupies a large share of the Industrial Engineer's time. It is here where his training and attention to details becomes of particular importance in providing management with a soundly based appraisal of the project's potential. It is at this point that data must be gathered and then rationally analyzed for answering four questions:

1. What is the cost and timing of the installation or expenditure?
2. What is the amount and timing of the revenue or cost savings to be achieved?
3. Does it meet the company's standards of appraisal?
4. What constraints should be recognized and evaluated in other areas of the organization before proceeding with the proposal?

Answering these four questions successfully implies that all reasonable alternatives have been considered and evaluated; that a systems approach has been used in evaluating the alternatives; and that all factors affecting cash flow have been recognized and accounted for in the analysis.

These implications cannot be overemphasized. No analysis of a capital expenditure can be any better than the reliability and completeness of the data on which the analysis is based. If we have overlooked a better alternative, failed to consider the proposal's effect upon all aspects of the business, or neglected to include all items of cost, the results of our analysis will be misleading and inconclusive.

There are many acceptable methods for resolving problems and each one of us, I guess, has developed his own specific format depending upon the industry we are serving and the type of problem we are solving. There are a number of considerations in evaluating alternatives, however, which may have general application.

1. The analysis should be confined to cost differences or differential "out-of-pocket" costs. The inclusion of cost factors which are the same for each alternative only introduces an unnecessary complication into the projection. Figure 9-A-3 illustrates a typical differential cost comparison.
2. The scope of the proposal should consider the effect of the alternatives on all functions of the business. Will they raise industrial relations

	Current Method of Packaging (Base)	With Proposed A. B. Smith Packaging Equipment	With Proposed X. Y. Jones Packaging Equipment
ESTIMATED COMPARATIVE DIFFERENTIAL COSTS FOR PRODUCING XXX PACKAGES			
Total XXX Packages to Satisfy 1967 Demand:			
Local	64,000	64,000	64,000
Export	6,000	6,000	6,000
Total	70,000	70,000	70,000
Estimated Loss in Packaging and Handling	3.7%	2.5%	3.0%
Total Packages Required	72,600	71,800	72,100
Estimated Cost/Cwt.: Direct Packing Labor (Schedule I)	$ .050	$ .048	$ .049
Container Materials (1) (Schedule II)	.150	.068	.070
Closing Materials (Schedule III)	.020	.014	.011
Maintenance (Schedule I)	.025	.025	.030
Total Estimated Cost/Cwt.	$ .245	$ .155	$ .160
Savings/Cwt.	Base	$0.90	$0.85
Estimated Annual Savings		(Actual Cwt. x Savings/Cwt.)	

(1) Including wastage.

Figure 9-A-3.

hurdles? Will the necessary skills be available? Is sufficient warehousing capability available and what materials handling problems will be introduced? Or finally—will customer relations be affected as the result of possible changes in product or packaging specifications? These are the types of questions which should be answered during the early stages of the analysis. Otherwise they raise their ugly heads to embarrass us when the proposal is submitted for top management review.

3. The analysis should consider all factors influencing the rate of return on investment. Aside from the operating cost differentials, there are the factors of wastage, product give-away, maintenance, insurance and taxes, salvage value, obsolescence, start-up or debugging, power and utilities, floor space, and other indirect costs which should be considered and reviewed with those who are closest to these aspects of the business.

   A less thorough study of these factors is probably required at the preselection stage than during preparation of the feasibility study for final approval. They should be considered in sufficient depth, however, to provide management with a fairly accurate index of the proposal's worth for budgeting purposes.

If there are difficult-to-evaluate risk factors involved, it is sometimes advantageous to determine a project's worth on a "most optimistic," "most pessimistic," and "most probable" basis. Figure 9-A-4 illustrates the development of such an analysis.

4. And finally, there should be a sound basis for measuring the cash flow—for comparing the desirability of one project or alternative over another, investmentwise. This is a critical requirement.

| | | Mobey Dick Lines Replaced with Dick Tracy Lines | | |
ESTIMATED ANNUAL DIFFERENTIAL COSTS AND SAVINGS FOR REPLACING MOBEY DICK FLAT STOCK LINES WITH DICK TRACY ROLL STOCK LINES	Base	Most Optimistic Basis	Most Pessimistic Basis	Most Probable Basis
Number Lines	4	3	3	4
Line Speed	145	180	140	150
Manning: Head Operator	1	1	1	1
Assistant	1	1	1	1
Packing (W)	2	2	2	2
Floor Opr. (W)	1	–	1	1
Total	5	4	5	5
Adjusted Cost Per Shift	$125.00	$100.00	$125.00	$125,00
Items/Shift	65	60	51	68
Annual Items Required	38M	38M	38M	38M
Number Shifts Required	585	634	745	559
Total Cost	$73,125	$63,400	$93,125	$69,875
Savings or (Loss)	Base	$ 9,725	($20,000)	$ 3,250

Figure 9-A-4.

Less critical is the method which is used. There are many acceptable methods ranging from the simple "payback" (the length of time required for the cash proceeds to equal the investment) or the "average earnings" (the total cash proceeds divided by the number of earning years, and these average earnings divided by the total investment) to the more sophisticated "discounted cash flow" method which compares the present worth of disbursements and receipts over a future time period in arriving at a return on investment.

What the discounted cash flow method actually says is that a "bird in the hand is worth two in the bush." If receipts are delayed due to high start-up costs or there is a long period of installation and payout without revenue, the discounted cash flow method reflects this in a lesser but probably more accurate rate of return.

The discounted cash flow or "investor's method" of determining rate of return is used at C&H, along with a minimum acceptable return of 20%. The principal disadvantage of the discounted cash flow concept is the com-

SCHEDULE OF ESTIMATED CASH FLOW, PRODUCTION RATES AND MANNING RATES DURING THE PURCHASE, INSTALLATION AND PHASING-IN OF TWO XX/MINUTE A. B. SMITH PACKAGING LINES					
Time from Approval Date		Event	Estimated Capital Expenditure or (Credit)	Estimated Savings or (Loss) at Annual Rate	Estimated Capacity Per Day in Packages
Year	Month				
	1	1st purchase payment	$ 50,000		18,000
	2				
	3				
	4				
	5				
	6				
	7			No change	
	8				
	9				
	10				
	11				
1	12	1st unit shipped	100,000		
	1				12,000
	2				
	3				
	4				
	5	1st line installed	75,000		
	6				16,000
	7	2nd unit shipped	100,000		
	8				
	9				10,000
	10			$ 60,000 Loss	
	11	2nd line installed	75,000		
2	12				
	1				
	2				17,000
	3	Old equipment salvaged	60,000		
	4				
	5				
	6				
	7				
	8			Savings at $75,000 Rate	
	9				
	10	Savings commence at 100% Rate		$110,000 Thereafter	20,000 Thereafter

Figure 9-A-5.

plexity of the technique. It requires the use of compound or continuous interest tables against which disbursements and receipts are factored over the life of the investment. Where the time periods are uniform and definite, obtaining a solution is comparatively simple. In many situations, however, a precise cash flow prediction may look something like that shown in Fig. 9-A-5, in which case the solution becomes more complex.

Of particular importance in the estimating of cash flow is this matter of start-up losses which may result during the installation due to a phase-in/phase-out gap, and, following installation, due to the debugging and extra operator attention required.

Figure 9-A-6 reflects this start-up loss in a typical investment and earnings graph.

How do we know what these losses are going to be? Well, the best we can go on is historical experience and hunch—and we have found that it pays to be more pessimistic than optimistic in our hunches. For the more

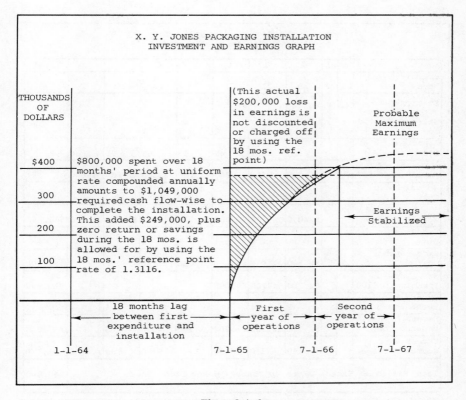

Figure 9-A-6.

Basic Capital Project Evaluation Techniques

complex installations, a learning curve projection is made with gradually increasing performance rates along with gradually decreasing labor requirements until objectives are reached. This projection is then costed out for inclusion in both the cash flow estimate and the operating budget. If this is not done, the rate of return on investment is inflated and unnecessary cost variance explanations will be required when the monthly cost control statements are issued.

Figure 9-A-7 illustrates one method of estimating start-up costs. Estimated actual performance is plotted against objective performance by months and the differences determined for inclusion in the station budgets.

Rate of return on investment is not always the determining factor. There may be other important project incentives which are difficult to evaluate from a dollar return standpoint. These include such things as safety of persons and property, continuity of operations, working conditions, quality improvement, state and federal regulations, and company goals.

ESTIMATED 1967 EXCESS STARTING-UP COSTS
FOR THE NEW MOBEY DICK LINES

Month	A	M	J	J	A	S	O	N	D	Total
Estimated No. Days	21	22	22	21	21	21	23	20	20	
STATION A										
Shifts Operated			1	2	2	2	2	2	2	
Expected % Efficiency			25	35	45	55	65	75	80	
Items @ 1,000 per Shift Std.			250	700	900	1,100	1,300	1,500	1,600	
Normal Labor Cost @ $125			$125	$250	$250	$250	$250	$250	$250	
Start-up Loss - Normal Labor			$2,070	$3,420	$2,900	$2,370	$2,020	$1,260	$1,000	$15,040
Excess No. Oprs./Shift			2	1	1	1	1	1	–	
Excess Labor Cost @ $25			$1,100	$1,050	$1,050	$1,050	$1,150	$1,000	–	$6,400
Start-up Training @ $100			$2,200	$4,200	$4,200	–	–	–	–	$10,600
Excess No. Mechanics @ $30			2	4	2	2	1	1	–	
Excess Maintenance Cost			$1,320	$2,520	$1,260	$1,260	$690	$600	–	$7,650
Excess over Normal Wastage			$150	$300	$200	$200	$130	$80	$50	$1,110
Total Estimated Excess Start-up Costs - Mobey Dick Lines										$40,800

Figure 9-A-7.

Screening and Establishing of Priorities and Final Approval

Preparing the various cost reduction proposals for inclusion in the Approved Projects Budget and the Long-Range Budget is an interdepartmental effort ending at the General Manager's desk. During this "preview" phase,

1. the availability of construction and maintenance skills for installing and debugging is reviewed by the Engineering Department;
2. the economics of each cost reduction proposal are developed by the Methods and Standards Department;
3. the Accounting Department assembles a cost summary of the proposed budget with a condensed description of each project for submitting to the General Manager; and
4. the General Manager reviews the assembled budget and determines its feasibility. If it appears that the budget is excessive from the standpoint of available funds or resources, marginal items are deleted or transferred from the Approved Projects Budget to the Long-Range Budget.

All steps in the program are carried out against a rigid time schedule in order that the final budget can be reviewed and approved by the company's executive officers before submission to the Board of Directors at their annual meeting in December.

Implementation

Final approval of the proposed capital improvement budget by the Board of Directors does not mean that the money can be spent without further authorization. It only means that we can now proceed, project by project, to:

1. obtain final engineered cost estimates and installation schedules;
2. prepare final economic feasibility studies; and
3. submit the foregoing with a "project expenditure authorization" request to the General Manager for his approval and recommendation to the Capital Appropriations Committee for its review and approval.

The "project expenditure authorization" (Fig. 9-A-8) constitutes a brief description of the project and expected benefits. It is used for collecting the various approvals needed to loosen the company's pursestrings.

Much of the work at this stage is a repetition, on possibly a more detailed scale, of the steps which were taken to get the proposals in the Approved Projects Budget in the first place. Engineering estimates are more refined and, for this reason, may differ slightly from initial estimates. If the new estimate is outside an allowable overexpenditure limit, the proposal may require

CALIFORNIA AND HAWAIIAN SUGAR REFINING CORPORATION, LTD.
PROJECT EXPENDITURE AUTHORIZATION

Title of Project _____ No. _____

Requested by _____ Date _____
(DEPARTMENT OR PERSON)

Authorization
Required: Labor $_____ Material $ _____ Contract $ _____ TOTAL $_____

Budget Year_____ APB ☐   MEB ☐

Listed as Item_____ for $ _____   Unforeseen ☐   Balance $_____

DESCRIPTION OF PROJECT
(Describe briefly; supplement with report if necessary.)

JUSTIFICATION
(Indicate basic reason for expenditure)

Increased Throughput Capacity ☐	Quality Improvement ☐	New Product-Package ☐
Economy	Increased Service Capacity	Replacement or Renewal
Protection of Assets ☐	Employee Safety and Conditions ☐	Improved Process and Control ☐
	Other	

(Describe briefly; supplement with report if necessary.)

ENGINEERING	ESTIMATED BY	STAFF ENGINEER	CHIEF ENGINEER	URGENT ☐	PRIORITY
				Highly ☐	IMPORTANT ☐
APPROVALS	ACCOUNTING DEPT.	DEPARTMENT HEAD		Moderately ☐	DESIRABLE ☐
	CKT. ASST. GEN. MGR.	CROCKETT GEN. MGR.	DIV. VICE PRESIDENT	VICE PRESIDENT AND TREASURER	

Figure 9-A-8.

resubmission for initial approval. Funds can also be drawn from an "unforeseen" budget allowance at the General Manager's discretion.

The final feasibility study also updates and refines previous analyses. Any project status changes which have taken place since the original feasibility study are taken into account.

Here again, the final feasibility analysis does not necessarily constitute the last word. The proposal at this point, particularly if it involves a large capital expenditure or marketing considerations, is turned over to the Operations–Cost Analysis Department. Here a group of experts determine the proposal's effect upon sales, inventories, taxes, and other areas. A complete cash flow analysis is also made to check the accuracy of the predicted return on investment.

The proposal is then submitted to the Capital Appropriations Committee and/or a higher-ranking official (depending upon the magnitude of the investment) for final approval.

Following this, the wheels start turning, commencing with engineering design, ordering of materials and system components, scheduling of construction, etc.

Control and Postcompletion Review

No matter how carefully a program may be planned or analyzed, there are unforeseen delays and hurdles which constantly crop up to set back an estimated completion date, reduce or delay payback, or otherwise alter the complexion of a proposal as it was originally conceived.

A good system of control and auditing does not necessarily prevent miscalculations or delays. It does, however, alert these things for prompt attention and possible corrective action. It also keeps management informed as to whether or not program objectives are being accomplished.

Referring back to Fig. 9-A-1, let us take a look at some of the supplemental reports and procedures which have been designed to measure the rate of progress, as well as assist in reaching objectives.

Forecast of manning requirements

Periodically, a forecast of manning changes is prepared for the Industrial Relations Department, which estimates the effect of all cost reduction projects on labor requirements for about 3 years ahead. The forecast lists each project, the estimated completion date, and the estimated number of employees by departments who will either be added or released as a result of the expansion or improvement.

The forecast has two purposes:

1. to assist the Industrial Relations Department in its hiring program, and
2. to plan ahead as far as possible for assimilating on other jobs those employees released because of method improvements.

Up to the present time all employees released because of technological change have been absorbed into other jobs through natural attrition of the work force.

Periodic project audit during start-up

A periodic audit is made of projects with a high investment and a slower-than-estimated rate of return. The audit compares the savings at an annual rate which are currently being obtained with those predicted in the feasibility study. Here again, comparisons are confined to differential costs only. Those costs which apply equally to the original and the new methods are ignored.

It will be noticed in the example (Fig. 9-A-9) that comparisons are confined to the differential cost factors of direct packing labor, maintenance, and containers.

A glance also seems to show that the cost reductions being realized are in containers only and that improvement is required in the other areas to achieve the originally estimated savings.

These reports keep management abreast of learning curve progress and provide data for the quarterly summary of cost reduction proposals, which will be discussed next.

JULY 1, 1967'

TO: THOSE CONCERNED
FROM: METHODS AND STANDARDS DEPARTMENT
SUBJECT: CURRENT SAVINGS RATE - X. Y. JONES STATION

      The X. Y. Jones packaging station is currently performing at an annual savings rate of $23,700, which is 93% of the $25,500 savings objective.

      The comparative differential costs are summarized in the following table:

	Old Method of Packing Base	X. Y. Jones Station
Differential Costs/Cwt.:		
Direct Packing Labor	$.050	$.056
Container Materials	.150	.069
Closing Materials	.020	.013
Maintenance	.025	.028
Total Differential Costs	$.245	$.166
Differential Savings/Cwt.	Base	$.079
Annual Cwt. Required		300,000
Annual Savings Rate		$23,700

      These data have been developed for inclusion in the Second Quarter 1967 Cost Reduction Summary.

METHODS AND STANDARDS DEPARTMENT

Figure 9-A-9.

Quarterly cost reduction summary

The quarterly cost reduction summary is a program status report issued four times a year, which shows the following for the three preceding months:

1. the cost reduction projects completed and the current estimated savings at an annual rate which are being achieved;
2. a list of the projects previously scheduled for completion which were deferred, and the reasons for deferment;
3. a list of the projects and their annual savings rates, scheduled for completion during the next two quarters;
4. a summary of the annual savings scheduled and completed by quarters since the inception of the control in 1962, both in tabular and graphic form; and
5. a complete schedule of all current and pending cost reduction projects which identifies the project, shows the updated potential savings, the savings which have already commenced, and the estimated timing of the savings yet to be realized.

This schedule is reviewed with all departments prior to issuance and each project is updated to reflect any status changes which may have altered either the timing or the savings potential. (See Fig. 9-A-10 for example.)

COST REDUCTION PROGRAM
SCHEDULE OF COMPLETED AND UNCOMPLETED PROJECTS

CR No.	Proj No.	APB if Listed	Project of Item	Total Savings Potential at Annual Rate	Amount Already Commenced	Balance to be Completed		
						This Quarter	Next Quarter	Thereafter
84	213	66-27	X. Y. Jones Packaging Equipment	$25,500	$11,500	$12,200	–	$1,800
85	221	66-13	Improved Checkweighing	14,500	3,400	5,000	$6,100	–
86	140	65-24	Rearrange Casing Equip.	8,000	–	–	8,000	–
87	187	66-1	Improved Decolorization	50,000	–	–	25,000	25,000
201	137	64-3	Reduce Basis Weight	10,000	–	–	–	10,000
202	200	–	Container Storage Reorganization	8,000	8,000	–	–	–
203	189	66-10	Reduce Boiler Blowdown	4,000	–	4,000	–	–

Figure 9-A-10.

Occasionally an item is deleted because changed circumstances have removed its economic justification.

The quarterly cost reduction summary constitutes a complete record of all cost reduction items, their annual savings potential and their approximate completion dates. It is used for the following purposes:

1. to keep all concerned posted as to the progress of the cost reduction program;
2. to highlight projects which are behind schedule or not yielding expected savings;
3. to develop long-term estimates of potential economies and manning requirements;
4. to assist in the preparation of annual departmental budgets; and
5. to adjust cost control standards.

Postcompletion review of selected projects

Each year and within 3 years of their installation, a number of projects are selected by the Operations–Cost Analysis Department for economic review. Projects with an investment of $25,000 or over, or those with a high risk factor, are selected for auditing.

The audit consists of comparing the actual savings and benefits being realized with the estimates contained in the original feasibility study.

A summary of the investment expenditure by quarters and the amount of the total under- or overexpenditure is also noted, as shown in Fig. 9-A-11. A supporting work sheet showing the derivation of cost savings is developed for each item. Figure 9-A-12 illustrates the type of data included.

These data are assembled by the Methods and Standards and Accounting Departments. Sometimes the audits reflect a favorable comparison—occasionally they do not. If a project is not performing as expected, the reasons are noted and the sponsoring department provides a detailed explanation of why expected benefits are not being realized and the recommended steps for effecting an improvement.

In addition to the foregoing controls and auditing procedures, the Accounting and Engineering Departments issue periodic progress reports which summarize the outlay of funds by plant order numbers and the status of the various programs which are in the construction stage.

All of this work has one objective in common—to insure that the efforts of management in providing for the requirements of tomorrow are carried out as efficiently and effectively as possible.

There probably is no such thing as an effective "canned" capital expenditure program. Each company's program has to be built around its own set

RECAP OF INVESTMENTS AND SAVINGS
FOR SELECTED 1965 APB ECONOMY ITEMS
(Adjusted to 1967 Volume and Costs)

Project	Better Weighers	Improved Takeaway System	Dust Control	Direct Sugar Feed	Improved Baling	Relocate XYZ Station
Supporting Work Sheets	I	II	III	IV	V	VI
APB Number	65-13	65-3	64-30	65-6	65-9	64-5
P.O. Number	1101	1210	0904	1150	1304	1050
Investment Expenditure: 1st Q. 1965	$150	–	$1,100	–	–	–
2nd Q.	1,230	–	2,700	–	–	2,000
3rd Q.	2,310	$1,980	5,460	$3,480	–	2,700
4th Q.	650	3,720	4,320	2,970	–	5,000
1st Q. 1966	–	520	150	675	$400	67
2nd Q.	–	–	1,275	–	2,300	4
3rd Q.	–	–	–	1150	1,800	–
4th Q.	–	–	–	275	500	–
Total Expended	$4,340	$6,220	15,005	$8,550	$5,000	10,4
Amount Authorized	4,000	6,400	14,500	9,000	5,000	9,50
Under or (Over) Expended	($340)	$180	($505)	$450	–	($950
Annual Savings 1967 Basis	$3,570	$675	$3,000	$8,000	$1,500	$4,
Less Taxes and Insurance	70	100	225	130	75	16
Net Annual Savings	$3,500	$575	$2,785	$7,870	$1,425	$3,83
Original Estimated Savings	$2,400	$1,800	$2,500	$7,000	$1,400	$5,000
Principal Reason for Variance	Better than anticipated weights	Mechanical trouble with system	–	Increase in production requirements	–	Subnormal station performance

Figure 9-A-11.

of corporate objectives and business requirements. There are a few elements, however, which should be considered in any program. These include

1. the development of a climate for creating investment opportunities;
2. the use of a standard and acceptable method for evaluating proposals and alternatives;
3. a control and periodic review of expenditures and program status;
4. a planned postcompletion review for comparing actual performance with estimated performance.

The program at C&H recognizes these elements and has been designed

SCHEDULE I

REVIEW OF 1965 ECONOMY PROJECTS

ESTIMATE OF REDUCED COSTS - 1967 BASIS

BETTER WEIGHERS

Line No.	Avg. Overweight/Pkg. in Ounces (1)			Total M Pkgs.	Pounds Product Saved
	Before	Last 6 Months	Reduction		
X	$\frac{3.5}{16}$	$\frac{.8}{16}$	$\frac{2.7}{16}$	1,155	12,182
Y	$\frac{3.9}{16}$	$\frac{1.3}{16}$	$\frac{2.6}{16}$	1,200	12,188
Z	$\frac{3.0}{16}$	$\frac{.8}{16}$	$\frac{2.2}{16}$	130	1,117
TOTAL POUNDS PRODUCT SAVED					25,487
VALUE @ $14/CWT.					$3,570

(1) From Technical Department Quality Control Records.

Figure 9-A-12.

to stimulate creative thinking, encourage sound analysis, and exert the necessary pressures to achieve planned results.

References

1. Baker, Kenneth A., "Management Reviews Capital Expenditures," *Automation* (May 1965).

2. Dean, Joel, "Measuring the Productivity of Capital," *Harvard Business Review* (January–February 1954).

3. Healy, Thomas H., "Analysis of Capital Investment Opportunities," *Management Controls* (September 1963).

4. Grant, Eugene, and W. Grant Ireson, *Principles of Engineering Economy*, Fourth Edition, (New York: Ronald Press Company, 1960).

APPENDIX 9-B

Giddings & Lewis DCF Investment Evaluation Plan*

Introduction

The plan has been developed to provide a uniform method of evaluating investment opportunities within the corporation and to provide a standard format for review and grading of projects requiring capital funding.

The Giddings & Lewis DCF Investment Evaluation Plan is a modification of the conventional discounted cash flow technique which is gaining popularity in industry, particularly in multiplant concerns.

The discounted cash flow approach recognizes effective cash flow in business performance and the time value of money as an important factor in financial decisions. A prime feature of the DCF method is that it expresses evaluations in a term of common financial understanding, "compound interest":

The discounted cash flow procedure develops a "True Rate of Return," *sometimes referred to as* "Profitability Rate." *This is equivalent to after-tax compound interest earnings over the analysis period, including full recovery of invested funds (i.e., compound interest earned plus recovery of investment—all after tax).*

As a separate and additional calculation, the Giddings & Lewis DCF Plan also expresses "Years to Pay Back," or years to recover the investment (after tax), primarily as one measure of risk of investment rather than profitability.

It is not intended that the procedure should replace executive judgment in the company's capital investment program, but is adopted as an aid to

---

*Reprinted from Giddings and Lewis, Inc., *Instruction Manual—DCF Plan* (May 1, 1969) by permission of Giddings and Lewis, Fond Du Lac, Wisconsin. Only certain illustrative segments of the manual are shown herein. Special thanks are due to Mr. Loren Matthews, staff vice president–manufacturing.

the many investment decisions involved in maintaining and planning growth of the firm's fixed assets.

Policy For Use

Economic evaluations, using the G&L DCF Plan, are to be developed for all proposals involving capital expenditures of $2,000 or more. (Except for projects approved for reasons other than for tangible return on investment.)

Component equipment and all supporting facilities isolatable to a common purpose shall be considered as one project and should be covered by not more than one appropriation request. A single appropriation request may be used for a group of projects serving an overall common purpose and where this approach will simplify analysis.

Approvals

The President and General Manager of Giddings & Lewis Machine Tool Company and of Gisholt Machine Company shall approve all Capital Expenditures of $2,000 and over for their divisions, when not in excess of the approved Capital Budget.

The Chairman of the Board shall approve all Capital Expenditure Projects in excess of $50,000 and also Capital Expenditure Projects of lesser amounts which are not covered by the Capital Budget for a respective Division Company.

Post Audit

The real potential of the DCF Capital Investment Evaluation System will not be realized until a general confidence in the evaluations is achieved.

A Post Audit Procedure will be issued to aid in attaining this confidence.

The plan will be to Post Audit each evaluation, 1 year after the Zero Point, and a report of the findings will be issued to those who have signed the appropriation request.

-EXAMPLE-

Request for Approval of Capital Asset Addition	Location: PLANT #12

GIDDINGS & LEWIS Discounted Cash Flow Capital Investment Evaluation Procedure	

Ⓖ SHORT-CUT METHOD
For use only when Annual Income from Operations (exclusive of tax and salvage credits) is assumed to be level, year to year.

Page No.
1-S

1. DESCRIPTION OF PROJECT:

Replace Model #1, G&L Widget Machine, in North end of plant #12, with New Model #12. Equip with G&L Electronic Inspection device. Propose to have machine available for customer demonstrations an average of 12 hrs/mo. Will involve rearranging 3 machines in Dept 99 as per attached sketch.

APPROPRIATION NO.	
CAPITAL PLAN NO.	70-12-1
YEAR TO FUND	1970
Date Submitted	4-25-69
Date Approved	

7. COSTS

CAPITALIZED Items	line 1d page 2S	77,500
EXPENSED Items	line 2d page 2S	1,700
TOTAL TO BE AUTHORIZED		79,200
WORKING FUNDS	line 4c page 4S	1,200

8. CREDITS

INVESTMENT Credit	line 6a	5,425
EXPENSE Tax Credit	line 6b	935
SALVAGE Credit --"OLD" ASSETS	line 6c page 2S	4,478
OTHER Credits	line 6d page 2S	

9. NET FUNDS REQUIRED 69,562

10. PROFIT IMPROVEMENT

TRUE (DOF) RATE OF RETURN	line 16 page 3S	18.0 %
Equivalent PRE-TAX RATE OF RETURN		40.0 %

YEARS TO PAY BACK 4.5 (After tax)

2. REASON FOR EXPENDITURE:

☐ NEW PRODUCT ☒ OBSOLESCENCE ☒ PROFIT IMPROVEMENT ☐ SAFETY
☒ REDUCED COSTS ☒ CAPACITY INCREASED ☒ REPLACEMENT ☐ OTHER

Cost reduction detailed on page 4-5 & covered by attachments shows reduction in direct & Indirect labor, use of less costly alloy, reduced overtime premium. less spoilage, less maunal inspection & reduced maintenance

Note: (Model #1 is a prototype)

3. ☐ This is part of an approved project See Appropriation No. ___

4. Request Submitted By S. D. Jones 4/25	**5.** Analysis Checked & Approved By J. E. Smith 4/10

6. APPROVALS

_____ _____ _____

_____ _____

11. ASSETS REPLACED

Description & Proposed Disposition:

Propose to sell old Model #1 thru Goldberg-Emniernion

Date Acquired	1965
Present Book Value	$ 7200
Potential Salvage Value	$ 9950

Page 2-S	SUMMARY OF ACTUAL CASH FLOW (Short Cut Form Procedure)

SUMMARY OF INVESTMENTS

CAPITALIZED ITEMS: (Totals By Depreciation Schedule)

1a	Sched. *12* Yr. *G & L WIDGET MACHINE MODEL #2*	*74,500*	1a
1b	Sched. *3* Yr. *G & L ELECTRONIC INSPECTION DEVICE*	*3,000*	1b
1c	Sched. ___ Yr.		1c
1d	TOTAL Capitalized Items	*77,500*	1d

EXPENSED ITEMS: (Site Prep., Relocation, Inventory Loss, etc.)

2a	*Re-arrange 3 machines in Dept 99*	*1,700*	
2b			
2c			
2d	TOTAL Expensed Items	*1,700*	2d
3a	TOTAL TO BE AUTHORIZED	*79,200*	3a

Increase in Working Funds: (Acct.'s Rec., parts supply, Inventory, etc.)

4a	*Spare parts Supply*	*1,200*	
4b			
4c	TOTAL WORKING FUNDS	*1,200*	4c
5a	GROSS FUNDS REQUIRED FOR PROJECT	*80,400*	5a

SUMMARY OF CREDITS IN THE INVESTMENT CASH FLOW (At Start of Operation)

6a	INVESTMENT CREDIT: (1d) $ *77,500* x *7* %	*5,425*	6a
6b	Tax Credit from Expense: (2d) $ *1,700* x (Tax Rate) *55* %	*935*	6b
6c	Disposal Value of Assets Replaced: $ *9,750* x (1.0-Tax Rate) *45* %	*4,478*	6c
6d	Other		6d
6e	TOTAL CREDITS (Before Depr. Tax Credits)	*10,838*	6e
7a	NET FUNDS REQUIRED FOR PROJECT	*67,562*	7a

EXPECTED TIMING OF EXPENDITURES

Qtr	Yr.	Description	Capital Items by Depr. Schedule *12* Yr.	*3* Yr.	___ Yr.	Expense Item	Working Funds	TOTAL
1	*70*	*Widget Machine*	*74,500*					*74,500*
1	*70*	*Inspection Device*		*3,000*				*3,000*
1	*70*	*Rearrange Dept*				*1,700*		*1,700*
3	*70*	*Spare Parts Supply*					*1,200*	*1,200*
		Note - Dispose of old asset by Jan 1971						
		Note - More facility in operation by - 8-1-70						
		TOTALS	*74,500*	*3,000*		*1,700*	*1,200*	*80,400*

TERMINAL CREDITS:

9a	Salvage Value of New Asset *(10Yr)* $ *27,055* x (1.0-Tax Rate) *45* %	*12,175*	
9b	Return of Working Funds (4c) $	*1,200*	
9c	*(1/4 of 9,950)* $ *2,488* x (1.0-Tax Rate) *45* %	*(1,120)*	
9d	TOTAL TERMINAL CREDITS	*12,255*	9d

10a	ANNUAL (Level) INCOME FROM OPERATIONS--Page 4 (31) $ *24,890* x (1.0-Tax Rate) *45* %	*11,200*	10a

GIDDINGS & LEWIS Discounted Cash Flow Capital Investment Evaluation Procedure	Page No.
SHORT-CUT METHOD For use only when Annual Income from Operations (exclusive of tax and salvage credits) is assumed to be level, year to year.	3-S

CALCULATION OF TRUE RATE OF RETURN (After Tax)

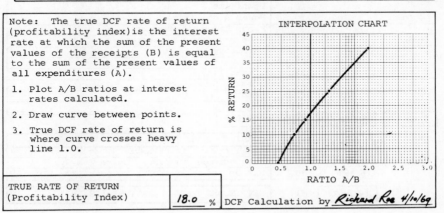

COMPARISON PERIOD *10* Yrs. ZERO DATE *8-1-70*		TRIAL NO. 1 0% INTEREST RATE		TRIAL NO. 2 10% INTEREST RATE		TRIAL NO. 3 15% INTEREST RATE		TRIAL NO. 4 25% INTEREST RATE		TRIAL NO. 5 40% INTEREST RATE	
		ACTUAL AMOUNT	FACTOR PRESENT WORTH	FACTOR	PRESENT WORTH	FACTOR	PRESENT WORTH	FACTOR	PRESENT WORTH	FACTOR	PRE. EN! WORTH
A	**CASH OUTFLOW** *See page 2-5*										
1	Capitalized Items (1d)	77,500	1.052 81,530	1.079	83.623	1.136	88.040	1.230	95,325		
2	Expensed Items (2d)	1,700	1.052 1,788	1.079	1.834	1.136	1,931	1,230	2.091		
3	Working Funds (4d)	1,200	1.000 1,200	1.000	1.200	1.200	1,200	1.000	1.200		
4	TOTAL A (5a)	80,400	84,518		86,657		91,171		98,616		
B	**CASH INFLOW**										
	Annual (Level) Income										
5	(10a) *11,200* x *10* Yrs.	112,000	.632 70,784	.518	58.016	.367	41,104	.246	27,552		
6	Investment Credit (6a)	5,425	1.000 5,425	1.000	5,425	1.000	5,425	1.000	5,425		
7	Expense Tax Credit (6b)	935	1.000 935	1.000	935	1.000	935	1.000	935		
8	Disposal-"Old" Asset (6c)	4,478	.952 4,263	.929	4.160	.885	3,963	.824	3,690		
9	Other (6d) Depreciation Tax Credit:										
10	*12* Yr. (1a) x *55*% Tax =	40,975	.642 26,306	.531	21,758	.377	15,448	.263	10,776		
11	*3* Yr. (1b) x *55*%	1,650	.873 1,440	.818	1,350	.721	1,190	.603	.995		
12	___ Yr. (1c) x ___										
13	Terminal Credits (9d)	12,255	.387 4,743	.241	2,953	.093	1,140	.023	.281		
14	TOTAL B	177,718	113,896		94,597		69,205		49,654		
	* Comparison Period										
15	RATIO A/B	.45	.74		.92		1.32		1.99		
		0%	10%		15%		25%		40%		

CHART NO.5 CHART NO.1 CHART NO. 4b CHART NO.3 CHART NO.2

Note: The true DCF rate of return (profitability index) is the interest rate at which the sum of the present values of the receipts (B) is equal to the sum of the present values of all expenditures (A).

1. Plot A/B ratios at interest rates calculated.

2. Draw curve between points.

3. True DCF rate of return is where curve crosses heavy line 1.0.

INTERPOLATION CHART

% RETURN vs RATIO A/B

TRUE RATE OF RETURN (Profitability Index)	*18.0* % DCF Calculation by *Richard Roe 4/10/69*

Page 4-S	SHORT CUT FORM DCF INVESTMENT EVALUATION	GIDDINGS & LEWIS, INC.

SUMMARY SHEET - ANNUAL (Level) Income from OPERATIONS - Pre-Tax

INCREASE	DECREASE	Item No.	ANALYST *John Doe* DATE 4/8/69
			Effect of Project on REVENUE
		1.	PRODUCT QUALITY (Potential loss or gain of profit through change is product quality.)
		2.	PRODUCTION CAPACITY (Potential loss or gain as result of change in capacity.)
3,500		3.	FLOOR DEMONSTRATION(Potential profit from having G& L machine available for Customer Demonstration.) Hrs./Mo. *12*
3,500 X	Y	4.	TOTAL
			Effect of Project on DIRECT COSTS
	11,500	5.	Direct Labor Hrs. x(D.L. Rate + Fringes)
	4,500	6.	Direct Material
		7.	Sub-Contracting
		8.	Other
Y	16,000 X	9.	TOTAL
			Effect of Project on INDIRECT COSTS
	650	10.	Indirect Labor(Incl.Fringe)
	2,500	11.	Overtime (Premium, etc.)
1,200		12.	Indirect Materials & Supplies
		13.	Tooling
	300	14.	Tool Repairs
	2,700	15.	Scrap & Rework
	2,000	16.	Inspection
	350	17.	Maintenance
		18.	Down Time
420		19.	Power & Utilities
		20.	Floor Space & Occupancy
1490		21.	Property Taxes & Insurance
		22.	Inventory
		23.	Safety
		24.	Flexability
		25.	Working Conditions
		26.	Other
3,110 Y	8,500 X	27.	TOTAL
			COMBINED EFFECT
	3,500	28.	Net Increase in REVENUE (4x-4y)
	16,000	29.	Net Decrease in DIRECT Costs (9x-9y)
	5,390	30.	Net Decrease in INDIRECT Costs (27x-27y)
	24,890	31.	NET INCOME FROM OPERATIONS (28+29+30)

	GIDDINGS & LEWIS Discounted Cash Flow Capital Investment Evaluation Procedure	Page No.
	CALCULATION SHEET FOR PAY BACK (Non-Discounted Cash Flow Basis)	6-S&L

NET FUNDS REQUIRED FOR PROJECT (See Line 2-S or Page 2-L)   **69,562**

AFTER TAX CASH FLOW RECOVERY OF INVESTED FUNDS

		COLUMN 1	COLUMN 2	COLUMN 3	COLUMN 4	COLUMN 5	COLUMN 6	COLUMN 7	COLUMN 8	COLUMN 9	
		Depreciation Schedules Involved in Project	Total Depreciation % Tax Credit from Request Form Pages 3-S or 3-L (lines 10, 11, & 12)	Specific Year % Depreciation from CHART 6	Specific Year Depreciation Tax Credit Col. 2 X Col. 3	After Tax Income From Operating Asset Request Form Pages 2-S (line 10a) or 1-L (specific year)	Interest On Unrecovered Invested Funds @ 3.2% * (After Tax) X Prev. Balance Col. 8)	Net Cash In-Flow Each Specific Year To Recover Invested Funds Col. 4 & Col. 5 Minus Col. 6	Year End Balance of Unrecovered Invested Funds Prev. Balance from Col. 8 Minus Col. 7	% Recovery of Invested Funds	
FIRST YEAR	10 Yr.	40,975	.1000	4,098						FIRST YEAR
	3 Yr.	1,650	.3333	550	11,200	⟨2,226⟩	13,622	55,940	19.6%	
	Yr.									
SECOND YEAR	10 Yr.	40,975	.1800	7,376						SECOND YEAR
	3 Yr.	1,650	.4444	733	11,200	⟨1,790⟩	17,519	38,421	44.8%	
	Yr.									
THIRD YEAR	10 Yr.	40,975	.1440	5,900						THIRD YEAR
	3 Yr.	1,650	.1482	245	11,200	⟨1,229⟩	16,116	22,305	67.9%	
	Yr.									
FOURTH YEAR	10 Yr.	40,975	.1152	4,720						FOURTH YEAR
	3 Yr.	1,650	.0741	122	11,200	⟨714⟩	15,328	6,977	89.9%	
	Yr.									
FIFTH YEAR	10 Yr.	40,975	.0922	3,778						FIFTH YEAR
	Yr.				11,200	⟨223⟩	14,755	⟨7,778⟩	111.2%	
	Yr.									
SIXTH YEAR	Yr.									SIXTH YEAR
	Yr.									
	Yr.									
SEVENTH YEAR	Yr.									SEVENTH YEAR
	Yr.									
	Yr.									
EIGHTH YEAR	Yr.									EIGHTH YEAR
	Yr.									
	Yr.									
NINTH YEAR	Yr.									NINTH YEAR
	Yr.									
	Yr.									
TENTH YEAR	Yr.									TENTH YEAR
	Yr.									
	Yr.									

* 7% X (1.0 - Tax Rate) 45% = 3.2%

INTERPOLATION FOR PAY BACK

NOTE:
"Pay Back" or number of years to recover investment is one measure of risk of investment. Not a good measure of profitability.

YEARS TO PAY BACK **4.5 (After Tax)**

"Yrs. to Pay Back" is read from graph at point where curve crosses the 100% line.

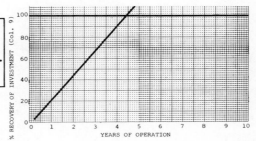

part II

EXTENDED TECHNIQUES, CONCEPTS, AND ANALYSIS PROCEDURES

ten

Estimation
and Introduction to
Risk and Uncertainty

All of the economy study methods and illustrations in the chapters of Part I were for conditions of "assumed certainty"; i.e., all elements (parameters) considered were estimated or specified by a single figure. Generally, such elements as life, salvage value, and periodic incomes and costs are random variables rather than known constants. Hence, in many economy studies it is necessary or desirable to extend the result of assumed certainty analyses by directly considering the risk and uncertainty involved due to variability in the outcome of elements. This chapter discusses techniques of estimating and introduces the inclusion of risk and uncertainty in project economic analyses.

Estimation

The term *estimate*, when applied to economic analyses, can have a multiplicity of meanings. At one extreme it can be used to indicate a carefully considered computation of some quantity for which the exact magnitude cannot be determined. At the other extreme it can be used to denote what are actually just offhand approximations that are little better than outright guesses.

173

The basic difficulty in estimating for economic analyses is that most prospective projects for which estimations are to be made are unique; that is, substantially similar projects have not been undertaken in the past under conditions that are the same as expected for the future. Hence, outcome data that can be used in estimating directly and without modification often do not exist. It may be possible, however, to gather data on certain past outcomes which are related to the outcomes being estimated, and to adjust and project that data based on expected future conditions. Techniques for collecting and projecting estimation data and also for making probabilistic estimates are rooted in the field of statistics.

Whenever an economic analysis is for a major new product or process, the estimating for that analysis should be an integral part of comprehensive planning procedure. Such comprehensive planning would require the active participation of at least the marketing, design engineering, manufacturing, finance, and top management functions. It would generally include the following features:

1. a realistic master plan for product development, testing, phase into production, and operation;
2. provision for working capital and facilities requirements;
3. integration with other company plans;
4. evaluation against company objectives for market position, sales volume, profit, and investment; and
5. provision of a sound basis for operating controls if project is adopted.

Obviously, such comprehensive planning is costly in time and effort, but when a new product or process has major implications for the future of a firm, it is generally a sound rule to devote a greater rather than a lesser amount of effort to complete planning, including estimates for the economic analysis which is a partial result of that planning. The application of this rule, of course, is bounded by constraints of limited time and talent; however, following the rule will tend to minimize the chance of poor decisions or lack of preparedness to implement projects once the decision to invest has been made.

Estimation Reliability

Estimates or forecasts, by their nature, are evaluations of incomplete evidence indicating what the future may hold. They may be based on empirical observations of only somewhat similar or analogous situations, adjusted on the basis of the kind of personal hunch that grows out of the accumulation of the experiences. Or they may be inferences drawn from various kinds of available objective data, such as trade statistics, results experienced in analogous situations, or personal observations.

Regardless of the estimate source, the estimate user should have specific recognition that the estimate will be in error to some extent. Even the use of formalized estimation techniques will not, in itself, eliminate error, although it will hopefully reduce error somewhat, or will at least provide specific recognition of the anticipated degree of error.

Approaches to Estimation

Techniques of estimation are highly diverse and depend strongly on the nature of the element to be estimated, the type of firm, data-handling facilities and analysis skills available, and types of information which may exist. Some common techniques (approaches) are discussed below.

Single estimate

This approach, as its name indicates, involves making the single best estimate of the element(s) in question. Direct use of these single estimates results in the *assumed certainty* procedure of economic evaluation. This approach is very common in practice because of its simplicity. It has the great weakness, however, of failing explicitly to recognize probable error. Indeed, it is notable that some persons are reluctant to make only single estimates, as they do not like to be tied to a single outcome when they know uncertainty prevails.

Single estimate and range

This approach involves first making the best single estimate for each element, and then setting limits to bracket these estimates. The limits may be established either intuitively or by statistical analysis. As an example, suppose the most probable life of a project is estimated to be 8 years. As an indication of variability, it is further estimated that the life could be as low as 3 years or as high as 10 years.

This approach to estimating is essentially the same as that used for the optimistic–pessimistic method of economic analysis explained in Chapter 11. It has the advantage of forcing the estimator to think in terms of reasonable variability of outcomes. In order to use it, the estimator should adopt a philosophy of what extremes to consider in specifying the range.

Subjective probability distributions

It is reasonable to estimate many element outcomes in terms of subjective, usually continuous, probability distributions. This can be most useful, either for purposes of calculating measures of merit which directly take these distributions into account or for purposes of merely judging the degree and effect of probable outcome variation. When it is desired to estimate the subjective probability distribution of an element and that element is not thought to fit one of the computationally convenient distributions, one good way is to estimate in terms of a cumulative probability distribution function and then convert the results to other forms if needed. For example, suppose you desire to estimate the life of a project (such as the length of time before your car will have a major breakdown). After considering the experience records for similar cars and making your subjective adjustments for future conditions, you may decide that, say, there is practically nil probability that the life will be equal to or less than 2 years; 0.10 probability that the life will be equal to or less than 3 years; and you keep making similar estimates until the life is reached at which you feel there is 100% chance that the life will not be exceeded. A complete set of estimates for this example is given in Table 10-1, and then graphed, assuming a continuous distribution, in Fig. 10-1.

Table 10-1

EXAMPLE ESTIMATES EXPRESSED IN CUMULATIVE PROBABILITY FORM

Life (yr)	Probability that life will be equal to or less than life given
2	0.0
3	0.1
4	0.3
5	0.7
6	0.9
7	1.0

Figure 10-2 shows the same estimates converted into the more commonly-portrayed probability density form. The reader may recall that the probability density function (height of the curve) for a continuous distribution equals the slope of the cumulative probability distribution function over the entire range of the element estimated.

The following two sections give simplified approximation procedures for estimating parameters of elements thought to be distributed according to the Beta distribution and to the normal distribution.

Beta II distribution. The Beta II distribution is of interest because it can describe a wide range of left-skew and right-skew conditions of differing variances.*

*Whereas the Beta I (normally called just Beta) distribution applies to variables ranging between 0 and 1, the Beta II distribution applies to variables ranging over any set of outcomes.

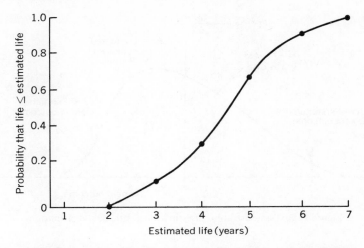

Figure 10-1. Example estimates graphed in cumulative probability form.

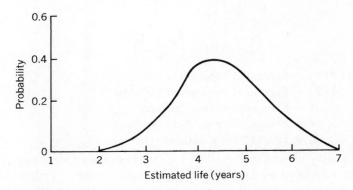

Figure 10-2. Example estimates graphed in probability density form.

The following Beta estimation procedure is based on a system developed for the PERT network planning and scheduling technique. It involves first making an "optimistic" estimate, a "pessimistic" estimate, and a "most likely" estimate for the element. These estimates are to correspond to the lower (or upper) bound, upper (or lower) bound, and mode, respectively, of the assumed Beta II distribution describing the element. Figure 10-3 shows an assumed Beta distribution for a typical element together with the meaning of the above types of estimates. In this case, the distribution happens to be left-skewed.

Once the three estimates of element outcome have been made, the approxi-

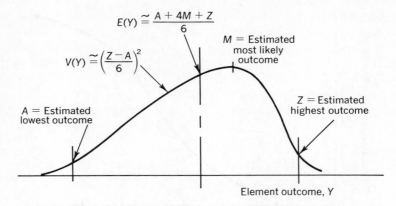

Figure 10-3. Demonstration of estimations with Beta distribution.

mate mean and variance of the Beta distribution for the element may be calculated as

$$E(Y) \approx \frac{A + 4M + Z}{6} \qquad (10\text{-}1)$$

and

$$V(Y) \approx \left(\frac{Z - A}{6}\right)^2 \qquad (10\text{-}2)$$

where $E(Y)$ = Estimated expected outcome
$V(Y)$ = Estimated variance of outcome
A = Estimated lowest outcome
M = Estimated most likely outcome
Z = Estimated highest outcome

It is worthy of note that the difference between the approximate expected values as calculated by Eq. (10-1) and the exact formula is relatively small for a wide range of Beta II distribution conditions. On the other hand, the difference between the approximate variance as calculated by Eq. (10-2) and the exact formula can be quite high, and the difference usually is in the direction of underestimation of the exact value.

If several elements, as estimated by the above procedure, are assumed to be independent and are added together, the distribution of the total outcome so obtained is, according to the central limit theorem, approximately normal. The mean of this total outcome distribution can be calculated by adding the means of the individual elements. Further, the variance of this total outcome distribution can be calculated by adding the variances of the distributions of the individual elements.

Normal distribution. Quite often the best subjective estimate of the shape of the distribution of an element that can be made in practice is that the distribution is normal. It can be observed from tables of area under the normal distribution that the middle 50% of a normal distribution is within ±0.675 standard deviations of the mean of that distribution as shown in Fig. 10-4. Thus, for a normally distributed element, if one is willing to estimate the smallest range r within which that variable is expected to occur with 50% probability, then the standard deviation σ for that variable can be calculated by the relation $0.675\sigma = r/2$. In practice, it is generally sufficiently close to approximate the 0.675 with $\frac{2}{3}$.

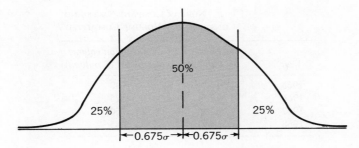

Figure 10-4. Normal distribution.

This same idea for estimating the variance for normally distributed variables could be applied using any other number of standard deviations and the associated probabilities. The values suggested above, however, are probably most useful because of the relative ease of visualizing the minimum range which would include 50% probability of occurrence.

As an example, suppose that the investment for a project is estimated to be normally distributed, and it is thought that there is a 50% chance it will be between $9,000 and $12,000. The standard deviation for this distribution is calculated as $\frac{2}{3}\sigma = (\$12,000 - \$9,000)/2$; or $\sigma = \$2,250$. The mean for the distribution is, of course, $(\$12,000 + \$9,000)/2 = \$10,500$.

Statistical and mathematical methods

Statistical methods for forecasting have been given a mixed reception in business, although most forecasters make use of these procedures to some degree. Two common methods are shown below.

Correlation analysis. Sometimes it is possible to correlate an element, such as revenue for a firm, with one or more economic indices, such as construction contracts awarded, disposable personal income, the Federal Reserve Board Index of Industrial Production, etc. When an index can be found to which an element to be estimated is highly correlated, but with a time lag, formal correlation techniques may be highly useful. In cases where the lag is insufficient for longer-term forecast requirements, correlation of an element to be estimated with the available index still leaves the forecaster with the need to predict or obtain a prediction of future value(s) of the index itself.

As an example, suppose that comparison of Norcar Company sales with many economic indicators shows that sales correlate best with, say, the state's construction volume committed. The nature of the correlation is shown in Table 10-2.

Table 10-2

NORCAR COMPANY SALES AND
CONSTRUCTION VOLUME COMMITTED

Year	Sales ($ million)	Construction volume committed ($ million)
1965	3	40
1966	2	25
1967	5	50
1968	4	45

The volume of sales as a function of the construction volume committed (together with the regression line to be calculated later) is shown in the scatter diagram of Fig. 10-5. Let us assume that a linear regression is thought to express the correlation adequately. A least-squares linear regression line can be fitted to the data to find the equation of the relationship in the general

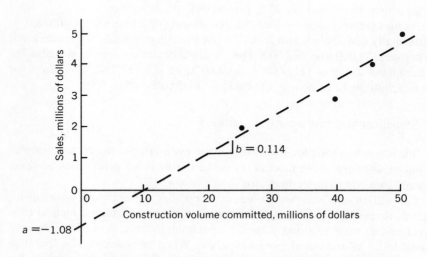

Figure 10-5. Norcar Company sales versus construction volume committed (with least squares regression line shown).

form $Y = a + bX$. Calculations to find a and b can be made by solving the following normal equations:

$$\sum Y = Na + b \sum X \tag{10-3}$$

and

$$\sum XY = a \sum X + b \sum X^2 \tag{10-4}$$

where N is the number of data points. The calculations of $\sum Y$, $\sum X$, $\sum X^2$, and $\sum XY$ are performed in Table 10-3.

Table 10-3

CALCULATIONS FOR LINEAR LEAST-SQUARES REGRESSION—NORCAR COMPANY

Y Sales ($ million)	X Construction volume committed ($ million)	X^2	XY
3	40	1,600	120
2	25	625	50
5	50	2,500	250
4	45	2,025	180
$\sum Y = 14$	$\sum X = 160$	$\sum X^2 = 6,750$	$\sum XY = 600$

Thus, the normal equations become

$$14 = 4a + 160b$$

and

$$600 = 160a + 6,750b$$

and solution of the simultaneous equations shows that $a = -1.08$ and $b = 0.114$. Thus, the linear relationship is Sales $= -\$1.08$ million $\times$ 0.114 (construction volume committed in $ million). The line showing this relationship is drawn in Fig. 10-5.

A standard quantitative measure of the "goodness of fit" of a linear regression is called the *coefficient of correlation*. If the absolute value of the coefficient of correlation is 1, this means there is perfect correlation between the dependent and independent variables; while if it is 0, this means no correlation exists; while any absolute value between 1 and 0 gives a measure of relative correlation or lack of it. The coefficient of correlation p for this two-variable case can be most readily calculated from Eq. (10-5).

$$p = \frac{N \sum XY - (\sum X)(\sum Y)}{\sqrt{N \sum X^2 - (\sum X)^2} \sqrt{N \sum Y^2 - (\sum Y)^2}} \tag{10-5}$$

$$= \frac{4(600) - (160)(14)}{\sqrt{4(6,750) - (160)^2} \sqrt{4(54) - (14)^2}} = 0.52$$

Thus, only a fair degree of correlation is indicated.

Finally, to illustrate the use of the calculated regression line results in estimating, suppose it is predicted that the construction volume committed for the coming period will be \$35 million. The indicated sales corresponding to this is $Y = -\$1.08$ million $+ 0.114(\$35$ million) $= \$2.92$ million.

Correlation analysis should be applied with good judgment, particularly with respect to whether the correlation exhibited in the past can be reasonably expected to continue on the basis of future conditions.

To conclude this section on estimation by correlation analysis, let us consider the topic of extrapolation, which is the process of estimating by projecting outside the range of past data. Extrapolation forecasts can be made by either graphical or mathematical methods. Further, extrapolation can be made for an element correlated to some index or for an element which exhibits a trend over a time series.

As an example of a mathematical linear extrapolation for an element correlated to an index, consider the Norcar Company case above in which the linear regression of Sales (Y) as a function of construction volume committed (X) was found to be $Y = -\$1.08$ million $+ 0.114X$, based on data for the construction volume committed index ranging from \$25 million to \$50 million. Suppose that it is desired to obtain a mathematical projection of sales for a construction volume committed index of \$70 million. This is easily calculated as

$$Y = -\$1.08 \text{ million} + 0.114(\$70 \text{ million}) = \$6.90 \text{ million}$$

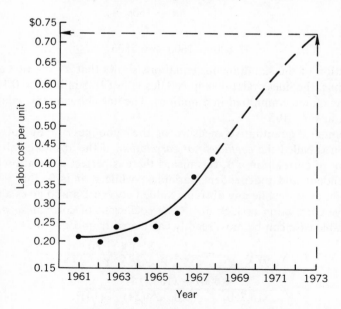

Figure 10-6. Time series data for unit labor cost.

As an example of a graphical and nonlinear extrapolation of time series data (i.e., data arranged according to time order), consider the labor cost data in Fig. 10-6. This data shows a pronounced increase in unit labor cost over time; indeed, the trend seems to be at a greater rate than a linear increase. Suppose it is desired to obtain an estimate of the unit labor cost in, say, 1973. A possible graphical nonlinear extrapolation which results in an estimate of approximately $0.72 is shown in Fig. 10-6.

Time series extrapolations are valid only if nonrecurring distortions have been removed from the data. Also, unless the forces which caused the underlying patterns continue into the future unchanged, supplementary analyses of causative factors and sound judgment should be applied to adjust extrapolations for changes which are expected to occur.

Exponential smoothing. It is commonly thought that more recent data is more relevant to estimates for a given element than is older data, and that the more recent data should receive greater weight. There are many mathematical methods of accomplishing this. One common technique of forecasting with time series data is called exponential smoothing.

The exponential smoothing model gives an estimate of the expected element outcome, $\bar{X}$, as

$$\bar{X} = CX_0 + C(1 - C)X_1 + C(1 - C)^2 X_2 + \cdots + C(1 - C)^n X_n + \cdots$$
(10-6)

where X_0 = Actual outcome for the most recent time period
X_1 = Actual outcome in the first preceding time period
X_2 = Actual outcome in the second preceding time period, etc.
C = Weighting constant, between 0 and 1

The above expression can be reduced for computational simplicity to

$$\bar{X} = CX_0 + (1 - C)\bar{X}_1$$
(10-7)

where $\bar{X}_1$ is the estimate made at the end of the first preceding period (which applied to the most recent time period).

This means that to obtain a new estimate of the expected outcome, we multiply the estimate for the most recent time period by $(1 - C)$ and add to it the actual outcome during the most recent time period multiplied by C.

As an example, suppose that a cost item for last year was estimated to be $600,000 and actually turned out to be $700,000. The estimate for the next year using the exponential smoothing model is $\bar{X} = C(\$700,000) + (1 - C)$ ($600,000) where C is a subjectively determined weighting constant between 0 and 1.

A great advantage of this technique of forecasting is its flexibility of weighting. If the weighting constant C is 1, the mathematical model reduces to using the most recent period's outcome as the forecast. If C is very close to 0, this is essentially equivalent to using an arithmetic average of actual outcome over a large number of previous periods as the best estimate of the future outcome. Intermediate choices for C between 0 and 1 provide forecasts which have more or less emphasis on long-run average outcomes vs. current outcomes.

Estimation of Correlation Coefficients

Dependence between two variables can often be best expressed by estimating a coefficient of correlation, ρ, for the two variables. Below is shown a systematic procedure for estimating those correlation coefficients.

If X_1 and X_2 are two random variables with variances σ_1^2 and σ_2^2, respectively, and if the joint probability distribution of X_1 and X_2 is bivariate normal, it can be shown that

$$E(X_2 \mid X_1 = x) = E(X_2) + \rho\left\{\frac{\sigma_2}{\sigma_1}[X - E(X_1)]\right\} \tag{10-8}$$

The above expression can be manipulated so that X_1 and X_2 are normalized as

$$\frac{E(X_2 \mid X_1 = x) - E(X_2)}{\sigma_2} = \rho\left[\frac{X_1 - E(X_1)}{\sigma_1}\right] \tag{10-9}$$

Thus, after normalization, the expected value of X_2, given the value of X_1, is just ρ times the value of X_1. Expressed in terms of the actual variable, if X_1 lies s standard deviations from its mean, the expected value of X_2 given X_1 will lie $\rho \times s$ standard deviations from the unconditional mean of X_2.

By trying various values of s and estimating the corresponding conditional expected value of X_2, it should be possible to generate a subjective estimate of ρ. As an example of how this can be done using just one value of s, suppose that the parameter estimates are $E(X_1) = \$7,000$, $\sigma_1 = \$1,000$, $E(X_2) = \$6,500$, and $\sigma_2 = \$3,000$. For an arbitrary s value of $+1.0$, the outcome of $X_1 = x = \$7,000 + 1.0(\$1,000) = \$8,000$. Now, a final estimate required is $E(X_2 \mid X_1 = \$8,000)$, which for example, will be supposed to be $\$5,600$. Using Eq. (10-9),

$$\frac{\$5,600 - \$6,500}{\$3,000} = \rho\left(\frac{\$8,000 - \$7,000}{\$1,000}\right)$$

Thus, the estimate of the coefficient of correlation, ρ, can be calculated to be -0.3. For more reliable estimates of ρ, parallel estimates and calculations should be made using other values of s.

If the joint distribution of X_1 and X_2 is not bivariate normal, the expression for $E(X_2 \mid X_1 = x)$ given above does not hold in general. However, this expression does provide the best linear estimate of $E(X_2 \mid X_1 = x)$ according to the principle of least squares.

The Delphi Method of Estimating

The Delphi method is a relatively new technique for the use of a group of persons to make estimates which are of substantial importance, and for which each of the estimators is thought to have some reasonable basis of judgment. It attempts to improve the panel or committee approach in arriving at a forecast or estimate by subjecting the views of individuals to each other's criticism in ways that avoid face-to-face confrontation and provide anonymity of opinions and of arguments in defense of those opinions. Direct debate is generally replaced by the interchange of information and opinion through a carefully designed sequence of questionnaires. The participants are asked to give their opinions and the reasons for their opinions, and at each successive interrogation they are given new and refined information, in the form of opinion feedback, which is derived from a computed consensus. The process continues through successive iterations until further progress toward a consensus appears to be of questionable value in view of the worth of further accuracy of the estimate.

To illustrate this technique, suppose that, say, sales of a new product are critical to the success of a proposed investment project. Further, there are nine persons whose judgments are thought to be approximately equally valid for this critical estimate. Each of these persons is asked to estimate this, and the results on a quantity interval scale are shown as S_1, S_2, S_3, S_4, S_5, S_6, S_7, S_8, S_9 in Fig. 10-7. Once these results are known, the median, upper quartile, and lower quartile can be calculated and the results shown as Q_l, M, and Q_u in Fig. 10-7(a).

The values of Q_l, M, and Q_u should then be communicated to each estimator and each should be asked to reconsider his previous estimate and, if his new estimate lies outside the interquartile range between Q_l and Q_u, to state briefly the reason why, in his opinion, the answer should be lower

(a) First round estimates

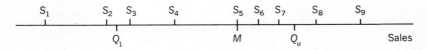

(b) Second round estimates

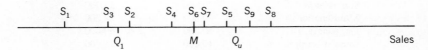

Figure 10-7. Illustration of Delphi method.

(or higher) than corresponds to the 75% majority opinion expressed in the first round.

The results of this second round of estimates as depicted in Fig. 10-7(b) (and which will usually be less dispersed than the first round) are again fed back to each estimator in summary form, including the new quartiles and median. In addition, the reasons for raising or lowering the values, elicited in the second round, are given to the estimators in edited form while still preserving the anonymity of the individual estimators. Now the estimators are asked to revise individually their estimates after considering and weighting the reasoning of the others. Moreover, if any revised estimate falls outside the second round's interquartile range, the estimator in question is asked to state briefly why he found unconvincing the arguments that might have drawn his estimate toward the median. These revised estimates consitute the third round.

The above process can be continued for as many additional rounds as thought worthwhile. The median (or perhaps computed mean) of the final round can then be taken as the estimated quantity (sales), and the remaining dispersion around this value is generally a conservative indication of the risk involved.

Use of Accounting Data for Estimates

It should be emphasized again that although accounting data is a prime source of information for economic analyses, this data is often not suitable for direct, unadjusted use in economic analyses. Not only must this data be adjusted from the past to expected future conditions, but also the data often contains arbitrary allocations or exists in categories which are not suitable for the needs of the economic analysis.

As an example, consider the XYZ Corporation, which experienced certain 19X1 actual overhead costs and has certain 19X2 projected overhead costs as shown in Table 10-4.

Table 10-4

OVERHEAD COSTS FOR XYZ CORPORATION

Type	19X1 actual	19X2 projected
Indirect labor	$40,000	$54,000
Indirect material	30,000	26,000
Supervision	30,000	33,000
Maintenance	20,000	22,000
Depreciation	50,000	50,000
Interest on debt	10,000	15,000
Total:	$180,000	$200,000

To continue the example, the XYZ Corporation allocates its overhead costs to individual projects on the basis of direct labor dollars. For 19X1 the actual direct labor dollars expended was $360,000, which means that the correct "after-the-fact" rate would be $180,000/$360,000, or $0.50 per dollar labor cost. For 19X2, the projected number of direct labor dollars is $500,000. This means that the overhead rate for 19X2 should be $200,000/$500,000, or $0.40 per dollar of direct labor cost. Suppose that a prospective job requires $10,000 of direct labor by the machine generally used, but only $6,000 by a proposed new machine, and it is desired to determine the change in overhead costs due to the proposed change. Using the overhead rate directly, the traditionally used machine would show an overhead cost of $10,000 × 0.40, or $4,000, while the new machine would show an overhead cost of $6,000 × 0.40, or $2,400, for the job. Thus, the change in machine will supposedly reduce overhead costs by $1,600. This amount is probably in marked error, for a decrease in direct labor cost due to change in machine will not necessarily result in a corresponding decrease in actual overhead costs for the job. To emphasize this point, it should be recognized that the overhead rate is merely a paper allocation of costs on an average basis for accounting purposes.

The correct approach to estimation of overhead costs in the above situation is to examine how the individual cost types included in the total overhead cost are expected to be affected by the proposed change in machines. Let us assume that the change in machine used is not expected to change the costs of supervision, depreciation, and interest on debt, while it is expected to increase actual expenditure for indirect labor by $600, decrease actual expenditure for indirect material by $200, and increase actual maintenance expenditure by $600. Hence, the change in methods is expected to increase true overhead costs by $1,000 rather than decrease those costs by $1,600, as calculated by straight application of overhead rates.

Consideration of Inflation in Estimating

In most free-world economic systems, it is reasonable to expect inflation or future increases in currency prices for given units of value, such as labor and equipment. Inflation can, indeed, affect the economic choice of projects. Hence, the nature of inflation and methods for taking inflation into account will be considered below.

Nature of inflation

Whenever future investment receipts are predetermined by contract, as in the case of a bond or a fixed annuity, these receipts do not respond to inflation. In cases where the future receipts are not predetermined, however, they may respond to inflation. The degree of response varies from case to case. To illustrate the nature of inflation, let us consider two annuities: The first annuity is fixed (unresponsive to inflation) and yields $2,000 per yr for 10 years. The second annuity is of the same duration and yields enough future dollars to be equivalent to $2,000 in the value of dollars of investment (constant worth dollars). Assuming an inflation of 3% per annum, pertinent values for the two annuities over a 10-year period are shown in Table 10-5.

Table 10-5

ILLUSTRATION OF FIXED AND RESPONSIVE ANNUITY
WITH INFLATION RATE OF 3% PER YR

	Fixed annuity		Responsive annuity	
Year	In then-current dollars	In value of dollars of investment (constant worth dollars)*	In then-current dollars	In value of dollars of investment (constant worth dollars)*
1	$2,000	$1,942	$2,060	$2,000
2	2,000	1,886	2,122	2,000
3	2,000	1,830	2,186	2,000
4	2,000	1,776	2,252	2,000
5	2,000	1,726	2,318	2,000
6	2,000	1,674	2,388	2,000
7	2,000	1,626	2,460	2,000
8	2,000	1,578	2,534	2,000
9	2,000	1,532	2,610	2,000
10	2,000	1,488	2,688	2,000

*Constant worth dollars = Then-current dollars $\times \left[\dfrac{1}{1 + \text{Inflation rate}}\right]^{\text{yr}}$

Thus, when the receipts are constant in then-current dollars (unresponsive to inflation), their equivalent in value of constant worth dollars of investment declines over the 10-year interval to $1,488 in the final year. When receipts are fixed in value of constant worth dollars of investment (responsive to inflation) their equivalent in then-current dollars rises to $2,688 by year 10.

Methods for consideration of inflation

In the economic analyses illustrated in this book as well as in usual practice, inflation, if relevant, is taken into account by one of the two following methods:

1. estimating outcomes in terms of "then-current" dollar amounts and combining the inflation rate with the monetary interest rate to form a single discount rate for economic calculation and comparison purposes; or

2. estimating outcomes in terms of "constant worth" dollars and using a straight monetary interest rate for economic calculation and comparison purposes.

Thus, inflation, if considered, can be virtually hidden in an analysis. To use the first method above, one needs first to determine the combined discount rate, which is often referred to as *interest rate* or *minimum rate of return* with no specific reference to inflation.

Combining monetary interest rate and inflation rates

If i is the interest rate per period and d is the inflation rate per period, then the discount rate which considers both rates is $(1 + i)(1 + d) - 1$. For example, if $i = 10\%$ and $d = 5\%$, the combined discount rate is $(1.10)(1.05) - 1 = 15.5\%$.

This combined discount rate is often conveniently approximated as $i + d$. For the above example figures, this would mean that the combined discount rate is approximated as $10\% + 5\% = 15\%$. This approximation can be used with confidence for low values of inflation and the monetary interest rate, especially in view of the fact that neither rate can be estimated with great precision. The lower the monetary interest and inflation rates, the better the approximation.

Example:

To illustrate the relationship of the two approaches to consideration of inflation, consider a project requiring an investment of $10,000 which is expected to return, in terms of future or "then-current" dollars, $3,000 at the end of the first year, $4,000 at the end of the second year, and $6,000 at the end of the third year. The rate of inflation is 5% per yr, and the monetary interest rate is 10% per yr. (Thus, from the above section, the combined discount factor is 15.5%.) Table 10-6 shows how the net present worth of the project would be calculated to be −$520 using the first method above.

Table 10-6

CALCULATION OF NET PRESENT WORTH
WITH ESTIMATES IN "THEN-CURRENT" DOLLARS

Year (N)	Outcome in then-current dollars	Discount factor for interest and inflation (P/F,15.5%,N)	Present worth
0	−$10,000	1.000	−$10,000
1	3,000	0.867	2,600
2	4,000	0.745	2,990
3	6,000	0.647	3,880
		$\Sigma =$	−$520

If the second method for considering inflation is used, then the outcomes should be estimated in terms of constant worth dollars.

For the above example, with the inflation rate of 5%, if the estimator is precisely consistent, his outcome estimates in terms of constant worth dollars, as of time of investment, should be $10,000, $2,860, $3,620, and $5,180 for each year, respectively. Table 10-7 shows how the net present worth of the project would be calculated to be the same − $520 using the second method, which involves straightforward present worth calculations with the monetary interest rate of 10%.

Table 10-7

CALCULATION OF NET PRESENT WORTH
WITH ESTIMATES IN CONSTANT WORTH DOLLARS

Year (N)	Outcome in constant worth dollars	Discount factor for interest only (P/F,10%,N)	Present worth
0	− $10,000	1.000	− $10,000
1	2,860	0.909	2,600
2	3,620	0.826	2,990
3	5,180	0.751	2,980
			$\Sigma = -\$520$

It is worthy of note that had the outcomes in then-current dollars been discounted by only the monetary interest rate of 10%, then the net present worth for the example would have been calculated to be $540, indicating a favorable project. This is in contrast with the − $520 net present worth (indicating an unfavorable project) calculated when inflation was considered by either of the two methods. This illustrates the potential importance of considering inflation directly in economic analyses.

Difference Between Risk and Uncertainty

The classical distinction between risk and uncertainty is that an element or analysis involves *risk* if the probabilities of the alternative, possible outcomes are known, while it is characterized by *uncertainty* if the frequency distribution of the possible outcomes is not known. The distinction between conditions of assumed certainty, risk, and uncertainty for a given element such as project life is portrayed graphically in Fig. 10-8.

Another less restrictive distinction between risk and uncertainty is that *risk* is the dispersion of the probability distribution of the element being

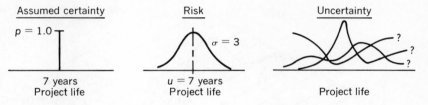

Figure 10-8. Illustrations of assumed certainty, risk, and uncertainty as applied to life of a project.

estimated or calculated outcome(s) being considered, while *uncertainty* is the degree of lack of confidence that the estimated probability distribution is correct. The word *risk* can be used to apply to the outcome of any element or measure of merit. Colloquially, the word is often used merely to denote variability of outcome, and oftentimes the only variability which is of concern is variability in an unfavorable direction.

There are several combinations of risk and assumed certainty which can specify a given element estimate over time. For example, Fig. 10-9 represents an assumed certain outcome amount (e.g. , cash flow) at an assumed certain point in time, while Fig. 10-10 shows a risk amount at an assumed certain point in time. Figure 10-11 represents an assumed certain amount at risk (discrete) points in time, while Fig. 10-12 represents random amounts at each of risk (discrete) points in time.

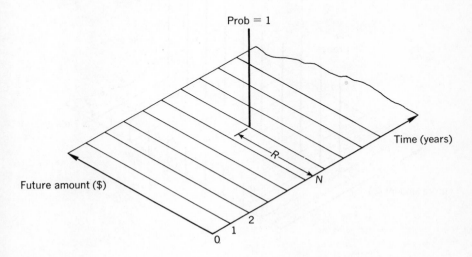

Figure 10-9. Assumed certain case.

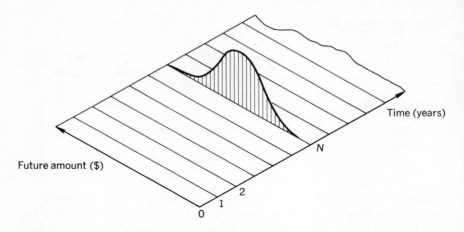

Figure 10-10. Risk amount, assumed certain time.

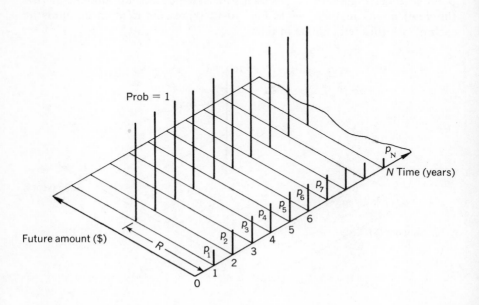

Figure 10-11. Assumed certain amount, risk time.

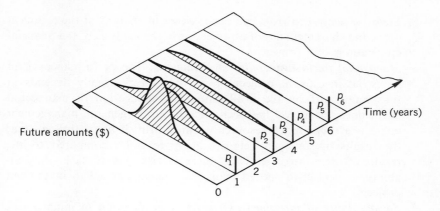

Figure 10-12. Risk amount, risk time.

Causes of Risk and Uncertainty

Risk and uncertainty in project investment decisions are attributable to many possible sources. Below is a brief description of some main causes.

1. *Insufficient numbers of similar investments.* In general, a firm will have only a few investments of a particular type. This means that there will be insufficient opportunity for the results of a particular investment type to "average out," i.e. , for the effect of unfavorable outcomes to be virtually cancelled by favorable outcomes. This type of risk is dominant when the magnitude of the individual investment commitment is large compared to the financial resources of the firm.

2. *Bias in the data and its assessment.* It is common that individuals making or reviewing economic analyses have biases of optimism or pessimism or are unconsciously influenced by factors which should not be a part of an objective study. A pattern of consistent undue optimism or pessimism on the part of an analyst should be recognized through analysis review procedures.

3. *Changing external economic environment, invalidating past experience.* Whenever estimates are made of future conditions, the usual bases are past results for similar quantities, whenever available. While the past information is often valuable, there is risk in using it directly without adjustment for expected future conditions.

4. *Misinterpretation of data.* Misinterpretation may occur if the underlying factors behind elements to be estimated are so complex that the relationship of one or more factors to the desired elements is misunderstood.

5. *Errors of analysis.* Errors can occur either in analysis of the technical operating characteristics of a project or in the analysis of the financial implications of a project.
6. *Managerial talent availability and emphasis.* The performance of an industrial investment project or set of projects usually depends in substantial part on the availability and application of managerial talent once the project has been undertaken. In general, management talent is a very limited resource within a firm; hence, it follows that the results of some projects are going to suffer compared to the results of other projects. Thus, there is risk due to lack of availability or neglect in needed managerial talent applied to investment projects.
7. *Salvageability of investment.* Of prime consideration in judging risk is the relative recoverability of investment commitments if a project, for performance considerations or otherwise, is to be liquidated. For example, an investment in special-purpose equipment which has no value to other firms entails more risk than an investment in general-purpose equipment which would have a high percentage salvage value if sold because of poor operating results. A descriptive synonym is "bail-outability."
8. *Obsolescence.* Rapid technological change and progress are characteristic of our economy. Not only do products become superseded, thus rendering productive facilities for those products less needed or useless, but also changes in process technology can render existing facilities obsolete.

Weakness in Probabilistic Treatment of Project Analyses Involving Risk

While the use of probabilities is freely made in analyses of projects involving risk, it should be pointed out that these probabilities are not generally objectively verifiable, and hence are generally *subjective* (sometimes called *personal*) probabilities. A further weakening fact is that the evidence supporting any given probability in an analysis may differ markedly in both quality and quantity from that for any other probability.

When probabilities are used, the risk and uncertainty concerning outcomes in question are not eliminated, but rather the uncertainty then becomes uncertainty connected with the probabilities on which the analysis is based. Nevertheless, it is often worthwhile to express degree of confidence in estimates through the use of probability distributions rather than through subjective verbal expressions.

Ways to Change or Influence Degree of Uncertainty

It is usually possible for the firm to take actions which will decrease the degree of uncertainty to which it is subject as a result of investment project selection. Several notable ways are

1. by increasing information obtained before decision, such as through additional market research or investigation of technical performance characteristics;
2. by increasing size of operations so as to have enough different investment projects to increase expectation that results will "average out"; and
3. by diversifying products, particularly by choosing product lines for which sales are affected differently by changes in business activity (i.e., when sales of some products decrease, then sales of other products can be expected to increase).

Return, Risk, and Choice

It is generally accepted that the riskier a project, the higher the apparent return it must promise to warrant acceptance. It would be desirable to determine differential risk allowances which would reduce all projects to a common basis. This cannot be done precisely, however, for the statement of differential risk allowances is very much a matter of subjective judgment.

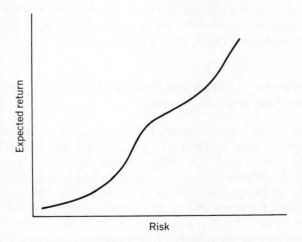

Figure 10-13. Relationship between return and risk.

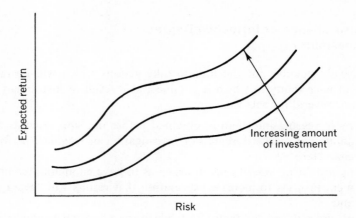

Figure 10-14. Relationship between return and risk, considering amount of investment.

Before a firm can make investment decisions to include allowances for risk, the firm's policy toward risk should be determined. The amount of risk a firm is prepared to undertake to secure a given actual or apparent monetary return is a general question of values. There is no rational or logical criterion by which the choice can be made. Rather, this is largely a function of the preferences of the decision-makers of the firm and the amount of risk to which the firm is already exposed.

In general, the relationship between expected return and risk (degree of variability of the return) can be represented as in Fig. 10-13.

A refinement of the concept of Figure 10-13 can be made if risk is sub-categorized into the quantitative components of variability of returns and amount of investment. This is shown in Figure 10-14.

Decision Guides on When and How Much to Consider Risk and Uncertainty

The question of the extent to which risk and uncertainty should be directly considered in economic analyses is of great concern and cannot be answered categorically. The concern stems from the fact that the risk and uncertainty of the future pervades most capital projects for which analyses are made. The impossibility of categorical answers stems from the fact that there is an infinite variety of sources of risk and relative degrees of risk for various projects and firms.

It is sometimes felt that the risk and uncertainty inherent in most investment decisions make it not worthwhile to engage in any complex or "sophisticated" methods of analysis. While this may be true in particular situations, the position is strongly suggested that it is, in general, very worthwhile to supplement judgment quantitatively and explicitly in the analysis of risk and uncertainty for investment projects. Analysis is needed to insure that the implementation of judgment is not accompanied by errors in quantification and omissions in factors considered. Indeed, with the increasing complexity and economic size of individual projects compared to the worth of the firm as a whole, quantitative consideration of risk and uncertainty in capital project analyses becomes increasingly important. This section provides some qualitative decision guides regarding this question.

A conceptual answer to the question of when and how much risk and uncertainty should be considered can be reduced to simple economics—that is, put more study effort into the analysis as long as the savings from further study is greater than the cost of further study (i.e., as long as marginal savings is greater than marginal cost). Since the marginal savings (and possibly marginal cost also) for a given amount of added study is a variable, it is necessary to modify the rationale. A reasonable modification is suggested then to be the consideration of expected values. Thus the rationale can be restated as: put more study effort into the analysis as long as the expected savings from further study is greater than the expected cost of that further study.

The great problem in applying this rationale in practice is that it is quite difficult to estimate the expected savings from further study. In economic analyses of mutually exclusive projects (i.e., when at most one project can be chosen), savings from further study occur if the further study correctly causes a reversal or change in decision as to the project accepted. In economic analyses of non-mutually exclusive projects (i.e., when the choice of one project does not affect the desirability of choice of any other project), savings from further study occur if the further study correctly causes the decision-maker to drop one or more projects previously accepted and/or correctly to add one or more projects not previously accepted. By "correctly" is meant "with favorable consequences." Other savings can be created by the added study. For example, the added study may provide information which will prove useful in future operating decisions and/or investment analyses.

The savings from further study can be conceptually determined as the discounted present value of the new project(s) accepted after the further study minus the present value of the project(s) accepted before the further study. However, the practical problem of determination of the expected savings from further study, as based on the amount of savings and the likelihood or probability of those savings, is generally quite difficult. It should be noted that the expected savings from added study may well not be a continuous function of the amount of the added study, but rather it is likely to change in discrete steps.

The expected cost of added study is more readily determinable than the expected savings from that study; nevertheless, it is not always apparent. Two common viewpoints on this cost are that it is equal to the direct cost of the resources devoted to the added study or that it is essentially zero on the grounds that the resources are available and paid for regardless of whether or not they are used on that added study. The most defensible cost of added study is based on the opportunity cost principle; that is, the cost of the added study should be determined by the value to the company of those study resources if put to best productive use on work other than that added study. While this opportunity cost is often hard to evaluate, it seems reasonable that in a well-managed company the cost will be at least as great as the direct cost of those resources.

Figure 10-15 shows a flow diagram which depicts a general recommended sequence of steps in making economic analyses and shows qualitative test points regarding the extent of the analysis. This sequence would be applicable to analyses of either groups of mutually exclusive or non-mutually exclusive projects. Note that the recommended sequence shown in the figure shows four different points at which the decision could be made concerning which project(s) to accept. Also, there are four stages at which provision is made for dropping from further consideration projects which analysis indicates are clearly not contenders worthy of further study.

The meaning of the test points included is worthy of discussion. The test points are depicted as diamond shapes and are numbered in parentheses. Test point 1 considers the magnitude of the fixed monetary commitments involved in the decision for purposes of deciding whether further study is justified. The relevant amount of money to consider is the total present value of the nonsalvageable investment costs as well as other fixed costs which the company would incur if it should accept that project. If the magnitude of the fixed commitments for each of the projects being considered is low compared to the cost of further study, then it may be decided that further study is not justified and that the choice(s) should be made. The break-even point concerning the size of fixed commitments to use as this criterion is rather subjective. Determined intuitively, it appears that this point would be related to the company's financial health, the size of the projects usually considered, and the availability of resources for further analysis.

Test point 2 in Fig. 10-15 considers how close is the choice between projects. In this case, "close" can be defined as the nearness of the measure of merit for the most preferred alternative to the next most preferred alternative. If the assumed certainty analysis results up to that point show that the decision is not at all close [i.e., the choice(s) is (are) apparent], then further study is hardly justified and the choice(s) should be made.

Test point 3 is concerned with the decision of whether the results of an initial analysis considering variation of elements (which would be essentially

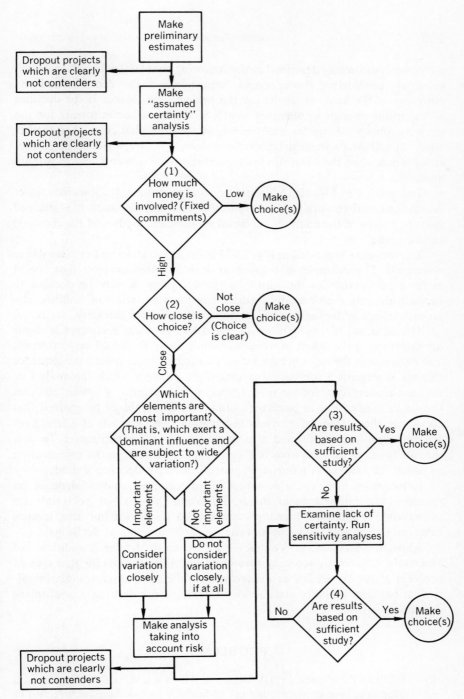

Figure 10-15. Recommended sequence of steps for economic analyses showing decision points on extent of analysis. This may be used for groups of either mutually exclusive or non-mutually exclusive projects.

199

a risk analysis such as described in the following chapters) is based on sufficient study considering the economic importance of the decision and the closeness of the analysis results for the projects considered. If the decision is important enough in terms of worth of the fixed commitments for the projects considered and the analysis results are somewhat close, then further study should be performed before the choice(s) is (are) made. The further study would take the form of closer estimations of elements and sensitivity analyses.

Test point 4 in Fig. 10-15 is repetitious of test point 3. It shows that closer estimations and sensitivity analyses would be continued until it is decided that the results of the analyses are based on sufficient study and the choice(s) can be made.

The sequence suggested in Fig. 10-15 is subject to shortcuts in cases where warranted. For example, if a given analysis involves projects that are of extreme importance to the future of the company, it may be decided to perform directly a risk analysis which considers variation of multiple elements without bothering to perform an initial "assumed certainty" study.

The sequence of steps shown in Fig. 10-15 provides a conceptual basis for determining the extent to which economic analyses should be performed. The decisions in the sequence are rather intangible; nevertheless, the sequence of steps represents a formalized structure for thinking which the analyst or decision-makers can follow in determining the extent to which analyses should be carried out in particular situations. It should be recognized that all of the above steps of analyses involving a particular set of alternatives are not necessarily performed at a single level in the organization. In fact, the more money which is involved, the higher is the level in the organization to which the analysis is referred, in general, before a decision is made.

In summary, the justifiable extent of an economic analysis depends on the economic importance of the study. When the risks or potentials are substantial, systematic procedures are needed to reduce the uncertainties inherent and to give them appropriate weight in arriving at decisions.

Appendix 9-A, "Cost–Volume–Profit Analysis Under Conditions of Uncertainty," shows interesting uses of probability concepts for that type of problem. It also serves as a basic exposition of the use of discrete and normally distributed probability distributions for the reader desiring a brief introduction or review.

PROBLEMS

10-1. Estimate the expected total remaining life of a given car, either one you happen to own or some other car with which you are familiar, in terms of
    a. single best estimate;
    b. single estimate and range;

c. subjective continuous probability distribution (estimate the cumulative probabilities and then graphically convert this into an approximate probability density function);

d. Beta II distribution (calculate the approximate mean and variance);

e. normal distribution (calculate the approximate mean and variance).

10-2. Work Prob. 10-1 except change the variable estimated to the number of basketball (or football) games to be won next year by the team of your choice. Of course, the variable is discrete, so the Beta II and normal distributions are only approximations.

10-3. Total operating costs and the corresponding production volumes for a particular process has been found to be as follows:

Operating costs ($M)	Production volume (hundreds of units)
800	10.0
1,000	11.0
700	9.0
600	8.5

a. Calculate the least-squares linear regression line to relate total operating costs as a function of production volume.

b. From the line in Prob. 10-3(a), estimate the operating costs for a production volume of 950 units.

c. Calculate the coefficient of correlation and comment on whether this indicates a relatively good or poor fit of the regression line to the data.

10-4. Use the Delphi method for obtaining the best composite estimate by four to six associates of some variable which is familiar to those associates, but for which they do not know the exact value. Examples of variables which could be estimated are the number of cars in a given community or the total amount of new industrial employment in a given state for a given year. Make at least three cycles of estimates.

10-5. State main advantages for each of the two methods for consideration of inflation. Which method do you feel is more desirable and why?

10-6. What distinction between risk and uncertainty do you think is most useful? Why?

10-7. Which of the eight causes of risk and uncertainty listed in this chapter may be said to be generally within the control (power to affect) of the economic analyst or the people from whom he obtains estimates?

10-8. Which of the three listed ways for a firm to change or influence degree of uncertainty is generally within the control of the economic analyst?

10-9. Under what circumstances might it be reasonable to start the analysis at the point immediately following decision point 2 in the sequence of steps shown in Fig. 10-15?

10-10. In Fig. 10-15, are there any points at which the step "Drop-out Projects Which Are Clearly Not Contenders" might reasonably be added or deleted to make it a more reasonable representation of ideal general practice? Explain your reasoning.

APPENDIX 10-A

Cost–Volume–Profit Analysis
Under Conditions of Uncertainty*

Cost–volume–profit analysis is frequently used by management as a basis for choosing among alternatives such decisions as (1) the sales volume required to attain a given level of profits, and (2) the most profitable combination of products to produce and sell. The fact that traditional C–V–P analysis does not include adjustments for risk and uncertainty may, in any given instance, severely limit its usefulness. Some of the limitations can be seen from the following example.

Assume that the firm is considering the introduction of two new products, either of which can be produced by using present facilities. Both products require an increase in annual fixed cost of the same amount, say $400,000. Each product has a $10 selling price and variable cost per unit of, say, $8 and $8 respectively and each requires the same amount of capacity. Using these data, the break-even point of either product is 200,000 units. C–V–P analysis helps to establish the break-even volume of each product, but this analysis does not distinguish the relative desirability of the two products for at least two reasons.

The first piece of missing information is the *expected* sales volume of each product. Obviously, if the annual sales of A are expected to be 300,000 units and of B are expected to be 350,000 units, then B is clearly preferred to A so far as the sales expectation is concerned.

However, assume that the expected annual sales of each product is the same—say 300,000 units. Is it right to conclude that management should be indifferent as far as a choice between A and B is concerned? The answer is

*By Robert K. Jaedicke and Alexander A. Robichek. Reprinted by permission of the publisher from *The Accounting Review*, No. 39 (October 1961), 917–926.

no, unless each sales expectation is certain. If both sales estimates are subject to uncertainty, the decision process will be improved if the relative risk associated with each product can somehow be brought into the analysis. The discussion which follows suggests some changes which might be made in traditional C–V–P analysis so as to make it a more useful tool in analyzing decision problems under uncertainty.

Some Probability Concepts Related to C–V–P Analysis

In the previous section, it was pointed out that the *expected* volume of the annual sales is an important decision variable. Some concepts of probability will be discussed using the example posed earlier.

The four fundamental relationships used in the example were (1) the selling price per unit, (2) the variable cost per unit, (3) the total fixed cost, and (4) the expected sales volume of each product. In any given decision problem all four of these factors can be uncertain. However, it may be that, *relative* to the expected sales quantity, the costs and selling prices are quite certain. That is, for analytical purposes, the decision-maker may be justified in treating several factors as certainty equivalents. Such a procedure simplifies the analysis and will be followed here as a first approximation. In this section of the paper, sales volume will be treated as the only uncertain quantity. Later, all decision factors in the above example will be treated under conditions of uncertainty.

In the example, sales volume is treated as a *random variable*. A random variable can be thought of as an *unknown quantity*. In this case, the best decision hinges on the value of the random variable, sales volume of each product. One decision approach which allows for uncertainty is to estimate, for each random variable, the likelihood that the random variable will take on various possible values. Such an estimate is called a subjective probability distribution. The decision would then be made by choosing that course of action which has the highest *expected monetary value*. This approach is illustrated in Table 10-A-1.

The expected value of the random variables, sales demand for each product, is calculated by weighting the possible conditional values by their respective probabilities. In other words, the expected value is a weighted average. The calculation is given in Table 10-A-2.

Based on an expected value approach, the firm should select product B rather than A. The expected profits of each possible action are as follows:

Product A:
  ($10 — $8)(300,000 units) — $400,000 = $200,000
Product B:
  ($10 — $8)(305,000 units) — $400,000 = $210,000

Table 10-A-1

PROBABILITY DISTRIBUTION FOR
PRODUCTS A AND B

Event (units demanded)	Probability distribution	
	Product A	Product B
50,000	——	0.1
100,000	0.1	0.1
200,000	0.2	0.1
300,000	0.4	0.2
400,000	0.2	0.4
500,000	0.1	0.1
	1.00	1.00

Table 10-A-2

EXPECTED VALUE OF SALES DEMAND FOR PRODUCTS A AND B

(1) Event	(2) P(A)	(1) × (2) E.V.(A)	(3) P(B)	(1) × (3) E.V.(B)
50,000	——	——	0.1	5,000
100,000	0.1	10,000	0.1	10,000
200,000	0.2	40,000	0.1	20,000
300,000	0.4	120,000	0.2	60,000
400,000	0.2	80,000	0.4	160,000
500,000	0.1	50,000	0.1	50,000
	$\Sigma = 1.00$		$\Sigma = 1.00$	
Expected value:	$\Sigma = 300,000$ units		$\Sigma = 305,000$ units	

Several observations are appropriate at this point. First, the respective probabilities for each product, used in Table 10-A-1, add to 1.00. Furthermore, the possible demand levels (events) are assumed to be mutually exclusive and also exhaustive. That is, the listing is done in such a way that no two events can happen simultaneously and any events *not* listed are assumed to have a zero probability of occurring. Herein are three important (basic) concepts of probability analyses.

Second, the probability distributions may have been assigned by using historical demand data on similar products, or the weights may be purely subjective in the sense that there is no historical data available. Even if the probability distributions are entirely subjective, this approach still has merit. It allows the estimator to express his uncertainty about the sales estimate. An estimate of sales is necessary to make a decision. Hence, the question is *not* whether an estimate must be made, but simply a question of the best way to make and express the estimate.

Now, suppose that the expected value of sales for each product is 300,000, as shown in Table 10-A-3. In this example, it is easy to see that the firm

Table 10-A-3

Demand	P(A)	E.V.(A)	P(B)	E.V.(B)
100,000 units	0.1	10,000	——	——
200,000	0.2	40,000	——	——
300,000	0.4	120,000	1.00	300,000
400,000	0.2	80,000	——	——
500,000	0.1	50,000	——	——
	1.00		1.00	
Expected sales demand:		$\Sigma = 300,000$		$\Sigma = 300,000$

would *not* be indifferent between products A and B, even though the expected value of sales is 300,000 units in both cases. In the case of product A, for example, there is a 0.1 chance that sales will be only 100,000 units, and in that case, a loss of $200,000 would be incurred (i.e. , $2 \times 100,000$ units — $400,000). On the other hand, there is a 0.3 chance that sales will be above 300,000 units and if this is the case, higher profits are possible with product A than with product B. Hence, the firm's attitude toward risk becomes important, but so is the "spread" in the distribution. Typically, the greater the "spread," the greater the risk involved. A quantitative measure of the spread is available in the form of the standard deviation of the distribution and this concept and its application will be refined later in the paper.

The Normal Probability Distribution

The preceding examples were highly simplified and yet the calculations are relatively long and cumbersome. The possible sales volumes were few in number and the probability distribution was discrete, that is, a sales volume of 205,762 units was considered an impossible event. The use of a continuous probability distribution is desirable not only because the calculation will usually be simplified but because the distribution may also be a more realistic description of the uncertainty aspects of the situation. The normal probability distribution will be introduced and used in the following analysis which illustrates the methodology involved. This distribution, although widely used, is not appropriate in all situations. The appropriate distribution depends on the decision problem and should, of course, be selected accordingly.

The normal probability distribution is a smooth, symmetric, continuous, bell-shaped curve as shown in Fig. 10-A-1. The area under the curve sums to 1. The curve reaches a maximum at the mean of the distribution and one-half the area lies on either side of the mean.

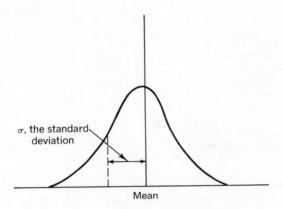

Figure 10-A-1. The normal probability distribution.

On the horizontal axis are plotted the values of the appropriate unknown quantity or random variable; in the examples used here, the unknown quantity is the sales for the coming periods.

A particular normal probability distribution can be completely determined if its mean and its standard deviation σ are known. The standard deviation is a measure of the dispersion of the distribution about its mean. The area under any normal distribution is 1, but one distribution may be "spread out" more than another distribution. For example, in Fig. 10-A-2, both normal distributions have the same area and the same mean. However, in one case the σ is 1 and in the other case the σ is greater than 1. The larger the σ, the more spread out is the distribution. It should be noted that the standard deviation is not an area but is a measure of the dispersion of the individual observations about the mean of all the observations—it is a distance.

Since the normal probability distribution is continuous rather than discrete, the probability of an event cannot be read directly from the graph. The unknown quantity must be thought of as being in an interval. Assume, for example, that the mean sales for the coming period is estimated to be 10,000 units and the normal distribution appears as in Fig. 10-A-3. Given Fig. 10-A-3, certain probability statements can be made. For example:

1. The probability of the actual sales being between 10,000 and 11,000 units is 0.20. This is shown by area C. Because of the symmetry of the

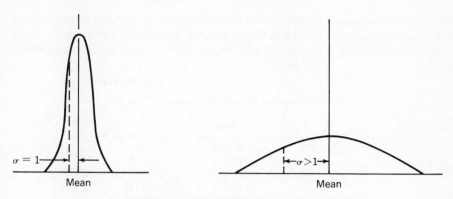

Figure 10-A-2. Normal probability distributions with different standard deviations.

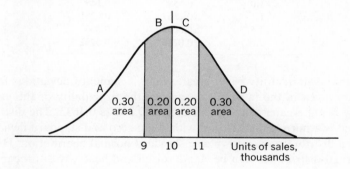

Figure 10-A-3.

curve, the probability of the sales being between 9,000 and 10,000 is also 0.20. This is shown by shaded area *B*. These probabilities can be given a frequency interpretation. That is, area *C* indicates that the actual sales will be between 10,000 and 11,000 units in about 20% of the cases.

2. The probability of the actual sales being greater than 11,000 units is 0.30 as shown by area *D*.
3. The probability of the sales being greater than 9,000 units is 0.70, the sum of areas *B*, *C*, and *D*.

Given a specific normal distribution, it is possible to read probabilities of the type described above directly from a normal probability table.

Another important characteristic of any normal distribution is that approximately 0.50 of the area lies within ±0.67 standard deviations of the mean; about 0.68 of the area lies within ±1.0 standard deviations of the mean; 0.95 of the area lies within ±1.96 standard deviations of the mean.

As was mentioned above, normal probabilities can be read from a normal probability table. A partial table of normal probabilities is given in Table 10-A-4. This table is the "right tail" of the distribution; that is, probabilities

Table 10-A-4

AREA UNDER THE NORMAL PROBABILITY FUNCTION

X	0.00	0.05
0.1	0.4602	0.4404
0.3	0.3821	0.3632
0.5	0.3085	0.2912
0.6	0.2743	0.2578
0.7	0.2420	0.2266
0.8	0.2119	0.1977
0.9	0.1841	0.1711
1.0	0.1587	0.1469
1.1	0.1357	0.1251
1.5	0.0668	0.0606
2.0	0.0228	0.0202

of the unknown quantity being greater than X standard deviations from the mean are given in the table. For example, the probability of the unknown quantity being greater than the mean plus 0.35σ is 0.3632. The distribution tabulated is a normal distribution with mean zero and standard deviation of 1. Such a distribution is known as a standard normal distribution. However, any normal distribution can be standardized and hence, with proper adjustment, Table 10-A-4 will serve for any normal distribution.

For example, consider the earlier case where the mean of the distribution is 10,000 units. The distribution was constructed so that the standard deviation is about 2,000 units.* To standardize the distribution, use the following formula, where X is the number of standard deviations from the mean:

$$X = \frac{\text{Actual sales} - \text{Mean sales}}{\text{Standard deviation of the distribution}}$$

To calculate the probability of the sales being greater than 11,000 units, first standardize the distribution and then use the table.

$$X = \frac{11,000 - 10,000}{2,000}$$

$$= 0.50 \text{ standard deviations}$$

*To see why this normal distribution has a standard deviation of 2,000 units, remember that the probability of sales being greater than 11,000 units is 0.30. Now examine Table 4, and it can be seen that the probability of a random variable being greater than 0.5 standard deviation from the mean is 0.3085. Hence, 1,000 units is about the same as $\frac{1}{2}$ standard deviation. So, 2,000 units is about 1 standard deviation.

The probability of being greater than 0.50 standard deviations from the mean, according to Table 10-A-4, is 0.3085. This same approximate result is shown by Figure 10-A-3; that is, area D is 0.30.

The Normal Distribution Used in C–V–P Analysis

The normal distribution will now be used in a C–V–P analysis problem, assuming that sales quantity is a random variable. Assume that the per-unit selling price is $3,000, the fixed cost is $5,800,000, and the variable cost per unit is $1,750. Break-even sales (in units) is calculated as follows:

$$S_B = \frac{\$5,800,000}{\$3,000 - \$1,750} = 4,640 \text{ units}$$

Furthermore, suppose that the sales manager estimates that the mean expected sales volume is 5,000 units and that it is equally likely that actual sales will be greater or less than the mean of 5,000 units. Furthermore, assume that the sales manager feels that there is roughly a $\frac{2}{3}$ (i.e., 0.667) chance that the actual sales will be within 400 units of the mean. These subjective estimates can be expressed by using a normal distribution with mean $E(Q)$ = 5,000 units and standard deviation $\sigma_Q = 400$ units. The reason that σ_Q is about 400 units is that, as mentioned earlier, about $\frac{2}{3}$ of the area under the normal curve (actually 0.68) lies within 1 standard deviation of the mean. The probability distribution is shown in Fig. 10-A-4.

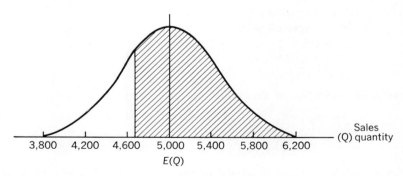

Figure 10-A-4.

The horizontal axis of Fig. 10-A-4 denotes sales quantity. The probability of an actual sales event taking place is given by the area under the probability distribution. For example, the probability that the sales quantity will exceed 4,640 units (the break-even point) is the shaded area under the probability distribution (the probability of actual sales exceeding 4,640 units).

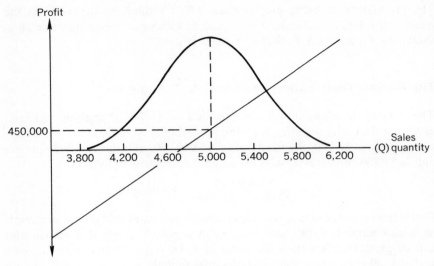

Figure 10-A-5.

The probability distribution of Fig. 10-A-4 can be superimposed on the profit portion of the traditional C–V–P; this is done in Fig. 10-A-5. The values for price-fixed costs and variable costs are presumed to be known with certainty. Expected profit is given by

$$E(Z) = E(Q)(P - V) - F = \$450,000$$

where $E(Z)$ = Expected profit
$E(Q)$ = Expected sales
P = Price
V = Variable cost
F = Fixed cost

The standard deviation of the profit (σ_z) is

$$\sigma_z = \sigma_Q \times \$1,250 \text{ contribution per unit}$$
$$= 400 \text{ units} \times \$1,250$$
$$= \$500,000$$

Since profits are directly related to the volume of sales, and since it is the level of profits which is often the concern of management, it may be desirable to separate the information in Fig. 10-A-5 which relates to profit. Figure 10-A-6 is a graphical illustration of the relationship between profit level and the probability distribution of the profit level. A number of important relationships can now be obtained in probabilistic terms. Since the probability distribution of sales quantity is normal with a mean of 5,000 units and a standard deviation of 400 units, the probability distribution of

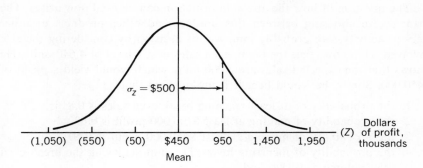

Figure 10-A-6.

profits will also be normal with a mean, as shown earlier, of \$450,000 and a standard deviation of \$500,000.

Using the probability distribution shown in Fig. 10-A-6, the following probabilities can be calculated (using Table 10-A-4).

1. *The probability of at least breaking even:* This is the probability of profits being greater than zero and can be calculated by summing the area under the distribution to the right of zero profits. This probability can be calculated as $1 -$ (Probability of profits being less than zero). Since the distribution is symmetric, Table 10-A-4 can be used to read left-tail as well as right-tail probabilities. Zero profits fall 0.9 standard deviations to the left of the mean, i.e. , ($450 - 0$)/$500 = 0.9. Hence, the probability of profits being less than zero is

$$P(\text{Profits} < 0.9\sigma \text{ from the mean}) = 0.184$$

   Therefore,

$$P(\text{Profits} > 0) = 1 - 0.184 = 0.816$$

2. *The probability of profits being greater than \$200,000:*

$$P(\text{Profits} > \$200,000)$$
$$= 1 - P\left[\text{Profits} < \left(\frac{450 - 200}{500}\right)\sigma \text{ from the mean}\right]$$
$$= 1 - P(\text{Profits} < 0.5\sigma \text{ from the mean})$$
$$= 1 - 0.3085$$
$$= 0.692$$

3. *The probability of the loss being greater than \$300,000:*

$$P(\text{Loss} > \$300,000)$$
$$= P\left\{\text{Loss} > \left[\frac{450 - (-300)}{500}\right]\sigma = 1.5\sigma \text{ from the mean}\right\}$$
$$= 0.067$$

The question of how the above information can be used now arises. The manager, in choosing between this product and other products or other lines of activity, can probably improve his decision by considering the risk involved. He knows that the break-even sales is at a level of 4,640 units. He knows that the expected sales are 5,000 units which would yield a profit of $450,000. Surely, he would benefit from knowing that

1. the probability of at least reaching break-even sales is 0.816;
2. the probability of making at least $200,000 profit is 0.692;
3. the probability of making at least $450,000 profit is 0.50;
4. the probability of incurring losses, i.e. , not achieving the break-even sales volume, is 0.184; and
5. the probability of incurring a $300,000 or greater loss is 0.067, etc.

If the manager is comparing this product with other products, probability analysis combined with C–V–P allows a comparison of the risk involved in each product, as well as a comparison of relative break-even points and expected profits. Given the firm's attitude toward and willingness to assume risk (of losses as well as high profits), the decision of choosing among alternatives should be facilitated by the above analysis.

Several Relevant Probabilistic Factors

It is evident from the above discussion that profit Z is a function of the quantity of sales in units, Q, the unit selling price P, the fixed cost F, and the variable costs V. Up to this point P, F, and V were considered only as given constants, so that profit was variable only as a function of changes in sales quantity. In the following discussion, P, F, and V will be treated in a manner similar to Q, i.e. , as random variables whose probability distribution is known. Continuing the example from the preceding section, let

Variable	Expectation (mean)	Standard deviation
Sales quantity (Q)	$E(Q') = 5,000$ units	$\sigma_{Q'} = 400$ units
Selling price (P)	$E(P') = \$3,000*$	$\sigma_{P'} = \$50*$
Fixed costs (F)	$E(F') = \$5,800,000*$	$\sigma_{F'} = \$100,000*$
Variable costs (V)	$E(V') = \$1,750*$	$\sigma_{V'} = \$75*$

*The mean and standard deviation for P, F, and V can be established by using the same method described earlier. That is, the sales manager may estimate a mean selling price of $3,000 per unit and, given the above information, he should feel that there is roughly a $\frac{2}{3}$ probability that the actual sales price per unit will be within $50 of this mean estimate.

This assumption is made to facilitate computation in the example. Where correlation among variables is present the computational procedure must take into account the values of the respective covariances.

For purposes of illustration, the random variables will be assumed to be independent, so that no correlation exists between events of the different random variables. In this case, the expected profit $E(Z')$ and the related standard deviation $\sigma_{Z'}$ can be calculated as follows:†

$$E(Z') = E(Q')[E(P') - E(V')] - E(F')$$
$$= \$450,000$$
$$\sigma_{Z'} = \$681,500$$

Note that when factors other than sales are treated as random variables, the expected profit is still \$450,000 as in the previous cases. However, the profit's risk as measured by the standard deviation is increased from \$500,000 to \$681,500. The reason for this is that the variability in all of the components (i.e., sales price, cost, etc.) will add to the variability in the profit. Is this change in the standard deviation significant? The significance of the change is a value judgment based on a comparison of various probabilistic measures and on the firm's attitude toward risk. Using a normal distribution, Table 10-A-5 compares expected profits, standard deviations of profits, and select probabilistic measures for three hypothetical products.

In all three situations, the proposed products have the same break-even quantity: 4,640 units. The first case is the first example discussed where sales quantity is the only random variable. The second case is the one just discussed, that is, all factors are probabilistic. In the third case, the assumed product has the same expected values for selling price, variable cost, fixed

Table 10-A-5

COMPARISON OF EXPECTED PROFITS, STANDARD DEVIATIONS OF PROFITS,
AND SELECT PROBABILISTIC MEASURES*

	Product		
	1	*2*	*3*
Expected profit:	\$450,000	\$450,000	\$ 450,000
Standard deviation of profit:	\$500,000	\$681,500	\$1,253,000
The probability of			
a. at least breaking even:	0.816	0.745	0.641
b. profit at least +\$250,000:	0.655	0.615	0.564
c. profit at least +\$600,000:	0.382	0.413	0.456
d. loss greater than \$300,000:	0.067	0.136	0.274

Note: The above probabilities, in some cases, cannot be read from Table 10-A-4. However, all probabilities come from a more complete version of Table 10-A-4, such as Appendix A-E.

†For the case of independent variables given here, $\sigma_{Z'}$ is the solution value in the following equation:

$$\sigma_{Z'} = \sqrt{\sigma_Q^2(\sigma_P^2 + \sigma_V^2) + [E(Q)]^2(\sigma_P^2 + \sigma_V^2) + [E(P') - E(V')]^2\sigma_Q^2 + \sigma_F^2}$$

cost, and sales volume, but the standard deviations on each of these random variables have been increased to $\sigma_{Q''} = 600$ (instead of 400 units); $\sigma_{P''} = \$125$ (instead of \$50); $\sigma_{F''} = \$200,000$ (instead of \$100,000); and $\sigma_{V''} = \$150$ (instead of \$75).

Table 10-A-5 shows the relative "risk" involved in the three new products which have been proposed. The chances of at least breaking even are greatest with product 1. However, even though the standard deviation of the profit on product 3 is [more than] twice that of product 1, the probability of breaking even on product 3 is only 0.17 lower than product 1. Likewise, the probability of earning at least \$250,000 profit is higher for product 1 (which has the lowest σ) than for the other two products.

However, note that the probability of earning profits above the expected value of \$450,000 (for each product) is *greater* for products 2 and 3 than for 1. If the firm is willing to assume some risk, the chances of high profits are improved with product 3, rather than with 2 and 1. To offset this, however, the chance of loss is also greatest with product 3. This is to be expected, since product 3 has the highest standard deviation (variability) as far as profit is concerned.

The best alternative cannot be chosen without some statement of the firm's attitude toward risk. However, given a certain attitude, the proper choice should be facilitated by using probability information of the type given in Table 10-A-5. As an example, suppose that the firm's position is such that any loss at all may have an adverse affect on its ability to stay in business. Some probability criteria can, perhaps, be established in order to screen proposals for new products. If, for example, the top management feels that any project which is acceptable must have no greater than a 0.30 probability of incurring a loss, then projects 1 or 2 would be acceptable but project 3 would not.

On the other hand, the firm's attitude toward risk may be such that the possibility of high profit is attractive, provided the probability of losses can be reasonably controlled. In this case, it may be possible to set a range within which acceptable projects must fall. For example, suppose that the firm is willing to accept projects where the probability of profits being greater than \$600,000 is at least 0.40, provided that the probability of a loss being greater than \$300,000 does not exceed 0.15. In this case, project 2 would be acceptable, but project 3 would not. Given statements of attitude toward risk of this nature, it seems that a probability dimension added to C–V–P analysis would be useful.

Summary and Conclusion

In many cases, the choice among alternatives is facilitated greatly by C–V–P analysis. However, traditional C–V–P analysis does not take account of the relative risk of various alternatives. The interaction of costs, selling prices, and volume are important in summarizing the effect of various alternatives on the profits of the firm. The techniques discussed in this paper preserve the traditional analysis but also add another dimension—that is, risk is brought in as another important decision factor. The statement of probabilities with respect to various levels of profits and losses for each alternative should aid the decision-maker, once his attitude toward risk has been defined.

eleven

Risk and Uncertainty—
Traditional Analysis
Procedures

There are numerous basic or traditional procedures (methods) for considering risk and uncertainty. The single procedure or combination of procedures which should be used for a particular problem depends upon the individual situation—the complexity and importance of the decision, and the preferences of analysts and decision-makers. Several of the most important are listed below and described in the sections which follow.

1. Intuitive judgment
2. Conservative adjustment
3. Optimistic–pessimistic
4. Sensitivity
5. Break-even
6. Risk discounting
7. Miscellaneous decision rules for complete uncertainty
8. Game theory

Intuitive Judgment Method

Probably the most common procedure for considering risk and uncertainty, if indeed it could even be called a procedure, is to make an assumed certainty analysis and then make an intuitive or subjective judgment as to whether the risk for any project or projects is great enough to change the decision based on the quantitative results of the analysis coupled with any consideration of intangibles.

Example:

> In the example comparison of a wood building vs. a brick building at the end of Chapter 7, assumed certainty calculations resulted in showing that the brick building, having an expected life of 40 years, was less economical than the wood building, having an expected life of 20 years. (Annual cost of $9,060 for brick vs. $8,012 for wood.) It is entirely possible that a subjective or intuitive consideration of the relative risks involved would result in the decision that the brick building was the better choice.
>
> *Note:* Of course, consideration of such irreducible factors as quality, safety, esthetic appeal, etc., could also serve to reverse the decision indicated by the economic analysis alone.

Conservative Adjustment Method

This procedure, as its name indicates, involves changing estimates of one or more elements in a conservative direction so as to decrease the risk that the actual outcome will not be as favorable as predicted in the prior economy study.

Example:

> The single project illustrated in the beginning of Chapter 3 on the annual worth method involved the following estimates which were presumably the expected or most likely estimated outcomes:

	Expectation estimates
Investment:	$10,000
Life:	5 yr
Salvage value:	$2,000
Annual receipts:	$5,000
Annual disbursements:	$2,200

> Using an interest rate of 8%, the net annual worth for the above estimates was calculated to be $630.
>
> Suppose an analyst is particularly concerned about the risk of the project and wants to adjust estimates of elements involving particularly high risk —say, life, annual receipts, and annual disbursements—in a conservative direction. Revised estimates might be

	Conservative-adjusted estimates
Investment:	$10,000
Life:	4 yr
Salvage value:	$2,000
Annual receipts:	$4,500
Annual disbursements:	$2,400

Using the conservative-adjusted estimates, the annual worth can be calculated as

Annual receipts:		$4,500
Annual disbursements:	$2,400	
C.R. cost $= (\$10,000 - \$2,000)(A/P,8\%,4)$		
$\quad + \$2,000(8\%)$:	2,570	
		−4,970
Net A.W.:		−$470

Thus, the calculated results indicate the project to be unfavorable (A.W. < 0) after the conservative adjustments.

Of course, the conservative adjustment procedure can be extended to any number of elements and any number of projects being compared. In fact, one may want to calculate results for more than one degree of conservatism—say, mildly conservative and strongly conservative.

Optimistic–Pessimistic Method

This procedure, as its name implies, involves changing estimates of one or more elements in a favorable outcome (optimistic) direction and in an unfavorable outcome (pessimistic) direction so as to investigate the effect of these various changes on the economy study result.

In using this method, it is desirable for the estimator to adopt a guideline philosophy of "how optimistic" and "how pessimistic" in making the estimates. One convenient way to do this is to adopt a probabilistic statement such as: "An optimistic estimate will mean a value of the element which we would expect to be bettered or exceeded in outcome no more than, say, 5% of the time, while a pessimistic estimate is a value of the element which we would expect to be more favorable than the final outcome no more than, say, 5% of the time."

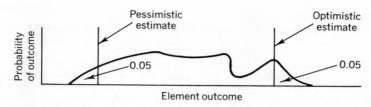

Figure 11-1. Illustration of estimates for optimistic-pessimistic method.

Example:

Suppose that for the single project example given above and in the first part of Chapter 3, the optimistic, pessimistic, and expected estimates are as follows:

	Estimation condition		
	Optimistic	*Expected*	*Pessimistic*
Investment:	$10,000	$10,000	$10,000
Life:	7 yr	5 yr	4 yr
Salvage value:	$2,000	$2,000	$2,000
Annual receipts:	$6,000	$5,000	$4,500
Annual disbursements:	$2,200	$2,200	$2,400
Interest rate:	8%	8%	8%

Note: The "pessimistic" estimates happen to be the same as the "conservative-adjusted" estimates in the section above. Hence, the net annual worth under the pessimistic conditions is −$470. The net annual worth for the expected estimates was calculated in Chapter 3 to be $630. The net annual worth for optimistic conditions can be calculated to be $2,100. These results should be useful to the decision-maker in determining the degree of risks and rewards for estimated extreme conditions.

The above example calculations are based on the assumption that the elements are going to turn out to be all per the pessimistic estimates, all per the expected estimates, or all per the optimistic estimates. Of course, one can investigate the effect on calculated results when various elements turn out per optimistic, expected, or pessimistic estimates in various combinations. When this is done, it is usually helpful to summarize results in tabular form.

Example:

For the above example, note that estimates for the three conditions differed only for the project life, annual receipts, and annual disbursements. Table 11-1 shows the calculated results for all combinations of estimating conditions—optimistic (*O*), expected (*E*), and pessimistic (*P*)—for all elements which vary significantly.

Table 11-1

CALCULATED RESULTS FOR ALL COMBINATIONS OF ESTIMATING CONDITIONS

Net annual worth

Life		Annual disb.—O			Annual disb.—E			Annual disb.—P		
		O	E	P	O	E	P	O	E	P
Annual receipts	O	$2,100	$1,630	$1,230	$2,100	$1,630	$1,230	$1,900	$1,430	$1,030
	E	1,100	630	230	1,100	630	230	900	430	30
	P	600	130	−270	600	130	−270	400	−70	−470

Key: *O* is optimistic outcome
E is expected outcome
P is pessimistic outcome

Sensitivity Method

The sensitivity method is merely an informal offshoot of the optimistic–pessimistic method in which estimates of one or more elements can be changed in a favorable or unfavorable direction or combinations of favorable and unfavorable directions so as to investigate the effect of any changes of concern on the economy study result.

Example:

Suppose, for the single project example given above which resulted in a net annual worth of $630 for expected estimating conditions, it was decided that critical elements are project life and interest rate, and that it is desired to determine the effect if the project life were decreased 40% below expectation to 3 years and the interest were increased by 50% to a rate of 12%.

Solution:

$$
\begin{array}{lrr}
\text{Annual receipts:} & & \$5,000 \\
\text{Annual disbursement:} & \$2,200 & \\
\text{C.R. cost} = (\$10,000 - \$2,000)(A/P,12\%,3) & & \\
\quad + \$2,000(12\%): & 3,573 & \\
\cline{2-2}
& & -5,773 \\
\text{Net A.W.:} & & -\$773
\end{array}
$$

Thus, the economy study result is highly sensitive to the 40% decrease in project life together with 50% increase in interest rate; i.e., it rather markedly reverses the indicated decision based on calculated results.

One concept of sensitivity which is often useful is that "sensitivity is the relative magnitude of the change in one or more elements of an economy study which will reverse a decision among alternatives."

Example:

Suppose it is desired to examine the sensitivity of the same single project example illustrated above to changes in interest rate alone by determining the relative change in interest rate for the project no longer to show a positive net annual worth, and thus reverse the decision to invest.

Solution:

$$\$5,000 - \$2,200 - [(\$10,000 - \$2,000)(A/P,i\%,5) + \$2,000(i\%)] = 0$$

$$@i = 12\%: \quad \$5,000 - \$2,200 - [\$8,000(0.277) + \$2,000(0.12)] = +\$330$$

$$@i = 20\%: \quad \$5,000 - \$2,000 - [\$8,000(0.334) + \$2,000(0.20)] = -\$300$$

Therefore,

$$i = 12\% + \left(\frac{\$330}{\$330 + \$300}\right)(20\% - 12\%) = 16.2\%$$

Thus, if the interest rate is increased by (16.2% − 8%)/8%, or 103%, the indicated decision to invest would be reversed. From this, one might infer that the decision is relatively insensitive to changes in the interest rate.

A good way to reflect sensitivity to various changes in elements is to graph the results and thus be able to examine the results visually.

Example:

For the single project example illustrated above, graph the net annual worth as a function of the interest rate over the range 0 to 25%.

Solution:

The reader will recall that the net A.W. at an interest rate of 8% is $630. Also, the above example showed that the net A.W. is $0 at an interest rate of 16.2%. Calculations can be made to determine the net A.W. for other interest rates as desired, and the results plotted as shown below.

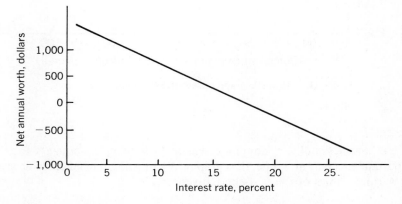

Figure 11-2. Example graph of sensitivity to interest rate.

Probably an even more valuable tool for examining sensitivity is to graph results for independent variation of all elements of concern while expressing the variation for each on a common abscissa as a percentage of the respective expected values.

Example:

For the single project example used previously in this chapter, graph the net A.W. as a function of the elements' life, annual disbursements, and interest rate for the range $\pm 100\%$ of the expected value of each.

Solution:

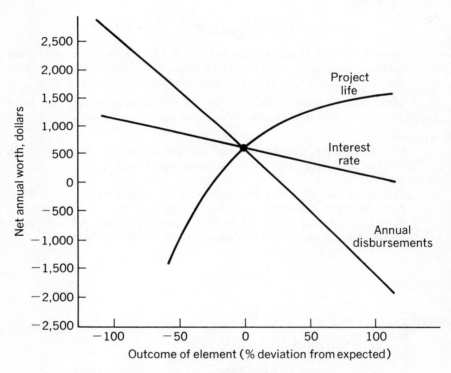

Figure 11-3. Example graph of sensitivity to multiple elements.

Yet another tool for examining sensitivity is to plot isoquants for two important elements at a time, thus graphically showing the indicated decision for various values of the two alternatives.

Example:

Develop an isoquant for the single project example shown above, where project lives of from 1 to 10 years and interest rates of from 4 to 20% are considered.

Solution:

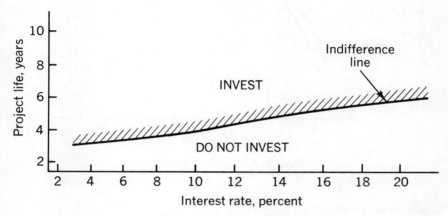

Figure 11-4. Example isoquant.

It is commonly desirable to plot the measure of merit as a function of a key element subject to variation, with various curves for selected values of other key elements subject to variation.

Example:

For the project illustrated above, the net annual worth for project lives ranging from 2.5 to 10 years with the following combinations of element conditions is shown in Fig. 11-5:

Condition	Annual receipts	Salvage value
A	$5,000	$ 2,000
B	5,500	2,000
C	4,500	10,000

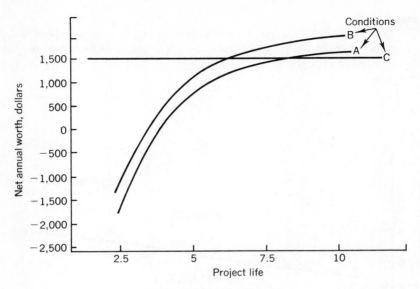

Figure 11-5. Sensitivity graphs.

Break-even Method

The *break-even method* of analysis is usually used in situations where there is particular uncertainty concerning one of the elements in an economy study. The break-even point for an element in an economy study of a single project can be defined as that value of the element at which the project is just marginal or barely justified.

Example:

Suppose that for the single project for which expected element estimates were shown above, the element for which there is particular uncertainty is the life of the project; hence, it is desired to find the minimum project life at which the project will barely be justified.

Solution:

$$\$5,000 - \$2,200 - (\$10,000 - \$2,000)(A/P,8\%,N) - \$2,000(8\%) = 0$$

$$(A/P,8\%,N) = \frac{-\$2,640}{-\$8,000} = 0.330$$

Therefore, interpolating in tables, $N = 3.7$ yr.

The break-even point for an element in the comparison of two alternatives can be defined as that value of the element at which the alternatives are equally desirable.

Risk Discounting Method

The *risk discounting procedure* involves using an interest rate appropriate for the associated degree of risk as the standard for the minimum acceptable rate of return. In general, the higher the risk in business, the higher the expected rate of return; however, the specification of what interest rate is appropriate for what degree of risk is difficult and subjective.

Because of the phenomena of higher interest rates resulting in lower equivalent present worths, the risk discounting method can possibly yield reasonable results only when the revenue or savings as well as the cost elements are known for each project; indeed, for comparisons of projects involving only costs, use of this method will influence each project in a manner opposite to what is reasonable; i.e., higher interest incident with higher risk will *lower* the equivalent present worth–cost of the project. Also, this method fails whenever a project has so short a life that discounting cannot take effect. Nevertheless, the method does represent an attempt to rationalize the consideration of risk.

Example:

The single project example given above results in a net A.W. of \$630 based on expected element estimates and an interest rate of 8%. Suppose it is decided to increase the interest rate to 12% to reflect an adjustment for consideration of risk. What is the risk-discounted net A.W.?

Solution:

Annual receipts:		\$5,000
Annual disbursements:	\$2,200	
C.R. cost = (\$10,000 − \$2,000)($A/P,12\%,5$)		
+ \$2,000(12%):	2,460	
		−4,660
Net A.W.:		\$340

Thus, the risk-discounted measure still reflects a favorable project, but not nearly so favorable as for the previous interest rate of 8%.

It should be noted that even though most of the example illustrations of application of the analysis procedures described in this chapter are applied to a single project, the procedures are equally appropriate for application to general cases in which two or more projects are being compared.

Miscellaneous Decision Rules for Complete Uncertainty

In this section, some arbitrary decision rules or principles for choosing from among alternatives in situations where there is the element of complete uncertainty about certain probabilities will be discussed. These decision rules apply to situations where there are a number of alternatives (*courses of action*) and a number of possible outcomes (*states of nature*), and where the effect of each alternative on each possible outcome is known but the probability of occurrence of each possible outcome is not known.

The most difficult aspect of using these decision rules is deciding which to use for making a decision. In effect, these decision rules reflect various degrees of optimism or pessimism, and should be chosen according to which reflect certain management views involving intuition and appropriateness for a particular situation. The greatest defense for the use of any of these rules is that their use will promote explicitness and consistency in decision-making under complete uncertainty.

A representation of a typical problem is given by the matrix in Table 11-2.

Table 11-2

EXAMPLE PROBLEM INVOLVING COMPLETE UNCERTAINTY
PAYOFFS—NET P.W. ($M)

Alternative	State of nature			
	E	G	F	P
I	3	−1	1	1
II	4	0	−4	6
III	5	−2	0	2

Note that this problem shows four possible states of nature (with presumably unknown probabilities of occurrence) and three alternative courses of action, one of which is to be chosen. The payoffs can be thought of as expressed in $M of net P.W. The following sections will explain and illustrate each of several decision rules for this type of problem.

Maximin or minimax rule

The *maximin rule* suggests that the decision-maker examine the minimum profit (payoff) associated with each alternative and then select the alternative which maximizes the minimum profit. Similarly, in the case of costs, the *minimax rule* suggests that the decision-maker examine the maximum cost associated with each alternative and then select the alternative which minimizes the maximum cost. These decision rules are conservative and pessimistic, for they direct attention to the worst outcome and then make the worst outcome as desirable as possible. However, they are widely discussed and form the usual basis for game theory analysis (to be covered later).

Example:

Given the payoffs for each of three alternatives and for each of four possible states of nature (chance occurrences) in Table 11-2, determine which alternative would maximize the minimum possible payoff.

Solution:

The minimum possible payoff for alternative I is -1, for alternative II is -4, for alternative III is -2. Hence alternative I would be chosen as maximizing these minimum payoffs.

Maximax or minimin rule

These rules are direct opposites of their counterparts discussed above, and thus reflect extreme optimism. The *maximax rule* suggests that the decision-maker examine the maximum profit associated with each alternative, and then select the alternative which maximizes the maximum profit. Similarly, in the case of costs, the *minimin rule* indicates that the decision-maker should examine the minimum cost associated with each alternative, and then select the alternative which minimizes the minimum cost.

Example:

Given the same payoff matrix as in Table 11-2, determine which alternative would maximize the maximum payoff.

Solution:

The maximum possible payoff for alternative I is 3. Similarly, for II the maximum payoff is 6, and for III it is 5. The highest of these is 6, which occurs with alternative II, so alternative II is the maximax choice.

Laplace principle or rule

This rule simply assumes that all possible outcomes are equally likely and that one can choose on the basis of expected outcomes as calculated using equal probabilities for all outcomes. There is a common tendency toward this assumption in situations where there is no evidence to the contrary, but the assumption (and, therefore, the rule) is of highly questionable merit.

Example:

Given the same payoff matrix as in Table 11-2, determine which alternative is best using the Laplace rule.

Solution:

$$E \text{ (alt. I):} \quad 3 \times \tfrac{1}{4} - 1 \times \tfrac{1}{4} + 1 \times \tfrac{1}{4} + 1 \times \tfrac{1}{4} = 1.00$$

$$E \text{ (alt. II):} \quad 4 \times \tfrac{1}{4} + 0 \times \tfrac{1}{4} - 4 \times \tfrac{1}{4} + 6 \times \tfrac{1}{4} = 1.50$$

$$E \text{ (alt. III):} \quad 5 \times \tfrac{1}{4} - 2 \times \tfrac{1}{4} + 0 \times \tfrac{1}{4} + 2 \times \tfrac{1}{4} = 1.25$$

Thus, alternative II, giving the highest expected payoff, is best.

Hurwicz principle or rule

This rule is intended to reflect any degree of moderation between extreme optimism and extreme pessimism which the decision-maker may wish to choose. The rule may be stated explicitly as

> Select an index of optimism, a, such that $0 \leq a \leq 1$. For each alternative, compute the weighted outcome: $a \times$ (Value of profit or cost if most favorable outcome occurs) $+ (1 - a) \times$ (Value of profit or cost if least favorable outcome occurs). Choose the alternative which optimizes the weighted outcome.

A practical difficulty of the Hurwicz rule is that it is difficult for the decision-maker to determine a proper value for a, the weighting factor. The Hurwicz rule also lacks several of the desirable properties of a good decision rule, and can even lead to results which are obviously counter to one's intuition.

Example:
> Given the same payoff matrix as in Table 11-2, calculate which alternative would be best, using the Hurwicz rule, for an index of optimism of 0.75. Also graph the calculated payoff for each alternative over the entire range of the index of optimism.

Solution:

$$\text{Alt. I:} \qquad 0.75(3) + 0.25(-1) = 2.0$$
$$\text{Alt. II:} \qquad 0.75(6) + 0.25(-4) = 3.5$$
$$\text{Alt. III:} \qquad 0.75(5) + 0.25(-2) = 3.25$$

Thus, alternative III, giving the highest payoff, is best.

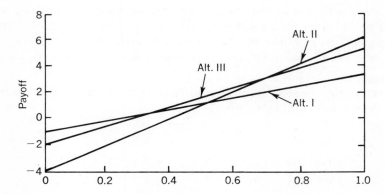

Figure 11-6. Graphed payoffs over range of optimism indices.

Minimax regret rule

This rule, proposed by L.J. Savage, is similar to the minimax and maximin rules, but is intended to counter some of the ultraconservative results given by those rules. This rule suggests that the decision-maker examine the maximum possible *regret* (loss because of not having chosen the best alternative for each possible outcome) associated with each alternative, and then select the alternative which minimizes the maximum regret.

Example:
Given the same payoff matrix as in Table 11-2, show which alternative would be chosen on the basis of minimizing the maximum regret. Develop a regret matrix to obtain a solution.

Solution:

Table 11-3

REGRET MATRIX FOR PROBLEM OF TABLE 11-2

Alternative	State of nature				Maximum of states
	E	G	F	P	
I	2 (= 5 − 3)	1	0	5	5
II	1 (= 5 − 4)	0	5	0	5
III	0 (= 5 − 5)	2	1	4	4 (Min. of all max.)

Thus, it can be seen that the worst (highest) regret for alternative I is 5, for alternative II is 5, and for alternative III is 4. The minimum of these maximum regrets is 4 for alternative III, and thus alternative III is the choice.

Game Theory

One important and special class of decisions under uncertainty consists of decisions which involve conflict or competition between two or more decision-makers. The philosophy and solution techniques for understanding these competitive decisions is called *game theory*.

The term *game* should not be construed to imply that game theory is limited to trivial parlor entertainment contests. Indeed, game theory can be applied to the study of strategies of war adversaries or business competitors. While game theory can be conceptually extended to situations in which there are numerous competitors, we shall limit our attention to situations involving only two competitors. The two-competitor situations serve to show the techniques and philosophy of analysis well without the greatly increased mathematical complexity of situations involving more than two competitors.

Actually, the two-competitor situation has great applicability in practice, for often the strategy of one competitor is designed to counter the interests of the most formidable opponent only, thus neglecting others among multiple opponents. At other times, a competitor may view an entire array of multiple business competitors as a single opponent, thus reducing the problem to a two-competitor contest.

Payoff matrix

In two-competitor games, the rows of the *payoff matrix* contain the outcomes (usually interpreted as gains) for one competitor and the columns show the outcomes (usually interpreted as losses) for the other competitor. As an example, consider Fig. 11-7, which shows that competitor X has four strategies (alternatives) and competitor Y has three strategies (alternatives). The outcomes are written in terms of payoffs to competitor X and losses to competitor Y. These payoffs can be in any units—for example, thousands of dollars. Thus, any negative outcome is interpreted as a negative payoff, or loss, to X and as a negative loss, or gain, to Y. Because the sum of the payoffs for any choice of alternatives is zero (when X gains, Y loses by the same amount, and vice versa), the game is called a *zero-sum game*.

		LOSS BY COMPETITOR Y		
	Strategies	*Y1*	*Y2*	*Y3*
	X1	4	1	0
Payoff to	X2	3	2	3
competitor X	X3	2	1	4
	X4	2	1	−1

Figure 11-7. Example two-competitor game problem.

There are several assumptions implied in the conflict situation represented by the two-competitor zero-sum payoff matrix, such as in Fig. 11-7. These are

1. each competitor has a finite number of alternative strategies;
2. both competitors know all the strategies available to each;
3. all payoffs or losses can be quantified to a single number; and
4. both competitors know all the potential payoffs and losses.

Dominance

The first step in analyzing a game matrix (or even a matrix describing a complete uncertainty situation for a single firm) is to check for *dominance*.

That is, for competitor X, we should check for any strategy (or strategies) which would clearly always be less desirable than some other strategy (or strategies). And the same thing should be done for competitor Y. If any such strategy is found, it should be eliminated from consideration. For example, in Fig. 11-7, strategy X4 is always less desirable to competitor X than strategy X2. That is, regardless of the strategy that competitor Y chooses, competitor X would rationally prefer strategy X2 to strategy X4. Similarly, strategy Y1 is always less desirable to competitor Y than strategy Y2. Once these dominated strategies (X4 and Y1) are eliminated, the matrix of interest becomes as shown in Fig. 11-8.

Loss by Competitor Y

	Strategies	Y2	Y3
Payoff to competitor X	X1	1	0
	X2	2	3
	X3	1	4

Figure 11-8. Problem of Fig. 11-7 after dominated strategies removed.

The assumption that allows dominance checks for both competitors is that both competitors are intelligent. That is, Y would recognize that X, if rational, would never choose X4, and X would recognize that Y, if rational, would never choose Y1.

Solution method when pure strategy is optimal

In determining the solution of a game such as in Fig. 11-8, it can be shown that if a normal conservative viewpoint is followed, competitor X will tend to choose the strategy or strategies which will maximize his minimum possible gain, while competitor Y will tend to choose the strategy or strategies which will minimize his maximum possible loss. Applied to the above problem, the minimum possible gains of X can be shown as row minimums, while the maximum possible losses of Y can be shown as column maximums. If the maximum of the row minimums (maximin) corresponds to the minimum of the column maximums (minimax), then this defines a unique solution (pure strategy) at a point called the *saddle point*. This is shown in Fig. 11-9 as the point at which strategies X2 and Y2 are followed. This means that the resulting *value of the game* will be 2. That is, each time the game is undertaken, competitor X will gain 2 units and competitor Y will lose 2 units.

LOSS BY COMPETITOR Y

	Strategies	Y2	Y3	Row minimum
Payoff to competitor X	X1	1	0	0
	X2	2	3	2 ◄ (Maximin)
	X3	1	4	1
Column maximum:		2	4	

(Minimax)

(Saddle point)

Figure 11-9. Pure strategy solution to problem of Fig. 11-7.

Solution methods for mixed-strategy zero-sum games

If a game does not have a saddle point and thus no pure strategy, then the optimal strategy of at least one competitor will be mixed (involve random alternation between more than one alternative or strategy according to pre-determined probabilities). There are several different methods for solving zero-sum games. For example, any two-competitor zero-sum game with a finite number of alternatives can be solved as a linear programming problem. In addition, there are special solution approaches appropriate to certain game conditions.

To illustrate a common method of computation of mixed strategies for two-person zero-sum games in which neither competitor has more than two alternatives (pure strategies), consider the two-competitor game problem of Fig. 11-10.

LOSS BY COMPETITOR B

	Strategies	B1	B2
Payoff to competitor A	A1	5	2
	A2	3	4

Figure 11-10. 2×2 game matrix.

The reader can examine the problem to see that there is no dominance among the alternatives and no saddle point. Thus, the problem is to find the proportion of time each player will use each of his alternative strategies. A simple method of calculating this is shown in Fig. 11-11.

The indicated solution from Fig. 11-11 is that competitor A should use alternative A1 $\frac{1}{4}$ of the time and alternative A2 $\frac{3}{4}$ of the time $(\frac{1}{4}, \frac{3}{4})$, and that competitor B should use each of his alternatives $\frac{1}{2}$ of the time $(\frac{1}{2}, \frac{1}{2})$.

Step 1: Obtain the absolute value of the difference in payoff for each row and column; and add the sum of the column differences (which is also equal to the sum of the row differences).

Strategies	B1	B2	Payoff difference
A1	5	2	$3 = \lvert 5 - 2 \rvert$
A2	3	4	$1 = \lvert 3 - 4 \rvert$
Payoff difference:	2	2	$4 = \Sigma$

Step 2: Form a fraction associated with each row and column by using the payoff difference as the numerator and the sum of the column or row differences as the denominator.

	B1	B2	
A1	5	2	$\frac{3}{4}$
A2	3	4	$\frac{1}{4}$
	$\frac{2}{4}$	$\frac{2}{4}$	

Step 3: Interchange the row fractions obtained in step 2. This specifies the proportions of the time that competitor A should randomly use each of the strategies A1 and A2. Similarly, interchange of the column fractions specifies the optimal mixed strategy for competitor B.

	B1	B2	
A1	5	2	$\frac{1}{4}$
A2	3	4	$\frac{3}{4}$
	$\frac{2}{4}$	$\frac{2}{4}$	

Figure 11-11. Solution steps for 2 × 2 games without a pure strategy, with application to problem in Fig. 11-10.

To determine the value of the game—i.e., the expected payoff to A and cost to B for each play of the game—one merely needs to sum the cross-products of probabilities and payoffs for all strategy conditions. Thus, the value of the game is

$$(\tfrac{1}{4})(\tfrac{2}{4})(5) + (\tfrac{1}{4})(\tfrac{2}{4})(2) + (\tfrac{3}{4})(\tfrac{2}{4})(3) + (\tfrac{3}{4})(\tfrac{2}{4})(4) = 3.5$$

In determining the value of the game, it can be shown that if A uses his optimal strategy, the game value will be determined regardless of the strategy B uses; and conversely, if B uses his optimal strategy, the game value will be determined regardless of the strategy A uses. To illustrate this mathematically, if B uses any strategy $(p, 1 - p)$ and A uses his optimal strategy, A will expect to gain:

$$\tfrac{1}{4}[(p)(5) + (1 - p)(2)] + \tfrac{3}{4}[(p)(3) + (1 - p)(4)] = 3.5$$

If A uses any strategy $(q, 1 - q)$ and B uses his optimal strategy, B will expect to lose:

$$\tfrac{1}{2}[(q)(5) + (1 - q)(3)] + \tfrac{1}{2}[(q)(2) + (1 - q)(4)] = 3.5$$

Further, it can be shown that if B, through ignorance or error, fixes upon any strategy other than his optimal, A may take advantage of this to improve his expected payoff. For example, if B plays $(\frac{1}{5}, \frac{4}{5})$, then A may play $(0, 1)$ to result in an expected game value of $3(\frac{1}{5}) + 4(\frac{4}{5}) = 3\frac{4}{5}$, which is higher than the game value of $3\frac{1}{2}$.

For games in which at least one of two competitors has more than two possible alternatives, it is not necessarily true, if one competitor uses his optimal strategy, that the game result will be determined regardless of the strategy followed by the other competitor. There are a variety of methods for solving such larger games. Probably the easiest way to solve games in which one competitor has two alternatives and the other competitor has n alternatives (where $n > 2$) is graphically. To illustrate, consider the game situation of Fig. 11-12 involving competitor S and competitor T.

| | Strategies | LOSS BY COMPETITOR T | |
		T1	T2
Payoff to competitor S	S1	1	4
	S2	2	3
	S3	6	1

Figure 11-12. 3×2 game matrix.

The graphical solution should be set up with an abscissa which represents the probability with which competitor T (the competitor with two alternatives) plays his alternative T1. The ordinate should represent the payoff to competitor S (the competitor with n alternatives). For each of competitor S's alternatives, the payoff is plotted for all values of the abscissa.

Thus, if p denotes the probability of $T1$, the payoff line for alternative S1 is

$$(p)(1) + (1-p)(4) = 4 - 3p$$

For alternative S2, the payoff line is

$$(p)(2) + (1-p)(3) = 3 - p$$

For alternative S3, the payoff line is

$$(p)(6) + (1-p)(1) = 1 + 5p$$

Figure 11-13 reflects the three payoff lines, and shows the solution point which minimizes the maximum loss to T.

Thus, the graph of Fig. 11-13 shows that competitor T can minimize the maximum payoff to S by using a mixture of S1 and S3 which fixes the payoff to S at the intersection of the payoff functions for S1 and S3. The probability of T1 (denoted p) at the intersection of lines S1 and S3 can be calculated by

$$4 - 3p = 1 + 5p$$
$$p = \tfrac{3}{8}$$

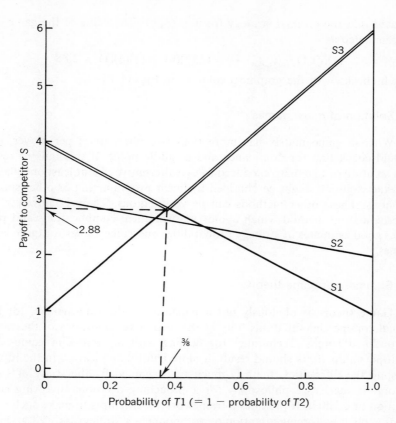

Figure 11-13. Graphical solution to problem of Fig. 11-12.

Once that it is seen that S2 is not part of the solution, the game can be reduced to a 2×2 case and solved by the same procedures previously explained. The results of that calculation are shown in Fig. 11-14 as probabilities with which each competitor should play his strategies.

Thus the optimal strategy for S is $(\frac{5}{8}, 0, \frac{3}{8})$, and we have previously cal-

LOSS BY COMPETITOR T

	Strategies	*T1*	*T2*	*Difference*	*Probability*
Payoff to	S1	1	4	3	$\frac{5}{8}$
Competitor S	S3	6	1	5	$\frac{3}{8}$
Difference:		5	3	8	
Probability:		$\frac{3}{8}$	$\frac{5}{8}$		

Figure 11-14. Solution of reduced problem of Figure 11-12.

culated that the optimal strategy for T is $(\frac{3}{8}, \frac{5}{8})$. The value of the game can be calculated as

$$(\tfrac{5}{8})(\tfrac{3}{8})(1) + (\tfrac{5}{8})(\tfrac{5}{8})(4) + (\tfrac{3}{8})(\tfrac{3}{8})(6) + (\tfrac{3}{8})(\tfrac{5}{8})(1) = 2.88$$

which checks with the graphical solution in Fig. 11-13.

Solution of $n \times n$ games

When a game matrix has more than two alternatives per player, one should check first for dominance and a saddle point. If this fails to result in a solution or in a matrix reduced to two alternatives for at least one player, an exact solution might be obtained by linear programming or other special methods. These other methods can be very tedious. There is, however, an approximation method which avoids mathematical complications and provides good estimates of strategy probabilities and game values for quite large games.*

Summary of game theory

Game theory is obviously not a panacea for decision-makers, for few actual commercial situations fully fit the restrictive conditions of the games as outlined herein. Techniques for dealing with nonzero-sum games and multiple competitors should result in more fruitful application in the future. Despite the difficulties, there is much to be gained by the study of game theory. It suggests a philosophy for approaching decisions involving competition or conflict. It provides a framework for attempts to make such decisions explicit by forcing attention to an opponent's strategy as well as one's own. It also introduces the very important notion of a mixed strategy as a means of countering competitive pressures. Its most important function is to give insights rather than to yield exact computation of optimal strategies.

PROBLEMS

11-1. Make an economic comparison of ownership of a particular relatively small car of your choice requiring an investment of no more than, say, $2,200 to ownership of a particular relatively large car of your choice requiring an investment of at least, say, $4,000. Assume that you would purchase either new and keep it for an economical period of time. Use your best data-synthesizing and intuitive resources for estimates. Consider all monetary factors as best as you can, recognizing that such nonmonetary factors as safety and prestige should also be considered before any final decision is

*For an explanation of the approximation method, see William T. Morris, *The Analysis of Management Decisions* (Homewood Ill.: R. D. Irwin, 1964), pp. 430–433.

made. Consider that a personal car has no effect on income taxes. Make your study using the methods listed below with an annual worth format; show all your assumptions in clear form; use your opportunity cost for any equity capital:
   a. Intuitive judgment
   b. Conservative adjustment
   c. Optimistic—pessimistic
   d. Sensitivity (showing the variation of elements which are of most critical importance)

11-2. Work Prob. 11-1 except consider that the alternatives are to keep an existing old car (one that you or an acquaintance presently owns) or to purchase a new car of your choice. Again, make your study using the following methods:
   a. Intuitive judgment
   b. Conservative adjustment
   c. Optimistic–pessimistic
   d. Sensitivity (showing the variation of elements which are of most critical importance)

11-3. For the most critical element of Prob. 11-1, make an analysis to determine the break-even value of that element. What does this indicate?

11-4. For the element in Prob. 11-2 which shows the greatest percentage variability per the optimistic–pessimistic method, calculate the break-even value of that element. What does this indicate?

11-5. Make an after-tax economic comparison of the desirability of renting an apartment or duplex of your choice vs. purchasing a house of your choice which has approximately the same facilities. Assume that your effective income tax rate is 20% and that capital gains or capital losses affect taxes at one-half that rate. Show all your assumptions in clear form and use an annual worth format with the following methods (use your opportunity cost for any equity capital):
   a. Intuitive judgment
   b. Conservative adjustment
   c. Optimistic–pessimistic
   d. Sensitivity (showing the variation of elements which are of most critical importance)

11-6. Assuming that the resale value of the house in Prob. 11-5 will remain constant over time and that you will pay a 6% broker's fee when you sell the house, what is the minimum length of time you should keep the house in order for it to be as economical as the apartment?

11-7. Using the expected or most likely estimates in Prob. 11-5, what is the highest opportunity cost of capital at which it is economical to purchase the house?

11-8. A certain potential investment project is critical to a firm. The following are "best" or "expected" estimates:

Investment:	$100,000
Life:	10 yr
Salvage value:	$20,000
Net annual cash flow:	$30,000
Minimum required rate of return:	10%

It is desired to show the sensitivity of a measure of merit (net annual worth) to variation, over a range of $\pm 50\%$ of the expected values, in the following elements: (a) life, (b) net annual cash flow, and (c) interest rate. Graph the results. To which element is the decision most sensitive?

11-9. Suppose that for a certain potential investment project the optimistic–pessimistic estimates are as follows:

	Optimistic	*Expected*	*Pessimistic*
Investment:	$90,000	$100,000	$120,000
Life:	12 yr	10 yr	6 yr
Salvage value:	$30,000	$20,000	0
Net annual cash flow:	$35,000	$30,000	$20,000
Minimum required rate of return:	10%	10%	10%

a. What is the net annual worth for each of the three estimation conditions?

b. It is thought that the most critical elements are life and net annual cash inflow. Develop a table showing the net annual worth for all combinations of estimates for those two elements assuming all other elements to be as expected.

11-10. Two pumps, A and B, are being considered for a given drainage need. Both pumps operate at a rated output of 6 hp (8 kw), but differ in initial cost and electrical efficiency. Electricity costs 2¢ per kwhr and the minimum before-tax rate of return is 15%.

a. The critical variable hardest to estimate is the number of hours of operation per yr. Determine the break-even point for this variable.

b. If the operating time is greater than the break-even point in part a, which pump is better?

c. Plot the total annual costs of each pump as a function of hours of operation.

	Pump A	*Pump B*
Cost installed:	$3,500	$4,500
Expected life to termination at zero salvage value:	10 yr	15 yr
Maintenance cost per 1,000 hr of operation:	$50	$30
Efficiency:	60%	80%

11-11. A new all-season hotel will require land costing $300,000 and a structure costing $500,000. In addition, fixtures will cost $150,000, and a working capital of 30 days' gross income at 100% capacity will be required. While the land is nondepreciable, the investment in fixtures should be recovered in 8 years, and the investment in the structure should be recovered in 25 years.

When the hotel is operating at 100% capacity, the gross income will be $1,400 per day. Fixed operating expenses, exclusive of depreciation and interest, will amount to $120,000 per yr. Operating expenses, which vary linearly in proportion to the level of operation, are $80,000 per yr at 100% capacity.

    a. At what percentage of capacity must the hotel operate to earn a before-tax minimum attractive rate of return of 20%?

    b. Plot the revenue and total cost (including cost of capital) as a function of percentage of capacity. (*Note:* The point at which revenue and the total of all costs, including capital, are equal is commonly called the *unhealthy point*.)

11-12. Given the matrix of costs below, for various mutually exclusive alternatives, show which is best using the following decision rules or principles:

    a. Minimax rule
    b. Minimin rule
    c. Laplace principle
    d. Hurwicz principle with $\frac{2}{3}$ optimism
    e. Minimax regret rule

	State of nature			
Alternative	*A*	*B*	*C*	*D*
I	18	18	10	14
II	14	14	14	14
III	5	26	10	14
IV	14	22	10	10
V	10	12	12	10

11-13. Given the following competitive game matrix, show the optimal strategy for each competitor:

		Loss by competitor Y	
	Strategies	*Y1*	*Y2*
Gain to	X1	4	7
competitor X	X2	3	9

11-14. Given the following competitive game matrix, show the optimal strategy for each competitor:

	Strategies	*Loss by competitor Y*	
		Y1	*Y2*
Gain to	X1	4	7
competitor X	X2	3	5

11-15. Given the following competitive game matrix, show the optimal strategy for each competitor:

	Strategies	*Loss by competitor Y*			
		Y1	*Y2*	*Y3*	*Y4*
Gain to	X1	−10	6	2	40
competitor X	X2	10	10	8	12
	X3	−8	−4	0	−10

11-16. Given the following competitive game matrix, show the optimal strategy for each competitor:

	Strategies	*Loss by competitor Y*		
		Y1	*Y2*	*Y3*
Gain to	X1	1	8	2
competitor X	X3	6	2	8
	X3	5	1	6

twelve

Risk and Uncertainty—
Advanced Analysis
Procedures

This chapter will introduce a number of advanced (nontraditional) procedures or methods of economic analysis with examples of application. These are as follows:

1. Probabilistic monetary
2. Expected utility
3. Expectation-Variance
4. Variable discounting

Probabilistic Monetary Method

The *probabilistic monetary procedure* involves estimating certain elements, the prospective variation of which is thought to be important to the analysis outcome, in terms of probabilities. These probabilistic estimates can then, in turn, be manipulated to obtain desired characteristics of the measure of merit (such as net annual worth). The results of a study using this method could be in the form of any of the following:

a. expected project outcomes;
b. expected project outcomes together with some measure of the variabilities of those outcomes; or

c. complete descriptions of probability distributions of the project outcomes.

Project comparison results based on a probabilistic monetary analysis
can be much more useful than similar results for assumed certainty. For
example, suppose it is calculated that project A has an expected net annual
worth of $10,000 with a standard deviation of $25,000, while project B has
an expected net A.W. of $8,000 with a standard deviation of $4,000. If the
decision-maker were particularly adverse to the possibility of a loss, he might
well choose project B even though he knows project A has the higher expected
net A.W.

If it is possible to determine or approximate the shape of the distribution
in addition to parameters such as expected value and standard deviation of
the measure of merit, the decision-maker is in an even better position to
judge the relative desirability of alternatives. For example, if the net A.W.
for projects A and B (parameters given above) are each distributed normally,
the situation could be depicted as in Fig. 12-1. It can be seen in Fig. 12-1

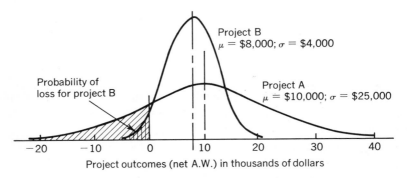

Figure 12-1. Two normally distributed projects.

that the probability of a loss (negative net A.W.) for project A is much
higher than for project B; hence, project B might be chosen. If the respective
distributions are extremely skewed rather than normally distributed, the
indicated decision may differ. For example, suppose that project A is skewed
to the right and project B is skewed to the left as shown in Fig. 12-2. On the
basis of these conditions, project B might no longer be considered the more
desirable.

If a probabilistic monetary model involves simple variation functions for
the individual elements considered, then it sometimes can be mathematically
manipulated so as to obtain directly the desired parameters or characteristics
of the measure of merit. Use of the Taylor series expansion is often convenient for obtaining analytical approximations (see Chapter 16).

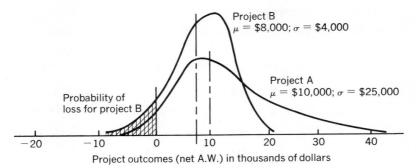

Figure 12-2. Two skewed projects with same means and standard deviations as for Fig. 12-1.

On the other hand, if the model involves variation functions such that the model cannot be handled feasibly by analytical mathematics, then a practical way to obtain approximations of the desired parameters or characteristics of the measure of merit is to use the Monte Carlo technique of simulation (see Chapter 13). The remainder of this section will be devoted to simple examples of applications of the probabilistic monetary method.

Example:
A single project is estimated to have a variable life and other element outcomes as follows:

Investment:	$10,000
Life:	3 yr, with probability = 0.3
	5 yr, with probability = 0.4
	7 yr, with probability = 0.3
Salvage value:	$2,000
Annual receipts:	$5,000
Annual disbursements:	$2,200

Find the expected annual worth and the standard deviation of the annual worth if interest on invested capital is 8%.

Solution:
For life = 3 yr, net A.W.:

$5,000 − $2,200 − [($10,000 − $2,000)(A/P, 8%, 3) + $2,000(8%)]

= − $460

For life = 5 yr, net A.W.:

$5,000 − $2,200 − [($10,000 − $2,000)(A/P, 8%, 5) + $2,000(8%)]

= $630

For life = 7 yr, net A.W.:

$5,000 − $2,200 − [($10,000 − $2,000)(A/P, 8\%, 7) + $2,000(8\%)]$

$$= \$1,110$$

Expected net A.W. $= E(\text{A.W.}) = \sum_{\text{yr}} \text{A.W.} \times P(\text{A.W.})$

$$= -\$460(0.3) + \$630(0.4) + \$1,110(0.3) = \$446$$

Variance of A.W. $= \sigma^2_{\text{A.W.}} = \sum_{\text{yr}} (\text{A.W.})^2 \times P(\text{A.W.}) - [E(\text{A.W.})]^2$

$$= (-\$460)^2 \times 0.3 + (\$630)^2 \times 0.4$$
$$+ (\$1,110)^2 \times 0.3 - (\$446)^2$$
$$= 401,000$$

Standard deviation of net A.W. $= \sqrt{\sigma^2_{\text{A.W.}}} = \sqrt{401,000} = \$631$

Note that the expected net A.W. at an expected life of 5 years, which is $446, is less than the net A.W. at the assumed certain life of 5 years, which is $630. Variation of project life can have a very marked effect on the results of an economic evaluation. In general, the greater the life variation the higher the expected capital recovery cost based on that variation compared to the capital recovery cost at the assumed certain life equal to the expected life.

Example:

Assume the same conditions as the example above except that annual receipts is also a random variable and is $7,000 with a probability of 0.33 or $4,000 with a probability of 0.67. Further, assume that the variation of project life occurs independently of variation of annual receipts. Show the net A.W. for all possible occurrences and compute the expected net A.W.

Solution:

	Net Annual Worth Project life		
Annual receipts	*3 yr (P = 0.3)*	*5 yr (P = 0.4)*	*7 yr (P = 0.3)*
$7,000 (P = 0.33)	$1,540	$2,630	$3,110
$4,000 (P = 0.67)	− 1,460	− 370	110

Expected net A.W. $= E(\text{A.W.}) = \sum_{\text{yr}} \sum_{\text{receipts}} \text{A.W.} \times P(\text{A.W.})$

$$= \$1,540(0.3)(0.33) + \$2,630(0.4)(0.33)$$
$$+ \$3,110(0.3)(0.33) - \$1,460(0.3)(0.67)$$
$$- \$370(0.4)(0.67) + \$110(0.3)(0.33)$$
$$= \$446$$

Note that the expected value for this example is the same as for the above example. This is because the expected value of the variable receipts is $7,000(0.33) + $4,000(0.67) = $5,000, which is the same as the assumed certain receipts previously used. However, the standard deviation of the net A.W. for this example is higher than that calculated in the previous example.

Chapter 13 will describe the use of the Monte Carlo technique for determining probabilistic monetary outcomes in situations not amenable to use of analytical mathematics. Chapter 16 will explain some special and simplified techniques for computing means and variances and selecting among projects using the probabilistic monetary method of comparison.

Expected Utility Method

The *expected utility procedure* has particular usefulness for analyzing projects in which the potential gain or loss is of significant size compared to the total funds available to the firm. More specifically, if the marginal utility or desirability of each dollar potentially to be gained or lost is not a constant, then the utility of dollars rather than just amount of dollars is relevant, and then it may be worthwhile to use the expected utility method rather than the probabilistic monetary method.

The expected utility method consists of determining the *cardinal utility*—e.g., relative degree of usefulness or desirability to the decision-maker—of each of the possible outcomes of a project or group of projects on some numerical scale and then calculating the expected value of the utility to use as the measure of merit.

The application of this method is based on the premise that it is possible to measure the attitudes of an individual or decision-maker toward risk. If the decision-maker is consistent with himself, then a relation between monetary gain or loss and the utility or relative desirability of that gain or loss can be obtained through the decision-maker's answers to a series of questions and resultant computations as explained below.

Steps in deriving utility-of-money function

1. Select two possible monetary outcomes within the range of interest. For example, say you pick $0 and $10,000.
2. Assign arbitrary utility indices to these monetary outcomes, the only restriction being that the index for the higher monetary outcome be higher than the index for the lower monetary outcome. For example, say you assign an index of 1 to a $0 outcome and 20 to a $10,000 outcome.
3. The utility value of other monetary outcomes can be found by having

the decision-maker answer questions and then making subsequent calculations as follows:

a. To obtain utility values for monetary outcomes within any two outcomes for which utility values have been assigned or calculated, ask questions such as, "What monetary outcome for certain would you desire just as highly as a $q\%$ chance of the first monetary outcome and an $r\%$ chance of the second monetary outcome?" For example, say you let $q = r = 50\%$ and suppose the decision-maker decides he would desire \$3,000 for certain just as much as a 50% chance of \$0 outcome and a 50% chance of \$10,000 outcome. The utility of \$3,000 can then be calculated as

$$U[\$3,000] = 0.5 \times U[\$0] + 0.5U \times [\$10,000]$$
$$= 0.5 \times 1 + 0.5 \times 20$$
$$= 10.5$$

b. To obtain utility values for monetary outcomes greater than or less than those for which utility values have been assigned or calculated, ask questions such as, "What relative chances of monetary outcomes of \$X vs. \$Z would be just as desirable as a certain monetary outcome of \$Y?" (*Note:* $\$X < \$Y < \$Z$, and \$Z is the amount for which the utility value is to be determined.)

   For example, suppose it is desired to find the utility of \$20,000 given the utility values which have been obtained above for \$0, \$3,000, and \$10,000. Suppose the question posed is, "What relative chances of monetary outcomes of \$3,000 vs. \$20,000 would be just as desirable as a certain outcome of \$10,000?" Suppose further that the considered answer by the decision-maker is 40% chance of \$3,000 and 60% chance of \$20,000. The utility value of \$20,000 can then be calculated as

$$0.4 \times U[\$3,000] + 0.6 \times U[\$20,000] = U[\$10,000]$$
$$0.4 \times 10.5 + 0.6 \times U[\$20,000] = 20$$
$$U[\$20,000] = 26.3$$

4. Questions and computations in step 3 above can be continued as long as utility values are needed. These can, in turn, be graphed to show utility values for the entire range of monetary outcomes of interest. A graph based on the above values is shown in Fig. 12-3.

In carrying out the utility derivation procedure, inconsistencies in the decision-maker's replies may be discovered (e.g., two or more utility values calculated for the same monetary outcome, or an extremely jagged utility-of-money function). If this happens, it becomes necessary to requestion to obtain judgments which are internally consistent.

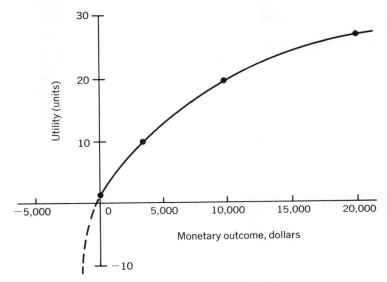

Figure 12-3. Utility of money function.

The use of expected utility value as a decision criterion has a real advantage over the expected monetary value such as annual worth or present worth. Procedures based on expected monetary values virtually overlook the severe consequences of widely varying possible outcomes and merely take a weighted average of all outcomes. The expected utility procedure overcomes this objection by incorporating these variance influences directly into the computations. A large loss may be assigned a large negative utility by the individual, or he may assign a very great positive utility to a large increment in wealth, thus automatically bringing variance influences into the calculated results. This is demonstrated in the example below.

Example:
As an example of calculation of expected utility, suppose the decision-maker having the utility-of-money function in Fig. 12-3 is faced with a project which is expected to have monetary outcomes according to the following probabilities.

Monetary outcome	Probability
$20M	0.05
10M	0.15
0M	0.30
— 2M	0.50

It is desired to compare the calculated results using the expected utility method with the expected outcome using the probabilistic monetary method.

Solution:

The necessary calculations are shown in Table 12-1. Thus the expected utility method indicates an unfavorable project (expected utility is negative, when the utility of a monetary outcome of $0 is one). In contrast, the expected monetary outcome using the probabilistic monetary method indicates a favorable project (expected outcome is greater than $0).

Table 12-1

CALCULATION OF EXPECTED MONETARY OUTCOME AND EXPECTED UTILITY

Monetary outcome	Probability of monetary outcome	Monetary outcome × Probability	Utility of outcome	Utility × Probability
$20M	0.05	$1.0M	26.3	1.31
10M	0.15	1.5M	20.0	3.00
0M	0.30	0M	1.0	0.30
— 2M	0.50	— 1.0M	—10.0	—5.00
	Expected monetary outcome: $\sum$ = $1.5M		Expected utility: $\sum$ = —0.39	

Again, it should be emphasized that the expected utility method is useful for analyzing projects in which the potential gain or loss is of significant size compared to the monetary resources of the individual or firm for which the analysis is made. If a graph of the utility-of-money function can be closely approximated by a straight line over the range between the maximum and minimum monetary returns under consideration, then the expected monetary outcome can be used in place of the expected utility without significant error.

The use of utility measurements

The method of assigning utilities to outcomes can be quite useful for gaining understanding of the rationale behind decisions made in situations involving risk. Indeed, if a decision-maker specifies a utility-of-money function and if the economic analyst can predict monetary outcomes of individual projects which are accepted or believed by the decision-maker, then the analyst can specify the project acceptance or rejection choices which would presumably turn out to be the same as those of the decision-maker (neglecting nonmonetary factors). Thus, the problem of the analyst in dealing with decisions under risk would be "solved." That is, he could provide the manager with recommendations which are consistent with the manager's own thinking, thus relieving the manager for other problems.

Several limitations to use of the expected utility method should be recognized. First, it is often time-consuming and it is difficult to obtain a consistent utility-of-money function for an individual or organization. Secondly, responses for determining utility-of-money functions may well change over time; indeed, they may change even from day to day because of changes in the mood or temporary outlook of the person being questioned. Finally, a utility function for a particular set of alternative projects is not necessarily valid for another set of alternatives. Many intangible considerations fringe the choice of any specific weighting. A decision-maker might indicate a utility function which clearly shows a conservative approach in his attitudes toward industrial actions, but he might have an entirely different set of attitudes for gambling with his own personal finances, such as on the stock market.

Under some conditions, it is expedient to employ methods that retain the concepts of utility functions without having to enumerate the full range of utilities and continuing through formal expected utility calculations. These informal uses can serve well to solidify subjective evaluations of risk situations.

Expectation-Variance Method

The *expectation-variance method* or procedure, sometimes called the *certainty equivalence method*, involves reducing the economic desirability of a project into a single measure which includes consideration of the expected outcome as well as variation of that outcome. One simple example is

$$V = \mu - A\sigma \tag{12-1}$$

where V = Expectation-variance
μ = Mean or expected monetary outcome
σ = Standard deviation of monetary outcome
A = Coefficient of risk aversion*

---

*Donald Farrar (*The Investment Decision Under Uncertainty*, Englewood Cliffs, N.J.: Prentice-Hall, Inc., 1962) and others have shown that as long as there is a diminishing marginal utility of money, the correspondence between a firm's coefficient of risk aversion and its utility function of monetary outcome is

$$A = -\frac{U''(\mu)}{2}$$

That is, the coefficient of risk aversion is equal to the negative of one-half of the second derivative of the utility function evaluated at the expected monetary outcome.

Example:

Suppose it is desired to evaluate projects A and B as given in Fig. 12-1 by the expectation-variance measure shown above. Suppose further that $A = 0.40$ at $E(A.W.) = \$10,000$ for project A, and 0.75 at $E(A.W.) = \$8,000$ for project B. Recall that for project A, $\sigma = \$25,000$, and for project B, $\sigma = \$4,000$.

Solution:

Project A:

$$V = \$10,000 - 0.4(\$25,000) = 0$$

Project B:

$$V = \$8,000 - 0.75(\$4,000) = \$5,000$$

On the basis of these figures, project B is indicated to be the more desirable. Indeed, project A is just marginal.

Cramer and Smith, in the article reprinted in Appendix 12-A, recognize that the desirability of an investment project is a function of not only the mean and variance but also of the investment amount in the indivdual project. Hence, they developed an evaluation model of the form

$$V = \mu - A\sigma^a I^b \tag{12-2}$$

where V = Certainty equivalence
μ = Expected monetary outcome
A = Coefficient of risk aversion
σ = Standard deviation of monetary outcome
I = Project investment amount
a and b = Constants

Cramer and Smith further show how one can empirically obtain all the constants for the use of the model. The following example is a simple application.

Example:

Suppose that for the same two projects A and B illustrated in Fig. 12-1 it is decided to use Cramer and Smith's model to determine the best project, and the constants a and b are each found to be approximately 0.5. The investment for project A is \$22,500, and for project B is \$40,000. The coefficients of risk aversion are again 0.75 for project A and 0.50 for project B.

Solution:

$$V = \mu - A\sigma^a I^b$$

Project A:

$$\$10,000 - 0.4(\$25,000)^{0.5}(\$22,500)^{0.5} = \$500$$

Project B:

$$\$8,000 - 0.75(\$4,000)^{0.5}(\$40,000)^{0.5} = \$1,600$$

Thus, on the basis of the above calculated results, project B is shown to be the more desirable of the two.

A variation of the model in Eq. (12-2) which has intuitive appeal is

$$V = \mu - (A_l\sigma_l^a + A_u\sigma_u^{a'})I^b \tag{12-3}$$

where A_l and σ_l^a apply to variations below μ, and A_u and $\sigma_u^{a'}$ apply to variations above μ.

Variable Discounting Method

One means for taking into account increasing risk with more distant future is by use of a varying rate of discounting such that the further one estimates in the future, the progressively higher will be the rate of discounting (and, thus, the lower will be the weighting of future outcomes relative to present outcomes). As an example of such a function, the interest at any time in the future, $r(n)$, could be said to vary according to the function

$$r(n) = r_0 e^{an} \tag{12-4}$$

where r_0 is the initial (risk-free) rate and a (which is greater than zero) is the coefficient which determines the rate of increase. The advantage of this approach is that it provides a way to reconcile the short-run and long-run viewpoints.

The function in Eq. (12-4) and other variable rate-of-discounting functions are subject to the criticism of not being readily useable. J. Morley English[*] acknowledges the deficiency and rather elaborately develops what he terms an "operationally useful discount function." That function expresses the interest rate as a function of time:

$$r(n) = \frac{1}{n} \ln \frac{1}{1 - r_0 n} \tag{12-5}$$

where all of the symbols are as defined for Eq. (12-4).

A great disadvantage of English's "operationally useful interest function" is that its use fixes a planning horizon T, which is the reciprocal of the initial, risk-free rate r_0. That is, $T = 1/r_0$, and $r_0 = 1/T$. This does not seem reasonable in many cases, for the existence of a low interest rate does not necessarily mean that there is a long planning horizon or vice versa.

Appendix 12-A is the reprinted article "Decision Models for the Selection of Research Projects" by Robert H. Cramer and Bernard E. Smith which reports excellent empirical work in deriving utility-of-money functions and relating these to expectation-variance models. The article also shows application to sequential-type projects in the manner of the decision tree analysis of Chapter 15.

---

[*]J. Morley English, "A Discount Function for Comparing Economic Alternatives," *Journal of Industrial Engineering*, Vol. 16, No. 2 (March–April, 1965).

PROBLEMS

12-1. A certain project requires an investment of $10,000, and is expected to have net annual receipts minus disbursements of $2,800. The salvage value as a function of life, together with associated probabilities, is

Life	Salvage value	Probability
3	$4,000	0.25
5	2,000	0.50
7	0	0.25

Find the expected net A.W. and the standard deviation of net A.W. if interest on invested capital is 8%.

12-2. Work Prob. 12-1 with the change that the net annual receipts minus disbursements is a random variable which is independent of the life, and is estimated to be $1,800 with probability 0.2, $2,800 with probability 0.6, and $3,800 with probability 0.2.

12-3. Project Stochastic is estimated to require an investment of $25,000, have a life of 5 years and 0 salvage value, and have an annual net cash flow of $5,000 with 30% probability, $10,000 with 50% probability, and $12,000 with 20% probability. If the minimum required rate of return is 15%, calculate the expected value and variance of the net A.W. for Project Stochastic.

12-4. Project Variate is estimated to require an investment of $25,000 and have an annual net cash flow of $16,000 and a 0 salvage value. The life for Project Variate is estimated to be 1 year with 10% probability, 5 years with 50% probability, and 10 years with 40% probability. If the minimum required rate of return is 15%, calculate the expected value and variance of the net A.W.

12-5. Plot a single-frequency histogram for the projects in Prob. 12-3 and 12-4, distinguishing between the two by shaded coding. Which project would probably be thought more desirable if the decision-maker were (a) conservative, thus not prone to take risks, and (b) a maximizer of expectations, regardless of risk.

12-6. Suppose that the expectation-variance decision function for a given project is equal to the net A.W. minus a constant times the standard deviation of the net A.W.
   a. For the projects in Prob. 12-3 and 12-4, determine which appears to be the more desirable if the constant coefficient is 0.6.
   b. At what value of the constant coefficient are the two projects equally desirable?

12-7. The mean and standard deviation of the rate of return for project X are estimated to be 15% and 5% respectively. Similarly, the mean and standard deviation of the rate of return for a competing project Y are estimated to be 25% and 18% respectively.

   a. If the expectation-variance function for the decision-maker is the expected rate of return minus 0.1 times the variance of the rate of return (in integer amounts), show which project would be more desirable.

   b. For the function in part a, at what value of the coefficient applied to the variance would the projects be considered equally desirable?

12-8. If the expectation-variance function of a firm is given by the relation $V = \mu - \frac{1}{2}A\sigma$, where μ and σ are in terms of net A.W., what is the value of A at which the project in Prob. 12-1 is exactly marginal?

12-9. Suppose that in Prob. 12-1 the interest on capital is 4% with probability 0.5 and 12% with probability 0.5, and that interest varies independently of the life of the project.

   a. Calculate the expected net A.W.

   b. Plot histograms of outcomes for Prob. 12-1 and for this problem to compare variability.

12-10. Entrepreneur Y has a utility index of 108 for $11,000, and 75 for $0. He is indifferent between a 0.5 chance at $11,000 plus a 0.5 chance at a $20,000 loss and a certainty of $0. What is his utility index for a loss of $20,000?

12-11. Entrepreneur Z has a utility index of 10 for $18,750, 6 for $11,200, and zero for $0. What probability combination of $0 and $18,750 would make him indifferent to $11,200 for certain?

12-12. Two economists, Alfred M. Dismal and J. Maynard Science, are arguing about the relative merits of their respective decision rules. Dismal says he always takes the act with the greatest expected monetary value; Science says he always takes the act with the greatest expected utility, and his utility function for money is $U = 10 + 0.2M$, where M is the monetary payoff. For decisions involving monetary payoffs, who will make the better choices?

12-13. You have a date for the economic analysis ball; the admission is $20, which you do not have. On the day of the dance your psychology instructor offers you either $16 for certain or a 50–50 chance at nothing or $24. Which choice would you make, assuming you had no other source of funds or credit. Why? If the utility of $16 is 20, and the utility of $0 is zero, what does this imply about the utility of $20?

12-14. Develop a utility function for yourself for the monetary outcomes of $-\$100,000$, $-\$10,000$, $+\$10,000$, $+\$40,000$, and $+\$200,000$. Start with the following monetary outcomes and arbitrarily assigned units:

Monetary outcome	Utility units
$ 1,000	10
15,000	30

Write out the questions which you ask yourself and show your calculations. Finally, plot the results with monetary outcome on the x-axis.

12-15. Suppose that the utility-of-money function of a decision-maker is described as Utility = ln (Monetary outcome in thousands of dollars) between the monetary outcome limits of $100 and $1,000,000. The monetary outcomes and associated probabilities for two competing projects are as follows:

Project	Monetary outcome (*gain*)	Probability
A	$ 1,000	0.33
	10,000	0.33
	19,000	0.33
B	$ 9,000	0.3
	10,000	0.4
	12,000	0.1
	13,000	0.2

Show which project is preferable by the expected monetary method and by the expected utility method.

APPENDIX 12-A

Decision Models
for the Selection of Research Projects*

Introduction

Research management is by nature a process of risk-taking. Each project offers an unknown and highly variable payoff for an often uncertain expenditure. This is in contrast to plant investment where expenditures may be

*By Robert H. Cramer, Socony Mobil Oil Company, and Barnard E. Smith, Massachusetts Institute of Technology. Reprinted from *The Engineering Economist*, Vol. 9, No. 2 (Winter 1964) by permission of the publisher.

Note: A more detailed account of the research on which this paper is based is given in Reference 3 at the end of this appendix.

accurately estimated and payoffs, while not certain, are at least determined within a reasonably narrow range.

Due to this difference, the techniques for decision-making which have been developed for plant expenditures offer little attraction to the research manager. Such techniques usually assume that revenues and expenses are precisely determined. If an estimate must be viewed as having a distribution, it is assumed adequate to use the expected value of this distribution as the cost certain. While this assumption seems harmless enough, it ignores a significant aspect of the decision process. Implicit in this assumption is that the decision-maker values every dollar as being equally important.

A research manager cannot accept this assumption. Today's research is characterized by massive expenditures with the hope of massive payoffs. Only at the lowest level of research activity are the expenses and rewards so modest that the loss of the entire investment would be viewed as no more important than an equivalent gain. While $100 might well be spent for a 20% chance at $1,000, a $100,000 research proposal might be rejected even if it were viewed as leading to a $1,000,000 payoff with a 20% chance of success. This is strictly not in accord with the decision procedures based on expected monetary value.

The problem is that all risky dollars are not viewed as having a constant value. A big loss is clearly worse than an equivalent big gain. The increment of pleasure to be gained through success is of less value than the increment of pain suffered if we lose. Research deals in big projects. To compare these it is necessary that the utility of money be taken into account.

Selection Among Risky Alternatives

Several methods have been proposed for dealing with risk. Some of the more popular methods are:

1. Act as if the most likely future would occur. Accept any project which has an acceptable present value provided the most likely outcome is obtained.
2. Compare projects according to the present worth of their expected outcome but require a higher rate of return for more risky alternatives.
3. Weigh each possible outcome of each project with the probability of its occurrence and by the utility of the outcome if it does occur. Select those projects which maximize the expected utility.
4. Reduce each project to its certainty equivalent by considering both the expected value and the variance of the outcomes. Compare projects through their certainty equivalents.

Method 1 is adequate when one outcome is extremely likely relative to any other outcome and when the outcomes do not differ substantially from one another. In research the odds might favor project failure yet the project might be attractive if the rewards for success were large. Thus this method could lead to serious errors in selection.

Method 2 is widely used. When project payoffs are far enough distant, a realistic discounting of risk may be possible. However, if the payoffs are immediately available, the method fails. No interest rate can discount for risk unless some time will elapse before the payoff is obtained.

Expected utility

Method 3 is the basis of statistical decision theory. It is generally attributed to von Neumann and Morgenstern (Ref. 8). The presentation of this method by Grayson (Ref. 5) puts it in context quite similar to that of research. Essentially, this method views the decision process as being the choice of an action from among a set of actions where the utility of outcome is determined partially by the action, and partly by some unknown choice of nature. Nature is viewed to make her choice according to a probability distribution over the available states.*

Moment method

Method 4 retains much of the reality of method 3 while offering several operational advantages. Farrar (Ref. 4) has demonstrated the application of this method to the selection of investment portfolios. This application allows any level of investment in the stock of any company. Research portfolios do not permit funds to be assigned in this way. Investment in a project is fairly much an all-or-nothing proposition. Method 4 will be extended to project selection in this paper.

Determination of Utility Functions

To make either the method of expected utility or the method of risk discounting operational, it is necessary to construct a utility function for the decision-maker or decision-making group. Such a utility function can be determined by examining actual decisions which have been made in the firm under consideration. They can also be developed by examining decisions concerning standard gambles. The presentation of standard gambles has the advantage of providing controlled conditions as well as eliminating bias toward individuals or projects as would be found under real conditions.

---

*Important facets of this method are explored by Green (Ref. 6) and Hicks and Steffens (Ref. 7).

Functional parameters can be developed, based on the behavior observed by either of these methods. These parameters can then be used to prescribe a rule for determining the utilities of subsequent decisions. Following the rule thus described assures a measure of consistency in decision-making. This consistency, as Bowman (Ref. 2) observes, is *the* advantage of management science.

It was decided to employ the standard gamble to determine the utility for money for a limited number of research and manufacturing executives. The executives were chosen from a leading U.S. corporation. Each had had extensive experience in decision-making involving risk. Both research and manufacturing executives were chosen since it was hypothesized that the two groups would tend to see utility in a different fashion. Intuition suggests that the manufacturing executive would be more interested in small but sure propositions while research executives would have less fear of loss and would be more willing to take the long shot. If this is true, joint action by the two groups would be difficult. If a single utility function can be agreed upon, then some of the difficulties can be resolved. To accomplish this a series of gambles were presented to eight executives of the subject company. The questions were styled after the procedure of Grayson (Ref. 5, Chapter 10). Each decision-maker was asked to give a probability of success which would make him indifferent to the investment required for each of a series of projects under a stated payoff. For instance, the first question asked the probability of winning $200,000 which would make him indifferent to investing $100,000 in the project. Thus he stands to win or lose $100,000. Presumably the response would be close but not equal to 0.5, indicating a nonlinear utility for money.

The results of these queries are displayed on Table 12-A-1. From these responses points on the utility curve were calculated.

As an example of the method of calculation, consider the probabilities taken from research supervisor A's response shown in Table 12-A-1. Two points are set arbitrarily: $0 at 0 utiles and the loss of 0.1 million at −1 utile, *utiles* being an arbitrary unit of utility. Balancing the net gain from the gamble against the possible loss, the equation for the first point is written as follows:

$$0.6 \times \text{utility}(\$0.1 \text{ million}) + 0.4 \times \text{utility}(-0.1 \text{ million}) = 0$$

Calculating from the above equation, the utility of a $0.1 million net gain is then two-thirds or 0.67 utile. The three utile points were plotted at the respective net payoffs. Similar points were calculated with other net payoffs at $0.1 million investment level. These were then connected to give a utility function over the range from −$0.1 million ot $0.9 million. This range is not wide enough to cover all situations executives may face. Consequently, several series of gambles in ascending, overlapping ranges were presented.

Table 12-A-1

INDIFFERENCE PROBABILITY OF SUCCESS RESPONSES TO UTILITY-OF-MONEY QUESTIONNAIRE

← Indifference probabilities of success →

Gamble			Research					Manufacturing				
Investment ($ million)	Total payoff ($ million)	Net payoff ($ million)	Policy-making	Adminis-tration	Super-vision A	Super-vision B	Average	HQ staff adminis-tration	HQ staff engineering	Line adminis-tration	Line supervision	Average
0.1	0.2	0.1	0.95	0.95	0.60	0.95	0.86	0.60	0.70	0.70	0.70	0.68
	0.3	0.2	0.85	0.90	0.50	0.90	0.79	0.40	0.65	0.40	0.60	0.51
	0.4	0.3	0.85	0.80	0.45	—	0.70	0.35	0.60	0.30	0.50	0.44
	0.6	0.5	0.70	0.60	0.35	—	0.55	0.25	0.60	0.30	0.40	0.39
	1.0	0.9	0.40	0.40	0.25	0.80	0.46	0.20	0.60	0.20	0.35	0.34
	10.0	9.9	—	0.05	0.10	0.15	0.10	—	—	—	—	—
0.2	0.4	0.2	0.95	0.95	0.65	—	0.85	0.60	0.75	0.60	0.70	0.66
	0.5	0.3	0.95	0.90	0.60	—	0.82	0.50	0.70	0.50	0.60	0.58
	1.2	1.0	0.75	0.60	0.35	0.80	0.62	0.25	0.65	0.25	0.40	0.39
	1.7	1.5	0.55	0.50	0.25	—	0.43	0.20	0.60	0.20	0.40	0.35
	10.0	9.8	—	—	—	0.20	—	—	—	—	—	—
0.5	1.0	0.5	0.95	0.95	0.70	0.80	0.87	0.65	0.75	0.60	0.70	0.68
	1.5	1.0	0.95	0.95	0.55	—	0.81	0.45	0.75	0.40	0.60	0.55
	4.0	3.5	0.60	0.60	0.35	0.50	0.51	0.20	0.70	0.30	0.50	0.42
	8.0	7.5	0.35	0.25	0.25	0.30	0.29	0.15	0.70	0.20	0.40	0.36
	40.0	39.5	—	0.05	0.05	0.05	0.05	—	—	—	—	—
0.75	1.65	0.9	—	0.95+	0.95	0.95	0.95	0.55	0.80	0.60	0.75	0.68
	4.25	3.5	—	0.90	0.65	0.70	0.75	0.30	0.80	0.30	0.60	0.50
	8.25	7.5	—	0.50	0.40	0.40	0.43	0.20	0.80	0.30	0.50	0.45
	10.0	9.25	—	0.30	0.30	0.30	0.30	0.20	0.75	0.30	0.40	0.41
	100.0	99.25	—	—	—	—	—	—	0.50	—	—	—
1.0	2.0	1.0	0.95	0.95+	0.95	0.95+	0.95	0.60	0.80	0.80	0.80	0.75
	3.5	2.5	0.95	0.95	0.90	—	0.93	0.35	0.80	0.60	0.70	0.61
	4.5	3.5	0.95	0.90	0.75	0.60	0.80	0.30	0.80	0.50	0.60	0.55
	6.0	5.0	0.90	0.70	0.55	0.50	0.66	0.25	0.75	0.40	0.50	0.48
	10.0	9.0	0.45	0.40	0.40	0.30	0.39	0.20	0.75	0.30	0.40	0.41
	100.0	99.0	—	0.05	0.10	0.05	—	—	—	—	—	—
1.5	3.0	1.5	0.95	0.95+	0.95	0.90	0.94	0.60	0.90	0.70	0.80	0.75
	5.0	3.5	0.95	0.95	0.90	0.60	0.85	0.40	0.85	0.50	0.70	0.61
	6.5	5.0	0.90	0.90	0.80	0.50	0.78	0.35	0.85	0.40	0.70	0.58
	10.0	8.5	0.60	0.70	0.70	0.30	0.58	0.25	0.85	0.40	0.50	0.50
	20.0	18.5	0.35	—	—	0.05	0.15	—	—	—	—	—
	100.0	98.5	—	—	—	—	—	—	—	—	—	—
2.5	4.0	1.5	—	0.95++	0.95	0.95	0.95	0.75	0.90	0.95	0.85	0.86
	5.0	2.5	0.95	0.95+	0.95	0.80	0.91	0.65	0.90	0.80	0.80	0.79
	7.5	5.0	0.95	0.90	0.90	0.50	0.81	0.50	0.90	0.80	0.70	0.72
	10.0	7.5	0.90	0.90	0.80	0.40	0.75	0.40	0.90	0.70	0.60	0.65
	12.5	10.0	0.80	0.85	0.70	0.35	0.68	0.35	0.90	0.60	0.50	0.59
	100.0	97.5	—	0.30	0.40	0.05	—	—	—	—	—	—

Table 12-A-1 (Cont.)

INDIFFERENCE PROBABILITY OF SUCCESS RESPONSES TO UTILITY-OF-MONEY QUESTIONNAIRE

Gamble			Research					Manufacturing				
Investment ($ million)	Total payoff ($ million)	Net payoff ($ million)	Policy-making	Administration	Supervision A	Super-vision A	Average	HQ staff administration	HQ staff engineering	Line administration	Line supervision	Average
5.0	10.0	5.0	No	0.95++	0.95	0.95	0.95	0.65	0.95	0.95+	0.95	0.88
	15.0	10.0	0.95	0.95++	0.90	0.70	0.88	0.50	0.95	0.95+	0.85	0.81
	20.0	15.0	0.95	0.95+	0.85	0.50	0.81	0.45	0.95	0.80	0.70	0.72
	100.0	95.0	0.30	0.50	0.50	0.10				0.50		—
10.0	20.0	10.0		0.95++	0.95	No	0.95	0.80	0.99	0.95+	0.95	0.92
	35.0	25.0	0.95	0.95++	0.95	No	0.95	0.70	0.99	0.95	0.90	0.88
	45.0	35.0		0.95++	0.90	No	0.93	0.60	0.99		0.85	0.81
	60.0	50.0	0.95	0.95+	0.85	0.30	0.92	0.50	0.99	0.80	0.75	0.76
	100.0	90.0	0.80		0.75		0.70	0.40	0.99	0.50		0.63
	200.0	190.0	0.70					0.25				
	400.0	390.0	0.50					0.20				
	500.0	490.0		0.50								

←Indifference probabilities of success→

If the executive were completely consistent, the results obtained at the overlap would be identical.

When plotting the second set of responses at the $0.2 million investment level, utility values were adjusted by trial and error to match previous responses. This process was repeated to calculate the utility curve over the entire range for each executive.

As would be expected, the responses of the research executives differed considerably from those of the manufacturing executives. Furthermore, *the executives within a group differed.**

The results of the pooled utility calculations were as shown by Fig. 12-A-1.

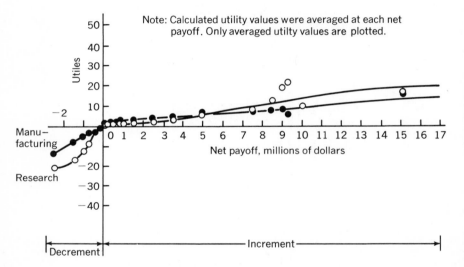

Figure 12-A-1. Utility curves calculated from averaged research and manufacturing department indifference probability responses.

Moment Method

The data from the standard gambles may also be used to develop a model for discounting for risk through the mean and variance. The net gains and

*In fact, the same person quizzed at two different *times might not be consistent with himself.* However, to provide consistent measure of utility, a single function must be provided for the group. This problem of pooling group attitudes has been the subject of much research, none of which provides a useful guide in this situation. Since our purpose was to capture in a gross sense the group attitude towards risk, a single utility curve was constructed *from the average of the probability responses.* The median might have been preferred had the group been larger or if manipulation was suspected of one or *more individuals in order to get his way as the average.*

indifference probabilities provided the necessary information to determine the mean and variance for each risk situation.

The mean μ of the gamble at indifference is $\mu = GP + L(1 - P)$, where P is the indifference probability of gaining G and $1 - P$ is the probability of losing L. The variance for this gamble is $\sigma^2 = P(1 - P)(G - L)^2$.

For instance, supervisor A indicated that he would be indifferent to a project which would yield either \$100,000 with a probability of 0.6 or $-\$100,000$ with a probability of 0.4. Therefore,

$$\mu = 0.1(0.6) - 0.1(0.4) = \$0.02 \text{ million}$$

and

$$\sigma^2 = 0.6(1 - 0.6)[0.1 - (-0.1)]^2 = 0.0096 \text{ million}^2$$

The moments were calculated in this manner for each response. As a first step it was decided to try to develop a model of the general form $U = \mu - K\sigma^a$, where a is a constant exponent of the standard deviation and K is the

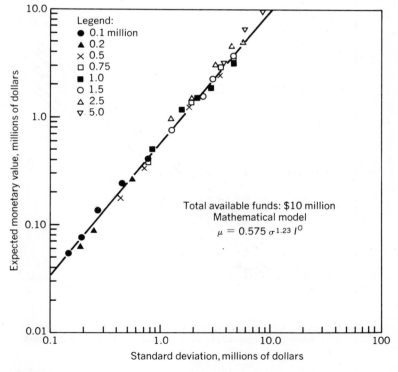

Figure 12-A-2. Comparison of mathematical model with averaged manufacturing department responses expected monetary value vs. standard deviation for outcome of gamble.

coefficient of risk aversion. Because the responses were at a point of indifference, utility is zero and $U = 0 = \mu - K\sigma^a$. Transposing, $\mu = K\sigma^a$, and taking the logarithm of both sides, $\log \mu = a \log \sigma + \log K$. If μ were plotted vs. σ on log–log coordinates, then a linear relationship of the standard form $y = mx + b$ should result, where m is the slope and b the y-intercept.

Attempts to correlate individual responses resulted in widely scattered data. It was therefore decided to average the means and variance within each department.* More work is needed to justify treating the individual responses in this way to arrive at a group response. However, if the responses are well grouped, the discrepancy between consensus arrived at by averaging indifference probabilities or by averaging mean and variance is small.

The group consensus data correlated in an orderly manner with a uniform

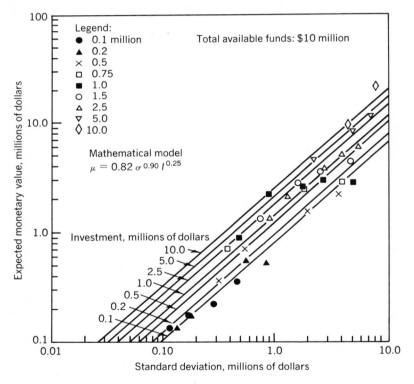

Figure 12-A-3. Comparison of mathematical model with averaged research department responses expected monetary value vs. standard deviation for outcome of gamble.

---

*Many other methods of achieving a consensus are possible (majority rule, etc.). See R. D. Luce, H. Raiffa, *Games and Decisions* (New York: John Wiley & Sons, Inc., 1957). Using the average assumes that the executives compromise.

slope over a range of about one-hundredfold in mean and variance. This permitted evaluation of the exponent *a*. These data are presented in Fig. 12-A-2 for the manufacturing department and in Fig. 12-A-3 for the research department.

It was noted that the research department responses corresponded with the proportion of funds invested. Consequently, a second equation of the form

$$\log \frac{\mu}{\sigma^a} = b \log I + \log K$$

was developed by plotting μ/σ^a vs. the diversification coefficient I (percentage available budget invested)* on log–log coordinates.

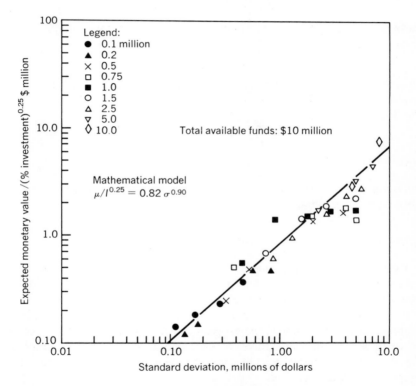

Figure 12-A-4. Comparison of mathematical model with averaged research department responses expected monetary value (1 % invested) vs. standard deviation for outcome of gamble.

*The diversification factor I represents the proportion of the research investment in a single project. It recognizes that the executive would prefer to pass on the research budget as a whole.

Again the data plotted approximately linearly for the research department. This permitted evaluation of the exponent b.

The multiplier constant K was evaluated by taking smoothed data and calculating

$$\frac{\mu I^b}{\sigma^a} = K$$

From these calculations, utility models of the form

$$U = \mu - K\sigma^a I^b$$

were developed for both departments*:

For research:

$$U = \mu - 0.82\sigma^{0.90}I^{0.25}$$

The model is compared with the research department data on Fig. 12-A-4.

For manufacturing:

$$U = \mu - 0.575\sigma^{1.23}I^0$$

Because I^0 is equal to 1, the relationship shown in Fig. 12-A-2 is not altered by plotting the ratio μ/I^0 versus σ. Figure 12-A-2 may be compared directly with Fig. 12-A-4.

Application

Equipped with a measure of utility it is now possible to compare research projects in a meaningful manner.

Selection among independent projects

Consider three projects involving the same applied research and development expenditures, but differing in payoff and the expense required to commercialize. Each involves a decision to start applied research, to start development, and then to undertake the laboratory expenditure involved with commercialization. These three projects are outlined by the tree diagram shown in Fig. 12-A-5 and have the outcomes and probabilities described. The examples are simple, but the same approach can be used for much more complicated situations.

Calculation of expected monetary value and certainty equivalence value. Considering Example I in Fig. 12-A-5, at the point of decision to start applied

---

*If the utility of a return on investment is desired, dividing the mean and standard deviation of the distribution of outcomes by the investment gives

$$U_R = \frac{\mu}{I} - K\left(\frac{\sigma}{I}\right)^a I^b \quad \text{or} \quad U_R = \frac{\mu}{I} - K\sigma^a I^{(b-a)}$$

Figure 12-A-5. Examples of selection among three independent research projects.

Project	Example I	Example II	Example III
Decision	$11.35 million ($10.00 net); $p = 0.9$; $p = 0.6$, $p = 0.1$, $-\$1.35$ million; $-\$0.35$ million; $p = 0.5$; $p = 0.4$, $-\$0.05$ million — Start commercialization / Start development / Start applied research	$13.65 million ($12.30 net); $p = 0.75$; $p = 0.6$, $-\$1.35$ million; $p = 0.25$, $-\$0.35$ million; $p = 0.5$; $p = 0.4$, $-\$0.05$ million — Start commercialization / Start development / Start applied research	$22.35 million ($20.00 net); $p = 0.6$; $p = 0.6$, $-\$2.35$ million; $p = 0.4$, $-\$0.35$ million; $p = 0.5$; $p = 0.4$, $-\$0.05$ million — Start commercialization / Start development / Start applied research

Criterion of choice	Example I			Example II			Example III		
Expected monetary value, $million	2.56	5.18	8.86	2.56	5.18	8.86	3.22	—	11.06
Expected utility, utiles									
Research	2.55	5.60	11.00	1.87	—	8.75	0.84	—	5.30
Manufacturing	—	—	7.49	—	—	6.89	—	—	3.80
Certainty equivalent, $million									
Research value	1.05	2.49	6.38	0.72	—	4.80	0.74	—	2.66
Manufacturing value	—	—	6.24	—	—	3.74	—	—	0.16

research, four outcomes are shown: a successful commercialization, resulting in a total payoff of $11.35 million; an unsuccessful commercialization, resulting in a net loss of $1.35 million; an unsuccessful development program, resulting in a net loss of $0.35 million; and finally, an unsuccessful applied research program resulting in a net loss of $0.05 million. The calculations of expected values of x and x^2 for the decision to start applied research are shown in the following table.

	$P(x)$	*Net payoff* x	$x\,P(x)$	$x^2\,P(x)$
$0.5 \times 0.6 \times 0.9 =$	0.27	10.00	2.70	27.00
$0.5 \times 0.6 \times 0.1 =$	0.03	−1.35	−0.0405	0.0548
$0.5 \times 0.4 \quad\;\; =$	0.20	−0.35	−0.0700	0.0245
$0.5 \quad\qquad\;\; =$	0.50	−0.05	−0.0250	0.0012
	1.00		2.564	27.08

$$E(x) = \sum x\,P(x) = \$2.564 \text{ million}$$
$$E(x^2) = \sum x^2\,P(x) = \$27.08 \text{ million}^2$$

The expected monetary value is calculated directly to be $2.56 million. The variance is calculated from the relationship shown below:

$$\sigma^2 = E(x^2) - [E(x)]^2$$
$$= 27.08 - 6.57$$
$$= \$20.51 \text{ million}^2$$

This results in a standard deviation of $4.54 million.

Substituting in the proposed model as shown below

$$U = \mu - 0.82\sigma^{0.90}I^{0.25}$$

where $\mu = $ $2.56 million
$\sigma = $ $4.54 million
$I = $ $0.05 million

results in a certainty equivalent of $1.05 million to the research department executives.

At the point of the decision to start development work, three outcomes exist as described above. Similarly, this decision can be calculated to have an expected monetary value of $5.18 million and a standard deviation of $5.24 million. A certainty equivalent value of $2.49 million to the research executives was calculated using the incremental investment for development. The applied research expenditure was regarded as sunk cost.

At the point of the decision to commercialize, two outcomes exist—a total payoff of $11.35 million, or a net loss of $1.35 million. By the procedure described above, an expected monetary value of $8.86 million, a standard deviation of $3.43 million, and certainty equivalent values of $6.38 million for the research executives and $6.24 million for the manufacturing executives can be calculated.

This project, by itself, would be regarded favorably because of the high expected monetary and certainty equivalent values calculated.

Calculations for the other two examples in Fig. 12-A-5 would be made in the same manner.

Calculation of expected utility. The calculation of expected utility at each point of decision is analagous to the calculation of expected monetary value. The difference lies in that the utility of each of the outcomes as read from Fig. 12-A-3 is substituted for a monetary value. This calculation is shown in tabular form.

$P(x)$	x	Research utility, U	$U \times P(x)$
0.27	10.00	14.00	3.78
0.03	−1.35	−16.00	−0.48
0.20	−0.35	−2.50	−0.50
0.50	−0.05	−0.50	−0.25
1.00			2.55

$$E(U) = \sum U \times P(x) = 2.55 \text{ utiles}$$

The expected utility of the decision to start applied research is 2.55 utiles. Since the utility value is positive, the project would be regarded favorably.

At the point of decision to start development work, the expected utility is similarly calculated to be 5.60 utiles.

At the point of decision to commercialize, the expected utility value for the research department executives is calculated to be 11.00 utiles, and for the manufacturing department executives 7.49 utiles. Since this is a large expected utility value in both cases, both groups would regard the project favorably.

The other two examples would be calculated in exactly the same manner.

Comparison of calculated results. The calculated expected monetary values, expected utilities, and certainty equivalent values for the three examples are shown in the following table.

Expected monetary value rates examples I and II equal and shows a decided preference for example III, which involves the greatest risk. An executive basing judgment on expected monetary value would clearly choose example III. However, how would he evaluate the risk involved?

Both the expected utility and the certainty equivalent rate the examples in the order I, II, III at the point of commercialization. By considering the element of risk, according to a defined policy, example III clearly becomes

	Expected monetary value ($ million)	Expected utility (utiles)		Certainty equivalent ($ million)	
		Research	Manufacturing	Research	Manufacturing
Example I					
Start applied research:	2.56	2.55	——	1.05	——
Start development:	5.18	5.60	——	2.49	——
Start commercialization:	8.86	11.00	7.49	6.38	6.24
Example II					
Start applied research:	2.56	1.87	——	0.73	——
Start commercialization:	8.86	8.75	6.89	4.80	3.74
Example III					
Start applied research:	3.22	0.84	——	0.74	——
Start commercialization:	11.06	5.30	3.80	2.66	0.16

less desirable. This demonstrates the advantage of these two criteria over expected monetary value.

The difference in relative desirability of the three projects to the research and manufacturing executives becomes readily apparent as the element of risk increases. This demonstrates the effect of different policies on risk. As expected, projects which involve the greatest risk are regarded more conservatively by the manufacturing executives.

Differences of opinion between research and manufacturing as to the desirability of a project at the point of commercialization involve much discussion and argument. If the difference cannot be resolved between the two groups, the issue must be taken to a higher executive level for decision. This is generally an unpleasant experience and leaves much residual ill will, regardless of the outcome of the decision. If a risk policy is agreed to beforehand, some of the difficulty is eliminated.

Selection of portfolios of projects

The goal of the research manager is to select the portfolio of projects which maximizes his chosen criterion subject to budget constraints. As long as projects are independent, no problem exists (as will be shown). However, when projects are interdependent, the selection is more complicated.

Dependent projects fall into two classifications, according to Bierman and Smidt (Ref. 1). If the decision to undertake a second project will increase the benefits from the first, then the second project is said to be a *complement* of the first. If the decision to undertake the second project will decrease the benefits expected from the first, then the second project is said to be a *substitute* for the first. In the extreme case where the potential benefits derived from the first project will completely disappear if the second project is accepted, or where it is technically impossible to undertake the first when the second has been accepted, then the two projects are said to be *mutually exclusive*.

Under the expected utility model an expected utility for each portfolio must be calculated using conditional probabilities. These probabilities are extremely difficult to estimate. In addition, they substantially increase the computational burden.

The certainty equivalent model provides a far more convenient procedure for evaluating dependent projects. Where such dependency exists, much of the effect can be accounted for in terms of the correlation between projects. Thus for two projects x and y, the measured correlation is given by

$$\rho = \frac{E[(x - \mu_x)(y - \mu_y)]}{\sigma_x \sigma_y}$$

where ρ is called the correlation coefficient. The correlation coefficient approaches 1 when projects complement each other. The correlation coefficient is near -1 when projects substitute; ρ is zero for independent projects. Thus, the estimator must furnish a statement of relative association through a ρ-value for every dependent project pair.

The correlation coefficient is used in the model to calculate the variance for groups of projects. We know that for a sum

$$z = \sum_{i=1}^{n} x_i$$

of n random variables the expected value is

$$\mu_z = \sum_{i=1}^{n} E(x_i)$$

and that the variance is

$$\sigma^2 = \sum_{i=1}^{n} \sigma_{x_i}^2 + 2 \sum \rho \sigma_{x_i} \sigma_{x_j}$$

where the second sum is over all i and j such that $i < j$. This relationship indicates that the variance is increased for values of ρ near 1 and is decreased for values of ρ near -1. In terms of the research projects this implies that complementing projects entail more risk than competing projects. Since the expected value is independent of the correlation coefficient, decreased variance implies increased utility.

If this tool were used by a sophisticated evaluation group, estimates of the correlation coefficient would provide for the synergistic effects which occur when several projects in the same field are being worked on (complementary) and the effects of using competing groups to work on the same project (substitution) which occurs in some research laboratories.

Conclusion

It is not claimed that the methods presented here are the ultimate in decision-making procedures. They do, however, offer a way of discounting risk when comparing research alternatives. In particular, the certainty equivalent model provides convenience with a comparatively modest demand for data. To be sure, a rather violent compromise with reality is made by using only two moments of the payoff distribution. However, when the uncertainty involved in estimating the input data is considered, the compromise becomes reasonable. What is most important is that the model provides an objective device for delegation as it offers a statement of attitude toward risk which can be communicated to others.

References

1. Bierman, H. J. and S. Smidt, *The Capital Budgeting Decision* (New York: The Macmillan Company, 1960).

2. Bowman, E. H., "Consistency and Optimality in Managerial Decision Making," *Management Science* (January 1963), 310–321.

3. Cramer, R. H., "An Application of Decision Theory to the Selection of Research Projects," Master's thesis, School of Industrial Management, Massachusetts Institute of Technology, 1963.

4. Farrar, Donald, *The Investment Decision Under Uncertainty* (Englewood Cliffs, N.J.: Prentice-Hall, Inc., 1962).

5. Grayson, Jr., C. Jackson, *Decisions Under Uncertainty* (Boston: Harvard Business School Press, 1960).

6. Green, P. E., "Risk Attitudes and Chemical Investment Decisions," *Chemical Engineering Progress*, Vol. 59, No. 1 (January 1963), 35.

7. Hicks, J. S. and L. R. Steffens, "Cost Estimating and Decision Making," *Chemical Engineering Progress*, Vol. 52, No. 5 (May 1956).

8. Von Neumann, John and Oskar Morgenstern, *Theory of Games and Economic Behavior*, 2nd edition (Princeton University Press, 1947).

thirteen

Monte Carlo Technique for Comparison of Projects Involving Risk

Introduction

The Monte Carlo technique is an especially useful means of simulating situations involving risk so as to obtain approximate answers when a physical experiment or the use of analytical mathematics is either too burdensome or not feasible. It has enjoyed widespread acceptance in practice because of the analytical power it makes possible without the necessity for complex mathematics. It is especially adaptable to computation by digital computers. Indeed, computer languages have been developed especially to facilitate Monte Carlo simulation.

The technique is sometimes descriptively called the *method of statistical trials*. It involves, first, the random selection of an outcome for each variable (element) of interest, the combining of these outcomes with any fixed amounts, and calculation if necessary to obtain one trial outcome in terms of the desired answer (measure of merit). This, done repeatedly, will result in enough trial outcomes to obtain a sufficiently close approximation of the mean, variance, distribution shape, or other characteristic of the desired answer. Figure 13-1 schematically shows this process applied to investment project analysis.

The key requisite of the Monte Carlo technique is that the outcomes of

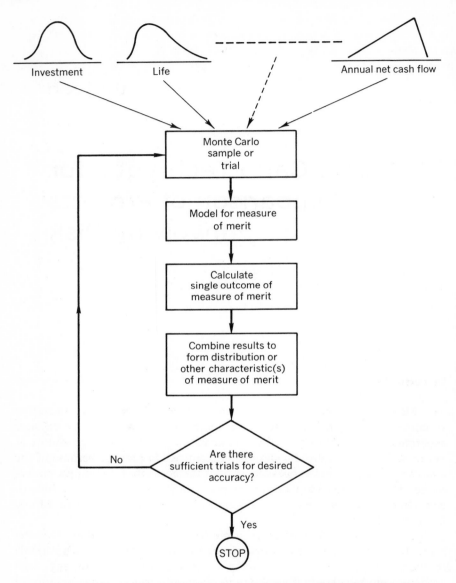

Figure 13-1. Schematic of Monte Carlo technique applied to investment project analysis.

all variables of interest be *randomly* selected, i.e., that the probability of selection of all possible outcomes be in exact accord with their respective probability distributions. This is accomplished through the use of tables of random numbers and relating these numbers to the distributions of the variables. *Random numbers* are numbers which have been generated in such a way that there is an equal probability of any number appearing each time, regardless of what sequence is experienced at any prior time. Appendix A–B contains one page of these numbers. The simple example below will demonstrate the Monte Carlo technique.

Example:

> As an illustration of Monte Carlo simulation applied to one variable or element, suppose the annual net cash flow for a project is estimated to have the distribution shown in Table 13-1.

Table 13-1

EXAMPLE FREQUENCY DISTRIBUTION FOR
ANNUAL NET CASH FLOW

Net cash flow	P(Net cash flow)
$10,000	0.10
15,000	0.50
20,000	0.25
25,000	0.15

This random simulation can be accomplished through tabular methods by assigning random numbers to each outcome in proportion to the probability of each outcome. Because two-digit probabilities are given in this case, sets of only two random digits are needed, and are shown in Table 13-2.

Table 13-2

ASSIGNMENT OF RANDOM NUMBERS FOR
EXAMPLE IN TABLE 13-1

Net cash flow	Random numbers
$10,000	00–09
15,000	10–59
20,000	60–84
25,000	85–99

Now one can generate net cash flow outcomes by picking random numbers* and determining the net cash flow which corresponds to each according to the above list. Table 13-3 lists ten two-digit random numbers

Note: The random numbers should be taken from the table in a way to assure randomness or nonrepetitiveness by randomly selecting a point to begin in the table and randomly selecting the direction of movement within the table (such as up, down, to right, etc.).

taken arbitrarily from a table of random numbers such as Appendix A–B, together with the corresponding net cash flows, taken from Table 13-2.

Table 13-3

GENERATION OF OUTCOMES FOR EXAMPLE IN TABLE 13-1

Random number	Net cash flow outcome
47	$15,000
91	25,000
02	10,000
88	25,000
81	20,000
74	20,000
24	15,000
05	10,000
51	15,000
74	20,000

It may be of interest to note that the mean net cash flow based on the above simulated outcomes is $175,000/10 = $17,500. This compares with a mean of $17,250 for the known distribution shown in Table 13-1. Results for ten simulated outcomes would not always turn out this close. However, in general, the larger the number of Monte Carlo trials, the closer the approximation to the desired answer(s).

For Monte Carlo simulations in which a computer is not used, it is sometimes helpful to use a graph of the distribution function (cumulative frequency function) instead of a table matching random numbers to the various out-

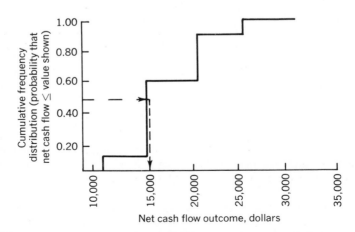

Figure 13-2. Sample cumulative frequency distribution for net cash flow.

comes. Figure 13-2 contains a graph of the distribution function for the example in Table 13-1. Once a graph such as in Fig. 13-2 has been constructed, outcomes are generated as follows: A random number table such as Appendix A–B is used to obtain random values which correspond to the ordinate scale (vertical axis) with the decimal removed. For each random number, a horizontal line is drawn until it meets the curve. Then a vertical line is dropped to the abscissa (horizontal axis) and the outcome thus determined. The dotted line in Fig. 13-2 illustrates the generation of a sample cash flow outcome.

The above example is for a discrete outcome distribution, but it should be noted that the same principle applies for continuous distributions. For continuous distributions, the tabular method is usually impractical, but the graphical method is readily applicable as is shown in the next section.

Generation of Random Normal Values

It is quite common for random phenomena to possess a normal distribution and for element outcomes to be estimated as normally distributed. The Monte Carlo technique can be conveniently used for simulation of random outcomes in such cases.

The basic quantity needed to generate randomly distributed normal outcomes is called a *random normal deviate*, or random normal number. A random normal deviate is merely a random number of standard deviations from the mean of a standard normal distribution. Random normal deviates can be obtained directly from a graph of the cumulative standard normal distribution. Such a graph is shown in Fig. 13-3.

For a normal distribution, the probability of an occurrence near the mean is greater than the probability of an occurrence further from the mean. This is reflected in Fig. 13-3, for the relative frequency of occurrence at each outcome value is proportional to the slope of the cumulative frequency curve.

To obtain random normal deviates, a table of random numbers is used to select numbers between 0.000 and 0.999 on the ordinate scale of the cumulative frequency distribution. (*Note:* More or less than three decimal places can be used as desired for accuracy.) For each random number a horizontal and vertical line can be drawn to find the corresponding random normal deviate. This is shown for two example random numbers in Fig. 13-3, and the results are summarized below.

Random number	*Random normal deviate*
405	−0.24
877	1.16

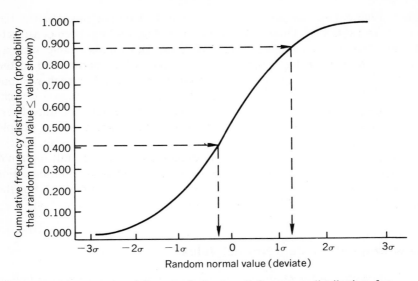

Figure 13-3. Cumulative standard normal frequency distribution for generation of random normal deviates.

Tables of random normal deviates can be generated by a procedure such as the above. Such a table is presented in the Appendix A–C. Tables of random normal deviates save much effort, for they enable us to generate a Monte Carlo sample from a normal distribution merely by using the relation, Outcome value = Mean + R.N.D. × Standard deviation, where R.N.D. denotes the random normal deviate. As an example, suppose a project has a mean life of 8 years and a standard deviation of 2 years. Generated lives using the above random normal deviates, for example, can then be calculated as

$$8 - 0.24(2) = 7.52 \text{ yr}$$

and

$$8 + 1.16(2) = 10.32 \text{ yr}$$

Generation of Uniformly Distributed Values

Whenever the cumulative distribution function of a random variable can be expressed mathematically, random outcomes of that variable can be generated from random numbers by direct mathematical substitution. An example is the following development of a mathematical model for the generation of uniformly distributed values.

A uniform continuous distribution with a minimum value *a* and a maxi-

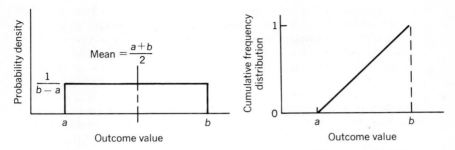

Figure 13-4. Density and distribution function for uniform continuous distribution.

mum value b has a density function and cumulative frequency distribution as shown in Fig. 13–4. For this distribution, the mean equals $(a+b)/2$ and the range equals $(b - a)$.

To illustrate the generation of outcomes according to this distribution, let R. N. denote a random number, and R. N.$_m$ denote the largest-numbered random number. By similar triangles, it can be seen that

$$\left. \begin{aligned} \text{Outcome value} &= a + \frac{\text{R. N.}}{\text{R. N.}_m}(b - a) \\ &= a + (\text{R. N. expressed as a decimal})(b - a) \end{aligned} \right\} \quad (13\text{-}1)$$

An equivalent statement is

$$\text{Outcome value} = \frac{a + b}{2} - \frac{(b - a)}{2} + \frac{\text{R. N.}}{\text{R. N.}_m}(b - a) \quad (13\text{-}2)$$

If an element or variable is uniformly distributed with a mean of 8 and a range of 6, random outcomes can be generated using the relation

$$8 - \frac{6}{2} + \frac{\text{R. N.}}{\text{R. N.}_m}(6) = 5 + (\text{R. N. expressed as a decimal})(6)$$

Example:

Example of the use of Monte Carlo simulation for nonindependent elements: One of the valuable features of the Monte Carlo technique is that it provides an analysis tool for cases in which elements are not independent and thus are difficult or impossible to manipulate so as to obtain the desired answers analytically. For example, suppose that the life of a project is described by some distribution with a mean which is a function of the annual cash flow of the project. Further, suppose the annual cash flow itself is described by some distribution, and that it is desired to determine the distribution of the net P.W. (present worth) of those cash flows over the life of the project. The following illustrates the use of the Monte Carlo technique for this type of situation.

The annual net cash flow of a project is estimated to be normally distributed with a mean of $10,000 and standard deviation of $2,000. The life of the project is estimated to be uniformly distributed with a mean of 0.0005 of the annual net cash flow (rounded to the nearest integer year), and a range (difference between maximum and minimum life) of 6 years. Table 13-4 demonstrates use of the Monte Carlo technique for ten trials to obtain an estimate of the mean of the net P.W. of the cash flows, at an interest rate of 10%.

The estimated mean P.W. from the limited number of trials in Table 13-4 is $374,800/10 = $37,480. Repeated trials would doubtless result in a more accurate answer. It is worthy of note that the exact answer for this situation is not the same as $10,000 ($P/A$, 10%, 5) = $37,910, where $10,000 is the mean cash flow and 5 years is the mean life.

Example:

Example of Monte Carlo technique applied to economic analysis for a single project: To illustrate the use of the Monte Carlo technique to calculate the measure of merit for a single project for which the element outcomes are estimated as variables, consider a case in which the estimates are as follows:

Investment:	Normally distributed with mean of $100,000 and standard deviation of $5,000
Life:	Uniformly distributed with minimum of 4 yr and maximum of 16 yr (rounded to nearest integer)
Salvage value:	$10,000 (single outcome)
Annual net cash flow:	$14,000 with probability 0.4, $16,000 with probability 0.4, and $20,000 with probability 0.2.

It is assumed that all elements which are subject to variation vary independently of one another, and it is desired to obtain a good estimate of the distribution characteristics for the net A.W. using an interest rate of 10%. For purposes of the illustration, only five repetitions of the Monte Carlo simulation will be made. However, perhaps several thousand repetitions would be needed to obtain sufficiently accurate net A.W. distribution information. Table 13-5 shows the calculations.

The estimate of the net A.W. based on the very limited sample as calculated in Table 13-5 is $-$18,000/5 = -$3,600$.

An estimate of the standard deviation of the net A.W. can be obtained from the relation

$$\left. \sigma(\text{A.W.}) = \sqrt{\frac{\sum\limits_{i=1}^{k}[\text{A.W.}_{\cdot i} - E(\text{A.W.})]^2}{k-1}} \\ = \sqrt{\frac{58,100,000}{4}} = \$3,850 \right\} \quad (13\text{-}3)$$

This estimate should also come closer to the true standard deviation with increasing numbers of Monte Carlo trials.

Example of Monte Carlo technique applied to economic comparison of two independent projects: Suppose two competing projects, A and B, have the following estimated distributions of net A.W. and it is desired to estimate the

Table 13-4
Monte Carlo Example with Nonindependent Elements

Random normal deviate (R.N.D.)	Annual net cash flow (A.N.C.F.) $[\$10,000 + R.N.D.(\$2,000)]$	Three random numbers (R.N.)	Project life N $\left[0.0005(A.N.C.F.) - 3 + \dfrac{R.N.}{999}(6)\right]$	Project life N to nearest integer	$(P/A,10\%,N)$	P.W. of cash flows $[A.N.C.F. \times (P/A,10\%,N)]$
0.944	$ 8,112	443	3.65	4	3.170	$25,700
−1.140	7,720	511	3.64	4	3.170	24,500
1.353	12,706	549	6.54	7	4.868	62,000
0.466	10,912	169	3.48	3	2.487	27,100
0.732	11,464	656	6.65	7	4.868	56,000
−1.853	6,394	955	5.84	6	4.355	27,800
−0.411	9,188	783	6.29	6	4.355	40,100
0.488	10,976	197	5.92	6	4.355	48,000
−0.351	9,298	842	6.75	7	4.868	45,400
−1.336	7,328	372	2.89	3	2.487	18,200
						$\Sigma = \$374,800$

Table 13-5

MONTE CARLO EXAMPLE FOR A SINGLE PROJECT

Random normal deviate (R.N.D.)	Investment P [$100,000 + R.N.D.($5,000)]	Three random numbers (R.N.)	Project life N $\left[4 + \frac{R.N.}{999}(16-4)\right]$	Project life N nearest integer	One random number	Annual receipts A $\begin{bmatrix} \$14{,}000 \text{ for } 0\text{-}3 \\ 16{,}000 \text{ for } 4\text{-}7 \\ 20{,}000 \text{ for } 8\text{-}9 \end{bmatrix}$	Net A.W. $\begin{bmatrix} [-\{(P-F)(A/P, 10\%, N) \\ + F(10\%)\} + A] \end{bmatrix}$
0.30	$101,500	693	4 + 8.32	12	2	$14,000	−$ 400
−0.92	95,400	192	4 + 2.30	6	5	16,000	− 4,700
0.13	100,650	924	4 + 1.10	5	1	14,000	− 9,000
−0.16	99,200	490	4 + 5.87	10	4	16,000	+ 500
0.54	102,700	314	4 + 3.77	8	1	14,000	− 4,400
							$\Sigma = -\$18{,}000$

distribution of the difference in A.W. between the projects using Monte Carlo simulation and assuming that the outcomes are independent of each other.

Project A		Project B
A.W.	*P(A.W.)*	
−$ 5,000	0.10	A.W. is normally distributed
$10,000	0.30	with mean of $25,000 and
20,000	0.50	standard deviation of $10,000
30,000	0.10	

Table 13-6

MONTE CARLO COMPARISON OF TWO INDEPENDENT PROJECTS

One random number	*A.W. for project A* [−$5,000 for 0 / $10,000 for 1–3 / 20,000 for 4–8 / 30,000 for 9]	*Random normal deviate (R.N.D.)*	*A.W. for project B* [= $25,000 + R.N.D.($10,000)]	*Difference in A.W. for two projects*
4	$20,000	0.636	$31,360	$11,360
1	10,000	−0.179	22,210	11,210
4	20,000	−2.546	− 460	− 20,460
6	20,000	0.457	29,570	9,570
				$\Sigma = \$11,680$

Sample calculations to obtain the desired answers are shown in Table 13-6. The mean difference in A.W. based on the limited simulation in Table 13-6 is $11,680/5 = $2,816. To re-emphasize, a much larger number of Monte Carlo trials than illustrated is needed before meaningful estimates of the distribution of the difference in the A.W. for the two projects can be made.

Example of Monte Carlo technique applied to economic comparison of two projects with correlated elements: Two competing projects have the following outcome distribution characteristics:

	Project	
	A	*B*
Investment (normally distributed)		
Mean:	$50,000	$60,000
Standard deviation:	$20,000	$5,000
Life (uniformly distributed and rounded to the nearest year)		
Minimum:	3 yr	2 yr
Maximum:	7 yr	12 yr

It is thought that the investment outcomes are completely correlated for the two projects; i.e., when the investment for one project occurs high, the investment for the second project occurs correspondingly high, etc. On the other hand, the lives for the two projects are thought to be independently distributed. Table 13-7 demonstrates the use of the Monte Carlo technique for generating the distribution of the difference in the capital recovery costs for the two projects. For purposes of the illustration, zero salvage value and 10% interest is assumed and only three trials are shown. Note that the investment amounts for the two projects are generated using the same random normal deviates, thus reflecting complete correlation. On the other hand, the lives for the two projects are generated using independent random digits, reflecting the independence of life outcomes.

Table 13-7

MONTE CARLO COMPARISON OF PROJECTS WITH CORRELATED ELEMENTS

Random normal deviate (R.N.D.)	*Investment (P) for A* [$50,000 + R.N.D. ($20,000)]	*Investment (P) for B* [$60,000 + R.N.D. ($5,000)]	*Two random numbers*	*Life for A* $\left[3 + \dfrac{R.N.}{99}(4)\right]$ *(rounded)*
0.178	$53,560	$60,890	95	8
−0.507	49,860	57,460	04	4
0.362	57,240	61,810	08	4

Two random numbers	*Life for B* $\left[2 + \dfrac{R.N.}{99}(10)\right]$ *(rounded)*	*Capital recovery cost for A* [P (A/P,10%,N)]	*Capital recovery cost for B* [P (A/P,10%,N)]	*Difference in capital recovery cost [project B − project A]*
16	4	$10,000	$19,150	$ 9,150
98	12	15,550	8,400	− 7,150
00	2	18,030	35,000	16,970

Use of Computers

For typical practical problems, hundreds or even thousands of Monte Carlo trials are required in order to reduce sampling variation to a sufficiently low level so that the desired answers possess the level of accuracy thought necessary. This is often too laborious a task by hand methods, but can be done very efficiently with digital computers. Appendix 13-A contains a short exposition on simulation languages and programs available for economic analyses.

Method for Determining Approximate Number of Monte Carlo Trials Required

An easy method for determining the approximate number of Monte Carlo trials required to obtain sufficiently accurate answers is to keep a running tally (plot) on the average answer(s) of interest for increasing numbers of trials, and judge the number of trials at which those answer(s) have become stable enough to be within the accuracy required.

It is to be expected that the average outcome(s) will dampen or stabilize with increasing numbers of trials. This phenomenon is illustrated in Fig. 13-5 by the wavy line. Figure 13-5 also shows how a given typical permissible range of error can result in an indicated approximate number of trials required.

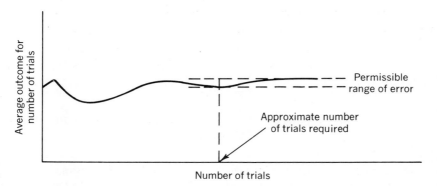

Figure 13-5. Number of trials.

Limitations

The Monte Carlo technique possesses real limitations which should be recognized. As for any analysis technique, the results can be no more accurate than the model and estimates used. The technique also inherently possesses the same problems of statistical variation and the need for experimental design that is encountered in direct physical experimentation. Finally, it should be emphasized that a sufficiently large number of Monte Carlo trials must be performed to reduce sampling variation (range of error) to a level which is tolerable in view of the accuracy needed and economically justified.

PROBLEMS

13-1. The salvage value of a prospective asset is a random variable dependent upon the life of the asset according to the following table:

Life	$5,000	$10,000	$15,000	$20,000	$25,000
2	——	——	0.20	0.50	0.30
4	——	0.20	0.50	0.20	0.10
6	0.30	0.30	0.30	0.10	——
8	0.30	0.50	0.20	——	——

Probability of salvage value

It is thought that each of the asset lives are equally likely to occur. If the investment in the asset is $50,000 and the interest rate is 15%, show how one can obtain a distribution of the capital recovery cost for the asset by setting up a table and generating five trial outcomes.

13-2. The estimated element outcomes for a key project are as follows:

Investment:	Normally distributed with a mean of $1,000,000 and a variance of 16,000,000
Life:	5 yr with probability 0.2
	7 yr with probability 0.7
	9 yr with probability 0.1
Net annual cash flow:	Uniformly distributed between $120,000 and $340,000 per yr
Salvage value:	0

All element outcomes are independent of each other. Demonstrate how to obtain a distribution of the net A.W. by generating five outcomes. From this, obtain estimates of the mean and variance of the net A.W. Assume a minimum attractive rate of return of 10%.

13-3. A certain project is expected to require an investment of $100,000 and to have a life which can be best described by a uniform distribution with a minimum of 5 years and a maximum of 15 years. This salvage value is expected to be $40,000 if the life is less than 8 years, $20,000 if the life is 8 to 12 years, and $15,000 if the life is 13 or more years. Show how to build a distribution of the capital recovery cost for this project by generating five outcomes using the Monte Carlo technique. Use an interest rate of 10% and round the project lives to the nearest whole year. From your results estimate the expected value and variance of the distribution of capital recovery cost.

13-4. Project X is expected to require an investment of $30,000 and to have a life which is normally distributed with a mean of 5 years and a standard deviation of 1 year (rounded to the nearest integer). The salvage value is expected to vary according to the relationship $5,000 − $1,000 × (life in yr).

Project Y is expected to require an investment of $45,000 and to have a life which is uniformly distributed between 5 and 15 years (rounded to the nearest integer). The salvage value is expected to be nil regardless of life. Show how to build a distribution of the difference in capital recovery costs for the two projects (X minus Y) by generating three outcomes using the Monte Carlo technique. Interest is 15%.

13-5. The net A.W. measures of merit for two competing projects are each normally distributed with the following parameters:

Project	Expected A.W.	Variance of A.W.
A	$10,000	490,000
B	12,000	360,000

Show how to use the Monte Carlo technique to estimate parameters of the distribution of the A.W. difference between the two projects (B minus A) by generating at least five sets of random outcomes (a) when the project outcomes are completely independent, and (b) when the project outcomes are perfectly correlated. If possible, compare your results with exact calculations of these parameters.

13-6. The estimated rate of return for project Q is normally distributed with a mean of 18% and a standard deviation of 8%. For competing project R, the estimated rate of return is uniformly distributed with a mean of 22% and a range of 20%. Show how to use the Monte Carlo technique to estimate parameters of the distribution of the difference in rates of return for the two projects (R minus Q) by generating five sets of random outcomes (a) where the project outcomes are completely independent, and (b) where the project outcomes are perfectly correlated.

13-7. Suppose that you desire to approximate the distribution of the annual cost of ownership of a new car or new house of your choice. Estimate at least three elements in terms of probabilistic outcomes, and assume that at least one of the elements is normally distributed and that at least one element has some irregular discrete distribution. State all your assumptions, including outcomes and probabilities and set up table(s) for generating five sets of outcomes. From these, estimate the mean and variance of the annual cost.

13-8. Records for a certain inventory item type indicate that the number of days lead time required for replenishment can be expected to have the following probability distribution:

Lead time (days)	Probability
1	0.25
2	0.50
3	0.25

Demand during any day of lead time is a normally distributed random variable independent of the number of days lead time and with a mean of 4 units and a standard deviation of 1 unit of the item. Inventory holding costs average $100 per unit per yr and the opportunity cost of a stock-out (failing to have a unit when demanded) is estimated at $70 per unit. Show how to use the Monte Carlo technique to determine the most economical size of safety stock for the item, where safety stock is defined as the difference between the number of units in inventory when the item is reordered and the expected demand during the lead time period. Illustrate by simulating five reorder periods with safety stocks of 0 units and then 4 units.

APPENDIX 13-A

Computer Simulation Languages and Available Programs for Capital Investment Analyses

There are many simulation languages and programs to facilitate the use of digital computers in making economic analyses. Two of the most common simulation languages used as of 1970 were GPSS III and SIMSCRIPT. GPSS III was developed by IBM for its 7040/44, 7090/94, and 360 series of computers. SIMSCRIPT was developed by the Rand Corporation for the IBM 709/7090 series of computers. Such special languages reduce programming effort by providing routines to perform certain operations unique to simulation which would otherwise have to be programmed in detail. GPSS is used primarily for queuing and scheduling simulations, but requires no previous knowledge of computer programming for use unless certain special features are desired. SIMSCRIPT, on the other hand, does require some knowledge of computer programming, but it allows for greater flexibility than GPSS. If one desires the ultimate in program flexibility, a general-purpose language, such as Fortran IV, can be used for simulation.

The following is a listing of pre-prepared library or "canned" computer programs, most of which perform Monte Carlo simulations for capital investment analyses.* When a suitable pre-prepared program such as one of

*The author wishes to thank N. C. State University graduate students Frederick H. Binder and Allan H. Rinne for their valuable assistance in the compilation of this list of computer programs.

those listed is available, it is the quickest and least expensive way to implement a computer simulation study. However, such programs can lose some of their desirability if an error is encountered in the program or if the program must be modified. If such problems occur, sufficiently detailed program description or documentation must be available to allow one to understand the internal logic of the program so that proper adjustments can be made. Although this listing is not necessarily complete, it does represent programs known by the author as of 1970. Of course, it is to be fully expected that additional programs will become available.

Program name	Description	Source
The capital risk program	Provides for Monte Carlo simulation of up to 25 random elements (variables) in each of up to 30 time periods to determine the distribution of measure of merit. Includes many useful options such as depreciation method, sensitivity testing features, sample size determination, and plotted distribution functions.	Control Data Corporation; Data Centers Division
Capital investment risk analysis applied to real estate	Determines the distribution of the rate of return and net present value for capital investments subject to uncertain incomes and expenses for up to a 50-yr period. Uncertainties may be uniform, skewed, normal, or not subject to fluctuation. Written specifically for real estate investments but easily modifiable to encompass any capital investment.	IBM 360 catalog of programs no. 360D-19.1.002
Discounted cash flow economic evaluation	Provides a means, through the application of the present worth method, of generating the financial information required to evaluate the economic worth of potential business investments. Instantaneous discounting is employed to obtain the expected present value and effective interest rate of return. Present value and payout time may be determined for each of three specified discount rates, and thus a sensitivity analysis showing the effect of discount rate can be generated. Output is complete in regard to all input assumptions, annual profit and loss statements, nondiscounted and discounted cash flows. Projects having anticipated cash flows from 1 to 20 years can be evaluated.	IBM 360 catalog of programs no. 360D-15.1.006
LESEE$	Makes present worth comparison of leasing with alternative of borrowing to purchase an asset. Sensitivity analysis can be performed on purchase price, lessee's income tax rate, inter-	GE 265 time-sharing system

Program name	Description	Source
	est rate on loan, after-tax opportunity rate, monthly rent, depreciable life of the asset, salvage value for tax purposes, and actual salvage value.	
LESOR$	Essentially the same as LESEE$ except that it calculates the after-tax rate of return measure of merit.	GE 265 time-sharing system
LESIM$	Essentially the same as LESOR$ except it takes into account a lease factor associated with the lessee.	GE 265 time-sharing system
PARSIM	Provides evaluations for comparison of alternative plant expansions using Monte Carlo simulation with options regarding measure of merit. Inputs include expected value and standard deviation estimates of depreciation duration, total market, market share, unit variable cost and price, growth rates, discount rates, and capitalization and expenses of alternatives.	GE 265 time-sharing system
PARSEN	Performs sensitivity analysis. Varies inputs and calculates effect on outputs, i.e., total market, market share, price, etc.	GE 265 time-sharing system
PARENT	Performs analysis similar to PARSIM except equipment is assumed to be rented instead of sold.	GE 265 time-sharing system

fourteen

Statistical Decision Techniques*

Numerous statistical techniques to aid in decision-making have been developed in the last two decades. Some of the more powerful of these techniques are included in the body of knowledge called *statistical decision theory*. Statistical decision theory is commonly characterized as the mathematical analysis of decision-making when, although the state of the world is uncertain, further information can yet be obtained by experimentation.

Statistical decision theory also often involves the use of subjective probabilities to express the decision-maker's degree of belief in the possible outcomes. A practice that is commonly associated with statistical decision theory is the use of Bayesian statistics, which is described briefly below.

Bayesian Statistics

Bayesian statistics is characterized by the adjustment of "prior" probabilities for an unknown parameter or factor to more reliable "posterior" probabilities based on the results of sample evidence or evidence from further study. Bayes' theorem, usually employed in this adjustment, is developed with applications below.

*This chapter was written primarily by Nathan Wolf, International Business Machines Corp., Raleigh, N.C.

Bayes' theorem

Bayes' theorem is an extension of joint and conditional probability theory. The probability of two events occuring is given by probability theory as

$$P(A, B) = P(A \mid B)P(B) \qquad (14\text{-}1)$$

where $P(A,B)$ = Probability of the two events A and B occurring together
$P(A \mid B)$ = Probability of A occuring given that B has occurred
$P(B)$ = Probability of B occuring

It can be quickly reasoned that the probability of drawing the ace of spades from a standard deck of 52 cards is one in 52. As an example of the application of Eq. (14-1), this probability can also be computed as follows:

$$P(\text{Ace, Spade}) = P(\text{Ace} \mid \text{Spade})P(\text{Spade})$$
$$= (1 \text{ Ace}/13 \text{ Spades})(13 \text{ Spades}/52 \text{ cards})$$
$$= (1/13)(13/52) = 1/52$$

Note that the condition of getting the ace of spades is equivalent to drawing the spade ace. This leads to a second axiom:

$$P(A,B) = P(B,A)$$

Since $P(B,A) = P(B \mid A) \cdot P(A)$, then

$$P(A \mid B)P(B) = P(B \mid A)P(A) \qquad (14\text{-}2)$$

Bayes' theorem is derived from Eq. (14-2). Provided that $P(B)$ and $P(A) \neq 0$, then

$$\left. \begin{aligned} P(A \mid B) &= \frac{P(B \mid A)P(A)}{P(B)} \\[2mm] P(B \mid A) &= \frac{P(A \mid B)P(B)}{P(A)} \end{aligned} \right\} \qquad (14\text{-}3)$$

Thus, the probability of an ace, given a spade, can be computed in an indirect way using Eq. (14-3) as

$$P(\text{Ace} \mid \text{Spade}) = \frac{P(\text{Spade} \mid \text{Ace})P(\text{Ace})}{P(\text{Spade})}$$
$$= \frac{(1 \text{ Spade}/4 \text{ Aces})(4 \text{ Aces}/52 \text{ Cards})}{(13 \text{ Spades}/52 \text{ Cards})}$$
$$= \frac{(1/4)(1/13)}{(1/4)} = 1/13$$

In general, if there are n mutually exclusive, exhaustive possible outcomes $S_1, S_2, \ldots, S_n$, and the results of additional study, such as sampling, is X, such that X is discrete and $P(X) \neq 0$, and prior probabilities $P(S_i)$ have been established, then Bayes' theorem for the discrete case can be written as

$$P(S_i|X) = \frac{P(X|S_i)P(S_i)}{P(X)} \qquad (14\text{-}4)$$

The posterior probability $P(S_i|X)$ is the probability of outcome S_i given that additional study resulted in X. The probability of X and S_i occurring, $P(X|S_i)P(S_i)$, is the "joint" probability of X and S_i. The sum of all the joint probabilities is equal to the probability of X. Therefore, Eq. (14-4) can be written

$$P(S_i|X) = \frac{P(X|S_i)P(S_i)}{\sum_i P(X|S_i)P(S_i)} \qquad (14\text{-}5)$$

A format for application is presented in Table 14-1.

Table 14-1

FORMAT FOR APPLYING BAYES' THEOREM IN DISCRETE OUTCOME CASES

(1) State	(2) Prior probability	(3) Probability of sample outcome X	(4) Joint probability	(5) Posterior probability, $P(S_i \mid X)$
S_1	$P(S_1)$	$P(X\mid S_1)$	$P(X\mid S_1)P(S_1)$	$P(X\mid S_1)P(S_1)/P(X)$
S_2	$P(S_2)$	$P(X\mid S_2)$	$P(X\mid S_2)P(S_2)$	$P(X\mid S_2)P(S_2)/P(X)$
.	.	.	.	.
.	.	.	.	.
S_i	$P(S_i)$	$P(X\mid S_i)$	$P(X\mid S_i)P(S_i)$	$P(X\mid S_i)P(S_i)/P(X)$
.	.	.	.	.
.	.	.	.	.
S_n	$P(S_n)$	$P(X\mid S_n)$	$P(X\mid S_n)P(S_n)$	$P(X\mid S_n)P(S_n)/P(X)$
	$\sum_{i=1}^{n} P(S_i) = 1.0$		$\sum_{i=1}^{n} P(X\mid S_i)P(S_i) = P(X)$	$\sum_{i=1}^{n} P(S_i\mid X) = 1.0$

The columns in Table 14-1 are as follows:

Column
(1) S_i: the potential states of nature
(2) $P(S_i)$: the prior probability of S_i which is estimated (*Note:* This column sums to unity)
(3) $P(X|S_i)$: the conditional probability of getting sample or added study results X, given that S_i is the true state
(4) $P(X|S_i)P(S_i)$: the joint probability of getting X and S_i; the summation of this column is $P(X)$, which is the probability that the sample or added study results in outcome X
(5) $P(S_i|X)$: the posterior probability of S_i given that additional study resulted in X; numerically, the ith entry is equal to the ith

entry of column (4) divided by the sum of column (4)
(*Note:* Column (5) sums to unity)

As a side note of interest, when X has a continuous density function $f_1(X)$, and S has a continuous density function $f_2(S)$, such that all conditional density functions are continuous, then the continuous equivalent of Bayes's theorem states that

$$f_2(S|X) = \frac{f_1(X|S)f_2(S)}{\int_s f_1(X|S)f_2(S)\,dS} \tag{14-6}$$

Most examples in the remainder of this chapter will be devoted to discrete outcome cases.

Example:

Example involving sampling to revise probabilities for production process: Let us consider the following application: A production process requires that equipment be set up for a fixed run of 200 units. If the setup is good, defects occur with a probability of 0.05 and in a random fashion. A bad setup occurs randomly with a probability of 0.2 and then the random defect rate is 0.25. Letting S_1 represent a good setup, S_2 a bad setup, and X the event that a sample of one is found to be defective, it is desired to calculate the posterior probabilities that the setup is good or bad given that X has occurred. Table 14-2 shows the necessary calculations where $P(S_1)$ equals 0.8 and $P(S_2)$ equals 0.2.

Table 14-2

POSTERIOR PROBABILITY CALCULATION FOR PRODUCTION PROCESS

S_i	$P(S_i)$	$P(X\|S_i)$	$P(X\|S_i)P(S_i)$	$P(S_i\|X)$
S_1	0.80	0.05	0.04	$4/9 = 0.44$
S_2	0.20	0.25	0.05	$5/9 = 0.56$
	$\sum_i = 1.00$		$\sum_i = P(X) = 0.09$	$\sum_i = 1.00$

Thus, the prior probability that the setup is good, 0.8, is revised to a posterior probability of 0.44 based on the evidence that a sample unit is defective.

Example:

Example of use of Bayes' theorem for discrete outcome investment analysis: As a further example, consider an investment project with a return (expressed in net P.W.) of $6,000 if event S_1 occurs and $-\$4,000$ if event S_2 occurs. The prior probability estimates are 0.4 for S_1 and 0.6 for S_2. Thus, the expected return, denoted $E(R)$, is

$$E(\text{R}) = 0.4(\$6,000) + 0.6(-\$4,000) = 0$$

The alternative of not investing also has an expected return of zero, for there would be no gain or loss. Additional study will result in either X_1, which indicates a net P.W. of \$6,000, or X_2, which indicates a net present worth loss of \$4,000. If S_1 will occur, then X_1 will be indicated with a probability of 0.8. Similarly, if S_2 will occur, X_2 will be indicated with a probability of 0.6. The problem is summarized as follows:

$$P(S_1) = 0.4 \qquad P(X_1 \mid S_1) = 0.8$$
$$P(S_2) = 0.6 \qquad P(X_2 \mid S_1) = 1.0 - P(X_1 \mid S_1) = 0.2$$
$$E(S_1) = \$6,000 \qquad P(X_2 \mid S_2) = 0.6$$
$$E(S_2) = -\$4,000 \qquad P(X_1 \mid S_2) = 1.0 - P(X_2 \mid S_2) = 0.4$$

The posterior probabilities resulting from the additional study can now be computed from the above information. New expected returns then can be computed and the decision to invest or not invest in the project can be determined as a function of the additional study outcome X.

Table 14-3

COMPUTATION OF POSTERIOR PROBABILITIES GIVEN X_1

S_i	$P(S_i)$	$P(X_1 \mid S_i)$	$P(X_1 \mid S_i)P(S_i)$	$P(S_i \mid X_1)$
S_1	0.4	0.8	0.32	0.32/0.56 = 0.57
S_2	0.6	0.4	0.24	0.24/0.56 = 0.43
	$\sum_i = 1.0$		$\sum_i = P(X_1) = 0.56$	$\sum_i = 1.00$

Table 14-3 shows the computation of posterior probabilities if the added study results in X_1. When X_1 occurs, the probability of S_1 is revised from the "prior" 0.4 to the "posterior" 0.56. The expected return given X_1, denoted $E(R \mid X_1)$, can then be computed as

$$E(R \mid X_1) = 0.57(\$6,000) + 0.43(-\$4,000) = \$1714$$

Hence, if X_1 occurs, the project should be undertaken to obtain the positive expected net P.W. return.

The computation of posterior probabilities if the additional study results in X_2 is presented in Table 14-4. The occurrence of X_2 results in a posterior

Table 14-4

COMPUTATION OF POSTERIOR PROBABILITIES GIVEN X_2

S_i	$P(S_i)$	$P(X_2 \mid S_i)$	$P(X_2 \mid S_i)P(S_i)$	$P(S_i \mid X_2)$
S_1	0.4	0.2	0.08	0.18
S_2	0.6	0.6	0.36	0.82
	$\sum_i = 1.0$		$\sum_i = P(X_2) = 0.44$	$\sum_i = 1.00$

probability of S_1 of 0.18, and the expected return given X_2, denoted $E(R \mid X_2)$, is computed to be

$$E(R \mid X_2) = 0.18(\$6,000) + 0.82(-\$4,000) = -\$2,182$$

Since $E(R \mid X_2)$ is negative, the decision would be not to invest in the project if X_2 occurs, thus resulting in an expected return of zero.

Considering the decision rule, to invest if additional study results in X_1, and to reject the project if X_2 occurs, the overall expected return is now positive and is calculated to be

$$E(R) = \begin{cases} \$0 & \text{if } X = X_2 \\ \$1,714 & \text{if } X = X_1 \end{cases}$$

From Tables 14-3 and 14-4, $P(X_1) = 0.56$ and $P(X_2) = 0.44$. Thus, with sampling or additional study,

$$E(R) = E(R \mid X_1)P(X_1) + E(R \mid X_2)P(X_2)$$
$$= (\$1,714)0.56 + (\$0)0.44 = \$960$$

In general, the overall expected return, given additional study or sample information resulting in X_j is

$$E(R \mid SI) = \sum_j \max [E(\text{alternatives}) \mid X_j]P(X_j) \qquad (14\text{-}7)$$

where $E(R \mid SI)$ is the expected return given sample information.

The change in the expected value from \$0 to \$960 is often called the *expected value of sample information* (EVSI). Expressed symbolically,

$$\text{EVSI} = E(R \mid SI) - E(R) \qquad (14\text{-}8)$$

Expected Value of Perfect Information

The *expected value of perfect information* (EVPI) is the maximum possible EVSI and is the maximum expected loss due to imperfect information as to what will be the state of nature in a situation involving risk. Interpreted another way, the expected value of perfect information is the amount which could be gained, on the average, if the future regarding a particular decision situation became perfectly predictable and decisions changed to the optimal choice(s) based on the new known conditions. Another term synonymous with the expected value of perfect information is the *expected opportunity loss* (EOL).

Figure 14-1 shows the steps for computation of the EVPI for the usual situation of multiple alternatives and discrete outcomes. The discrete outcome investment project above will be used as an example of the application of EVPI. In this case, the alternatives are to invest or not to invest. If perfect information were available, the project would be accepted and have a net present value of $6,000 when S_1 is to occur or it would be rejected when S_2 is to occur. The expected present worth, given perfect information (certainty), denoted $E(R|PI)$, is thus $6,000 with an expected frequency of occurrence of 0.4, or it is $0, occurring with a probability of 0.6. Overall,

$$E(R|PI) = 0.4(\$6,000) + 0.6(\$0) = \$2,400$$

This reasoning process corresponds to the right-hand side of Fig. 14-1.

Prior to sampling or added study, the expected return for the above investment project was computed to be $0. This corresponds to the left-hand

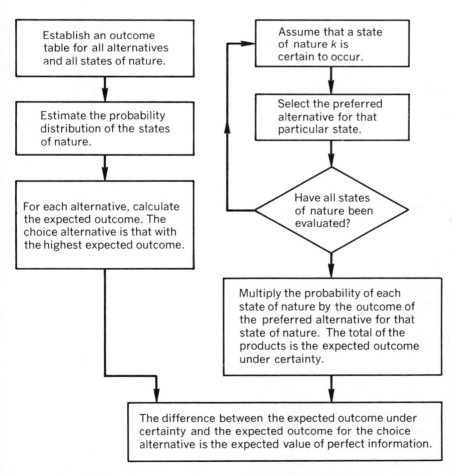

Figure 14-1. Computation of expected value of perfect information for multiple alternatives and discrete outcomes.

side of Fig. 14-1. Thus the EVPI is $2,400 — $0 or $2,400. This is a measure of the maximum possible expected to be gained by sampling for further information. It should be noted from the previous section that the $960 EVSI is expected to be gained (out of the $2,400 EVPI) by sampling one unit.

In general, EVPI (EOL) can be expressed as

$$\text{EVPI} = \text{EOL} = E(\text{R} \mid \text{PI}) - E(\text{R}) \qquad (14\text{-}9)$$

The general formula for computation of expected return under certainty is

$$E(\text{R} \mid \text{PI}) = \sum_i P(S_i) \cdot \max [\text{return } (A_1, \ldots, A_j, \ldots, A_m \mid S_i)] \quad (14\text{-}10)$$

where
$$E(\text{R} \mid \text{PI}) = \text{Expected return given perfect information}$$
$$P(S_i) = \text{Probability of the } i\text{th outcome}$$
$$A_j = \text{The } j\text{th alternative}$$
$$\text{return } (A_j \mid S_i) = \text{Value of alternative } j \text{ given that } S_i \text{ outcome occurs}$$
$$\max [\text{return } (A_1, \ldots, A_j, \ldots, A_m \mid S_i)] = \text{Decision rule that the value of the returns, given that } S_i \text{ occurs, is the maximum return over all } m \text{ alternatives}$$

Table 14-5

OUTCOMES IN NET P.W. FOR THREE ALTERNATIVES GIVEN
DISCRETE BUSINESS CONDITIONS

	Business Condition		
	Good $P(Good) = 0.25$	*Average* $P(Average) = 0.50$	*Poor* $P(Poor) = 0.25$
Alternative I	$300M	$200M	−$ 80M
Alternative II	400M	200M	− 200M
Alternative III	100M	240M	0M

Example:

Additional example of computation of EOL *through use of opportunity loss concept:* The *expected opportunity loss* (EOL) concept will be further demonstrated with the multiple-alternative, discrete outcome example given in Table 14-5. In this example the returns (expressed in net P.W.) depend on whether business conditions are good, average, or poor. The probabilities of these three possible business conditions are given as 0.25, 0.50, and 0.25 respectively. The expected return for each alternative can be calculated as

Alternative I: $300M(0.25) + $200M(0.50) − $80M(0.25) = $155M
Alternative II: $400M(0.25) + $200M(0.50) − $200M(0.25) = $150M
Alternative III: $100M(0.25) + $240M(0.50) + $0M(0.25) = $145M

Using the maximum expected return decision criterion, alternative I would be chosen. The *opportunity loss* (OL) for each business condition can be derived by the following rationale:

If good conditions prevail, alternative II would be preferred, and having chosen I incorrectly represents an OL of $400M − $300M or $100M. Similarly, if average business conditions occur, failure to select the optimal alternative III rather than alternative I represents an OL of $240M − $200M = $40M. If poor conditions resulted, alternative III would be the best choice at $0M. Choice of alternative I instead would cause an OL of $0M − (−$80M) = $80M.

Thus, for the above problem EOL is computed to be

$$\text{EOL} = (\$100M)0.25 + (\$40M)0.50 + (\$80M)0.25 = \$65M$$

In general, EOL can be computed as

$$\text{EOL} = \sum_i (\text{OL} \mid S_i)P(S_i) \qquad (14\text{-}11)$$

This implies that the expected return for the above alternatives, given perfect information, would be $65M greater than the expected return with no added information. To confirm this implication, the expected return with perfect information should be equal to the expected return with no added information ($155M) plus the EOL ($65M), or $220M. The computation of $E(R \mid PI)$ is shown in Table 14-6 to be $220M.

Table 14-6

EXPECTED RETURN WITH PERFECT INFORMATION

	Business condition (S_i)		
	Good	*Average*	*Poor*
Best alternative | Si	II	III	III
$P(S_i)$	0.25	0.50	0.25
Outcome for best alternative, $E(R \mid PI)_i$	$400M	$240M	$0M

$E(R \mid PI) = \sum_i E(R \mid PI)_i P(S_i) = \$100M(0.25) + \$120M(0.50) + \$0M(0.25) = \$220M$

Example:

As an example of evaluation of sample information schemes, suppose the Seyab Company is expanding its product line and a decision has to be made as to the size of additional facilities to add. The alternatives are to build a large plant (A_1), a modest plant (A_2), or to lease facilities as required (A_3). The possible outcomes in the strategy period are that demand will be high (S_1), good (S_2), fair (S_3), or low (S_4). Table 14-7 summarizes the net present value for each alternative for each of the four outcomes and also the best assessment by management of the (prior) probabilities of each possible demand outcome. From the data in Table 14-7, one can calculate the expected outcomes for each alternative as

$$E(A_1) = 0.2(\$18 \text{ million}) + 0.45(\$12 \text{ million}) + 0.25(\$6 \text{ million})$$
$$+ 0.1(-\$12 \text{ million}) = \$9.30 \text{ million}$$

$$E(A_2) = 0.2(\$12 \text{ million}) + 0.45(\$12 \text{ million}) + 0.25(\$9 \text{ million})$$
$$+ 0.1(-\$6 \text{ million}) = \$9.45 \text{ million}$$

$$E(A_3) = 0.2(\$13 \text{ million}) + 0.45(\$10 \text{ million}) + 0.25(\$6 \text{ million})$$
$$+ 0.1(-\$1 \text{ million}) = \$8.50 \text{ million}$$

Thus, based on the prior probabilities and expected outcomes, the indicated decision would be to build a modest plant (A_2) for an expected net P.W. of $9.45 million.

Table 14-7

SEYAB COMPANY RETURNS (IN NET P.W.)

Alternative	Demand and probability of demand			
	High, S_1 $P(S_1) = 0.2$ ($ million)	Good, S_2 $P(S_2) = 0.45$ ($ million)	Fair, S_3 $P(S_3) = 0.25$ ($ million)	Poor, S_4 $P(S_4) = 0.1$ ($ million)
Large plant (A_1)	$18	$12	$6	−$12
Modest plant (A_2)	12	12	9	− 6
Lease (A_3)	13	10	6	− 1

Suppose that a scheme for further consideration is that a market consultant be called in for further study. It is judged that the consultant will predict one of three possible ranges of demand outcome: good to high (X_1), fair to good (X_2), or poor to fair (X_3). The performance of the consultant based on management's subjective belief (or history) is given in Table 14-8. The interpretation of Table 14-8 is that if the demand is going to turn out to be high, the consultant will predict good–high with a probability of 0.6, i.e., $P(X_1 | S_1) = 0.6$; or he will predict fair–good with a probability of 0.3, i.e., $P(X_2 | S_1) = 0.3$; or he will predict poor–fair with a

Table 14-8

SEYAB COMPANY—INDICATIONS OF CONFIDENCE IN CONSULTANT'S STUDY

Given the demand will turn out to be _____ ...	... the probabilities the consultant will predict _____ are		
	Good–high X_1	Fair–good X_2	Poor–fair X_3
High (S_1)	0.6	0.3	0.1
Good (S_2)	0.3	0.5	0.2
Fair (S_3)	0.1	0.3	0.6
Poor (S_4)	0.1	0.1	0.8

probability of 0.1, i.e., $P(X_3 | S_1) = 0.1$. Similarly, $P(X_1 | S_2) = 0.3$, $P(X_2 | S_2) = 0.5$, etc.

The expected value of the project, using the sample information (further study results) from the consultant can be computed by determining what the optimal expected return will be for each possible prediction (X_j) by the probability of each prediction occurring. Tables 14-9, 14-10, and 14-11 present the computations of posterior probabilities given that X_1, X_2, or X_3 occur, respectively.

Table 14-9

SEYAB COMPANY—COMPUTATION OF POSTERIOR PROBABILITIES GIVEN THAT THE CONSULTANT PREDICTS X_1

S_i	$P(S_i)$	$P(X_1 | S_i)$	$P(S_i)P(X_1 | S_i)$	$P(S_i | X_1)$
S_1	0.20	0.60	0.120	0.414
S_2	0.45	0.30	0.135	0.466
S_3	0.25	0.10	0.025	0.086
S_4	0.10	0.10	0.010	0.034
			$P(X_1) = 0.290$	

Table 14-10

SEYAB COMPANY—COMPUTATION OF POSTERIOR PROBABILITIES GIVEN THAT THE CONSULTANT PREDICTS X_2

S_i	$P(S_i)$	$P(X_2 | S_i)$	$P(S_i)P(X_2 | S_i)$	$P(S_i | X_2)$
S_1	0.20	0.30	0.060	0.162
S_2	0.45	0.50	0.225	0.608
S_3	0.25	0.30	0.075	0.203
S_4	0.10	0.10	0.010	0.027
			$P(X_2) = 0.370$	

Table 14-11

SEYAB COMPANY—COMPUTATION OF POSTERIOR PROBABILITIES GIVEN THAT THE CONSULTANT PREDICTS X_3

S_i	$P(S_i)$	$P(X_3 | S_i)$	$P(S_i)P(X_3 | S_i)$	$P(S_i | X_3)$
S_1	0.20	0.10	0.020	0.059
S_2	0.45	0.20	0.090	0.265
S_3	0.25	0.60	0.150	0.441
S_4	0.10	0.80	0.080	0.235
			$P(X_3) = 0.340$	

If X_1 is predicted, then the posterior probabilities of S_1, S_2, S_3, and S_4 are given in Table 14-9 as 0.414, 0.466, 0.086, and 0.034 respectively. The expected value of the alternatives can then be calculated as

$$E(A_1) = 0.414(\$18 \text{ million}) + 0.466(\$12 \text{ million}) + 0.086(\$6 \text{ million})$$
$$+ 0.034(-\$12 \text{ million}) = \$13.15 \text{ million}$$
$$E(A_2) = 0.414(\$12 \text{ million}) + 0.466(\$12 \text{ million}) + 0.086(\$9 \text{ million})$$
$$+ 0.031(-\$6 \text{ million}) = \$11.13 \text{ million}$$
$$E(A_3) = 0.414(\$13 \text{ million}) + 0.466(\$10 \text{ million}) + 0.086(\$6 \text{ million})$$
$$+ 0.034(-\$1 \text{ million}) = \$10.52 \text{ million}$$

Therefore, given X_1 is predicted, A_1 (large plant) would be the choice with an expected net P.W. of \$13.15 million.

Similarly if X_2 is predicted, then the posterior probabilities of S_1, S_2, S_3, and S_4 are calculated in Table 14-10 as 0.162, 0.608, 0.203, and 0.027 respectively. The expected return of each alternative can be similarly computed as \$11.11 million for A_1, \$10.91 million for A_2, and \$9.38 million for A_3. Thus, alternative A_1 is again preferred, but with an expected return of \$11.11 million.

Finally, if X_3 is predicted, the posterior probabilities of S_1, S_2, S_3, S_4 are calculated in Table 14-11 as 0.059, 0.265, 0.441, and 0.235 respectively. The expected returns in this instance are \$4.07 million for A_1, \$6.45 million for A_2, and \$5.83 million for A_3. Hence, A_2 is the optimal alternative with an expected return of \$6.45 million.

It should be noted from the summations in the fourth columns of Tables 14-9, 14-10 and 14-11 that the probabilities that X_1, X_2, and X_3 will be predicted are, respectively, 0.29, 0.37, and 0.34.

The expected return given sample information $E(\text{R} \mid \text{SI})$, can now be computed using the general relationship

$$E(\text{R} \mid \text{SI}) = \sum_j \max [E(A_i \mid X_j)P(X_j)] \qquad (14\text{-}11)$$

Thus, $E(\text{R} \mid \text{SI}) = (\$13.15 \text{ million})(0.29) + (\$11.11 \text{ million})(0.37) + (\$6.45 \text{ million})(0.34) = \$10.12 \text{ million}$. To determine the EVSI, one need only compute

$$\text{EVSI} = E(\text{R} \mid \text{SI}) - E(\text{R})$$
$$= \$10.12 \text{ million} - \$9.45 \text{ million} = \$0.57 \text{ million}$$

This result indicates that management, based on the expected monetary principle, should be willing to pay up to \$0.67 million for the consultant's services in performing the added study if no other added study alternatives are available.

Suppose that the Seyab Company, rather than hiring a consultant, could follow the scheme of engaging its own staff in a fresh intensive study to predict outcomes. To evaluate the expected value of this new (sampling) information, management of the firm will again need to determine conditional probabilities that this type of added study will result in certain predictions given that the demand will turn out either high, good, fair, or poor. Table 14-12 shows the expected performance which reflects management's

Table 14-12

SEYAB COMPANY—INDICATIONS OF CONFIDENCE IN STAFF STUDY

Given the demand will turn out to be _____ . . .	. . . the probabilities the staff will predict _____ are			
	High X_1	Good X_2	Fair X_3	Poor X_4
High (S_1)	0.7	0.2	0.1	0.0
Good (S_2)	0.3	0.5	0.1	0.1
Fair (S_3)	0.1	0.3	0.4	0.2
Poor (S_4)	0.0	0.2	0.3	0.5

confidence in the added study. In this case, the staff will predict four possible outcomes corresponding to the actual expected demand—high, good, fair, or poor.

The posterior probabilities of demand turning out to be either S_1, S_2, S_3 or S_4 for each possible staff study prediction X_1, X_2, X_3, or X_4 can be calculated as shown in previous examples. Table 14-13 summarizes the results of these calculations. The expected returns for each alternative and each staff study prediction are summarized in Table 14-14.

Table 14-13

SEYAB COMPANY—SUMMARIZATION OF CALCULATED POSTERIOR PROBABILITIES FOR STAFF STUDY

S_i	Posterior probability			
	$P(S_i \mid X_1)$	$P(S_i \mid X_2)$	$P(S_i \mid X_3)$	$P(S_i \mid X_4)$
S_1	0.467	0.111	0.103	0.000
S_2	0.450	0.625	0.231	0.310
S_3	0.083	0.208	0.513	0.345
S_4	0.000	0.056	0.153	0.345

Table 14-14

SEYAB COMPANY—SUMMARIZATION OF EXPECTED RETURNS FOR STAFF STUDY

Alternative	Prediction ($ million)			
	X_1	X_2	X_3	X_4
$E(A_1)$	$14.30	$10.07	$5.87	$1.65
$E(A_2)$	11.75	10.37	7.71	4.76
$E(A_3)$	11.07	8.89	6.51	4.83

Table 14-15

SEYAB COMPANY—CALCULATION OF EXPECTED RETURN
FOR STAFF STUDY

Staff prediction (X_j)	Expected return of best alternative ($ million)	$P(X_j)$	Expected return $\times P(X_j)$ ($ million)
X_1	$14.30	0.300	$4.29
X_2	10.37	0.360	3.73
X_3	7.71	0.195	1.50
X_4	4.83	0.145	0.71
		$\sum_j =$	$10.23 million

Table 14-15 indicates the expected return of the best alternative and also probabilities of staff prediction for X_1, X_2, X_3, and X_4 respectively. The expected returns come directly from Table 14-14, but the probabilities are the result of the posterior probability calculations not shown but for which the results were summarized in Table 14-13. The right-hand column of Table 14-15 shows the computation of the expected return given the sample (added study) information to be $10.23 million. From this the expected value of sample information can be calculated as $10.23 million − $9.45 million = $0.78 million.

The difference between EVSI and the cost of additional study is called the *expected net value of sample information*, denoted ENVSI. Symbolically,

$$\text{ENVSI} = \text{EVSI} - \text{Cost of sample information} \qquad (14\text{-}12)$$

which is a more valuable decision criterion than EVSI alone. Suppose that for this example problem it is thought that the consultant would cost $0.50 million for the added study and that if the firm's staff conducted the study it would cost $0.65 million. In this event, the two alternatives for the added study can be compared through the following calculation:

Consultant:
  ENVSI = $0.67 million − $0.50 million = $0.17 million
Staff:
  ENVSI = $0.78 million − $0.65 million = $0.13 million

Thus, the expected net value of the sample information (added study) is slightly greater for the consultant alternative, and thus the consultant should be chosen on the basis of expectations.

Inventory example application: Consider a rather typical retailer's inventory problem with variable demand in which the objective is to minimize the sums of carrying costs and stock-out costs. Table 14-16 shows the costs totaled for each of four possible levels of demand S_i and four amounts of starting inventory A_k, as well as the prior probabilities of each level of demand. It is assumed that the product is highly seasonal and that the demand in a given time period is independent of demand in previous periods. The problem is to determine the optimal starting inventory.

Table 14-16

COSTS OF INVENTORY FOR LEVELS OF DEMAND
AND STARTING INVENTORY ALTERNATIVES

		Demand level			
Starting inventory	$P(S_i)$:	S_1 0.3	S_2 0.2	S_3 0.25	S_4 0.25
A_1		$ 0	$2	$6	$9
A_2		6	0	4	5
A_3		9	2	0	4
A_4		11	5	1	0

The expected costs of each alternative can be calculated to be

$$E(A_1) = 0.3(\$0) + 0.2(\$2) + 0.25(\$6) + 0.25(\$9) = \$4.15$$
$$E(A_2) = 0.3(\$6) + 0.2(\$0) + 0.25(\$4) + 0.25(\$5) = \$4.05$$
$$E(A_3) = 0.3(\$9) + 0.2(\$2) + 0.25(\$0) + 0.25(\$4) = \$4.10$$
$$E(A_4) = 0.3(\$11) + 0.2(\$5) + 0.25(\$1) + 0.25(\$0) = \$4.55$$

The objective, to minimize expected costs, is thus satisfied by inventory level A_2.

Suppose it is observed that the industry's output (production) level for a given period is a modest basis for prediction of the retailer's level of demand for the next period. The nature of this leading correlation is reflected in Table 14-17.

Table 14-17 can be interpreted as follows: If the industry output level for a given period is, say, X_3, then the probability the retailer's demand level for the next period will be S_1 is 0.2; the probability the retailer's demand will be S_2 is 0.3, etc. Another way of stating, which is more in line with

Table 14-17

PROBABILITIES OF INDUSTRY OUTPUT LEVEL
FOR EACH LEVEL OF RETAILER'S DEMAND IN FOLLOWING PERIOD

Given the retailer's demand level for the next period will turn out to be _____ . . .	. . . the probabilities the industry output level is _____ are			
	X_1	X_2	X_3	X_4
S_1	0.5	0.2	0.2	0.1
S_2	0.2	0.4	0.3	0.1
S_3	0.1	0.3	0.4	0.2
S_4	0.0	0.2	0.3	0.5

previous examples, is that, given the retailer's demand level will turn out to be, say, S_3, the probability the industry produced, say, X_4 in the previous period is 0.2.

Using the results of Table 14-17, posterior probabilities can be calculated using the format suggested in Table 14-1 for each of the four outcome levels. The results are summarized in Table 14-18.

Table 14-18

INVENTORY EXAMPLE—SUMMARIZATION OF CALCULATED POSTERIOR PROBABILITIES OF RETAILER'S DEMAND FOR EACH INDUSTRY OUTPUT LEVEL

S_i	$P(S_i \mid X_1)$	$P(S_i \mid X_2)$	$P(S_i \mid X_3)$	$P(S_i \mid X_4)$
S_1	0.698	0.226	0.203	0.133
S_2	0.186	0.302	0.203	0.089
S_3	0.116	0.283	0.340	0.222
S_4	0.000	0.189	0.254	0.556

Skipping the illustration of several computational steps, Table 14-19 summarizes the expected inventory costs for each alternative given the industry output level and also indicates the best alternative and probability for each output level.

Table 14-19

EXPECTED COSTS FOR EACH RETAILER'S INVENTORY LEVEL ALTERNATIVE, GIVEN INDUSTRY OUTPUT LEVEL IS X_j

	Industry output level			
Alternative	X_1	X_2	X_3	X_4
$E(A_1)$	\$1.07	\$4.00	\$4.73	\$6.51
$E(A_2)$	\$4.65	\$3.43	\$3.85	\$4.47
$E(A_3)$	\$6.65	\$3.39	\$3.25	\$3.60
$E(A_4)$	\$8.72	\$4.28	\$2.13	\$2.13
Best alternative:	A_1	A_2	A_3	A_4
$P(X_j)$:	0.215	0.265	0.295	0.225

The expected cost given the sample information (industry output level) is calculated to be

(Expected cost $\mid$ SI) $= \$1.07(0.215) + \$3.39(0.265) + \$3.25(0.295)$
$$+ \$2.13(0.225) = \$2.57$$

The savings due to the additional study is

$$\text{EVSI} = \min E(A_i) - E(\text{cost} \mid \text{SI})$$
$$= \$4.05 - \$2.57 = \$1.48$$

An interpretation of the above result is that if there is, say, a financial newsletter reporting service which publishes this industry's output level, their information would be expected to be worth up to $1.48 per demand period to the retailer. The numbers for this hypothetical problem are arbitrary and may appear to be insignificant. However, it is noteworthy that the EVSI of $1.48 represents 36% of the expected inventory costs before the additional study.

Classical and Bayesian Statistical Decision Approaches Compared

Implicit in all statistical decision techniques is that there are risks whenever information is less than perfect. Both classical and Bayesian techniques involve decision rules to minimize risk. Classical inference techniques are more widely used than Bayesian techniques, but Bayesian techniques are widely acknowledged as the more powerful. They will be compared briefly below.

Classical inference technique categorizes error as either Type I, the error due to the rejection of a hypothesis incorrectly, or Type II, the error of accepting a hypothesis when it is not correct. For example, consider a quality control situation where the hypothesis is that a production lot is acceptable from a defect standpoint. In this case a Type I error occurs when a good lot is rejected, while a Type II error occurs when a bad lot is accepted. Typically, the classical technique objective is to minimize the Type II error subject to a restriction on the probability of committing a Type I error.

The Bayesian technique, on the other hand, is concerned with minimizing the expected opportunity loss (EOL) defined in Eq. 14-11. Another, more detailed definition is

$$\text{EOL} = \sum_i [P(e_i|S_i)\text{OL}(e_i|S_i)P(S_i)] \tag{14-13}$$

where $P(e_i|S_i)$ = Probability of erring given that state S_i is present
$\text{OL}(e_i|S_i)$ = Opportunity loss of not knowing that S_i is present
$P(S_i)$ = Prior probability of S_i occurring

Hence, the Bayesian technique is concerned not only with the probabilities of committing errors of accepting or rejecting the hypothesis incorrectly, but also with the opportunity losses due to error. Additionally, the prior probability of each hypothesis (state S_i) is factored into the decision rule.

As an example comparing the classical and Bayesian approaches, consider the following problem which neglects the time value of money. A firm, entering into a new product line, is trying to decide whether to buy fully automatic or semiautomatic equipment. The costs of equipment are $830,000 and $250,000, respectively. The variable unit costs of production are $60 for the fully automatic process; and $80 per unit for the first 29,000 units and $85 per unit in excess of the first 29,000 units for the semiautomatic equipment. The selling price is $100, and the estimated market ranges from 20,000 to 40,000 units. A sample technique is devised, and from this it is estimated that the probabilities of the total market demand being in the range of 20,000–25,000 units is 0.20, between 25,000–30,000 is 0.40, 30,000–35,000 is 0.30, and from 35,000–40,000 is 0.10. The expected demand determined by using the midpoints of each of these ranges is 29,000 units. At this quantity the profits using fully automatic equipment (A_1) can be calculated to be $330,000. The profit using semiautomatic equipment (A_2) also happens to be $330,000. Since this is a problem of uncertainty, the application of statistical decision techniques can be used as input for the decision as to which equipment to purchase.

The classical technique requires the establishment of a null hypothesis H_0 and an alternate hypothesis H_1. For this example suppose H_0 is taken to be that the market demand is at least 29,000 units. The alternative hypothesis H_1 would be that the demand is less than 29,000 units. The classical analyst has the problem of establishing a specific point for H_1 that is tested by sampling through setting an acceptable Type I error level.

When the decision rule is to accept the alternative hypothesis H_1 if the sample indicates 29,000 units or less, the probability of committing a Type I error, denoted α, approaches 0.50 as the true demand approaches 29,000. Similarly, the probability of accepting the null hypothesis incorrectly, denoted β, is also a maximum of 0.50 when the true demand is 29,000 units. The analyst can change his cut-off point for the acceptance of H_1 to a lower

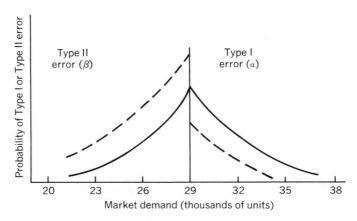

Figure 14-2. Probability of committing Type I and Type II errors for decision rule accept H_1 at or below 29,000 (solid line) and for decision rule accept H_1 at or below 27,000 (dashed line).

value—for example, 27,000 units. If this policy is adopted, the probability of α is reduced but β is increased. Figure 14-2 illustrates this point and indicates how α and β values change for varying levels of market demand.

To apply the Bayesian technique to this problem, one must consider the opportunity losses as well as the probabilities. If the demand is greater than 29,000 units and the semiautomatic equipment was chosen, then OL would be $(S - 29,000) \cdot \$25$, where S is true market demand and $25 is the $85 — $60 difference in unit costs. If the demand is less than 29,000 units and fully automatic equipment is chosen, the OL would be $(29,000 - S) \cdot \$20$. Figure 14-3 illustrates this loss function. The Bayesian technique would require

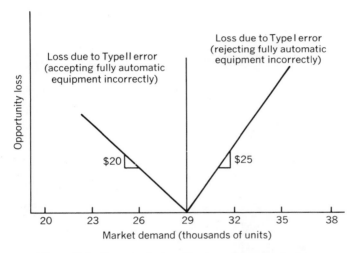

Figure 14-3. Opportunity loss if wrong alternative is chosen.

further sampling, computation of the posterior probabilities, and calculation of the EOL for each alternative. The decision would be to choose that alternative which would minimize the EOL. The following section gives convenient means of calculating the EOL when the possible outcomes are normally distributed. After that section, yet another example will be used to illustrate the calculation of EOL for a general two-alternative decision problem.

EOL With Continuous Distribution of Outcomes

If a project has a distribution of outcomes (expressed, say, in net P.W.) which ranges from positive to negative, then opportunity loss occurs whenever the outcome of the project is negative (or below some break-even cut-off point S_b). If the distribution of outcomes, denoted $f(S)$, is continuous, then the expected opportunity loss (expected value of perfect information) is the product of the amount the outcome is on the unfavorable side of the break-even point times $f(S)$ summed over all possible outcomes on that side of the break-even point. Thus,

$$\text{EOL} = \int_{-\infty}^{S_b} |S_b - S| \cdot f(S)\, dS \qquad (14\text{-}14)$$

As an example, suppose project Z has an expected net P.W., $E(S)$, of $20 million, that the outcomes are continuous, that the standard deviation $\sigma(S)$ is $15 million, and that the project is acceptable if the return in net P.W. is greater than or equal to the break-even value ($S_b = \$0$). Figure 14-4

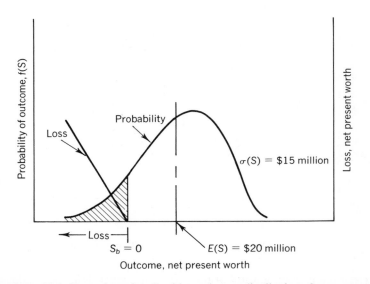

Figure 14-4. Example project Z, with continuous distribution of outcome.

represents this belief in the outcome of the project. Figure 14-5 represents the curve of the product of the distribution of S and the magnitude of the loss $S_b - S$. The area under the curve in Fig. 14-5 represents EOL.

When the outcome is normally distributed, convenient utilization of a "unit normal loss integral"* table (see Appendix A-D) can be made by the formula

---

*The "unit normal loss integral" is derived on p. 453 of Robert Schlaifer, *Probability and Statistics for Business Decisions* (New York: McGraw-Hill Book Company, 1958), and is equal to

$$f(S_b)\left[\frac{E(S) - S_b}{\sigma(S)}\right]\int_{-\infty}^{S_b} f(S)\, dS$$

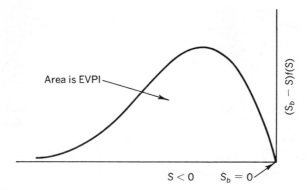

Figure 14-5. Product of the probability of outcome S by the magnitude of loss, $S_b - S$.

$$\text{EOL} = \sigma(S) \cdot \text{UNLI at } D \qquad (14\text{-}15)$$

where UNLI denotes the *unit normal loss integral*, and D equals $[E(S) - S_b]/\sigma(S)$. For the project Z example, given the outcome is normally distributed, UNLI at $D = (\$20 \text{ million} - 0)/\$15 \text{ million} = 1.33$ and can be found to be 0.0427 in Appendix A-D, and the expected opportunity loss can now be calculated as

$$\text{EOL} = \$15 \text{ million} \cdot \text{UNLI at } D = 1.33$$
$$= \$15 \text{ million}(0.0427) = \$0.6405 \text{ million}$$

Thus, the expected gain is $0.6405 million if the outcomes were known with certainty so that the investment in project Z could be averted when the net P.W. outcome is going to be negative.

The concept of UNLI can also be applied when the difference between the outcomes for the two projects can be expressed as a continuous normal distribution. For example, suppose two projects are each distributed normally as in Fig. 14-6.

The expected difference between the two projects is $7M − $6M = $1M. If the outcomes for the two projects are statistically independent, then the standard deviation of the distribution of the difference between the two projects is

$$\sigma_d(S) = \sqrt{(\$3\text{M})^2 + (\$4\text{M})^2} = \$5\text{M}$$

and that distribution is normal. Thus, the distribution of the difference between the two projects is as shown in Fig. 14-7.

The expected opportunity loss for the difference between the two projects can be calculated as

$$\$5\text{M} \times \text{UNLI at } D = \frac{\$1\text{M} - 0}{\$5\text{M}} = \$5\text{M} \times 0.3069 = \$1.535\text{M}$$

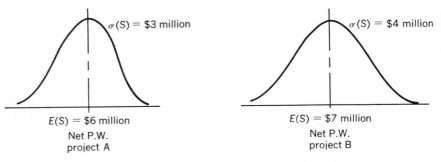

Figure 14-6. Outcome distributions for example projects.

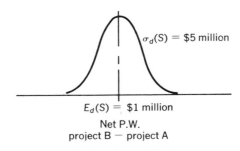

Figure 14-7. Distribution of difference between example projects.

This is a measure of the expected amount which can be gained by the perfect prediction of when project A will turn out better than project B (even though project B has a higher expected outcome) and then choosing project A at those times.

Appendix 14-A shows how one can conveniently determine the parameters of a posterior distribution when both the prior and added study distributions are normal.

Example:

An example two-alternative problem in which outcome is normally distributed: As a further example of the use of expected opportunity loss concepts and computational tools, suppose a firm is confronted with a decision as to which type of advertising contract to take with a trade journal. The first alternative A_1 is to pay a fixed rate of $3,000. The second alternative A_2 is to pay $30 per unit for the first 100 units sold and $5 per unit thereafter. The usual range of units sold is from 60 to 150 units because of the journal advertising. Additional information from the publisher gives the firm confidence that the number of units of this type and price sold through advertisement in this journal is normally distributed with a mean of 105 units and standard deviation of 15 units.

The loss functions can be generated from the above information. The break-even quantity S_b is 100 units at which the advertisement cost is \$3,000 for either contract. The opportunity loss function for A_1 occurs if the number of units sold is less than 100 and is

$$\mathrm{OL}(A_1 \mid S \le 100) = \$30(S_b - S)$$

Similarly, the loss function for A_2 occurs if the number of orders received is greater than 100 and is

$$\mathrm{OL}(A_2 \mid S \ge 100) = \$5(S - S_b)$$

Both the opportunity losses and the outcome function are depicted in Fig. 14-8.

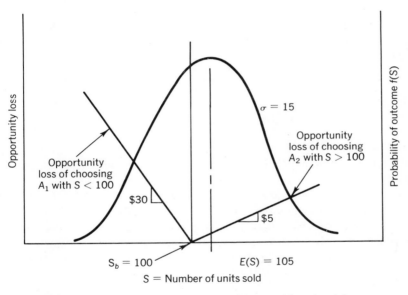

Figure 14-8. Example two-alternative decision problem involving two steps in determination of UNLI.

The characteristics of this type of problem in general are:

1. S is a random decision variable which is normally distributed.
2. There are two alternatives available. One alternative is preferred over one range of S, the other alternative is preferred over a second range of S.
3. There is a value of S, denoted S_b, at which the two alternatives are equally desirable.
4. A loss function equal to the opportunity loss due to the selection of the wrong alternative is definitive and is one or more linear functions of $|S - S_b|$.

The EOL for each alternative in the example depicted in Fig. 14-8 can now be computed. The UNLI for choosing the fixed contract A_1 is 0.2555 from the table in Appendix A-D when $D = (105 - 100)/15 = 0.33$. The UNLI for A_2 has to be calculated by adding two segments. Since the loss for choosing A_2 occurs when S is above 100 and since the mean is 105, then the section between 100 and 105 is one segment and from 105 to infinity or the right half of the normal curve is the other segment. From Appendix A-D, the UNLI at $D = 0.0$ is 0.3989. The UNLI at $D = (105 - 100)/15 = 0.33$ beyond the mean is the complement of the UNLI for one-half the curve less the UNLI for the portion beyond $D = 0.33$. From Appendix A-D, this is $0.3989 - 0.2555$, or 0.1434. Thus the total UNLI for A_2 is $0.3989 + 0.1434$ or 0.5423.

The loss value of one standard deviation from the break-even value S_b is equal to \$30 per unit times 15 units or \$450 for A_1, and is \$5 per unit times 15 units or \$75 for A_2. The EOL for each alternative can now be computed as

$$EOL(A_1) = \$\sigma(A_1) \cdot UNLI(A_1)$$
$$= \$450(0.2555) = \$115$$

and

$$EOL(A_2) = \$\sigma(A_2) \cdot UNLI(A_1)$$
$$= \$75(0.5423) = \$41$$

where (A_1) and (A_2) denote "for those alternatives," respectively. Since $EOL(A_2)$ is less than $EOL(A_1)$, alternative A_2, the variable rate contract, should be chosen.

Note that the probability of getting orders in excess of 100 is more likely than getting orders of less than 100—i.e., $P(S_i \geq 100) = 0.63$, per Appendix A-E. Thus, the probability that A_2 is the wrong alternative is 0.63 even though the indicated decision is to choose A_2. This decision considers not only probability of error, but also the magnitude of loss due to error. Herein lies the main difference between the classical inference and the Bayesian techniques.

PROBLEMS

14-1. The Quick Key Lock Company produces two types of locks and two models of each type. Below are summarized the probabilities of demand for each type and model:

Model	Type Cartridge (C)	Bolt (B)
Standard (S)	0.5	0.1
Pick-proof (P)	0.2	0.2

   a. What is $P(S)$? $P(P)$? $P(C)$? $P(B)$?

   b. What is the conditional probability of a lock being type B given that the lock is model P?

   c. What is $P(B|S)$?

   d. What is the joint probability of the bolt type being the pick-proof model?

   e. If one knew that a lock drawn randomly was of the bolt type, what is the probability that that particular lock is the standard model?

14-2. The Parcel Delivery Service has analyzed costs and longevity of their trucks. The length of service varies from $2\frac{1}{2}$ to $4\frac{1}{2}$ years with rare exception. The average cost per mile ranges from $0.105 to $0.165. The following matrix summarizes experience with 1,000 vehicles in which the ages and costs are shown discretely for simplicity.

	Cost per mile	
Length of service	*$0.12*	*$0.15*
3 yr	120	280
4	270	330

   a. What is the prior probability of the cost of $0.12 per mile? of $0.15 per mile? of 3 yr of service? of 4 yr?

   b. What are the following conditional probabilities: $P(\$0.12|3\ \text{yr})$? $P(\$0.15|3\ \text{yr})$? $P(\$0.12|4\ \text{yr})$? $P(\$0.15|4\ \text{yr})$?

   c. A truck at retirement is found to be in the $0.12 per mile category. What is the posterior probability that it is 4 yr old?

14-3. The Carolina Clay Company manufactures brick. A grading process occurs after each firing. A sample is drawn and a quality test is made. Grades A, B, and C have a 0.95, 0.75 and 0.50 proportion passing the quality test, respectively. Historically, the distribution of grade A, B, and C lots has been 32%, 44%, and 24% respectively.

   a. One brick is randomly drawn from each of 1,000 random lots. Fill in the matrix with the expected results.

	Pass	*Fail*	*Total*
Grade A			
Grade B			
Grade C			
Total			

   b. What is the probability of pass? fail?

   c. A lot of unknown grade was sampled once. The brick passed the test.

What are the posterior probabilities that the brick was drawn from a grade A lot? grade B lot? grade C lot?

14-4. The returns (in P.W.) for three investment alternatives are summarized below:

	Business condition		
Alternative	Good ($P = 0.25$)	Fair ($P = 0.55$)	Poor ($P = 0.20$)
A_1	$120,000	$60,000	$-$100,000
A_2	90,000	70,000	$-$ 40,000
A_3	$-$ 30,000	50,000	90,000

a. Based on the decision rule to maximize expected return, which alternative is best?

b. Which alternative(s) would be chosen if it were known with certainty that business conditions would be good, fair, or poor respectively?

c. What would be the expected return if perfect information were available?

d. What is the expected value of perfect information?

e. Construct an opportunity loss matrix.

f. On the basis of the decision rule to minimize EOL, which alternative should be chosen?

14-5. In Prob. 14-4, additional information conditional upon sample outcomes X_1 and X_2 is obtainable. The prior and posterior probabilities are presented below:

	Business conditions		
Probability	Good	Fair	Poor
Prior probability	0.25	0.55	0.20
Posterior probability if X_1 occurs	0.40	0.50	0.10
Posterior probability if X_2 occurs	0.10	0.60	0.30

The probabilities of X_1 or X_2 occurring are equally likely:

$$[P(X_1) = P(X_2) = 0.5]$$

a. Compute the $E(R)$ for each alternative if X_1 occurs; if X_2 occurs.

b. What is the $E(R)$ if sample information is obtained?

c. What is the value of the sample information?

d. What is the expected net gain if the sample information cost $5,000?

14-6. The net A.W. for project A is estimated to be normally distributed with a mean of $12,000 and a standard deviation of $8,000. What is the expected opportunity loss?

14-7. The net A.W. for project B is estimated to be normally distributed with a mean of $10,800 and a standard deviation of $6,000. What is the expected opportunity loss?

14-8. Given the two projects in Probs. 14-6 and 14-7, which is the better investment? Assuming that the outcomes for the two projects are independent, what is the expected opportunity loss for the difference between the two projects?

APPENDIX 14-A

Determining Posterior Distribution from Prior Distribution When Both Prior and Added-study Distributions Are Normal

This appendix contains a modification of developments by Schlaifer* for the determination of a posterior distribution when prior and sampling (added-study) distributions are normal and the sampling variance is known. In the usual economic analysis, there is no distribution of outcomes to actually sample from, but rather added study can be made and a subjective probability distribution formulated based on that added study. In this adaptation, Schlaifer's "sampling distribution" is replaced with what will be called an *added-study distribution*, i.e. , a distribution of the estimated outcomes based on the added study. The outcome of any variable or element pertinent to an economic analysis could be considered in this manner.

The same symbols as used by Schlaifer are used in this adaptation and are defined as

$E_1(\tilde{\mu})$ = Mean of posterior distribution
$E_0(\tilde{\mu})$ = Mean of prior distribution
$\bar{x}$ = Mean of distribution based on added study
$\sigma_1^2(\tilde{\mu})$ = Variance of posterior distribution
$\sigma_0^2(\tilde{\mu})$ = Variance of prior distribution
$\sigma^2(\tilde{x})$ = Variance of distribution based on added study

*Robert Schlaifer, *Probability and Statistics for Business Decisions* (New York: McGraw-Hill Book Company, 1958), pp. 440–448.

Schlaifer shows that when both the prior and added-study distributions of an outcome are normal with known means and variances, then the posterior distribution of the outcome is normal with the following parameter relations:

$$E_1(\tilde{\mu}) = \frac{E_0(\tilde{\mu})[1/\sigma_0^2(\tilde{\mu})] + \bar{x}[1/\sigma^2(\tilde{x})]}{1/\sigma_0^2(\tilde{\mu}) + 1/\sigma^2(\tilde{x})} \qquad (14\text{-}16)$$

and

$$1/\sigma_1^2(\tilde{\mu}) = 1/\sigma_0^2(\tilde{\mu}) + 1/\sigma^2(\tilde{x}) \qquad (14\text{-}17)$$

As an example of the use of the above adaptation of Schlaifer's developments, suppose that a certain cost element is to be estimated. Prior estimates (i.e., estimates before added study is undertaken) are that the distribution is normal with $E_0(\tilde{\mu}) = \$7,000$ and $\sigma_0^2(\tilde{\mu}) = 200,000$. Results of added study are that the outcome is normally distributed with $\bar{x} = \$6,000$ and $\sigma^2(\tilde{x}) = 66,667$. The posterior distribution resulting from these estimates is normal with the following calculated parameters:

$$E_1(\tilde{\mu}) = \frac{\$7,000(1/200,000) + \$6,000(1/66,667)}{1/200,000 + 1/66,667} = \$6,250$$

$$\frac{1}{\sigma_1^2(\tilde{\mu})} = \frac{1}{200,000} + \frac{1}{66,667}$$

Therefore,

$$\sigma_1^2(\tilde{\mu}) = 50,000$$

Note from the results of the above example that the posterior mean is closer to the mean based on added study than to the mean of the prior distribution. This is because the variance of the distribution based on the added study is less than the variance of the prior distribution, reflecting the greater confidence in the mean of the distribution based on added study. Note also that the variance of the posterior distribution is less than the variance of either the prior distribution or the distribution based on added study. This is because the combined information of the prior estimates and the estimates based on added study should provide a basis for as much (or more) confidence as the information of either one of those estimates alone.

Figures 14-A-1 and 14-A-2 demonstrate the effect of a wide range of conditions on parameters of the posterior distribution. Figure 14-A-1 shows the behavior of the posterior mean compared to the prior mean for various ratios of the means and the variances respectively. The ratios of variances that are of greatest interest are those between 0.00 and 1.00, since it is unlikely that the variance of the added-study distribution would be greater than the variance of the prior distribution. Figure 14-A-2 shows the variance of the posterior distribution as a function of the variances of the prior distribution and the added-study distribution.

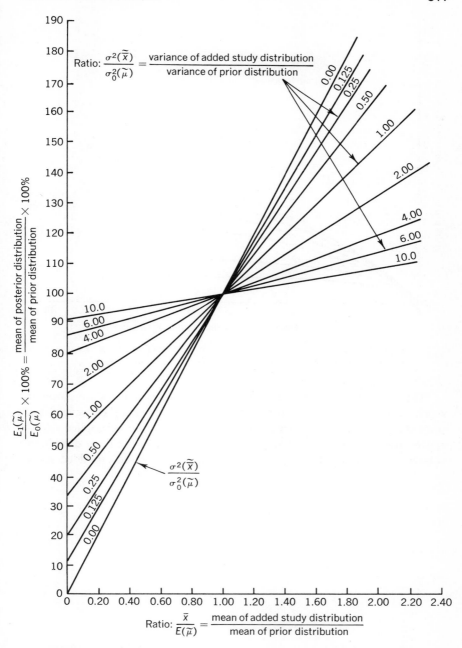

Figure 14-A-1. Posterior mean expressed as a percentage of prior mean for a wide range of $\frac{\bar{x}}{E_0(\tilde{\mu})}$ and $\frac{\sigma^2(\tilde{\tilde{x}})}{\sigma_0^2(\tilde{\mu})}$ conditions.

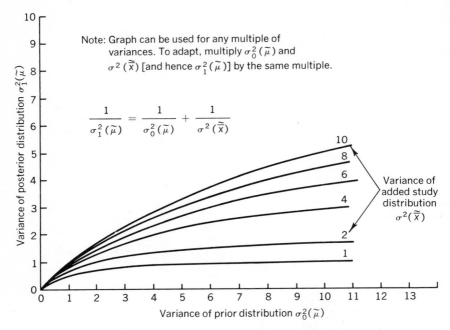

Figure 14-A-2. Variance of posterior distribution as a function of variance
of prior distribution and variance of added study distribution.

The formulas for the above adaptation of Schlaifer's developments
strictly apply when both input distributions are normal. However, if the
prior distribution is nonnormal, the same formulas can be applied without
appreciable loss in accuracy as long as the variance of the prior distribution
is large compared to the variance of the distribution based on added study.

fifteen

Use of Decision Tree Technique in Capital Project Evaluation*

The *decision tree technique* results from explicit recognition of the future alternatives, possible outcomes, and decisions which can result from an initial or "present" decision under question. It has great potential for practical development and application because it enables one to make an initial decision which includes explicit consideration of the risk and effect of the future.

The name *decision tree* stems from the appearance of a graphical portrayal, which shows branches for each possible alternative for a given decision and branches for each possible outcome (event) which can result from each alternative. To describe the concept and methodology of decision tree analysis, examples will be shown below.

Deterministic Example

The most basic form of decision tree occurs when each alternative can be assumed to result in a single outcome—that is, when certainty is assumed. The replacement problem in Fig. 15-1 illustrates this. The problem as shown

*This chapter is based largely on J. R. Canada, "Decision Tree Methodology in Capital Project Evaluation," *Proceedings of the 18th Annual Conference and Convention*, American Institute of Industrial Engineers, (May 1967), by permission of the publisher.

reflects that the decision on whether to replace the old machine with the new machine is not just a one-time decision, but rather one which recurs periodically. That is, if the decision is made to keep the old machine at decision point 1, then later, at decision point 2, a choice again has to be made. Similarly, if the old machine is chosen at decision point 2, then a choice again has to be made at decision point 3. For each alternative, the cash inflow is shown on the top of the arrow and the cash investment opportunity cost is shown below the arrow.

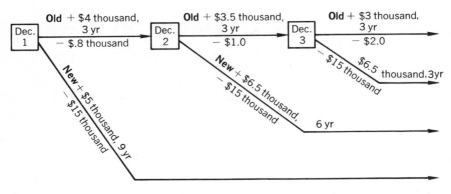

Figure 15-1. Deterministic replacement example.

For this problem one is concerned initially with which alternative to choose at decision point 1. But an intelligent choice at decision point 1 should take into account the later alternatives and decisions which stem from it. Hence, the correct procedure in analyzing this type of problem is to start at the most distant decision point, determine the best alternative and quantitative result of that alternative, and then "roll back" to each successive decision point, repeating the procedure until finally the choice at the initial or present decision point is determined. By this procedure, one can make a present decision which directly takes into account the alternatives and expected decisions of the future.

For simplicity in this example, timing of the monetary outcomes will first be neglected, which means that a dollar has the same value regardless of the year in which it occurs. Table 15-1 shows the necessary computations and decisions. Note that the monetary outcome of the best alternative at decision point 3 ($7.0M for the "Old") becomes part of the outcome for the "Old" alternative at decision point 2. Similarly, the best alternative at decision point 2 ($24.0M for the "New") becomes part of the outcome for the "Old" alternative at decision point 1.

By following the computations in Table 15-1, one can see that the answer is to keep the "Old" now and plan to replace it with the "New" at the end

Table 15-1

MONETARY OUTCOMES AND DECISIONS AT EACH
POINT—DETERMINISTIC REPLACEMENT EXAMPLE OF FIG. 15-1

Decision point	Alternative	Monetary outcome		Choice
3	Old	$3M(3) − $2M	= $ 7.0M	Old
	New	$6.5M(3) − $15M	= $ 4.5M	
2	Old	$7M + $3.5M(3) − $1M	= $16.5M	
	New	$6.5M(6) − $15M	= $24.0M	New
1	Old	$24M + $4M(3) − $0.8M	= $34.2M	Old
	New	$5M(9) − $15M	= $30.0M	

of 3 years. But this does not mean that the old machine should necessarily be kept for a full 3 years and then a new machine bought without question at the end of 3 years. Conditions may change at any time, thus necessitating a fresh analysis—probably a decision tree analysis—based on estimates which are reasonable in light of conditions at that later time.

Deterministic Example Considering Timing

For decision tree analyses, which involve working from the most distant decision point to the nearest decision point, the easiest way to take into account the timing of money is to use the present worth approach and thus

Table 15-2

DECISIONS AT EACH POINT WITH INTEREST = 25% PER YR FOR
DETERMINISTIC REPLACEMENT EXAMPLE OF FIG. 15-1

Decision point	Alternative	P.W. of monetary outcome		Choice
3	Old	$3M(P/A, 3) − $2M $3M(1.95) − $2M	= $3.85M	Old
	New	$6.5M(P/A, 3) − $15M $6.5M(1.95) − $15M	= −$2.30M	
2	Old	$3.85(P/F, 3) + $3.5M(P/A, 3) − $1M $3.85(0.512) + $3.5M(1.95) − $1M	= $7.89M	Old
	New	$6.5M(P/A, 6) − $15M $6.5M(2.95) − $15M	= $4.20M	
1	Old	$7.89M(P/F, 3) + $4M(P/A, 3) − $0.8M $7.89M(0.512) + $4M(1.95) − $0.8M	= $11.05M	Old
	New	$5.0M(P/A, 9) − $15M $5.0M(3.46) − $15M	= $2.30M	

discount all monetary outcomes to the decision points in question. To demonstrate, Table 15-2 shows computations for the same replacement problem of Fig. 15-1 using a discount rate of 25 % per yr.

Note from Table 15-2 that when taking into account the effect of timing by calculating present worths at each decision point, the indicated choice is not only to keep the "Old" at decision point 1, but also to keep the "Old" at decision points 2 and 3 as well. This result is not surprising since the high interest rate tends to favor the alternatives with lower initial investments, and it also tends to place less weight on long-term returns.

Consideration of Random Outcomes

The deterministic replacement example of Fig. 15-1 discussed above did not include one of the most powerful elements in the use of decision trees: the formal consideration of variable outcomes to which probabilities of occurrence can be assigned. Suppose that for each alternative there are two possible monetary outcomes, depending on whether the demand is "high" or "low." In such a case the decision tree problem of Fig. 15-1 would appear as in Fig. 15-2. Note that for each alternative in Fig. 15-2 there is shown a circle from which are drawn arrows to represent each possible chance event or state of nature which can result, such as demand being either "high" or "low."

In order to solve this problem—that is, to determine the best alternative for each decision point, etc.— it is necessary first to determine the outcome (usually expressed in monetary units) and the probability of occurrence for each possible chance event. Then the criterion (measure of merit) for choice (usually expected P.W. of monetary outcomes) can be decided and the solution computed by the same procedure as before; that is, criterion outcomes and decisions are determined for the most distant decision points first, and then the procedure is successively repeated, moving back in time until the decision for decision point 1 is determined.

Use of Bayesian Method to Evaluate the Worth of Further Investigation Study

One alternative that frequently exists in an investment decision problem is further research or investigation before deciding on the investment. This means making an intensive objective study, hopefully by a fresh group of people. It may involve such aspects as undertaking additional research and development study, making a new analysis of market demand, or possibly studying anew future operating costs for particular alternatives. As explained

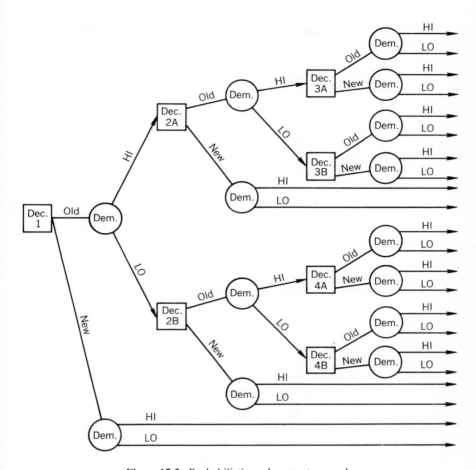

Figure 15-2. Probabilistic replacement example.

in Chapter 14, the concepts of Bayesian statistics provide a means for utilizing subsequent information to modify estimates of probabilities and also a means for estimating the value of further economic investigation study.

To illustrate, consider the one-stage decision situation shown in Fig. 15-3, in which each alternative has two possible chance outcomes: "high" or "low" demand. It is estimated that each outcome is equally likely to occur, and the monetary result expressed as P.W. is shown above the arrow for each outcome. Again, the amount of investment for each alternative is shown below the respective lines. Based on these amounts, the calculation of the expected monetary outcome (net P.W.) is shown in Table 15-3, which indicates that the "Old" should be chosen.

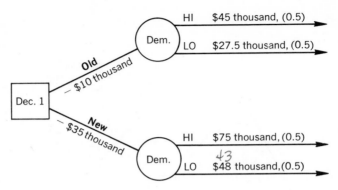

Figure 15-3. One-stage replacement problem.

Table 15-3

EXPECTED MONETARY OUTCOMES FOR PROBLEM IN FIG. 15-3

Old:	$45M(0.5) + $27.5M(0.5) − $10M = $26.25M
New:	$75M(0.5) + $48M(0.5) − $35M = $24.0M

To demonstrate the use of Bayesian statistics, suppose that one is considering the advisability of undertaking a fresh intensive investigation before deciding upon the "Old" versus the "New." Suppose also that this further study would cost $0.1M. In order to use the Bayesian approach, it is necessary for management to assess the conditional probabilities that the intensive investigation will yield certain results. These probabilities reflect explicit measures of management's confidence in the ability of the investigation to predict the outcome. Sample assessments are shown in Table 15-4. As an explanation, $P(h \mid H)$ means the probability that the predicted demand is "high," given that the actual demand will turn out to be "high."

Table 15-4

MANAGEMENT'S ASSESSMENT OF CONFIDENCE
IN INVESTIGATION RESULTS

$$P(h \mid H) = 0.70$$
$$P(h \mid D) = 0.20$$
$$P(d \mid H) = 0.30$$
$$P(d \mid D) = 0.80$$

Key:	*Investigation-predicted demand*	*Actual demand*
	h = High	H = High
	d = Low	D = Low

Once these assessments are obtained, then the Bayesian calculations for revised demand probabilities can be performed using Eq. 14-4. The calculations are shown in Table 15-5.

Table 15-5

BAYESIAN REVISION OF DEMAND PROBABILITIES

$$P(H\,|\,h) = \frac{P(h\,|\,H) \times P(H)}{P(h\,|\,H) \times P(H) + P(h\,|\,D) \times P(D)} = \frac{P(h\,|\,H) \times P(H)}{P(h)}$$

$$= \frac{0.7 \times 0.5}{0.7 \times 0.5 + 0.2 \times 0.5} = \frac{0.35}{0.45} = 0.78$$

$$P(d\,|\,h) = \frac{P(h\,|\,D) \times P(D)}{P(h)} = \frac{0.2 \times 0.5}{0.45} = 0.22$$

$$P(H\,|\,d) = \frac{P(d\,|\,H) \times P(H)}{P(d\,|\,H) \times P(H) + P(d\,|\,D) \times P(D)} = \frac{P(d\,|\,H) \times P(H)}{P(d)}$$

$$= \frac{0.3 \times 0.5}{0.3 \times 0.5 + 0.8 \times 0.5} = \frac{0.15}{0.55} = 0.27$$

$$P(D\,|\,d) = \frac{P(d\,|\,D) \times P(D)}{P(d)} = \frac{0.4 \times 0.5}{0.55} = 0.73$$

The probabilities calculated in Table 15-5 can now be used to assess the alternative of further investigation. Figure 15-4 shows a decision tree diagram for this alternative as well as the two original alternatives. Note the demand probabilities from Table 15-5 entered on the branches according to whether the investigation indicates "high" or "low" demand.

The expected outcome for the alternative of further investigation can now be calculated. This is done by the standard decision tree principle of determining the decision at the most distant points and working back. This is shown in Table 15-6. It is worthy of note that the 0.45 and 0.55 probabilities

Table 15-6

EXPECTED MONETARY OUTCOME FOR REPLACEMENT PROBLEM OF FIG. 15-4

Decision point	Alternative	Expected monetary outcome		Choice
2a	Old	$45M(0.78) + $27.5M(0.22) − $10M	= $31.13M	
	New	$75M(0.78) + $43M(0.22) − $35M	= $32.95M	New
2b	Old	$45M(0.27) + $27.5M(0.73) − $10M	= $21.20M	Old
	New	$75M(0.27) + $43M(0.73) − $35M	= $16.60M	
1	Further investigation	$32.95M(0.45) + $21.2M(0.55) − $0.1M	= $26.40M	Further investigation
	Keep old	(from Table 15-3):	26.25M	
	New	(from Table 15-3):	24.00M	

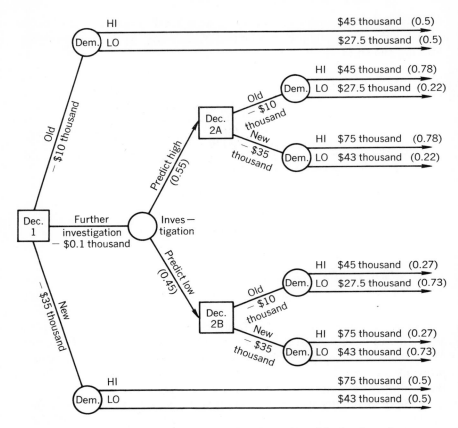

Figure 15-4. Replacement problem with alternative of further investigation.

that investigation-predicted demand will be "high" and "low," respectively, are obtained from the denominators of the Bayesian revision calculations shown in Table 15-5.

Thus, from Table 15-6, it can be seen that the alternative of further investigation, with an expected return of $26.40M, is the best present course of action by a slight margin. While the figures used here do not reflect much advantage to the further investigation, the advantage can be great.

Expected Opportunity Loss
(Value of Perfect Information)

It is possible to make calculations to aid judgment as to the maximum value further investigation, such as for the above problem, could be worth. One good approach is to calculate the expected opportunity loss (EOL), also denoted expected value of perfect information (EVPI) as explained in Chapter 14. Calculations of the EOL for the example replacement problem of Fig. 15-3 are shown in Table 15-7.

Table 15-7

EXPECTED OPPORTUNITY LOSS FOR ONE-STAGE
REPLACEMENT PROBLEM OF FIG. 15-3

If demand is	. . . then the preferred alternative is	And the monetary outcome is	The prior probability estimate is	Thus, the expected value is
High	New	$ 40M	0.5	$20.00M
Low	Old	17.5M	0.5	8.75M

Expected outcome with perfect foreknowledge: Σ = $28.75M
EOL = EVPI = $28.75M − $26.25M = $2.5M

Thus, the expected outcome with perfect foreknowledge, $28.75M, is greater than the expected value of the preferred alternative before the further investigation, $26.25M, by $2.5M, which is a measure of the maximum expected value of further investigation. For the example problem in Fig. 15-3 and Table 15-6, the further investigation resulted in an increase in the EVSI of only $0.25M of this $2.5M; i.e., $26.4M + $0.1M − $26.25M = $0.25M. The expected net value of sample information (ENVSI) in this case is $0.25M − $0.10M = $0.15M.

There is a practical limit to the amount of expenditure for further investigation which can be justified by the potential expected gains from that investigation. In general, the principle of diminishing marginal returns applies in this type of situation.

Examples of Decision Tree Applications

The decision tree technique can be useful in a very wide range of decision situations. To give some idea of the breadth of potential application, several examples follow.

Small vs. large asset

Figure 15-5 shows a situation in which a firm is initially faced with the decision between a small machine and a large machine for a use in which demand for the machine is uncertain but subject to probabilistic estimates. Further, if the firm should invest in a small machine now, it has the future

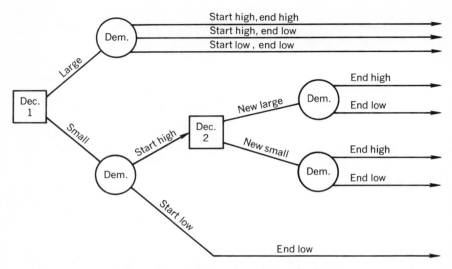

Figure 15-5. Small versus large machine example.

choice of whether to invest in another small machine according to the anticipated demand at the time of that future decision.

Facilities modernization

Figure 15-6 shows a situation in which a firm is faced with the decision
of whether to invest in major automation of the plant's facilities. The new
equipment is supposed to result in reduced labor cost, but its technical performance is critical and subject to variation. Also, the monetary outcome is
influenced strongly by the total market demand for the product and by
whether or not competitors also automate. The diagram shows two decision
stages, but, of course, further stages can be enumerated if that is thought
desirable.

Buy vs. lease building

Figure 15-7 depicts a simple buy vs. lease decision for building space in
which three stages are considered and the amount of use of the space is the
critical outcome subject to variation. Note that if initial use is high, there
is no further decision, regardless of whether the decision is to buy or lease
in the first stage. However, if use is low, then there are subsequent decisions
concerning whether to keep, abandon, or perhaps replace with a smaller
building.

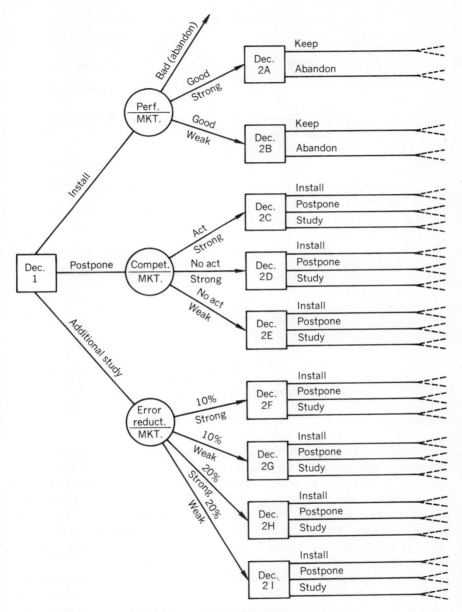

Figure 15-6. Facilities modernization example.

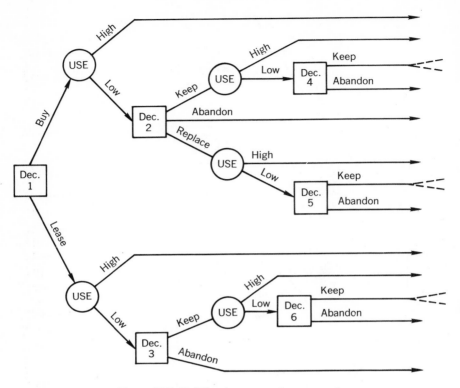

Figure 15-7. Building buy versus lease example.

Summary

The decision tree approach may appear to be complex, but it needs to be no more complex than the decision situation involved. Any investment problem can be examined at many levels of detail. A major difficulty in setting up a decision tree analysis is to strike the appropriate level. In general, the appropriate level is one which allows decision-makers to consider major future alternatives commensurate with the consequences of those alternatives without becoming so concerned with detail and refinement that the key factors are obscured.

Use of decision tree methodology as a basis for investment analysis, evaluation, and decision is a means for making explicit the process which should be at least intuitively present in good investment decision-making. Use of this methodology will help force a consideration of alternatives, define problems for further investigation, and clarify for the decision-maker the nature of the risks he faces and the estimates he must make.

Appendix 15-A contains the excellent article "Stochastic Decision Trees for the Analysis of Investment Decisions" by Richard F. Hespos and Paul A. Strassmann. Stochastic decision trees differ from the decision trees previously described in this chapter in that with the former the outcomes for any branch can be described in terms of a continuous probability distribution. The article also demonstrates the use of sensitivity analysis and computer simulation. It also provides a good supplement to the early part of this chapter regarding basic decision tree use and computation techniques.

PROBLEMS

15-1. Given the following two-stage decision situation, determine which is the best initial decision. Use the expected P.W. method and a minimum R.R. of 12%. To give the problem a physical context, the following letter symbols have been employed for each alternative:

BSW—Build small warehouse
RLW—Rent large warehouse
BA—Build addition
NC—No change

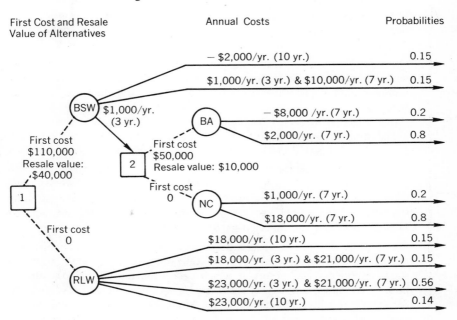

First Cost and Resale Value of Alternatives	Annual Costs	Probabilities
	− $2,000/yr. (10 yr.)	0.15
	$1,000/yr. (3 yr.) & $10,000/yr. (7 yr.)	0.15
BSW $1,000/yr. (3 yr.)	− $8,000 /yr. (7 yr.)	0.2
BA	$2,000/yr. (7 yr.)	0.8
First cost $110,000 Resale value: $40,000	First cost $50,000 Resale value: $10,000	
NC First cost 0	$1,000/yr. (7 yr.)	0.2
	$18,000/yr. (7 yr.)	0.8
First cost 0	$18,000/yr. (10 yr.)	0.15
	$18,000/yr. (3 yr.) & $21,000/yr. (7 yr.)	0.15
RLW	$23,000/yr. (3 yr.) & $21,000/yr. (7 yr.)	0.56
	$23,000/yr. (10 yr.)	0.14

15-2. A firm must decide between purchasing an automatic machine which costs $50,000 and will last 10 years and have 0 salvage value or purchasing a manual machine which costs $20,000 and will last 5 years and have 0 salvage value. If the manual machine is purchased initially, after 5 years a decision will have to be between a manual machine having the same characteristics affecting cost as the first manual machine and a semiautomatic machine costing $40,000 which would have a $20,000 salvage value after 5 years of life. The annual operating costs for each of the machines is as follows: automatic, $10,000; manual, $14,000; semiautomatic, $11,000.
   a. Graphically construct a decision tree to represent this situation.
   b. Determine which decision would be made at each point using the A.W. method and an interest of 10%.
   c. At what interest rate would the decision between the manual and semiautomatic machine be reversed?

15-3. Suppose one is faced with the same alternatives and dollar outcome consequences as in the replacement problem depicted in Fig. 15-4. However, the initial estimates of probability of demand are: high, 0.6; low, 0.4. Furthermore, management's assessment of confidence in further investigation results, using the notation in Table 15-4 are
   $$P(h\,|\,H) = 0.80$$
   $$P(h\,|\,D) = 0.40$$
   $$P(d\,|\,H) = 0.20$$
   $$P(d\,|\,D) = 0.60$$
   Calculate the choice at each decision point to determine the best initial decision. How close is the initial decision with these revised probabilities to the initial decision for the original problem depicted in Fig. 15-4?

15-4. On page 333 is a decision tree portrayal of a building lease vs. buy problem with input data supplied. Investment requirements are shown as negative numbers, and probabilities associated with each outcome are shown in parentheses. The annual cash savings and duration of those savings are shown together at each relevant outcome. Salvage values in the cases of abandonments are assumed to occur at the end of the 25-year study period. Determine the best decision using the expected net P.W. method with a minimum required R.R. of 0%.

15-5. On page 334 is a simplified portrayal of the relevant factors for deciding whether to start an applied research project. Determine the answer assuming that the decision points are each 1 year apart and the minimum required R.R. is 20%. Use the expected net P.W. method.

15-6. Set up a decision tree to reflect the personal automobile alternatives which you expect over the next several years. Carry the tree far enough in time to show several decision points at which a decision must be made between keeping an old car and buying a new car (from a possible choice of several). Show your roughly estimated assumed certain investment costs and salvage values and annual operating costs for each alternative and determine the best initial decision using the P.W. method and a 10% minimum personal opportunity cost of money.

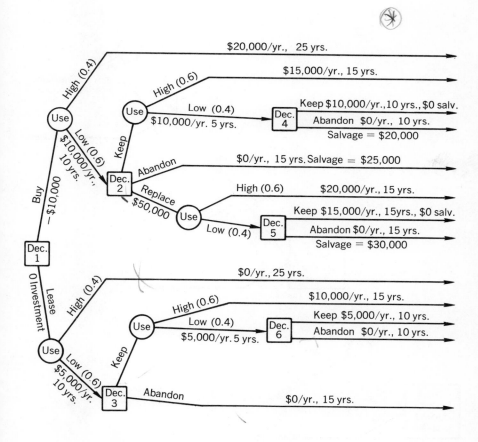

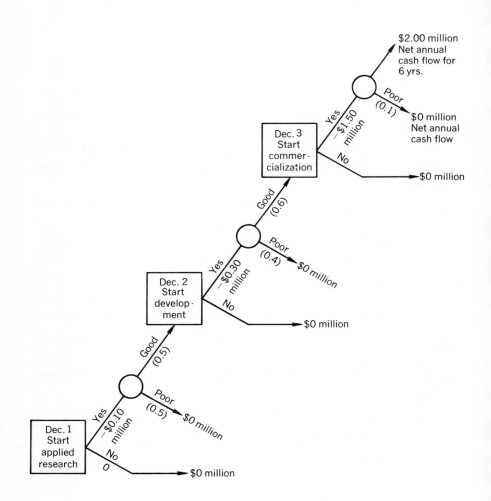

APPENDIX 15-A

Stochastic Decision Trees for the Analysis of Investment Decisions*

This paper describes an improved method for investment decision-making. The method, which is called the *stochastic decision tree method*, is particularly applicable to investments characterized by high uncertainty and requiring a sequence of related decisions to be made over a period of time. The stochastic decision tree method builds on concepts used in the risk analysis method and the decision tree method of analyzing investments. It permits the use of subjective probability estimates or empirical frequency distributions for some or all factors affecting the decision. This application makes it practicable to evaluate all or nearly all feasible combinations of decisions in the decision tree, taking account of both expected value of return and aversion to risk, thus arriving at an optimal or near-optimal set of decisions. Sensitivity analysis of the model can highlight factors that are critical because of high leverage on the measure of performance, or high uncertainty, or both. The method can be applied relatively easily to a wide variety of investment situations, and is ideally suited for computer simulation.

Investment decisions are probably the most important and most difficult decisions that confront top management, for several reasons. First, they involve enormous amounts of money. Investments of U.S. companies in plant and equipment alone are approaching $50 billion a year. Another $50 billion or so goes into acquisition, development of new products, and other investment expenditures.

Second, investment decisions usually have long-lasting effects. They often represent a "bricks and mortar" permanence. Unlike mistakes in inventory decisions, mistakes in investment decisions cannot be worked off in a short period of time. A major investment decision often commits management to a plan of action extending over several years, and the dollar penalty for reversing the decision can be high. Third, investments are implements of

*By Richard F. Hespos, McKinsey and Company, Inc., New York, and Paul A. Strassmann, National Dairy Products Corporation, New York. Reprinted from *Management Science*, Vol. 11, No. 10 (August 1965) by permission of the publisher.

strategy. They are the tools by which top management controls the direction of a corporation.

Finally, and perhaps most important, investment decisions are characterized by a high degree of uncertainty. They are always based on predictions about the future—often the distant future. And they often require judgmental estimates about future events, such as the consumer acceptance of a new product. For all of these reasons, investment decisions absorb large portions of the time and attention of top management.

Investment decision-making has probably benefited more from the development of analytical decision-making methods than any other management area. In the past 10 or 15 years, increasingly sophisticated methods have become available for analyzing investment decisions. Perhaps the most widely known of these new developments are the analytical methods that take into account the time value of money. These include the net present value method,* the discounted cash flow method, and variations on these techniques (Refs. 4, 13). Complementary to these time-oriented methods, a number of sophisticated accounting techniques have been developed for considering the tax implications of various investment proposals and the effects of investments on cash and capital position (Refs. 2, 12, 16). Considerable thought has been given to the proper methods for determining the value of money to a firm, or the cost of capital (Refs. 12, 13). The concepts of replacement theory have been applied to investment decisions on machine tools, automobile fleets, and other collections of items that must be replaced from time to time (Ref. 16).

In a somewhat different direction, techniques have been developed for the selection of securities for portfolios. These techniques endeavor to select the best set of investments from a number of alternatives, each having a known expected return and a known variability (Ref. 11). In this context, the "best" selection of investments is that selection that either minimizes risk or variability for a desired level of return, or maximizes return for a specified acceptable level of risk. (In general, of course, it is not possible to minimize risk and maximize return simultaneously.) The application of these techniques to corporate capital budgeting problems is conceivable but not imminent.

In the evolution of these techniques, each advance has served to overcome certain drawbacks or weaknesses inherent in previous techniques. However, until recently, two troublesome aspects of investment decision-making were not adequately treated, in a practical sense, by existing techniques. One of these problems was handling the uncertainty that exists in virtually all investment decisions. The other was analyzing separate but related investment decisions that must be made at different points in time.

*Author's Note: The net present value (denoted N.P.V. in this appendix) is the same as the net present worth (denoted net P.W.) used throughout the rest of this book.

Two recent and promising innovations in the methodology for analyzing investment decisions now being widely discussed are directed at these two problems. The first of these techniques is commonly known as risk analysis (Refs. 6, 8); the second involves a concept known as decision trees (Refs. 9, 10, 15). Each of these techniques has strong merits and advantages. Both are beginning to be used by several major corporations.

It is the purpose of this article to suggest and describe a new technique that combines the advantages of both the risk analysis approach and the decision tree approach. The new technique has all of the power of both antecedent techniques, but is actually simpler to use. The technique is called the *stochastic decision tree approach*.

To understand the stochastic decision tree approach, it is necessary to understand the two techniques from which it was developed. A review of these two techniques follows.

A Review of Risk Analysis

Risk analysis consists of estimating the probability distribution of each factor affecting an investment decision, and then simulating the possible combinations of the values for each factor to determine the range of possible outcomes and the probability associated with each possible outcome. If the evaluation of an investment decision is based only on a single estimate—the "best guess"—of the value of each factor affecting the outcome, the resulting evaluation will be at best incomplete and possibly wrong. This is true especially when the investment is large and neither clearly attractive nor clearly unattractive. Risk analysis is thus an important advance over the conventional techniques. The additional information it provides can be a great aid in investment decision making.

To illustrate the benefit of the risk analysis technique, Fig. 15-A-1 shows the results of two analyses of an investment proposal. First, the proposal was analyzed by assigning a single, "best-guess" value to each factor. The second analysis used an estimate of the probability distribution associated with each factor and a simulation to determine the probability distribution of the possible outcomes.

The best-guess analysis indicates a net present value of $1,130,000, whereas the risk analysis shows that the most likely combination of events gives the project an expected net present value of only $252,000. The conventional technique fails to take into account the skewed distributions of the various factors, the interactions between the factors, and is influenced by the subjective aspects of best guesses. Furthermore, the conventional analysis gives no indication that this investment has a 48% chance of losing money. Knowledge of this fact could greatly affect the decision made on

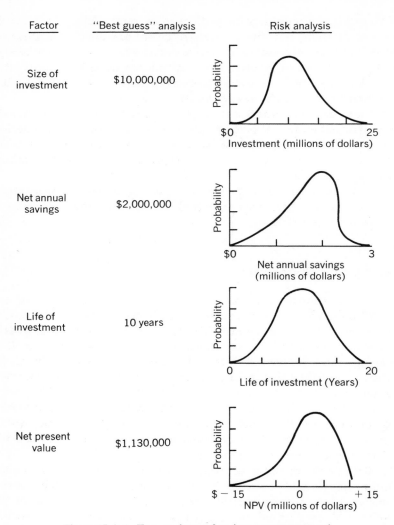

Figure 15-A-1. Two analyses of an investment proposal.

this proposal, particularly if the investor is conservative and has less risky alternatives available.

The risk analysis technique can also be used for a sensitivity analysis. The purpose of a sensitivity analysis is to determine the influence of each factor on the outcome, and thus to identify the factors most critical in the investment decision because of their high leverage, high uncertainty, or both. In a sensitivity analysis, equally likely variations in the values of each factor are made systematically to determine their effect on the outcome, or net

An unfavorable change of 10 percentiles from the mean value in this factor	*Which corresponds to a percentage change of*	*Would reduce N.P.V. by*
Annual net cash flow		
Sales level	12	17
Selling price	10	21
Manufacturing cost	18	58
Fixed cost	4	6
Amount of investment	5	12
Life of investment	12	30

Figure 15-A-2. Use of sensitivity analysis to highlight critical factors.

present value. Figure 15-A-2 shows the effect of individually varying each input factor (several of which are components of the net cash inflow).

This analysis indicates that manufacturing cost is a highly critical factor, both in leverage and uncertainty. Knowing this, management may concentrate its efforts on reducing manufacturing costs or at least reducing the uncertainty in these costs.

Risk analysis is rapidly becoming an established technique in American industry. Several large corporations are now using various forms of the technique as a regular part of their investment analysis procedure (Refs. 1, 3, 7, 17, 18). A backlog of experience is being built up on the use of the technique, and advances in the state of the art are continually being made by users. For example, methods have been devised for representing complex interrelationships among factors. Improvements are also being made in the methods of gathering subjective probability estimates, and better methods are being devised for performing sensitivity analysis.

One aspect of investment decisions still eludes the capabilities of this technique. This is the problem of sequential decision-making—that is, the analysis of a number of highly interrelated investment decisions occurring at different points in time. Until now no extension of risk analysis has been developed that can handle this problem well.

A Review of Decision Trees

The decision tree approach, a technique very similar to dynamic programming, is a convenient method for representing and analyzing a series of investment decisions to be made over time (see Fig. 15-A-3). Each decision point is represented by a numbered square at a fork or node in the decision tree. Each branch extending from a fork represents one of the alternatives that can be chosen at this decision point. At the first decision point the two

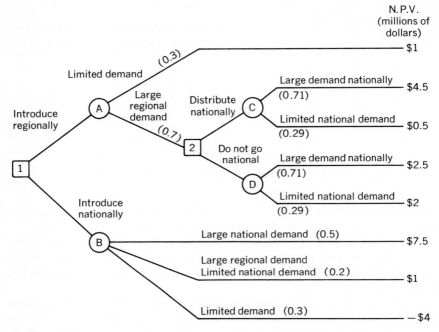

Figure 15-A-3. Use of decision tree to analyze investment alternatives for a new product introduction.

alternatives in the example shown in Fig. 15-A-3 are "introduce product nationally" and "introduce product regionally." (It is assumed at this point that the decision has already been made to introduce the product in *some* way.)

In addition to representing management decision points, decision trees represent chance events. The forks in the tree where chance events influence the outcome are indicated by circles. The chance event forks or nodes in the example represent the various levels of demand that may appear for the product.

A node representing a chance event generally has a probability associated with each of the branches emanating from that node. This probability is the likelihood that the chance event will assume the value assigned to the particular branch. The total of such probabilities leading from a node must equal 1. In our example, the probability of achieving a large demand in the regional introduction of the product is 0.7, shown at the branch leading from node A. Each combination of decisions and chance events has some outcome (in this case, net present value, or N.P.V.) associated with it.

The optimal sequence of decisions in a decision tree is found by starting at the right-hand side and "rolling backward." At each node, an expected

Alternative	Chance event	Probability of chance event	Net present value	Expected N.P.V.
Introduce product nationally	Large national demand	0.5	$ 7.5	
	Large regional, limited national demand	0.2	1.0	$2.75
	Limited demand	0.3	−4.0	
Introduce product regionally (and distribute nationally if regional demand is large)	Large national demand	0.5	4.5	
	Large regional, limited national demand	0.2	−0.5	2.44
	Limited demand	0.3	1.0	
Introduce product regionally (and do not distribute nationally)	Large national demand	0.5	2.5	
	Large regional, limited national demand	0.2	2.0	1.95
	Limited demand	0.3	1.0	

Figure 15-A-4. Net present value of investment alternatives for a new product introduction.

N.P.V. must be calculated. If the node is a chance event node, the expected N.P.V. is calculated for *all* of the branches emanating from that node. If the node is a decision point, the expected N.P.V. is calculated for *each* branch emanating from that node, and the highest is selected. In either case, the expected N.P.V. of that node is carried back to the next chance event or decision point by multiplying it by the probabilities associated with branches that it travels over.

Thus, in Fig. 15-A-3 the *expected* N.P.V. of all branches emanating from chance event node C is $3.05 million ($4.5 × 0.71 − $0.5 × 0.29). Similarly, the expected N.P.V. at node D is $2.355 million. Now "rolling back" to the next node—decision point 2—it can be seen that the alternative with the highest N.P.V. is "distribute nationally," with an N.P.V. of $3.05 million. This means that, if the decision-maker is ever confronted with the decision at node 2, he will choose to distribute nationally, and will expect an N.P.V. of $3.05 million. In all further analysis he can ignore the other decision branch emanating from node 2 and all nodes and branches that it may lead to.

To perform further analysis, it is now necessary to carry this N.P.V. backward in the tree. The branches emanating from chance event node A have an overall expected N.P.V. of $2.435 million ($1 × 0.3 + $3.05 × 0.7). Similarly, the expected N.P.V. at node B is 2.75 million. These computations, summarized in Fig. 15-A-4, show that the alternative that maximizes expected N.P.V. of the entire decision tree is "introduce nationally" at decision point 1. (Note that in this particular case there are *no* subsequent decisions to be made.)

One drawback of the decision tree approach is that computations can quickly become unwieldy. The number of end points on the decision tree increases very rapidly as the number of decision points or chance events increases. To make this approach practical, it is necessary to limit the number

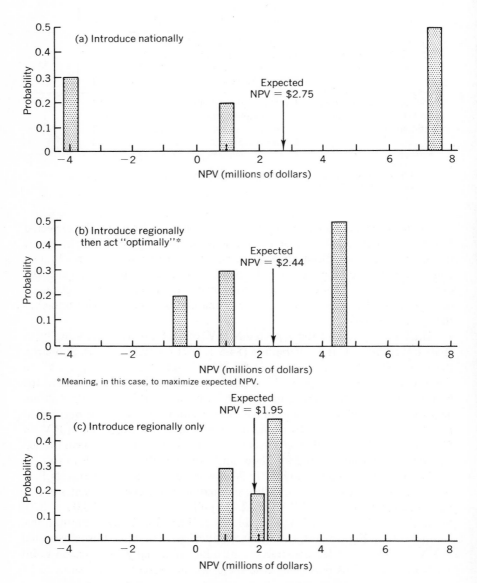

Figure 15-A-5. Range of possible outcomes for each of three alternatives.

of branches emanating from chance event nodes to a very small number. This means that the probability distribution of chance events at each node must be represented by a very few point estimates.

As a result, the answers obtained from a decision tree analysis are often inadequate. The single answer obtained (say, net present value) is usually close to the expectation of the probability distribution of all possible N.P.V.'s However, it may vary somewhat from the expected N.P.V., depending on how the point estimates were selected from the underlying distributions and on the sensitivity of the N.P.V. to this selection process. Furthermore, the decision tree approach gives *no* information on the range of possible outcomes from the investment or the probabilities associated with those outcomes. This can be a serious drawback.

In the example in Figs. 15-A-3 and 15-A-4, the decision tree approach indicated that introducing the product nationally at once would be the optimal strategy for maximizing expected N.P.V. However, the N.P.V. of $2.75 million is simply the mean of three possible values of N.P.V., which are themselves representative of an entire range of possible values, as shown in Fig. 15-A-5(a). Comparing the range of N.P.V.s possible under each possible set of decisions shows a vastly different view of the outcome. [See Figs. 15-A-5(b) and 15-A-5(c).]

Although the first alternative has the highest expected N.P.V., a rational manager could easily prefer one of the other two. The choice would depend on the utility function or the aversion to risk of the manager or his organization. A manager with a linear utility function would choose the first alternative, as shown in Fig. 15-A-6(a). However, it is probably true that *most* managers would *not* choose the first alternative because of the high chance of loss, and the higher utility value that they would assign to a loss, as shown

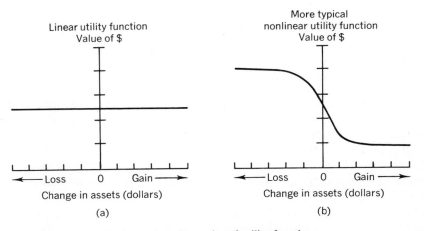

Figure 15-A-6. Examples of utility functions.

in Fig. 15-A-6(b). This conservatism in management is, to a large extent, the result of the system of rewards and punishments that exists in many large corporations today. Whether it is good or bad is a complex question, not discussed here.

In spite of these shortcomings, the decision tree approach is a very useful analytical tool. It is particularly useful for conceptualizing investment planning and for controlling and monitoring an investment that stretches out over time. For these reasons, the decision tree approach has been, and will continue to be, an important tool for the analysis of investment decisions.

Combining These Approaches: Stochastic Decision Trees

The complementary advantages and disadvantages of risk analysis and decision trees suggest that a new technique might be developed that would combine the good points of each and eliminate the disadvantages. The concept of stochastic decision trees, introduced in the remainder of this article, is intended to be such a combination.

The stochastic decision tree approach is similar to the conventional decision tree approach, except that it also has the following features:

1. All quantities and factors, including chance events, can be represented by continuous empirical probability distributions.
2. The information about the results from any or all possible combinations of decisions made at sequential points in time can be obtained in a probabilistic form.
3. The probability distribution of possible results from any particular combination of decisions can be analyzed using the concepts of utility and risk.

A discussion of each of these features follows.

Replacement of chance event nodes by probability distributions

The inclusion of probability distributions for the values associated with chance events is analogous to adding an arbitrarily large number of branches at each chance event node. In a conventional decision tree, the addition of a large number of branches can serve to represent any empirical probability distribution. Thus in the previous example, chance event node B can be made to approximate more closely the desired continuous probability distribution by increasing the number of branches, as shown in Figs. 15-A-7(a) and 15-A-7(b). However, this approach makes the tree very complex, and computation very quickly becomes burdensome or impractical. Therefore,

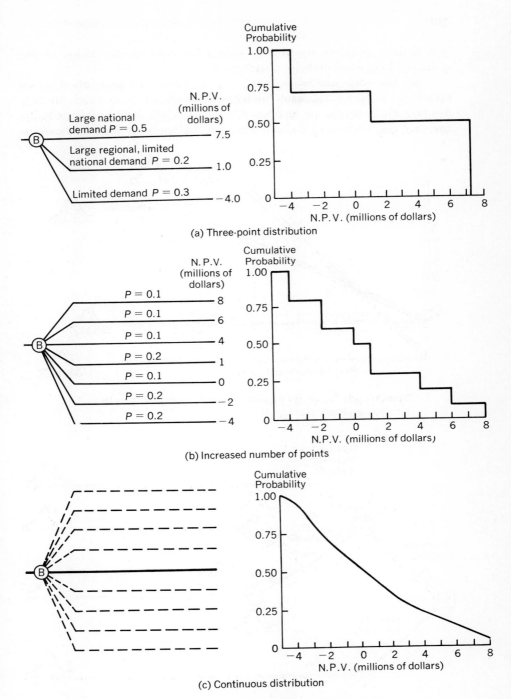

(a) Three-point distribution

(b) Increased number of points

(c) Continuous distribution

Figure 15-A-7. Probability distributions at chance event modes.

two or three branches are usually used as a coarse approximation of the actual continuous probability distribution.

Since the stochastic decision tree is to be based on simulation, it is not necessary to add a great many branches at the chance event nodes. In fact, it is possible to reduce the number of branches at the chance event nodes to *one*. [See Fig. 15-A-7(c).] Thus, in effect, the chance event node can be *elimi-*

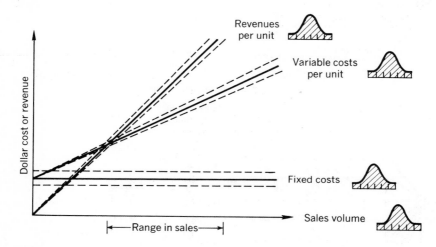

Figure 15-A-8. Typical probabilistic economic model used to select values of factors at chance event modes.

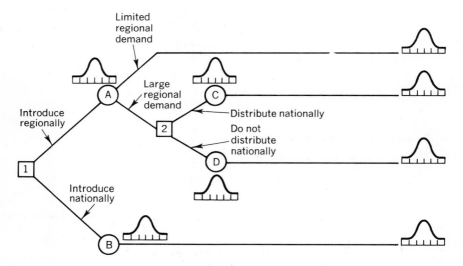

Figure 15-A-9. Simplified decision tree.

nated. Instead, at the point where the chance event node occurred, a random selection is made on each iteration from the appropriate probabilistic economic model such as the break-even chart shown in Fig. 15-A-8 and the value selected is used to calculate the N.P.V. for that particular iteration. The single branch emanating from this simplified node then extends onward to the next management decision point, or to the end of the tree. This results in a drastic streamlining of the decision tree as illustrated in Fig. 15-A-9.

Replacement of all specific values by probability distributions

In a conventional decision tree, factors such as the size of the investment in a new plant facility are often assigned specific values. Usually these values are expressed as single numbers, even though these numbers are often not known with certainty.

If the values of these factors could be represented instead by probability distributions, the degree of uncertainty characterizing each value could be expressed. The stochastic decision tree approach makes it possible to do this. Since the approach is basically a simulation, any or all specific values in the investment analysis can be represented by probability distributions. On each iteration in the simulation, a value for each factor is randomly selected from the appropriate frequency distribution and used in the computation. Thus, in the example, N.P.V. can be calculated from not only empirical distributions of demand, but also probabilistic estimates of investment, cost, price, and other factors.

Evaluating all possible combinations of decisions

Since this stochastic decision tree approach greatly simplifies the structure of the decision tree, it is often possible to evaluate by complete enumeration all of the possible paths through the tree. For example, if there are five sequential decisions in an analysis and each decision offers two alternatives, there are at most 32 possible paths through the decision tree. This number of paths is quite manageable computationally. And since most decision points are two-sided ("build" or "don't build," for example), or at worst have a very small number of alternatives, it is often feasible and convenient to evaluate all possible paths through a decision tree when the stochastic decision tree approach is used.

Why is it sometimes desirable to evaluate all possible paths through a decision tree? As the inquiry into the risk analysis approach showed, decisions cannot always be made correctly solely on the basis of a single expected value for each factor. The roll-back technique of the conventional decision tree necessarily deals only with expected values. It evaluates decisions (more exactly, sets of decisions) by comparing their expectations and selects the largest as the best, in all cases.

However, the stochastic decision tree approach produces *probabilistic* results for each possible set of decisions. These probability distributions, associated with each possible path through the decision tree, can be compared on the basis of their expectations alone, if this is considered to be sufficient. But alternative sets of decisions can *also* be evaluated by comparing the probability distributions associated with each set of decisions, in a manner exactly analogous to risk analysis. (The details of this technique are discussed in the next section.) Thus, the stochastic decision tree approach makes it possible to evaluate a series of interrelated decisions spread over time by the same kinds of risk and uncertainty criteria that one would use in a conventional risk analysis.

In a large decision tree problem, even with the simplifications afforded by the stochastic decision tree approach, complete enumeration of all possible paths through the tree could become computationally impractical, or the comparison of the probability distributions associated with all possible paths might be too laborious and costly.

In such a case, two simplifications are possible. First, a *modified* version of the roll-back technique might be used. This modified roll-back would take account of the probabilistic nature of the information being handled. Branches of the tree would be eliminated on the basis of dominance rather than simply expected value (Ref. 7). For example, a branch could be eliminated if it had both a lower expected return and a higher variance than an alternative branch. A number of possible sets of decisions could be eliminated this way without being completely evaluated, leaving an efficient set of decision sequences to evaluate in more detail.

Computation could also be reduced by making decision rules before the simulation, such that if, on any iteration, the value of a chance event exceeds some criterion, the resulting decision would not be considered at all. This has been done in the example shown in Fig. 15-A-3. If a limited demand appears at node A, national introduction of the product will not be evaluated. In the simulation, if demand were below some specified value, the simulation would not proceed to the decision point 2. This technique only saves computation effort—it does not simplify the structure of the tree, and if the criterion is chosen properly, it will not affect the final outcome.

Recording results in the form of probability distributions

It has already been shown that probability distributions are more useful than single numbers as measures of the value of a particular set of decisions. The simulation approach to the analysis permits one to get these probability distributions relatively easily. It is true that the method smacks of brute force. However, the brute force required is entirely on the part of the computer and not at all on the part of the analyst.

The technique is simply this: On each iteration or path through the decision tree, when the computer encounters a binary decision point node, it is instructed to "split itself in two" and perform the appropriate calculations along *both* branches of the tree emanating from the decision node. (The same logic applies to a node with three or more branches emanating from it.) Thus, when the computer completes a single iteration, an N.P.V. will have been calculated for each possible path through the decision tree. These N.P.V.'s are accumulated in separate probability distributions. This simulation concept is illustrated in Fig. 15-A-10.

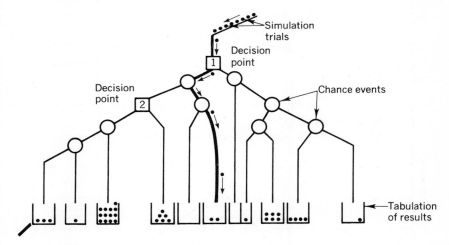

Figure 15-A-10. The GPSS concept of decision trees with risk simulation.

At the completion of a suitable number of iterations, there will be a probability distribution of the N.P.V. associated with each set of decisions that it is possible to make in passing through the tree. These different sets of decisions can then be compared, one against the other, in the usual risk analysis manner, as if they were alternative investment decisions (which in fact they are). That is, they can be compared by taking into account not only the expected return, but also the shape of each probability distribution and the effects of utility and risk. On the basis of this, one can select the single best set of decisions, or a small number of possibly acceptable sets of sequential decisions can then be evaluated and a decision whether or not to undertake the investment can be made by comparing it to alternative investments elsewhere in the corporation or against alternative uses for the money.

An example

To illustrate the kinds of results that can be expected from a stochastic decision tree analysis, the new product introduction problem described earlier has been solved using this method. The results are shown in Fig. 15-A-11.

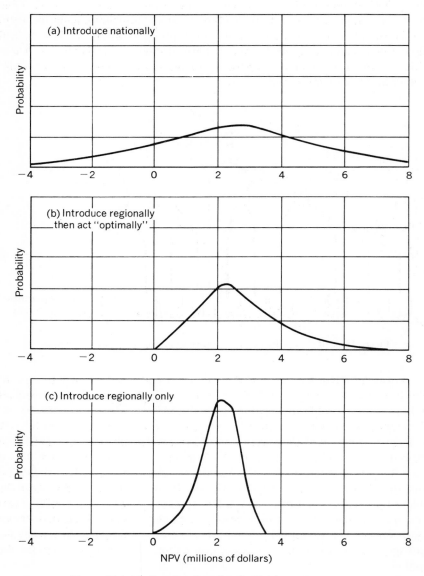

Figure 15-A-11. Results of stochastic decision tree analysis.

The differences in the expected values of the outcomes can now be seen in proper perspective, since the results show the relationship of the expected values to the entire distribution of possible outcomes. Moreover, the expected values of these distributions will not necessarily be identical with expectations resulting from the conventional decision tree approach, because

1. the interdependencies among the variables were not accounted for by the conventional approach;
2. the small number of point estimates used to approximate an entire distribution under the conventional approach did not utilize all the available information.

With the three alternatives presented in this form, it is easier to understand why a rational manager might choose an alternative other than the one with the highest expected value. Presented with the full range of possible outcomes related to each alternative, he can select that alternative most consistent with his personal utility and willingness to take risk.

Using the Stochastic Decision Tree Approach

Stochastic decision trees described here combine the best features of both risk analysis and conventional decision trees and are actually simpler to construct and use than either of these. The steps for collecting data and conceptualizing the problem are the same for the stochastic decision tree approach as they are for the risk analysis approach. These steps are:

1. Gather subjective probability estimates of the appropriate factors affecting the investment.
2. Define and describe any significant interdependencies among factors.
3. Specify the probable timing of future sequential investment decisions to be made.
4. Specify the model to be used to evaluate the investment.

The stochastic decision tree approach is ideally suited to the computer language known as General Purpose Systems Simulator (GPSS) (Refs. 5, 14). Although this language is not now capable of handling very complex interdependencies without certain modifications, it permits the solution of a very wide range of investment problems.

The structuring and solving of several sample problems have indicated that the stochastic decision tree approach is both easy to use and useful. The example in Fig. 15-A-4, 15-A-5, and 15-A-6 shows emphatically how the stochastic decision tree approach can detect and display the probable outcomes of an investment strategy that would be deemed optimal by the conventional decision tree approach, but that many managements would definitely regard as undesirable. Other work is being done on both sample problems and real world problems, and on the development and standardization (to a limited extent) of the computer programs for performing this analysis.

Summary

The stochastic decision tree approach to analyzing investment decisions is an evolutionary improvement over previous methods of analyzing investments. It combines the advantages of several earlier approaches, eliminates several disadvantages, and is easier to apply.

References

1. Anderson, S. L. and H. G. Haight, "A Two-by-Two Decision Problem," *Chemical Engineering Progress*, Vol. 57, No. 5 (May 1961).

2. Anthony, Robert N. (ed.), *Papers on Return on Investment* (Boston: Harvard Business School. 1959).

3. "Chance Factors, Meaning and Use," Atlantic Refining Company, Producing Department (July 1962).

4. Dean, Joel, *Capital Budgeting* (New York: Columbia University Press, 1951).

5. Gordon, G., "A General Purpose Systems Simulator," *IBM Systems Journal*, Vol. I (September 1962).

6. Hertz, David B., "Risk Analysis in Capital Investment," *Harvard Business Review* (January–February 1964).

7. Hess, Sidney W. and Harry A. Quigley, "Analysis of Risk in Investments Using Monte Carlo Technique," Chemical Engineering Progress Symposium Vol. 59, No. 42.

8. Hillier, Frederick, S., Stanford University, "The Derivation of Probabilistic Information for the Evaluation of Risky Investments," *Management Science* (April 1963).

9. Magee, John F., "Decision Trees for Decision Making," *Harvard Business Review* (July–August 1964).

10. Magee, John F., "How to Use Decision Trees in Capital Investment," *Harvard Business Review* (September–October 1964).

11. Markowitz, Harry, *Portfolio Selection, Efficient Diversification of Investments* (New York: John Wiley & Sons, 1959).

12. Masse, Pierre, *Optimal Investment Decisions* (Englewood Cliffs, N.J.: Prentice Hall, Inc., 1962.)

13. McLean, John G., "How to Evaluate New Capital Investments," *Harvard Business Review* (November–December 1958).

14. Reference Manual, General Purpose Systems Simulator II, IBM, 1963.

15. Schlaifer, Robert, *Probability and Statistics for Business Decisions* (New York: McGraw-Hill Book Company, 1959).

16. Terborgh, George, *Business Investment Policy* (Washington, D.C.: Machinery and Allied Products Institute, 1958).

17. Thorne, H. C. and D. C. Wise, American Oil Company, "Computers in Economic Evaluation," *Chemical Engineering* (April 29, 1963).

18. "Venture Analysis," Chemical Engineering Progress Technical Manual, American Institute of Chemical Engineers.

sixteen

Special Analytical Techniques for Project Probabilistic Monetary Comparison*

This chapter explains some special simplified analytical techniques for the calculation of means and variances and the selection among projects using probabilistic monetary comparison procedures. While these techniques are not now used commonly in practice, they have great potential for advancing the quantitative consideration of risk in project analyses because of their simplified features.

Mean and Variances

The net present worth of one life cycle for a project can be expressed as

$$\text{P.W.} = \sum_{n=0}^{N} X_n e^{-in} \tag{16-1}$$

where P.W. = Present worth (in dollars)
X_n = Cash flow for the nth yr
e^{-in} = Single sum present worth factor at $i\%$ interest for n yr (continuous compounding)

---

*This chapter is adapted from John R. Canada and Harrison W. Wadsworth, "Methods for Quantifying Risk in Economic Analyses of Capital Projects," *Journal of Industrial Engineering*, Vol. 19, No. 7 (January 1968), with the permission of the publisher.

A simplified form of Eq. (16-1) which is common in practical use is

$$\text{P.W.} = P + \frac{D(1 - e^{-iN})}{i} + Fe^{-iN} \tag{16-2}$$

where P = Initial investment (at the same time as P.W.)

   D = Net annual receipt or disbursement amount (assumed to be a constant flow through each year during the project life)

   F = Salvage or resale value (at end of life, N yr)

$(1 - e^{-iN})/i$ = Uniform series present worth factor at $i\%$ for N yr (for continuous compounding, continuous payment flow)

If the elements P, D, F, and N are all random variables with certain estimable characteristics, it is possible to obtain measures of the mean and variance of the distribution of P.W.

For most practical economic analyses, a sufficiently close approximation of the expected net P.W., $E(\text{P.W.})$, can be obtained merely by evaluating Eq. (16-2) at the expected values for each of the elements or variables. This is similar to the usual assumed certainty approach.

If F and D are each independent of N, the expected value of Eq. (16-2) may be accurately shown to be

$$E(\text{P.W.}) = E(P) + E(D) \cdot \frac{E(1 - e^{-iN})}{i} + E(F) \cdot E(e^{-iN}) \tag{16-3}$$

where E denotes the expected value.

If all of the four elements comprising P.W. are mutually independent variables, the variance of the distribution of P.W. may be conveniently and closely approximated by the use of the first two terms of the Taylor series expansion of P.W. as

$$V(\text{P.W.}) = \left(\frac{\partial \text{P.W.}}{\partial P}\right)^2 \cdot V(P) + \left(\frac{\partial \text{P.W.}}{\partial D}\right)^2 \cdot V(D)$$

$$+ \left(\frac{\partial \text{P.W.}}{\partial N}\right)^2 \cdot V(N) + \left(\frac{\partial \text{P.W.}}{\partial F}\right)^2 \cdot V(F) \tag{16-4}$$

where V denotes the variance and ∂ is the partial derivative operator. Equation (16-4) is a particularly good approximation when each of the elements—P, D, N, and F—is mutually independent. As a side note, if each of the elements is normally distributed as well as independent, then the distribution of P.W. is approximately normally distributed.

Note that the preceding formula does not consider variation in the interest rate. If it is desired to consider variation in interest rate or in any other element, another term similar to the four terms on the right-hand side of Eq. (16-4) may be added for each additional element considered. As a means of saving manual computations, Figs. 16-1 through 16-3 allow the reader to obtain $(\partial \text{P.W.}/\partial N)^2$, $(\partial \text{P.W.}/\partial F)^2$, and $(\partial \text{P.W.}/\partial D)^2$, respectively, for a

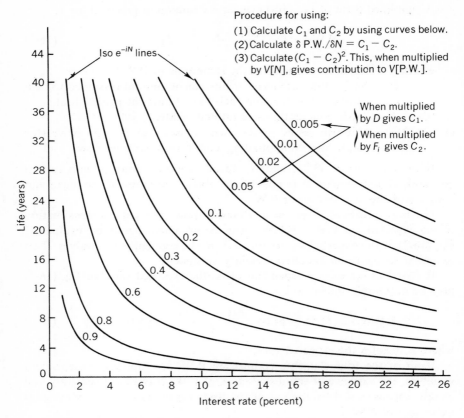

Figure 16-1. Contribution to variance of P.W. due to variance of T
$[(P.W.)/N]^2 = (De^{-iN} - Fie^{-iN})^2$.

wide range of conditions. These figures can also be used as an aid to examine visually the relative effect of different conditions on the various terms which contribute to $V(P.W.)$. Of course, $(\partial P.W./\partial P)^2$ is always unity.

Example:

> *Example to demonstrate formulas for calculating $E(P.W.)$ and $V(P.W.)$:*
> Given: $E(P) = -\$100,000,$ $V(P) = (\$1,000)^2$
> $E(N) = 10$ yr, $V(N) = (1$ yr$)^2$
> $E(F) = +\$10,000,$ $V(F) = (\$2,500)^2$
> $E(D) = +\$15,700,$ $V(D) = (\$2,000)^2$
>
> Interest is 10% and each of the above elements is independent of the others. It is desired to show how to calculate $E(P.W.)$ and $V(P.W.)$ through the use of the above formulas and shortcut figures.

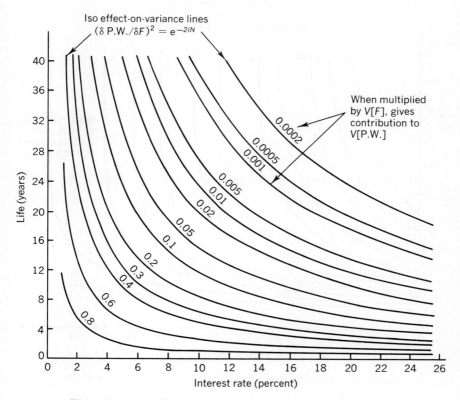

Figure 16-2. Contribution to variance of P.W. due to variance of F.

Solution:

$$E(\text{P.W.}) = -\$100{,}000 + \$15{,}700(6.32)(0.99)* + \$10{,}000(0.360)$$
$$= +\$800$$

$$V(\text{P.W.}) = \left(\frac{\partial \text{P.W.}}{\partial P}\right)^2 \cdot V(P) + \left(\frac{\partial \text{P.W.}}{\partial D}\right)^2 \cdot V(D)$$
$$+ \left(\frac{\partial \text{P.W.}}{\partial N}\right)^2 \cdot V(N) + \left(\frac{\partial \text{P.W.}}{\partial F}\right)^2 \cdot V(F)$$

$$\left(\frac{\partial \text{P.W.}}{\partial P}\right)^2 = (1)^2 = 1$$

*This factor is normally so close to 1.00 as to be inconsequential. For a graphical comparison of $E[(1 - e^{-iN})/i]$ compared to $(1 - e^{-iN})/i$ at $E(N)$ for a range of distributions of N, see John R. Canada and Harrison M. Wadsworth, "The Effect of Project Life Dispersion on Key Interest Factors for Economic Analyses of Capital Investments," *Engineering Economist*, Vol. 11, No. 4 (Summer 1966)

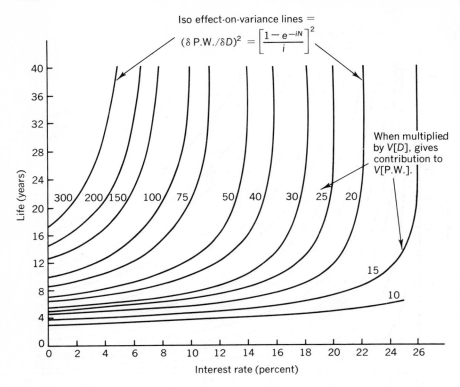

Figure 16-3. Contribution to variance of P.W. due to variance of D.

$$\left(\frac{\partial\text{P.W.}}{\partial D}\right)^2 = 39 \qquad \text{(from Fig. 16-3)}$$

$$\left(\frac{\partial\text{P.W.}}{\partial N}\right)^2 = (C_1 - C_2)^2 = [0.37(\$15,700) - 0.37(\$10,000)(0.10)]^2$$

$$= (\$5,440)^2 \text{ (From Fig. 16-1)}$$

$$\left(\frac{\partial\text{P.W.}}{\partial F}\right)^2 = 0.15 \qquad \text{(From Fig. 16-2)}$$

$$V(\text{P.W.}) = 1(\$1,000)^2 + 39(\$2,000)^2 + (\$5,440)^2(1)^2 + 0.15(2,500)^2$$
$$= 187,540,000$$

$$\text{Standard deviation of P.W.} = \sqrt{187,540,000} = \$13,700$$

From these results, it can be surmised that the project is barely acceptable based on $E(\text{P.W.}) = \$800$ (which is > 0). However, the relatively high variance indicates considerable dispersion which, together with the low $E(\text{P.W.})$, means that there is a relatively high probability of the project turning out to be unacceptable.

If, for example, each of the individual elements is estimated to be normally distributed so that **P.W.** is approximately normally distributed, then the calculation of the approximate probability that the project will turn out to be unacceptable (i.e., **P.W.** < 0) is

$$P(\text{P.W.} < 0) = P\left(S \leq \frac{0 - 800}{13,700}\right) = P(S \leq -0.0585)$$
$$= 1 - P[S \leq 0.0585] = 0.48$$

where S is the standard normal deviation tabled in Appendix A-E. Thus, if the distribution of **P.W.** is normal and other conditions are as stated in the problem, there is a 48% chance that the project will turn out to have a negative **P.W.**, and thus be unacceptable.

In determining $E(\text{P.W.})$ and $V(\text{P.W.})$, dependence or correlation among the elements can be taken into account if that is thought to be necessary. Means of accomplishing this are briefly discussed in the next two sections.

Effect of Correlation on E(P.W.)

The effect of covariance as well as variance of the individual elements on $E(\text{P.W.})$ can be determined exactly through evaluation of the expected value of the joint density functions. However, a valid estimate of these joint density functions might be quite difficult to obtain. Therefore, it seems feasible to use the Taylor series expansion and to evaluate higher-order terms of the expansion as necessary to approximate the effect of lack of independence.

Effect of Correlation on V(P.W.)

If correlation exists between any pair of elements in the analysis—say, N and F—the effect of that correlation on $V(\text{P.W.})$ can be approximated by adding a term of the form

$$2\left(\frac{\partial \text{P.W.}}{\partial N}\right) \cdot \left(\frac{\partial \text{P.W.}}{\partial F}\right) \cdot \text{Cov}(N,F)$$

to Eq. (16-4) for each pair of elements which are not independent. $\text{Cov}(N,F)$ denotes the covariance between elements N and F. To aid in performing computations, the squares of the partial derivatives with respect to N, F, and D are shown in Figs. 16-1 through 16-3. The covariance between any two elements—say, again, N and F—can be estimated by using the relation

$$\text{Cov}(N,F) = \rho_{N,F}\sqrt{V(N)}\sqrt{V(F)} \qquad (16\text{-}5)$$

where $\rho_{N,F}$ is the coefficient of correlation between N and F.

If it were desired to consider lack of independence between all possible pairs of the four elements in Eq. (16-4), there would be $\binom{4}{2} = 6$ terms of the preceding form. In most economic analyses, most of these terms would be either insignificant or difficult to estimate with reasonable confidence, and hence would be neglected. The term most likely to be significant is the term which considers the correlation of D and N. Intuitively, it seems that a larger D (higher net receipts or lower net disbursements) may well lead to a life longer than the unconditional expected life. Also, a strong correlation could exist between F and N, ordinarily reflecting that a larger N will cause a smaller F. However, if the value of F is so insignificant as to make this correlation irrelevant, then no term would be needed to reflect the effect of this correlation on $V(\text{P.W.})$.

Procedure for Selection Among Mutually Exclusive Projects

We shall now turn to a set of steps for quantitatively comparing two or more mutually exclusive projects with information on $E(\text{P.W.})$ and $V(\text{P.W.})$ for each of the projects.

Procedure step 1

Calculate the estimated mean and variance of P.W. for each project considered by using the methods discussed above. For project x call the mean and variance of present worth $E(\text{P.W.})_x$ and $V(\text{P.W.})_x$ respectively.

Procedure step 2

For the two projects with the largest positive $E(\text{P.W.})$, calculate the expected difference $E(\text{P.W.})_d$ and the variance of the difference, $V(\text{P.W.})_d$. The meaning of this difference is shown graphically in Fig. 16-6. The expected difference between projects x and y may be calculated as

$$E(\text{P.W.})_d = E(\text{P.W.})_x - E(\text{P.W.})_y \tag{16-6}$$

If the P.W. of the two projects are mutually independent, then the variance of the difference can be calculated as

$$V(\text{P.W.})_d = V(\text{P.W.})_x + V(\text{P.W.})_y \tag{16-7}$$

If the cash flows of the individual projects are not independent, the variance of the difference between projects x and y may be estimated by

$$V(\text{P.W.})_d = V(\text{P.W.})_x + V(\text{P.W.})_y - 2 \, \text{Cov}(\text{P.W.}_{\cdot x}, \text{P.W.}_{\cdot y}) \tag{16-8}$$

The covariance of the P.W. of cash flows for projects x and y might be estimated most effectively through estimation of the coefficient of correlation, ρ_{xy}. If this is done, then Eq. (16-8) becomes

$$V(\text{P.W.})_d = V(\text{P.W.})_x + V(\text{P.W.})_y - 2\rho_{xy}\sqrt{V(\text{P.W.})_x} \cdot \sqrt{V(\text{P.W.})_y}$$

$$(16\text{-}9)$$

Figure 16-4 is provided to demonstrate the behavior of $V(\text{P.W.})_d$ for $\rho_{xy} = 1.0$ over a continuous range of $V(\text{P.W.})_x$ and $V(\text{P.W.})_y$. Figure 16-5 considers the effect of the correlation between x and y, and can be used to aid graphically in determining $V(\text{P.W.})_d$ for any value of ρ_{xy}. Note from the explanation in Fig. 16-5 that

$$V(\text{P.W.})_d = V(\text{P.W.})_x + V(\text{P.W.})_y \qquad (16\text{-}10)$$

$$+ \rho_{xy} \qquad \text{(value found in Fig. 16-5)}$$

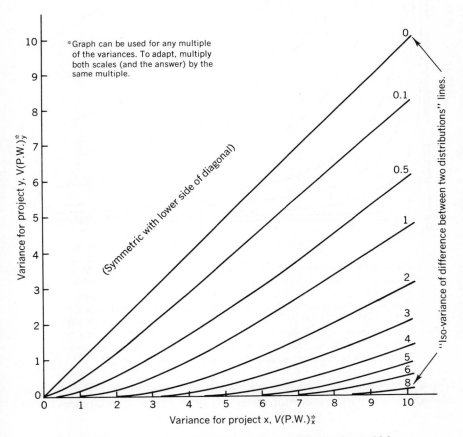

Figure 16-4. Variance of difference between two distributions which are perfectly correlated ($p = 1$)*. To use, find coordinate point corresponding to the variances of the two distributions. Visually interpolate to find the variance of the difference.

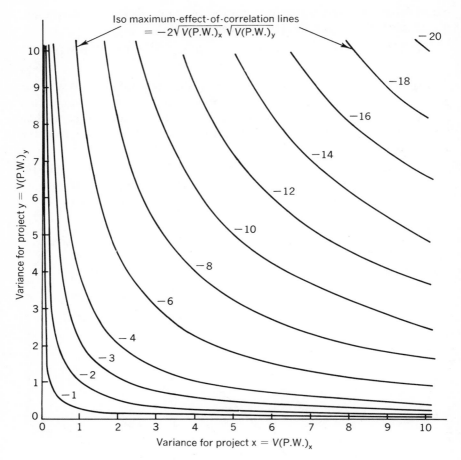

Figure 16-5. Effect of correlation on variance of difference between two distributions. To use, (1) for given variance for x and y, find maximum effect of correlation from graph; (2) multiply maximum effect of correlation by coefficient of correlation, ρ, to find effect of correlation $= -2\rho\sqrt{V(\text{P.W.})_x}\sqrt{V(\text{P.W.})_y}$. To find total variance of difference between two distributions, add effect of correlation to the sum of the variances of the two distributions. This graph can be used for any multiple of variances. Simply multiply both scales and the answer by the same multiple.

These figures enable one to obtain a rapid approximation of $V(\text{P.W.})_d$. They also serve as a partial indicator of sensitivity of $V(\text{P.W.})_d$ to changes in the relative variances in the P.W.'s for project x and project y.

Procedure step 3

With the information obtained in step 2, determine the "probability of reversal." *Probability of reversal* is the probability that between two projects the one with the greater E(P.W.) will actually turn out to be not as good as the other. Figure 16-6 shows how the probability of reversal is generated. The distributions of P.W. outcomes for two projects, x and y, are shown on the top of the figure. Although project x has a higher expected present worth than does project y, there is a certain probability that a single observation of P.W.$_x$ is less than an observation of P.W.$_y$. The distribution of P.W.$_d =$ P.W.$_x$ — P.W.$_y$ is shown in the bottom of the figure. The probability that P.W.$_d < 0$, the probability of reversal, is shown by the shaded area.

While E(P.W.)$_d$ and V(P.W.)$_d$ can be calculated by Eq. 16-6 and 16-8 respectively without regard to the shape of distribution for the individual projects, it is necessary to know the probability density function of P.W.$_d$ in order to be able to calculate the probability of reversal. The distribution of P.W.$_d$ depends upon the densities of P.W. for projects x and y as well as ρ_{xy}.

If P.W.$_x$ and P.W.$_y$ are normally distributed and independent of each other (that is, $\rho_{xy} = 0$), then P.W.$_d$ is also normally distributed. If P.W.$_d$

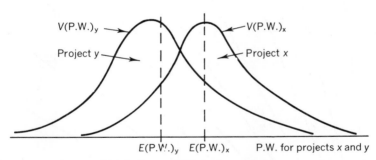

Distributions of P.W. for two projects

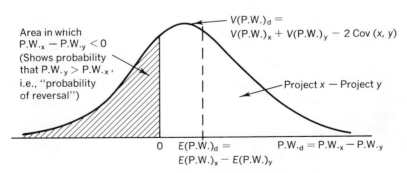

Distribution of P.W. for difference between two projects

Figure 16-6. Demonstration of meaning of probability of reversal.

is normally distributed, then the probability of reversal may be determined by the relation

$$P(\text{reversal}) = P\left[S \leq \frac{-E(\text{P.W.})_d}{V(\text{P.W.})_d} \right] = 1 - P\left[S \leq \frac{E(\text{P.W.})_d}{V(\text{P.W.})_d} \right] \quad (16\text{-}11)$$

where S is the standard normal deviate, which is commonly tabled, as in Appendix A-E. Figure 16-7 provides a convenient graph for determining the probability of reversal for a wide range of $E(\text{P.W.})_d$ and $V(\text{P.W.})_d$.

The probability of reversal is used, together with qualitative judgment considerations of pertinent intangible elements, to compare these two projects further. The more preferable of the two is then selected, using all the information now available.

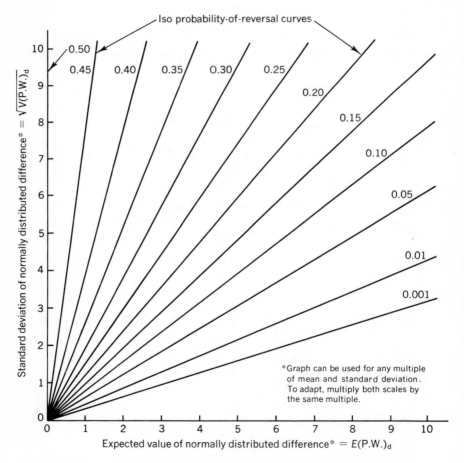

Figure 16-7. Probability of reversal according to mean and standard deviation of normal distribution of difference between two projects.

Procedure step 4

Once the more preferable of the two projects considered in step 3 has been selected, one can compare this project to the project having the next largest $E(P.W.)$. The comparison is made by repeating steps 2 and 3. This will result in a probability of reversal for this new pair of projects that can be compared with the $E(P.W.)_d$ and judgment on pertinent intangibles to decide which of these two projects is more desirable.

Procedure step 5

The procedure outlined in steps 2 through 4 can be repeated as long as alternative projects exist and it seems that the project having the next smallest $E(P.W.)$ is sufficiently competitive to the current most desirable project to warrant consideration of probability of reversal calculations and judgment on intangibles. The final choice should be the most desirable project remaining after the succession of comparisons. In other words, the final choice should be the project which has the most positive $E(P.W.)$ and which has not been judged to be less desirable than some other project due to consideration of the probability of reversal and pertinent intangibles.

Example:

Example of use of procedure for selection among mutually exclusive projects: Procedure step 1 calls for estimation or calculation of the mean and variance of P.W. for each project. These results to be used in this example are shown in Table 16-1. Assume that the P.W. for each project is normally distributed and independent. Hence, the distribution of differences between any two of the projects is normal.

Table 16-1

DATA FOR EXAMPLE MUTUALLY EXCLUSIVE PROJECTS

Project	$E(P.W.)$	$V(P.W.)$
A	$+\$2,000$	144,000,000
B	$+\ 600$	187,540,000
C	$+\ 100$	36,000,000
D	$+\ 50$	64,000,000

Procedure step 2 calls for comparison of projects A and B. This would consist of

$$E(P.W.)_d = \$2,000 - \$600 = \$1,400$$
$$V(P.W.)_d = \$144,000,000 + 187,540,000 - 0 = 331,540,000$$
$$\sqrt{V(P.W.)_d} = \$18,200$$

Procedure step 3 calls for calculation of the probability of reversal. Since the distribution of differences is normal, Fig. 16-7 can be used to find the probability of reversal equal to 0.47. This quite high probability of reversal together with consideration of the relative effects of intangibles on projects A and B should now be weighted by the decision-maker and a choice between the two projects should be made. For purposes of this illustration, suppose that it is decided that intangibles look very slightly more favorable to project B than to project A, but that this consideration together with the 47% probability of reversal is not enough to swing the choice to B. Hence, of the two, A is selected as the more desirable.

Procedure step 4 involves the comparison of the more desirable project selected in the last step, project A, with the project with the next less positive $E(P.W.)$, project C. This is done below:

$$E(P.W.)_d = \$2,000 - \$100 = \$1,900$$

$$V(P.W.)_d = 144,000,000 + 36,000,000 = 180,000,000$$

$$V(P.W.)_d = \$13,400$$

Using Fig. 16-7, the probability of reversal equals 0.44. This should now be considered together with the relative effects of intangibles to decide which is the more desirable project. Suppose that intangibles look markedly more favorable to project C than to project A so that the consideration of the probability of reversal together with these intangibles results in project C being selected as the more desirable.

Procedure step 5 involves successive comparison of the more desirable project selected in the last step with the project with the next less positive $E(P.W.)$. In this example problem, there is only one more project with a less positive $E(P.W.)$ to consider: project D. Project C compared to project D results in an $E(P.W.)_d$ of \$50 and a $V(P.W.)_d$ of 100,000,000. From Fig. 16-7, these conditions result in a probability of reversal of almost 0.50. If intangibles are, say, more favorable to project C, then project C would be the more desirable of the two projects. Concluding procedure step 5, the final choice among the alternative projects is project C.

It should be noted that this procedure is just as applicable to selection among projects where costs only are known. In such cases, the project with the most positive P.W. is actually the project with the least P.W. of costs, etc.

Procedure for Selection Among Non-Mutually Exclusive Projects

In selecting among non-mutually exclusive projects, the only projects on which the economics can be evaluated are those for which revenues or savings as well as costs can be estimated. If only costs are known, then there is no way quantitatively to say that a project has a positive net P.W. and is thus earning at least the minimum required rate of return.

Procedure step 1

Calculate estimated mean and variance of P.W. for each project considered by using the methods shown above.

Procedure step 2

Rank the projects in order of decreasing net $E(\text{P.W.})$. If investment funds are limited, include information on investment requirements.

Procedure step 3

For each project, determine the *probability of loss* (i.e. , the probability that P.W. will turn out to be < 0). This probability is analogous to, and can be calculated in the same manner as, the probability of reversal for mutually exclusive projects shown in the last section. The only difference is that in this case the distribution with which to work is the distribution of P.W. for an individual project rather than the distribution of P.W._d for pairs of projects.

Procedure step 4

Start with the project at the top of the list and subjectively weigh the combined criteria of $E(\text{P.W.})$, probability of loss, and consideration of intangibles, and make a decision as to whether or not tentatively to accept that project. Continue in this manner down the list, tentatively accepting those projects which meet the combined criteria of high enough $E(\text{P.W.})$ and sufficiently low risk of loss together with satisfactory intangibles.

If there is no limitation on the investment funds, all projects meeting the above combined criteria can be accepted. If there is some limitation on the investment funds, then projects can be considered as above down to the point where the available funds are exhausted. After that point, projects with lower $E(\text{P.W.})$ values should be considered on the basis of the same combined criteria and in light of whether or not those projects are better overall than one or more of the projects which have been tentatively accepted. If a project or projects with lower $E(\text{P.W.})$ values show up better, then they should be tentatively accepted and assigned the investment funds previously allocated to a project or projects with higher $E(\text{P.W.})$ values. This sequence is continued down the list until there are no other projects competitive enough to receive serious consideration.

The procedure for considering projects after all funds have been tentatively allocated is complicated by the fact that various projects typically require different investment amounts. Thus, it may be necessary to compare combinations of one or more projects against one or more tentatively accepted projects in order to stay within investment funds constraints and still select the group of projects which best meet the combined criteria. In judging combinations of projects to take the place of projects tentatively accepted, projects which were previously not accepted should again be considered because, in combination with others, one or more of those projects may be accepted.

Example:

As an example of use of the procedure for selection among non-mutually exclusive projects, consider Table 16-2 below which lists the pertinent data on five non-mutually exclusive projects which are ranked in order of decreasing E(P.W.). Investment funds are limited to $200,000; hence, information on investment requirements for each project are shown. Once this information is determined and tabulated, procedure steps 1 and 2 are complete.

Table 16-2

DATA FOR EXAMPLE NON-MUTUALLY EXCLUSIVE PROJECTS

Project	E(P.W.)	V(P.W.)	Investment required
Q	+$5,000	36,000,000	$100,000
R	+ 3,000	100,000,000	100,000
S	+ 2,500	169,000,000	200,000
T	+ 1,000	1,000,000	100,000
U	− 2,000	100,000,000	100,000

Procedure step 3 calls for the determination of the probability of loss for each project that has any likelihood of acceptance. Assume that the P.W. for each project is normally distributed, so that the probability of loss for each project can be determined directly from Fig. 16-7. Note again that what is called probability of reversal in Fig. 16-7 is the same as probability of loss when considering single projects. Table 16-3 shows the pertinent data together with probabilities of loss for the projects under consideration.

Table 16-3

DATA FOR EXAMPLE NON-MUTUALLY EXCLUSIVE PROJECTS AND PROBABILITIES OF LOSS

Project	E(P.W.)	Probability of loss	Investment required
Q	+$5,000	0.20	$100,000
R	+ 3,000	0.38	100,000
S	+ 2,500	0.42	200,000
T	+ 1,000	0.16	100,000
U	− 2,000	0.58 (= 1 − 0.42)	100,000

Procedure step 4 calls for the successive appraisal of each project according to the combined criteria. Suppose that projects Q and R are tentatively acceptable, using up the investment funds available. The remaining projects must now be examined in light of whether they are good enough to justify taking the investment funds from projects already tentatively accepted. Suppose that project S is judged not to be good enough, but that project T is judged to be better overall than project R. Project U, even though it has a negative $E(\text{P.W.})$, may still be a serious contender if the effect of intangibles is much more favorable to it than to project Q or T. In this case, suppose that project U is not considered sufficiently good through consideration of the composite criteria, and hence projects Q and T are the final selections.

Supplementary Criteria

In choosing between mutually exclusive projects or between non-mutually exclusive projects, there are refinements to supplement the probability of reversal or probability of loss information which can be useful. The particular refinement, to be discussed herein, is the use of the concept of expected opportunity loss—EOL (also called expected value of perfect information—EVPI) as covered in Chapter 14. Applied to the analysis of an individual project, the expected opportunity loss is a measure of how much could be saved, on the average, if the occurrence of the loss were perfectly predictable and the investment were not made if the loss were going to occur. If the distribution of P.W. is normal, the expected opportunity loss can be determined very readily by use of a table of the unit normal loss integral (UNLI) such as in Appendix A-D. The formula for expected opportunity loss is then reduced to

$$\text{EOL} = \sqrt{V(\text{P.W.})} \cdot \text{UNLI at } \frac{E(\text{P.W.}) - 0}{\sqrt{V(\text{P.W.})}} \qquad (16\text{-}12)$$

As an example of the use of this tool, consider a project with an $E(\text{P.W.})$ of \$4,000 and a $\sqrt{V(\text{P.W.})}$ of \$8,000, where P.W. is normally distributed. Thus,

$$\text{EOL} = \$8,000 \cdot \text{UNLI at } \frac{\$4,000}{\$8,000} = 0.5$$

$$= \$8,000 \cdot 0.1978 = \underline{\$1,582}$$

Another potentially useful type of information which can now be readily determined is the expected opportunity loss if a loss does occur. This can be calculated as

$$(\text{EOL} \mid \text{Loss occurs}) = \frac{\text{EOL}}{P(\text{Loss occurs})} \qquad (16\text{-}13)$$

The probability that a loss occurs is the same thing as the "probability of reversal," which can be conveniently read from Fig. 16-7 if the distribution is normal. In the example problem above, the probability of a loss occuring equals 0.31. Thus,

$$(\text{EOL} \,|\, \text{Loss occurs}) = \frac{\$1,582}{0.31} = \$4,970$$

The latter conditional loss information may be more useful than just EOL because it gives the decision-maker a feel for what is of vital concern if he is conservative about incurring losses—a measure of the expected loss if the loss should occur. In practice, one or both of these loss criteria may be valuable supplements to the combined criteria used in judging between projects.

PROBLEMS

16-1. Individual elements for an important prospective investment project A are estimated in terms of their respective means and variances as follows:

Element	Mean	Variance
Investment	$1,000,000	($120,000)^2
Life	20 yr	(5 yr)^2
Salvage value	$200,000	($90,000)^2
Net annual receipts	$145,000	($40,000)^2

    a. If the minimum R.R. is 12% and each of the elements is assumed to vary independently of the others, obtain approximations of the mean and variance of the net P.W. of project A through use of the first two terms of the Taylor series expansion.

    b. Assume also that each of the estimated elements is approximately normally distributed so that the distribution of the net P.W. is approximately normally distributed. Find the approximate probability that the net P.W. would turn out to be negative.

16-2. Estimates of outcomes of individual elements for an important prospective investment project B are made in terms of their respective means and standard deviations as follows:

Element	Mean	Standard deviation
Investment	$1,350,000	$300,000
Life	20 yr	3 yr
Salvage value	0	$110,000
Annual receipts	$390,000	$70,000
Annual disbursement	$150,000	$30,000

   a. If the minimum R.R. is 12% and each of the elements, including receipts and disbursement, is assumed to vary independently of the others, obtain approximations of the mean and variance of the net P.W. of project A through use of the first two terms of the Taylor series expansion.

   b. Assume also that each of the elements is approximately normally distributed. Find the approximate probability that the net P.W. would turn out to be negative.

16-3.   a. If projects A and B in Probs. 16-1 and 16-2 respectively were competing, which would be chosen on the basis of expected net P.W.?

   b. If the outcomes for the two projects above were assumed to be independent, what is the probability that the project with the lower net P.W. would actually turn out to be the more desirable?

16-4. Determine the variance of project A in Prob. 16-1 if the only nonindependence between element outcomes was between the project life and the net annual receipts, which have an estimated coefficient of correlation of 0.9.

16-5. Work Probs. 16-3(a) and (b) except assume that the net P.W. outcomes of the two projects have an estimated coefficient of correlation of -0.8.

16-6. Individual elements for competing investment projects I and II are estimated as follows:

Project	Element	Mean	Variance
I	Investment	$200,000	0
	Life	10 yr	$(2 \text{ yr})^2$
	Salvage value	0	0
	Net annual receipts	$42,000	$($7,000)^2$
II	Investment	$250,000	0
	Life	10 yr	$(3 \text{ yr})^2$
	Salvage value	$10,000	$($10,000)^2$
	Net annual receipts	$65,000	0

   a. If the minimum R.R. is 20% and each of the elements which is subject to variation is assumed to vary independently of the others, obtain approximations of the mean and variance of the net P.W. of each project through use of the first two terms of the Taylor series expansion.

   b. Assume also that each of the estimated elements is approximately normally distributed and that the outcomes for each project are independent. Which would be chosen on the basis of expected net P.W.? What is the "probability of reversal" of this choice?

   c. Suppose the decision-maker's expectation-variance function to be applied to any project equals expected P.W. minus a constant times the standard deviation of the net P.W. At what value of the constant are projects I and II equally desirable?

seventeen

Weighting and Evaluating Objectives and Nonmonetary Factors

It is a common phenomenon that there are many nonmonetary factors in addition to monetary factors which should be considered in an economic analysis. Also, it is widely recognized that a firm may have many objectives other than monetary ones. Some examples of firm objectives other than profit maximization or cost minimization are the following:

Minimize risk of loss
Maximize sales
Minimize cyclic fluctuations
Create a favorable public image
Maximize quality of service
Maximize growth rate
Maximize satisfaction of employees
Maximize firm prestige
Minimize air or water pollution

This chapter describes a rational way for weighting either objectives or nonmonetary factors according to importance, evaluating how well each alternative meets each factor, and then combining these results into a single weighted evaluation measure for each alternative.

Weighting Factors*

Consider k factors $F_1, F_2, \ldots, F_k$, such as objectives of a firm or nonmonetary factors, which should be considered in an analysis. The following method of weighting factors requires two assumptions:

A. It must be possible for the decision-maker to consider and judge the relative weight of any combination of factors. That is, it must be possible to consider not only the weight of F_1, but also the weight of both F_1 and F_2.

B. Weights are assumed to be additive. That is, given the weight of F_1 and the weight of F_2, the weight of both F_1 and F_2 is the sum of their individual weights.

The decision-maker should proceed in weighting the factors as follows:

1. Rank the factors according to decreasing weight (or importance). Once this is done, it would be desirable to reassign subscripts to indicate the rankings. Thus, F_1 is ranked first, F_2 is ranked second, etc.
2. Let the weight of F_1 equal 100 [i.e., $W(F_1) = 100$] and weight the other factors so as to reflect judgment of their weight relative to the weight of F_1. Thus, the weights of $F_2 \cdots F_n$ will range from a possible high value of 100 to a possible low value of 0. All further steps (3 through 6) serve to refine these initial weighting judgments and to insure that they are internally consistent.
3. Compare F_1 with the combination of $F_2 + F_3$ (the plus sign here means "and"). If F_1 is considered to have less weight than $F_2 + F_3$, then the weights assigned in step 2 above must satisfy the relation $W(F_1) < W(F_2) + W(F_3)$. If the assigned weights do not satisfy this relation, then $W(F_1)$ should be adjusted until the relation above corresponds to the judgment on relative weights. If, on the other hand, F_1 is considered to have greater weight than $F_2 + F_3$, then the inequality sign of the above relation would be reversed, and, if necessary, the weight of F_1 may be adjusted.
4. Compare F_1 with the combination $F_2 + F_3 + F_4$, and repeat the process of adjusting the value of $W(F_1)$ if necessary.
5. The process of comparison and adjustment is continued according to the following pattern (for a given problem, it is to be expected that many of these comparisons will not be needed, thus shortening the process):

*This section is adapted from William T. Morris, *The Analysis of Management Decisions* (Homewood, Ill.: Richard D. Irwin, Inc., 1964), pp. 417–424, with permission of the publisher.

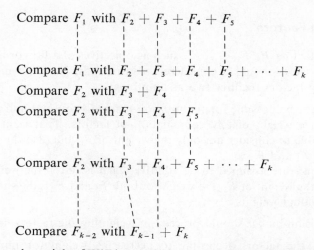

Compare F_1 with $F_2 + F_3 + F_4 + F_5$

Compare F_1 with $F_2 + F_3 + F_4 + F_5 + \cdots + F_k$

Compare F_2 with $F_3 + F_4$

Compare F_2 with $F_3 + F_4 + F_5$

Compare F_2 with $F_3 + F_4 + F_5 + \cdots + F_k$

Compare F_{k-2} with $F_{k-1} + F_k$

6. Once the weights $[W(F_1) + W(F_2) + \cdots + W(F_k)]$ have been adjusted and checked for consistency to the satisfaction of the decision-maker, it is common to "normalize" them to sum to 100 points by multiplying each individual weight by $\dfrac{100}{\sum\limits_{i=1}^{k} W(F_i)}$

Example:

Suppose management desires to establish weights for several main factors or objectives it considers important to its economic analyses, such as profit, employee safety, product quality, and stable employment. Further, management judges that the relative importance of these four factors is in the order of listing above, and that the initial weighting assignments should be

$$W(F_1) = 100$$
$$W(F_2) = 65$$
$$W(F_3) = 40$$
$$W(F_4) = 30$$

The first consistency check is to compare F_1 with $F_2 + F_3$. Suppose the decision-maker feels that F_1 is less important than the combination of F_2 and F_3. This judgment checks with the initial assignment of weights. That is,

$$W(F_1) = 100 < W(F_2) + W(F_3) = 65 + 40 = 105$$

The next comparison is between F_1 and $F_2 + F_3 + F_4$. It is reasonable that F_1 should be considered less important than the combination of F_2 and F_3 and F_4. This, too, checks with the initial assignment of weights. That is,

$$W(F_1) = 100 < W(F_2) + W(F_3) + W(F_4) = 65 + 40 + 30 = 135$$

The next comparison is between F_2 and $F_3 + F_4$. Suppose the decision-maker feels F_2 is more important than the combination of F_3 and F_4. A check of this compared to the assigned weights shows

$$W(F_2) = 65 < W(F_3) + W(F_4) = 40 + 30 = 70$$

Thus there is an inconsistency to be resolved. This might be done by increasing $W(F_2)$ by more than 5 points (i.e., $70 - 65$), by decreasing $W(F_3)$ and/or $W(F_4)$ by more than 5 points, or by some combination of these adjustments for consistency. Suppose it is judged that $W(F_2)$ should be increased by 5 points and that $W(F_4)$ should be decreased by 10 points. With these changes,

$$W(F_2) = 70 > W(F_3) + W(F_4) = 40 + 20 = 60$$

which agrees with the original judgment that F_2 is more important than the combination of F_3 and F_4. If adjustments in point assignments are sufficient, it may be necessary to redo prior consistency checks.

Table 17-1 shows the normalization of the factor weights which have been checked for consistency.

Table 17-1

CALCULATION OF NORMALIZED FACTOR WEIGHTS

Factor	Weight $[= W(F_i)]$	Normalized factor weight $\left[= \dfrac{W(F_i)}{\sum\limits_{i=1}^{4} W(F_i)} \times 100 \right]$
F_1	100	44
F_2	70	30
F_3	40	17
F_4	20	9
	$\sum\limits_{i=1}^{4} W(F_i) = 230$	$\Sigma = 100$

Evaluation of Alternatives for Factors

Once weights have been assigned to factors, the next step in applying them in an economic analysis is to assign numerical values to the evaluation of how well each alternative satisfies each factor. This is generally a difficult judgment task using an arbitrary scale of, say, between 0 and 10 or between 0 and 100 to reflect relative evaluations for each alternative and each factor.

Example:
Suppose we are comparing two alternatives on the basis of how well they satisfy the four factors with the weights developed in the example above. The factors, together with the subjective evaluation of how well each alternative meets each on the basis of a scale of 0 to 10 is shown in Table 17-2.

Table 17-2

EXAMPLE EVALUATION RATING OF HOW WELL EACH
ALTERNATIVE SATISFIES EACH FACTOR

	Alternative	
Factor	*A*	*B*
Profit	10	9
Employee safety	6	7
Product quality	5	10
Stable employment	7	7

Once the evaluations have been made, the results can be calculated as in Table 17-3 to arrive at weighted evaluations of factors for each alternative.

Table 17-3

CALCULATION OF WEIGHTED EVALUATIONS OF ALTERNATIVES

Factor	*Normalized factor weight (From Table 17-1)*	*Alternative A*		*Alternative B*	
		Evaluation rating	*Weighted evaluation**	*Evaluation rating*	*Weighted evaluation**
Profit	44	10	44.0	9	39.6
Employee safety	30	6	18.0	7	21.0
Product quality	17	5	8.5	10	17.0
Stable employment	9	7	6.3	7	6.3
			$\Sigma = 76.8$		$\Sigma = 83.9$

*Weighted evaluation = Normalized factor weight $\times \dfrac{\text{Evaluation rating}}{10}$

Thus, the summed weighted evaluation is 76.8 for alternative A and 83.9 for alternative B, indicating that alternative B is the better, even though it showed a lower profit in Table 17-2.

Example Application Considering Intangible Factors

Appendix 17-A, "Criteria for Investment in Handling Systems" by James M. Apple, gives an example application of the above weighting and evaluation technique as applied to the consideration of intangible factors. The article also provides an excellent discussion and checklist of what are called *direct cost factors*, *indirect cost factors*, and *indeterminate cost factors*, in addition to *intangible factors*.

Two weaknesses in Professor Apple's article are worth noting. First, in his Fig. 17-A-1, depreciation and interest is calculated by the approximation model of straight line depreciation plus interest on the initial investment. Compound interest techniques as explained in Chapter 3 of this book should have been used to determine the exact capital recovery cost. Secondly, in Fig. 17-A-5, the division of total cost factors by a weighted evaluation of intangible cost factors is suggested to obtain a single number for direct comparison of each alternative.

Appendix 17-B is a reprint of the author's "Reader's Comments" describing the latter deficiency in Professor Apple's article and suggesting a means of rectifying the weakness while retaining the main features.

Summary of Part II

Part II has concentrated on techniques and analysis procedures for quantifying the risk and uncertainty inherent in economic analyses of capital projects. While most of these techniques and procedures are candidates for straightforward and widespread application in practice, some are presented in the expectation that they will prove valuable with refinement and the increased inclination of progressive analysts to make use of these advances.

The extended analysis procedures included herein range from mere conservative adjustments to use of cardinal utilities and variable discounting. The techniques of approach range from statistical decision methods to Monte Carlo simulation and analytical approximations. For a given capital project economic evaluation, usually only a few procedures and techniques covered herein would be needed. Indeed, the burden is normally upon the resourceful analyst to determine which procedures and techniques are most appropriate for each analysis situation according to the magnitudes of prospective commitments, the uncertainties involved, and the desires of management. Correctly used, such procedures and techniques are extremely valuable in providing a rational basis for project investment decisions which, singularly or cumulatively, are vital to the welfare of the business firm.

PROBLEMS

17-1.   a. Weight the relative importance of the three or four most important factors you would consider in selecting a job. Assume these are the only factors you will quantitatively consider. Show how you make comparisons for internal consistency, and normalize the factor weights to sum to 100.

　　b. Using the factor weights developed above, obtain a weighted evaluation of two alternative jobs in which you might be interested by evaluating how well each job satisfies each factor using a scale of from 0 to 10.

17-2.　a. Weight the relative importance of the three to six most important factors you would consider in selecting a personal car. Assume these are the only factors you will quantitatively consider. Show how you make comparisons for internal consistency, and normalize the factor weights to sum to 1,000.

　　b. Using the factor weights developed above, obtain a weighted evaluation of three alternative makes of cars you might consider for purchase by evaluating how well each make of car satisfies each factor, using a scale of from 0 to 20.

17-3. Weight the relative importance of your significant personal goals or objectives. These should include work-related goals as well as those not related to your work. Show how you make comparisons for internal consistency and normalize the factor weights to sum to 1,000.

APPENDIX 17-A

Criteria for Investment in Handling Systems*

　　In the rapidly changing technology of present times, and with ever-intensifying competition, it is no longer economically appropriate to solve materials handling problems by implementing individual, isolated handling tasks with unrelated items of handling equipment. The total handling problem of a particular facility must be approached from an overall or systems point of view—one in which the complete handling function is visualized as a continuous cycle, and as an integral part of the total production process. This does *not* necessarily imply total automation of the complete activity, but it does imply the adoption of a "vision" in that general direction—that is, toward the theoretical ideal system. From this point, it is possible to "retreat" to what Professor Gerald Nadler (Ref. 2) identifies as the "technologically workable ideal system." This approach should result in a far superior

*By James M. Apple, Professor of Industrial Engineering, Georgia Institute of Technology. Reprinted from *The Journal of Industrial Engineering*, Vol. 19, No. 1 (January 1968), by permission of the publisher.

implementation of the handling functions than the traditional approach, which begins with the existing method and involves a step-by-step analysis, in a search for improvement opportunities in individual segments of the handling activity. Since this systems concept calls for a much higher level of planning activity, it also requires a more exacting consideration of the criteria to be selected for evaluation of the situation and the required investment.

Definition of a System

As previously intimated, most present-day materials handling activity can be characterized as a collection of individual, isolated, unrelated methods, techniques, and equipment selected to implement a series of independent handling tasks in moving materials from one point to another. In contrast, a production *system* is one in which the entire production activity is completely integrated with the related materials handling activity, distribution activity, and information processes, from the source of raw materials into the "hands" of the ultimate consumer. While such a goal is seldom achieved, it *should* serve as a long-range objective for those involved in any phase of the total system, whether manufacturer, shipper, or warehouseman. More specifically, each should investigate the possibility of planning *his* activity as an integral part of the entire system.

The materials handling system is that portion of the whole which implements the movement and storage phases of the total system—a materials flow network superimposed on or integrated with the whole. Perhaps in a more realistic sense, the present-day materials handling system should consist of a carefully planned network of integrated handling methods which will efficiently and economically move materials from the receiving area, through fabrication, to the shipping area. Practicable extensions of such a concept would include close cooperation with at least the related suppliers and customers in the design of the system and the necessary hardware for its implementation.

What Makes Systems Different

From an investment point of view, the typical handling problem of the past has been primarily concerned with the economic justification of single items of handling equipment. In a few cases it may have been concerned with two or more pieces of related equipment involved in a single handling project. However, the systems approach involves consideration of the *total* handling function as an entity, and of the physical implementation of the function as an entity. This means a conceptualization of a complete, integrated handling system in terms of equipment requirements. And this in turn will frequently mean the design of completely new handling devices—not merely the collection of a number of existing pieces of equipment.

Changing Criteria in Evaluation of Investments

Because of the implications of this more complex approach, the traditional ways of evaluating and comparing equipment alternatives also call for a new way of thinking. It must be one which will not only include the proven methods of economic evaluation, but which will also assure proper consideration of many factors that were not previously of significance, or which were not even recognized as having a bearing on the investment aspect of the problem.

In the past, evaluations of the types of installations implied in this discussion have been based on more-or-less commonly accepted criteria. Such criteria are acceptable because they are

1. easy to identify;
2. simple to evaluate;
3. easy to comprehend;
4. understood by all;
5. time-tested.

The more commonly accepted criteria include:

1. Return on investment
2. Reduced direct or indirect labor
3. Annual savings
4. Payback period
5. Additional capacity
6. Higher quality
7. Improved safety

However, as pointed out in the first paragraph of this paper, such commonplace criteria are no longer adequate—by themselves—in making investments in complex systems of equipment. The vision of management has become much too limited in light of present and future trends. Technology, competition, and increased concern for other than cost factors must be given proper consideration.

Criteria for Evaluation

If all factors of significance in evaluating either individual pieces of equipment or systems are to be taken into consideration, all must be properly identified. It is suggested that they be grouped into four categories:

1. *Direct cost factors*—commonly associated with the operation of a piece of equipment.
2. *Indirect cost factors*—associated with the investment or operation, but not in a direct relationship.
3. *Indeterminate cost factors* (Ref. 3)—although related, these factors cannot be precisely determined or fixed, are vague, frequently not known in advance, or do not lend themselves to the determination of a definite cost figure.
4. *Intangible factors*—in the ordinary sense, these defy quantification or calculation of a dollar value and therefore cannot be included as items in a cost comparison.

Table 17-A-1 is a listing of factors for consideration in investment analysis, including a large number of the more significant ones in the latter two categories.

Evaluation of Investment Criteria

The tremendous number of items shown on Table 17-A-1 certainly does not simplify the task of those who have the responsibility for making investment decisions. In fact, it may appear to complicate it unnecessarily. This need not be the case, *if* the problem is undertaken in an orderly fashion. This paper will present an approach to the consideration of this complex task.

Past practice in investment evaluation has been centered primarily on the direct costs (Fig. 17-A-1) and, to a certain extent, on the indirect costs (Fig. 17-A-2)—as outlined in Table 17-A-1. Even with such relatively easy-to-handle cost items, there is not uniform agreement on how the factors should be combined in a conveniently usable fashion, to provide a basis for decision-making. However, there are several approaches* to such cost factors, such as return on investment, profitability index, and the MAPI "formula." Therefore, the balance of this paper will concern itself with the indeterminate cost factors and the intangible factors.

Evaluation of Indeterminate Cost Factors

Indeterminate cost factors, it will be remembered, are those which *can* be reduced to a monetary value, but which are frequently omitted because of their vague relationships to costs. This group of costs consists primarily of those which are frequently "buried" in overhead, overlooked in analysis, or ignored because they are more difficult to identify and/or determine. In fact, in many cases, the analyst may not even be aware of them as possible cost components. Nevertheless, they are nearly all reducible to dollars and should be evaluated relatively easily with the aid of a form similar to that shown in Fig. 17-A-3. The columns are explained as follows:

*For details on these techniques, refer to one of the several engineering economy textbooks or Part I of this book.

Table 17-A-1

FACTORS FOR CONSIDERATION IN INVESTMENT ANALYSIS

Direct costs	Indirect costs	Indeterminate costs	Intangible factors
Fixed Depreciation Interest on investment Taxes Insurance Supervisory personnel Clerical help Maintenance personnel Other	**Equipment/Method** Space occupied Effect on taxes Effect on inventory value Value of repair parts Demurrage charges Downtime charges Changes in production rate	**Equipment/Method** Space lost or gained Changes in overhead Inventory control savings Inventory taking savings Production control savings Changes in product or material quality Life of job using equipment Reduction in physical effort	**Equipment/Method** Quality of equipment Durability of equipment Compatibility of equipment Standardization of equipment and components Flexibility Adaptability Complexity Safety	**Equipment/Method** Rate of obsolescence Manufacturer's reputation Availability of equipment Post-sale advice/service Availability of service Availability of repair parts Quality of service
Variable Operating personnel Fuel, power Lubrication Maintenance, parts and supplies Maintenance, labor	**Management** Travel expenses incurred in investigation Cost of follow-up Relayout costs Training of personnel Overtime required to make up for lost production Volume of work-in-process Charges to operation after full depreciation Handling returned goods	**Management** Lost production due to delay in installation Percentage of time equipment will be utilized Additional labor required for increased capacity Turnover of work in process Changes in line balance Trends in business volume Trends in equipment costs Improved work flow Ease of supervision Reduction in paper work	**Management** Financial policy Economic survival goals Effect of future changes Plans for expansion Labor relations aspects Effect on morale Increased salability of product Improved customer service Pride in installation	

Equipment Operating Cost Determination

Item	Alternative No. 1		Alternative No. 2	
Equipment Data				
Make	*Acme*		*Budget*	
Type	*direct*		*direct*	
Model	*46*		*B-3*	
Capacity	*5000 / HR*		*5200 / HR.*	
Accessories	—		—	
Attachments	—		—	
Operating characteristics	—		—	
Investment				
Invoice price	*$39,000*		*$33,000*	
Installation charges	*4000*		*5000*	
Maintenance facilities	*1000*		*1500*	
Fueling &/or power facilities	*2800*		*2800*	
Alterations to present	*6000*		*6000*	
Freight &/or transportation facilities	*600*		*1000*	
Design work	*1800*		*1400*	
Supplies	*1600*		*1800*	
Other charges *(travel + training)*	*3000*		*2500*	
Credits	—		—	
Total Investment Cost	*$60,000*		*$55,000*	
Fixed Charges	8 hours	16 hours	8 hours	16 hours
Depreciation *(5 yr.-st. line -20%)*	*$12,000*		*$11,000*	
Interest on investment *(10%)*	*6,000*		*5,500*	
Taxes *(25%) at 30% assessment*	*500*		*420*	
Insurance *(5%) at 75% coverage*	*230*		*180*	
Supervision *(50% x $5,000 wage)*	*2500*		*2500*	
Clerical *(25% x $4,000 wage)*	*1000*		*1000*	
Maintenance personnel *(10% x $8,000 wage)*	*800*		*800*	
Other	*170*		*100*	
Total Fixed Cost	*$23,200*		*21,500*	
Variable Charges				
Operating personnel *(% x $ wage)*	*$9750*	*(3 men)*	*$6500*	*(2 men)*
Power &/or fuel costs	*250*		*200*	
Lubricants	*100*		*100*	
Maintenance parts & materials	*500*		*600*	
Maintenance labor	*6200*		*5100*	
Other	—		—	
Total Variable Cost	*$16,800*		*$12,500*	
Other Overhead *(% x $)*	—		—	
Total Annual Cost	*$40,000*		*$34,000*	
Operating Hours per Year	*2000*		*2000*	
Cost per Hour of Operation	*$20.00*		*$17.00*	

Figure 17-A-1. Materials handling analysis.

Factors

In this column, list the indeterminate factors from the two general categories:

1. Those which are related in some way to the *equipment* being considered or to the *method* of handling.
2. Those in which the degree of importance and, therefore, the extent of their effect on the analysis, depends upon *management* decision or policies and the effectiveness of the management of the plant.

There are undoubtedly other factors which might be listed in specific situations, and probably the line of demarcation is debatable, in some instances.

Probable effect

This column provides for a consideration of the effect of the individual factor on the evaluation being considered. Care should be exercised here to

☒ Indirect   ☐ Indeterminate

Project *Warehouse handling* Alternative *No. 1* Analysis by *A.M.J.* Date *June 28*

Factors	Probable Effect on Analysis		Cost Basis (sq. ft., lbs., hrs., etc. in dollar/unit)	Evaluation Basis in No. of Units	Estimated Dollar Value of Factor		Remarks
	Adv. −	Dis- adv. +			Advant. −	Disadv. +	
Space occuped	✓		*$100/sq. ft. per year*	*5000 sq. ft.*	*$5000*		*less than previous method*
Increased taxes		✓		*Estimate*		*$3000*	*due to incr. in value of availability*
Repair parts inventory		✓	*$4000*	*25% Carrying charge*		*1000*	*over & above previous inventory*
Subtotals					*$ −5000*	*$ +4000*	
Total Evaluation of Cost Factors					*$ −1000*		*Savings = negative Cost*

Figure 17-A-2. Evaluation of indirect cost factors.

□ Indirect   ☒ Indeterminate

Project _Warehouse handling_ Alternative _No. 1_ Analysis by _A.M.J._ Date _June 28_

Factors	Probable Effect on Analysis		Cost Basis (sq. ft., lbs., hrs., etc. in dollar/unit)	Evaluation Basis in No. of Units	Estimated Dollar Value of Factor		Remarks
	Adv. −	Dis-adv. +			Advant. −	Disadv. +	
Higher overhead		✓	$83/mo	12 mo.		$1000	
Saving in taking inventory	✓		$4/HR	500 HR	$2000		
Reduced damage	✓		50% less	.50 × $2000	1000		based on last year
Reduced labor req'd	✓		$1.50/HR	10%×8000HR	1200		increased productivity
Lost production due to delay in installation		✓	$2000/WK	1 week		2000	
Additional labor req'd for increased capacity		✓	5% =/man @ $1.50/HR	2000 HR.		3000	
Easier supervision	✓		$2.80/HR	1000 HR saved	2800		
Reduction in paperwork	✓		$2.00/HR	250 HR	500		
			Subtotals		$−7500	$+6000	
			Total Evaluation of Cost Factors		$−1500		

Figure 17-A-3. Evaluation of indeterminate cost factors.

be *sure* the factor is interpreted in the proper "direction," in terms of its effect. A factor which is considered to be advantageous to the project at hand should be placed in the minus (−) column, since it results in a savings, or *negative* cost.

Cost basis

This column should contain the *basis* upon which the cost evaluation is to be made for each factor, in terms of the unit to be used and the dollar value per unit (that is, $5 per sq ft, $10 per hr, and so forth).

Evaluation basis

This column will show the number of "base units" (that is, 1000 sq ft, 40 hr, and so forth).

Estimated value

This column is the product of columns 3 and 4, and the value must be placed in the plus or minus column to correspond with the decision made in column 2, in terms of the effect of the factor on the evaluation.

Remarks

In this column may be entered a note to indicate the desired disposition of the factor and its resulting dollar value—that is, *if* it will be included in the total (any factor may be deleted, if deemed proper or desirable).

The total can now be determined for consideration along with the direct and indirect costs and the intangible factors, as will be shown later.

Evaluating Intangible Factors

This is the last category of factors to be evaluated, and that which practically defies quantification, or reduction to dollars. As has been suggested earlier, the intangible factors are the most difficult to take into consideration in their proper relationship to the problem of investment evaluation or equipment selection. In fact, their evaluation by any means is almost wholly subjective and therefore dependent on the judgment of the person making the evaluation. Undoubtedly some can be assigned a quantitative value, by means of educated estimates, but none is likely to be accurate enough to justify adding it into the real cost of the project being analyzed.

However, this does not justify omission of the factors from consideration, nor does it minimize their usefulness in contributing to the required decision. They are extremely important, and in many cases may outweigh or override the more easily determined cost items. The following outline (adapted from Ref. 1) suggests a method of evaluation which will permit their importance to be judged in proper perspective to the more tangible aspects of the problem:

1. *Determine from the list* (Table 17-A-1) *all factors that affect or apply to any of the alternatives under consideration*, adding any others which may be pertinent. This will simplify the problem.
2. *Review the factors* selected (in step 1) *and reword*, or restate them, if necessary, *to be sure they are well defined* and clearcut; that is, none should imply another—they should not be contradictory to each other (dependent on each other or have a cumulative effect on each other). This may mean the elimination of more factors or the combination of two or more into a new, single, more clearly stated factor.
3. *Determine the relative importance* of each factor, from most important

to least important. List them in this order, and double-check to be sure they are in their best order. This should most likely be done in cooperation with other persons acquainted with the project. Decide on final order.

4. *Assign an importance value to each factor*, using 100 for the most important, and a lesser value to each of the others, based on the judgment of the evaluator(s). (The preceding data can now be entered on the "intangible factor evaluation sheet"—Fig. 17-A-4, in columns 1 and 2.)

5. If desired, *adjust the values* so that the total is 100—for convenience. This is done by totaling the unadjusted values, dividing *each* by the sum, and multiplying the result by 100. Enter these values on the work sheet in column 3.

6. *Evaluate each factor for each alternative* in terms of its relative importance or *effect* on the project at hand, on the basis of 100 for the most important, and so forth. Enter these ratings in the columns numbered 4, for each alternative. Care must be taken in this evaluation to assure that the *best* or *most desirable* rating is at the high end of the "100% scale." That is, it is easy to become "mentally reversed" in evaluating some factors, and assign the best rating to a *low* value because a low number is more compatible with the nature of the factor. An example is "rate of obsolescence," where the tendency might be to evaluate the *most* longevity with the lowest obsolescence. A low obsolescence rate should be given a high value!

Project *Warehouse handling*

Evaluation(s) *A. M. J., M. E. M., J. J. J.* Date *June 28*

Factors (in order of importance)	Importance Value	Adjusted Importance Value	Alternatives Under Consideration					
			Altern 1		Altern 2		Altern 3	
			Eval- uation Rating	Weighted Eval. Rating	Eval. Rating	Wgt'd Eval. Rat'g	Eval. Rating	Wgt'd Eval. Rat'g
1	2	3	4	5	4	5	4	5
Improved Customer Service	100	23	90	20.7	95	21.9	100	23.0
Quality of equipment	90	21	80	16.8	85	17.9	90	18.9
Availability of Service	80	18	50	9.0	70	12.6	95	17.1
Availability of equipment	70	16	70	11.2	85	13.6	100	16.0
Effect on morale	50	11	80	8.8	90	9.9	95	10.5
Complexity	30	7	80	5.6	85	6.0	90	6.3
Flexibility	20	4	75	3.0	80	3.2	80	3.2
Totals	440	100	—	75	—	85	—	95

Figure 17-A-4. Intangible factor evaluation sheet.

7. *Determine weighted evaluation* rating by multiplying column 3 by column 4 and enter result in column 5.

8. *Total weighted evaluations* for each alternative at the bottom of each column 5.

Reaching the Final Decision

At this point, *all* factors—direct, indirect, indeterminate, and intangible—will have been evaluated. It is now possible to accumulate all four as bases for the final decision on which alternative should be chosen. All that has preceded is intended only to *guide* the analyst in his thinking. At this point, he (or they) must decide which alternative is to be chosen, on the basis of the information at hand. And, of course, there is always the likelihood that the evaluation of the intangibles may be "counter" to the cost aspects of the problem. Here again, the analyst must exercise *his* judgment in deciding whether or not the intangibles outweigh the cost factors, and to what extent.

If it is desired, the analyst may "weight" the cost results by the "value" of the intangible factors. At first glance, this may appear illogical, or even "illegal"—but due consideration will indicate the plausibility of such a procedure. If done, the calculation should be

$$\frac{\text{Total of cost factors}}{\text{Weighted evaluation of intangible factors}} = \frac{\text{Weighted evaluation of}}{\text{cost factors}}$$

The resulting values would appear as shown in Fig. 17-A-5. Examination will show that neither alternative 2 (lowest direct cost) nor alternative 1

	Alternative No. 1 ACME	Alternative No. 2 BUDGET	Alternative No. 3 DELUXE
1. Calculated value of direct cost factors	$40,000	$34,000	$41,000
2. Calculated value of indirect cost factors	1,000	+ 6,000 (disadvantage)	−3,000
3. Estimated value of indeterminate cost factors	1,500	−1,000	+2,000 (disadvantage)
4. Total of direct, indirect and indeterminate cost factors	$37,000	$39,000	$40,000
5. Weighted evaluation of intangible factors	75	85	95
6. Weighted evaluation of total of all cost factors	$50,000	$46,000	$42,000

Figure 17-A-5. Recap of investment costs.

(lowest total cost) comes out "best," *all* things considered. Alternative 3 (highest total cost) results in the lowest weighted evaluation of $42,000.00.

Conclusion

This paper has attempted to show that many factors must be given consideration in evaluating investment alternatives. In addition to the more common direct and indirect costs, a large number of indeterminate costs and intangible factors have been identified. Techniques have been developed for evaluating the last two categories and for taking them into consideration in arriving at an investment decision.

It is felt that more accurate results will be obtained by this method of analysis. It may also be found that, in many cases, the indeterminate cost factors and the intangible factors will alter the investment decision from that which might have been made without their due consideration.

References

1. Barish, Norman N., *Economic Analysis* (New York: McGraw-Hill Book Company, 1962), Chapter 27.
2. Nadler, Gerald, "What Systems *Really* Are," *Modern Materials Handling* (July 1965).
3. *Webster's Seventh New Collegiate Dictionary* (Springfield, Massachusetts: G. and C. Merriam Company), 1963.

APPENDIX 17-B

Comments on "Criteria for Investment in Handling Systems" (by James M. Apple)*

There is an important weakness in the main point of this article—the dividing of "total of . . . cost factors" by the "weighted evaluation of intangible factors" to give a "weighted evaluation of . . . cost factors" for use as the deci-

*By J. R. Canada. Reprinted from *The Journal of Industrial Engineering*, Vol. 19, No. 7 (July 1968), by permission of the publisher.

sion criteria. While this is an interesting approach to the tough problem of weighting intangibles with cost results, it is an over-simplification which I feel should not be propagated without a clear recognition of its weaknesses.

Professor Apple refers to his advocated division operation combining the effect of cost factors and intangibles by saying: "At first glance, this may appear illogical or even illegal, but due consideration will indicate the plausibility of such a procedure." To justify this, he demonstrates that a lower "weighted evaluation of intangible factors" will produce a higher "weighted evaluation of the total of all cost factors," thus making a project relatively less desirable. The fact that the advocated operation will adjust the weighted evaluation in the right *direction* does not mean it provides a correct or even fairly reasonably correct adjustment.

The fundamental problem with the division operation for combining the factors is that it does not provide for the relative importance of intangibles, taken as a whole, to the "total of . . . cost factors." To illustrate this, consider the same example results used in Fig. 17-A-5 of the article.

	Alt 1	Alt 2	Alt 3
4. Total of all direct, indirect and indeterminate cost factors	$37,500	$39,000	$40,000
5. Weighted evaluation of *intangible* factors	75	85	95

Suppose, for the sake of my illustration, that the intangible factors as a whole are of no significance compared to the cost factors. In this case, alternative 1 would be chosen *regardless* of the weighted evaluation concerning how well each alternative meets intangible criteria. At the other extreme, suppose that intangible factors are of overwhelming importance compared to cost factors. In this case, alternative 3, having the highest weighted evaluation of intangible factors, would be chosen *regardless* of the other cost factors. Admittedly, these are extreme conditions, but this points out the problem.

In an attempt to offer some replacement for Professor Apple's measure of alternative project desirability, which includes intangible factors as well as cost factors, I would like to suggest the following:

Weighted evaluation of all factors
$$= k[\text{Index of direct, indirect, and indeterminate cost factors}]$$
$$+ (1 - k)[\text{Weighted evaluation of intangible factors}]$$

where k is the relative importance of cost factors compared to intangible factors (ranging from 0 to 1.0), and "index of . . . cost factors" is the relative desirability of the total costs for all projects, and is a maximum of 1.0 for the lowest cost alternative and correspondingly lower for higher cost alternatives. The "index of . . . cost factors" can be subjectively estimated based on calculated costs in the same way that weights and evaluation ratings for intangibles are estimated.

Below is illustrated this suggested index procedure using Professor Apple's illustrative figures with estimated "indices of . . . cost factors" of 1.0, 0.96, and 0.94 for alternatives 1, 2, and 3 respectively.

If the evaluator feels that intangible factors are 4 times as important as the total of all cost factors, then k equals 0.2, and the weighted evaluation for each alternative can be calculated as

Alt. 1: $0.2(1.0) + 0.8(0.75) = 0.800$

Alt. 2: $0.2(0.96) + 0.8(0.85) = 0.862$

Alt. 3: $0.2(0.94) + 0.8(0.95) = 0.948$ (highest)

If, on the other hand, the evaluator feels that the cost factors are 4 times as important as intangible factors, then k equals 0.8; and the weighted evaluation for each alternative can be calculated as

Alt. 1: $0.8(1.0) + 0.2(0.75) = 0.950$ (highest)

Alt. 2: $0.8(0.96) + 0.2(0.85) = 0.940$

Alt. 3: $0.8(0.94) + 0.2(0.95) = 0.942$

Thus, alternative 3 is computed to be best when intangibles are weighted comparatively high, while alternative 1 is computed to be best when the total of all cost factors is weighted comparatively high.

appendix A-A

Tables of Discrete
Compound Interest Factors

Period N	Single sum compound amount (F/P,i,N) $(1 + i)^N$	Single sum present worth (P/F,i,N) $\dfrac{1}{(1 + i)^N}$	Uniform series compound amount (F/A,i,N) $\dfrac{(1 + i)^N - 1}{i}$	Sinking fund (A/F,i,N) $\dfrac{i}{(1 + i)^N - 1}$	Capital recovery (A/P,i,N) $\dfrac{i(1 + i)^N}{(1 + i)^N - 1}$	Uniform series present worth (P/A,i,N) $\dfrac{(1 + i)^N - 1}{i(1 + i)^N}$
1	1.005	0.9950	1.000	1.00000	1.00500	0.995
2	1.010	0.9901	2.005	0.49875	0.50375	1.985
3	1.015	0.9851	3.015	0.33167	0.33667	2.970
4	1.020	0.9802	4.030	0.24813	0.25313	3.950
5	1.025	0.9754	5.050	0.19801	0.20301	4.926
6	1.030	0.9705	6.076	0.16460	0.16960	5.896
7	1.036	0.9657	7.106	0.14073	0.14573	6.862
8	1.041	0.9609	8.141	0.12283	0.12783	7.823
9	1.046	0.9561	9.182	0.10891	0.11391	8.779
10	1.051	0.9513	10.228	0.09777	0.10277	9.730
11	1.056	0.9466	11.279	0.08866	0.09366	10.677
12	1.062	0.9419	12.336	0.08107	0.08607	11.619
13	1.067	0.9372	13.397	0.07464	0.07964	12.556
14	1.072	0.9326	14.464	0.06914	0.07414	13.489
15	1.078	0.9279	15.537	0.06436	0.06936	14.417
16	1.083	0.9233	16.614	0.06019	0.06519	15.340
17	1.088	0.9187	17.697	0.05651	0.06151	16.259
18	1.094	0.9141	18.786	0.05323	0.05823	17.173
19	1.099	0.9096	19.880	0.05030	0.05530	18.082
20	1.105	0.9051	20.979	0.04767	0.05267	18.987
21	1.110	0.9006	22.084	0.04528	0.05028	19.888
22	1.116	0.8961	23.194	0.04311	0.04811	20.784
23	1.122	0.8916	24.310	0.04113	0.04613	21.676
24	1.127	0.8872	25.432	0.03932	0.04432	22.563
25	1.133	0.8828	26.559	0.03765	0.04265	23.446
26	1.138	0.8784	27.692	0.03611	0.04111	24.324
27	1.144	0.8740	28.830	0.03469	0.03969	25.198
28	1.150	0.8697	29.975	0.03336	0.03836	26.068
29	1.156	0.8653	31.124	0.03213	0.03713	26.933
30	1.161	0.8610	32.280	0.03098	0.03598	27.794
35	1.191	0.8398	38.145	0.02622	0.03122	32.035
40	1.221	0.8191	44.159	0.02265	0.02765	36.172
45	1.252	0.7990	50.324	0.01987	0.02487	40.207
50	1.283	0.7793	56.645	0.01765	0.02265	44.143
55	1.316	0.7601	63.126	0.01584	0.02084	47.981
60	1.349	0.7414	69.770	0.01433	0.01933	51.726
65	1.383	0.7231	76.582	0.01306	0.01806	55.377
70	1.418	0.7053	83.566	0.01197	0.01697	58.939
75	1.454	0.6879	90.727	0.01102	0.01602	62.414
80	1.490	0.6710	98.068	0.01020	0.01520	65.802
85	1.528	0.6545	105.594	0.00947	0.01447	69.108
90	1.567	0.6383	113.311	0.00883	0.01383	72.331
95	1.606	0.6226	121.222	0.00825	0.01325	75.476
100	1.647	0.6073	129.334	0.00773	0.01273	78.543

Period N	Single sum compound amount (F/P,i,N) $(1 + i)^N$	Single sum present worth (P/F,i,N) $\dfrac{1}{(1 + i)^N}$	Uniform series compound amount (F/A,i,N) $\dfrac{(1 + i)^N - 1}{i}$	Sinking fund (A/F,i,N) $\dfrac{i}{(1 + i)^N - 1}$	Capital recovery (A/P,i,N) $\dfrac{i(1 + i)^N}{(1 + i)^N - 1}$	Uniform series present worth (P/A,i,N) $\dfrac{(1 + i)^N - 1}{i(1 + i)^N}$
1	1.010	0.9901	1.000	1.00000	1.01000	0.990
2	1.020	0.9803	2.010	0.49751	0.50751	1.970
3	1.030	0.9706	3.030	0.33002	0.34002	2.941
4	1.041	0.9610	4.060	0.24628	0.25628	3.902
5	1.051	0.9515	5.101	0.19604	0.20604	4.853
6	1.062	0.9420	6.152	0.16255	0.17255	5.795
7	1.072	0.9327	7.214	0.13863	0.14863	6.728
8	1.083	0.9235	8.286	0.12069	0.13069	7.652
9	1.094	0.9143	9.369	0.10674	0.11674	8.566
10	1.105	0.9053	10.462	0.09558	0.10558	9.471
11	1.116	0.8963	11.567	0.08645	0.09645	10.368
12	1.127	0.8874	12.683	0.07885	0.08885	11.255
13	1.138	0.8787	13.809	0.07241	0.08241	12.134
14	1.149	0.8700	14.947	0.06690	0.07690	13.004
15	1.161	0.8613	16.097	0.06212	0.07212	13.865
16	1.173	0.8528	17.258	0.05794	0.06794	14.718
17	1.184	0.8444	18.430	0.05426	0.06426	15.562
18	1.196	0.8360	19.615	0.05098	0.06098	16.398
19	1.208	0.8277	20.811	0.04805	0.05805	17.226
20	1.220	0.8195	22.019	0.04542	0.05542	18.046
21	1.232	0.8114	23.239	0.04303	0.05303	18.857
22	1.245	0.8034	24.472	0.04086	0.05086	19.660
23	1.257	0.7954	25.716	0.03889	0.04889	20.456
24	1.270	0.7876	26.973	0.03707	0.04707	21.243
25	1.282	0.7798	28.243	0.03541	0.04541	22.023
26	1.295	0.7720	29.526	0.03387	0.04387	22.795
27	1.308	0.7644	30.821	0.03245	0.04245	23.560
28	1.321	0.7568	32.129	0.03112	0.04112	24.316
29	1.335	0.7493	33.450	0.02990	0.03990	25.066
30	1.348	0.7419	34.785	0.02875	0.03875	25.808
35	1.417	0.7059	41.660	0.02400	0.03400	29.409
40	1.489	0.6717	48.886	0.02046	0.03046	32.835
45	1.565	0.6391	56.481	0.01771	0.02771	36.095
50	1.645	0.6080	64.463	0.01551	0.02551	39.196
55	1.729	0.5785	72.852	0.01373	0.02373	42.147
60	1.817	0.5504	81.670	0.01224	0.02224	44.955
65	1.909	0.5237	90.937	0.01100	0.02100	47.627
70	2.007	0.4983	100.676	0.00993	0.01993	50.169
75	2.109	0.4741	110.913	0.00902	0.01902	52.587
80	2.217	0.4511	121.672	0.00822	0.01822	54.888
85	2.330	0.4292	132.979	0.00752	0.01752	57.078
90	2.449	0.4084	144.863	0.00690	0.01690	59.161
95	2.574	0.3886	157.354	0.00636	0.01636	61.143
100	2.705	0.3697	170.481	0.00587	0.01587	63.029

Period N	Single sum compound amount (F/P,i,N) $(1 + i)^N$	Single sum present worth (P/F,i,N) $\dfrac{1}{(1 + i)^N}$	Uniform series compound amount (F/A,i,N) $\dfrac{(1 + i)^N - 1}{i}$	Sinking fund (A/F,i,N) $\dfrac{i}{(1 + i)^N - 1}$	Capital recovery (A/P,i,N) $\dfrac{i(1 + i)^N}{(1 + i)^N - 1}$	Uniform series present worth (P/A,i,N) $\dfrac{(1 + i)^N - 1}{i(1 + i)^N}$
1	1.020	0.9804	1.000	1.00000	1.02000	0.980
2	1.040	0.9612	2.020	0.49505	0.51505	1.942
3	1.061	0.9423	3.060	0.32675	0.34675	2.884
4	1.082	0.9238	4.122	0.24262	0.26262	3.808
5	1.104	0.9057	5.204	0.19216	0.21216	4.713
6	1.126	0.8880	6.308	0.15853	0.17853	5.601
7	1.149	0.8706	7.434	0.13451	0.15451	6.472
8	1.172	0.8535	8.583	0.11651	0.13651	7.325
9	1.195	0.8368	9.755	0.10252	0.12252	8.162
10	1.219	0.8203	10.950	0.09133	0.11133	8.983
11	1.243	0.8043	12.169	0.08218	0.10218	9.787
12	1.268	0.7885	13.412	0.07456	0.09456	10.575
13	1.294	0.7730	14.680	0.06812	0.08812	11.348
14	1.319	0.7579	15.974	0.06260	0.08260	12.106
15	1.346	0.7430	17.293	0.05783	0.07783	12.849
16	1.373	0.7284	18.639	0.05365	0.07365	13.578
17	1.400	0.7142	20.012	0.04997	0.06997	14.292
18	1.428	0.7002	21.412	0.04670	0.06670	14.992
19	1.457	0.6864	22.841	0.04378	0.06378	15.678
20	1.486	0.6730	24.297	0.04116	0.06116	16.351
21	1.516	0.6598	25.783	0.03878	0.05878	17.011
22	1.546	0.6468	27.299	0.03663	0.05663	17.658
23	1.577	0.6342	28.845	0.03467	0.05467	18.292
24	1.608	0.6217	30.422	0.03287	0.05287	18.914
25	1.641	0.6095	32.030	0.03122	0.05122	19.523
26	1.673	0.5976	33.671	0.02970	0.04970	20.121
27	1.707	0.5859	35.344	0.02829	0.04829	20.707
28	1.741	0.5744	37.051	0.02699	0.04699	21.281
29	1.776	0.5631	38.792	0.02578	0.04578	21.844
30	1.811	0.5521	40.568	0.02465	0.04465	22.396
35	2.000	0.5000	49.994	0.02000	0.04000	24.999
40	2.208	0.4529	60.402	0.01656	0.03656	27.355
45	2.438	0.4102	71.893	0.01391	0.03391	29.490
50	2.692	0.3715	84.579	0.01182	0.03182	31.424
55	2.972	0.3365	98.587	0.01014	0.03014	33.175
60	3.281	0.3048	114.052	0.00877	0.02877	34.761
65	3.623	0.2761	131.126	0.00763	0.02763	36.197
70	4.000	0.2500	149.978	0.00667	0.02667	37.499
75	4.416	0.2265	170.792	0.00586	0.02586	38.677
80	4.875	0.2051	193.772	0.00516	0.02516	39.745
85	5.383	0.1858	219.144	0.00456	0.02456	40.711
90	5.943	0.1683	247.157	0.00405	0.02405	41.587
95	6.562	0.1524	278.085	0.00360	0.02360	42.380
100	7.245	0.1380	312.232	0.00320	0.02320	43.098

3% Interest Factors

Period N	Single sum compound amount (F/P,i,N) $(1 + i)^N$	Single sum present worth (P/F,i,N) $\dfrac{1}{(1 + i)^N}$	Uniform series compound amount (F/A,i,N) $\dfrac{(1 + i)^N - 1}{i}$	Sinking fund (A/F,i,N) $\dfrac{i}{(1 + i)^N - 1}$	Capital recovery (A/P,i,N) $\dfrac{i(1 + i)^N}{(1 + i)^N - 1}$	Uniform series present worth (P/A,i,N) $\dfrac{(1 + i)^N - 1}{i(1 + i)^N}$
1	1.030	0.9709	1.000	1.00000	1.03000	0.971
2	1.061	0.9426	2.030	0.49261	0.52261	1.913
3	1.093	0.9151	3.091	0.32353	0.35353	2.829
4	1.126	0.8885	4.184	0.23903	0.26903	3.717
5	1.159	0.8626	5.309	0.18835	0.21835	4.850
6	1.194	0.8375	6.468	0.15460	0.18460	5.417
7	1.230	0.8131	7.662	0.13051	0.16051	6.230
8	1.267	0.7894	8.892	0.11246	0.14246	7.020
9	1.305	0.7664	10.159	0.09843	0.12843	7.786
10	1.344	0.7441	11.464	0.08723	0.11723	8.530
11	1.384	0.7224	12.808	0.07808	0.10808	9.253
12	1.426	0.7014	14.192	0.07046	0.10046	9.954
13	1.469	0.6810	15.618	0.06403	0.09403	10.635
14	1.513	0.6611	17.086	0.05853	0.08853	11.296
15	1.558	0.6419	18.599	0.05377	0.08377	11.938
16	1.605	0.6232	20.157	0.04961	0.07961	12.561
17	1.653	0.6050	21.762	0.04595	0.07595	13.166
18	1.702	0.5874	23.414	0.04271	0.07271	13.754
19	1.754	0.5703	25.117	0.03981	0.06981	14.324
20	1.806	0.5537	26.870	0.03722	0.06722	14.877
21	1.860	0.5375	28.676	0.03487	0.06487	15.415
22	1.916	0.5219	30.537	0.03275	0.06275	15.937
23	1.974	0.5067	32.453	0.03081	0.06081	16.444
24	2.033	0.4919	34.426	0.02905	0.05905	16.936
25	2.094	0.4776	36.459	0.02743	0.05743	17.413
26	2.157	0.4637	38.553	0.02594	0.05594	17.877
27	2.221	0.4502	40.710	0.02456	0.05456	18.327
28	2.288	0.4371	42.931	0.02329	0.05329	18.764
29	2.357	0.4243	45.219	0.02211	0.05211	19.188
30	2.427	0.4120	47.575	0.02102	0.05102	19.600
35	2.814	0.3554	60.462	0.01654	0.04654	21.487
40	3.262	0.3066	75.401	0.01326	0.04326	23.115
45	3.782	0.2644	92.720	0.01079	0.04079	24.519
50	4.384	0.2281	112.797	0.00887	0.03887	25.730
55	5.082	0.1968	136.072	0.00735	0.03735	26.774
60	5.892	0.1697	163.053	0.00613	0.03613	27.676
65	6.830	0.1464	194.333	0.00515	0.03515	28.453
70	7.918	0.1263	230.594	0.00434	0.03434	29.123
75	9.179	0.1089	272.631	0.00367	0.03367	29.702
80	10.641	0.0940	321.363	0.00311	0.03311	30.201
85	12.336	0.0811	377.857	0.00265	0.03265	30.631
90	14.300	0.0699	443.349	0.00226	0.03226	31.002
95	16.578	0.0603	519.272	0.00193	0.03193	31.323
100	19.219	0.0520	607.288	0.00165	0.03165	31.599

Period N	Single sum compound amount (F/P,i,N) $(1 + i)^N$	Single sum present worth (P/F,i,N) $\dfrac{1}{(1 + i)^N}$	Uniform series compound amount (F/A,i,N) $\dfrac{(1 + i)^N - 1}{i}$	Sinking fund (A/F,i,N) $\dfrac{i}{(1 + i)^N - 1}$	Capital recovery (A/P,i,N) $\dfrac{i(1 + i)^N}{(1 + i)^N - 1}$	Uniform series present worth (P/A,i,N) $\dfrac{(1 + i)^N - 1}{i(1 + i)^N}$
1	1.040	0.9615	1.000	1.00000	1.04000	0.962
2	1.082	0.9246	2.040	0.49020	0.53020	1.886
3	1.125	0.8890	3.122	0.32035	0.36035	2.775
4	1.170.	0.8548	4.246	0.23549	0.27549	3.630
5	1.217	0.8219	5.416	0.18463	0.22463	4.452
6	1.265	0.7903	6.633	0.15076	0.19076	5.242
7	1.316	0.7599	7.898	0.12661	0.16661	6.002
8	1.369	0.7307	9.214	0.10853	0.14853	6.733
9	1.423	0.7026	10.583	0.09449	0.13449	7.435
10	1.480	0.6756	12.006	0.08329	0.12329	8.111
11	1.539	0.6496	13.486	0.07415	0.11415	8.760
12	1.601	0.6246	15.026	0.06655	0.10655	9.385
13	1.665	0.6006	16.627	0.06014	0.10014	9.986
14	1.732	0.5775	18.292	0.05467	0.09467	10.563
15	1.801	0.5553	20.024	0.04994	0.08994	11.118
16	1.873	0.5339	21.825	0.04582	0.08582	11.652
17	1.948	0.5134	23.698	0.04220	0.08220	12.166
18	2.026	0.4936	25.645	0.03899	0.07899	12.659
19	2.107	0.4746	27.671	0.03614	0.07614	13.134
20	2.191	0.4564	29.778	0.03358	0.07358	13.590
21	2.279	0.4388	31.969	0.03128	0.07128	14.029
22	2.370	0.4220	34.248	0.02920	0.06920	14.451
23	2.465	0.4057	36.618	0.02731	0.06731	14.857
24	2.563	0.3901	39.083	0.02559	0.06559	15.247
25	2.666	0.3751	41.646	0.02401	0.06401	15.622
26	2.772	0.3607	44.312	0.02257	0.06257	15.983
27	2.883	0.3468	47.084	0.02124	0.06124	16.330
28	2.999	0.3335	49.968	0.02001	0.06001	16.663
29	3.119	0.3207	52.966	0.01888	0.05888	16.984
30	3.243	0.3083	56.085	0.01783	0.05783	17.292
35	3.946	0.2534	73.652	0.01358	0.05358	18.665
40	4.801	6.2083	95.026	0.01052	0.05052	19.793
45	5.841	0.1712	121.029	0.00826	0.04826	20.720
50	7.107	0.1407	152.667	0.00655	0.04655	21.482
55	8.646	0.1157	191.159	0.00523	0.04523	22.109
60	10.520	0.0951	237.991	0.00420	0.04420	22.623
65	12.799	0.0781	294.968	0.00339	0.04339	23.047
70	15.572	0.0642	364.290	0.00275	0.04275	23.395
75	18.945	0.0528	448.631	0.00223	0.04223	23.680
80	23.050	0.0434	551.245	0.00181	0.04181	23.915
85	28.044	0.0357	676.090	0.00148	0.04148	24.109
90	34.119	0.0293	827.983	0.00121	0.04121	24.267
95	41.511	0.0241	1012.785	0.00099	0.04099	24.398
100	50.505	0.0198	1237.624	0.00081	0.04081	24.505

Table A-A-6

5% INTEREST FACTORS

Period N	Single sum compound amount (F/P,i,N) $(1 + i)^N$	Single sum present worth (P/F,i,N) $\dfrac{1}{(1 + i)^N}$	Uniform series compound amount (F/A,i,N) $\dfrac{(1 + i)^N - 1}{i}$	Sinking fund (A/F,i,N) $\dfrac{i}{(1 + i)^N - 1}$	Capital recovery (A/P,i,N) $\dfrac{i(1 + i)^N}{(1 + i)^N - 1}$	Uniform series present worth (P/A,i,N) $\dfrac{(1 + i)^N - 1}{i(1 + i)^N}$
1	1.050	0.9524	1.000	1.00000	1.05000	0.952
2	1.103	0.9070	2.050	0.48780	0.53780	1.859
3	1.158	0.8638	3.153	0.31721	0.36721	2.723
4	1.216	0.8227	4.310	0.23201	0.28201	3.546
5	1.276	0.7835	5.526	0.18097	0.23097	4.329
6	1.340	0.7462	6.802	0.14702	0.19702	5.076
7	1.407	0.7107	8.142	0.12282	0.17282	5.786
8	1.477	0.6768	9.549	0.10472	0.15472	6.463
9	1.551	0.6446	11.027	0.09069	0.14069	7.108
10	1.629	0.6139	12.578	0.07950	0.12950	7.722
11	1.710	0.5847	14.207	0.07039	0.12039	8.306
12	1.796	0.5568	15.917	0.06283	0.11283	8.863
13	1.886	0.5303	17.713	0.05646	0.10646	9.394
14	1.980	0.5051	19.599	0.05102	0.10102	9.899
15	2.079	0.4810	21.579	0.04634	0.09634	10.380
16	2.183	0.4581	23.657	0.04227	0.09227	10.838
17	2.292	0.4368	25.840	0.03870	0.08870	11.274
18	2.407	0.4155	28.132	0.03555	0.08555	11.690
19	2.527	0.3957	30.539	0.03275	0.08275	12.085
20	2.653	0.3769	33.066	0.03024	0.08024	12.462
21	2.786	0.3589	35.719	0.02800	0.07800	12.821
22	2.925	0.3418	38.505	0.02597	0.07597	13.163
23	3.072	0.3256	41.430	0.02414	0.07141	13.489
24	3.225	0.3101	44.502	0.02247	0.07247	13.799
25	3.386	0.2953	47.727	0.02095	0.07095	14.094
26	3.556	0.2812	51.113	0.01956	0.06956	14.375
27	3.733	0.2678	54.669	0.01829	0.06829	14.643
28	3.920	0.2551	58.403	0.01712	0.06712	14.898
29	4.116	0.2429	62.323	0.01605	0.06005	15.141
30	4.322	0.2314	66.439	0.01505	0.06505	15.372
35	5.516	0.1813	90.320	0.01107	0.06107	16.374
40	7.040	0.1420	120.800	0.00828	0.05828	17.159
45	8.985	0.1113	159.700	0.00626	0.05626	17.774
50	11.467	0.0872	209.348	0.00478	0.05478	18.256
55	14.636	0.0683	272.713	0.00367	0.05367	18.633
60	18.679	0.0535	353.584	0.00283	0.05283	18.929
65	23.840	0.0419	456.798	0.00219	0.05219	19.161
70	30.426	0.0329	588.529	0.00170	0.05170	19.343
75	38.833	0.0258	756.654	0.00132	0.05132	19.485
80	49.561	0.0202	971.229	0.00103	0.05103	19.596
85	63.254	0.0158	1245.087	0.00080	0.05080	19.684
90	80.730	0.0124	1594.607	0.00063	0.05063	19.752
95	103.035	0.0097	2040.694	0.00049	0.05049	19.806
100	131.501	0.0076	2610.025	0.00038	0.05038	19.848

Period N	Single sum compound amount (F/P,i,N) $(1 + i)^N$	Single sum present worth (P/F,i,N) $\dfrac{1}{(1 + i)^N}$	Uniform series compound amount (F/A,i,N) $\dfrac{(1 + i)^N - 1}{i}$	Sinking fund (A/F,i,N) $\dfrac{i}{(1 + i)^N - 1}$	Capital recovery (A/P,i,N) $\dfrac{i(1 + i)^N}{(1 + i)^N - 1}$	Uniform series present worth (P/A,i,N) $\dfrac{(1 + i)^N - 1}{i(1 + i)^N}$
1	1.060	0.9434	1.000	1.00000	1.06000	0.943
2	1.124	0.8900	2.060	0.48544	0.54544	1.833
3	1.191	0.8396	3.184	0.31411	0.37411	2.673
4	1.262	0.7921	4.375	0.22859	0.28859	3.465
5	1.338	0.7473	5.637	0.17740	0.23740	4.212
6	1.419	0.7050	6.975	0.14336	0.20336	4.917
7	1.504	0.6651	8.394	0.11914	0.17914	5.582
8	1.594	0.6274	9.897	0.10104	0.16104	6.210
9	1.689	0.5919	11.491	0.08702	0.14702	6.802
10	1.791	0.5584	13.181	0.07587	0.13587	7.360
11	1.898	0.5268	14.972	0.06679	0.12679	7.887
12	2.012	0.4970	16.870	0.05928	0.11928	8.384
13	2.133	0.4688	18.882	0.05296	0.11296	8.853
14	2.261	0.4423	21.015	0.04758	0.10758	9.295
15	2.397	0.4173	23.276	0.04296	0.10296	9.712
16	2.540	0.3936	25.673	0.03895	0.09895	10.106
17	2.693	0.3714	28.213	0.03544	0.09544	10.477
18	2.854	0.3503	30.906	0.03236	0.09236	10.828
19	3.026	0.3305	33.760	0.02962	0.08962	11.158
20	3.207	0.3118	36.786	0.02718	0.08718	11.470
21	3.400	0.2942	39.993	0.02500	0.08500	11.764
22	3.604	0.2775	43.392	0.02305	0.08305	12.042
23	3.820	0.2618	46.996	0.02128	0.08128	12.303
24	4.049	0.2470	50.816	0.01968	0.07968	12.550
25	4.292	0.2330	54.865	0.01823	0.07823	12.783
26	4.549	0.2198	59.156	0.01690	0.07690	13.003
27	4.822	0.2074	63.706	0.01570	0.07570	13.211
28	5.112	0.1956	68.528	0.01459	0.07459	13.406
29	5.418	0.1846	73.640	0.01358	0.07358	13.591
30	5.743	0.1741	79.058	0.01265	0.07265	13.765
35	7.686	0.1301	111.435	0.00897	0.06897	14.498
40	10.286	0.0972	154.762	0.00646	0.06646	15.046
45	13.765	0.0727	212.744	0.00470	0.06470	15.456
50	18.420	0.0543	290.336	0.00344	0.06344	15.762
55	24.650	0.0406	394.172	0.00254	0.06254	15.991
60	32.988	0.0303	533.128	0.00188	0.06188	16.161
65	44.145	0.0227	719.083	0.00139	0.06139	16.289
70	59.076	0.0169	967.932	0.00103	0.06103	16.385
75	79.057	0.0126	1300.949	0.00077	0.06077	16.456
80	105.796	0.0095	1746.600	0.00057	0.06057	16.509
85	141.579	0.0071	2342.982	0.00043	0.06043	16.549
90	189.465	0.0053	3141.075	0.00032	0.06032	16.579
95	253.546	0.0039	4209.104	0.00024	0.06024	16.601
100	339.302	0.0029	5638.368	0.00018	0.06018	16.618

Period N	Single sum compound amount $(F/P,i,N)$ $(1 + i)^N$	Single sum present worth $(P/F,i,N)$ $\dfrac{1}{(1 + i)^N}$	Uniform series compound amount $(F/A,i,N)$ $\dfrac{(1 + i)^N - 1}{i}$	Sinking fund $(A/F,i,N)$ $\dfrac{i}{(1 + i)^N - 1}$	Capital recovery $(A/P,i,N)$ $\dfrac{i(1 + i)^N}{(1 + i)^N - 1}$	Uniform series present worth $(P/A,i,N)$ $\dfrac{(1 + i)^N - 1}{i(1 + i)^N}$
1	1.080	0.9259	1.000	1.00000	1.08000	0.926
2	1.166	0.8573	2.080	0.48077	0.56077	1.783
3	1.260	0.7938	3.246	0.30803	0.38803	2.577
4	1.360	0.7350	4.506	0.22192	0.30192	3.312
5	1.469	0.6806	5.867	0.17046	0.25046	3.993
6	1.587	0.6302	7.336	0.13632	0.21632	4.623
7	1.714	0.5835	8.923	0.11207	0.19207	5.206
8	1.851	0.5403	10.637	0.09401	0.17401	5.747
9	1.999	0.5002	12.488	0.08008	0.16008	6.247
10	2.159	0.4632	14.487	0.06903	0.14903	6.710
11	2.332	0.4289	16.645	0.06008	0.14008	7.139
12	2.518	0.3971	18.977	0.05270	0.13270	7.536
13	2.720	0.3677	21.495	0.04652	0.12652	7.904
14	2.937	0.3405	24.215	0.04130	0.12130	8.244
15	3.172	0.3152	27.152	0.03683	0.11683	8.559
16	3.426	0.2919	30.324	0.03298	0.11298	8.851
17	3.700	0.2703	33.750	0.02963	0.10963	9.122
18	3.996	0.2502	37.450	0.02670	0.10670	9.372
19	4.316	0.2317	41.446	0.02413	0.10413	9.604
20	4.661	0.2145	45.762	0.02185	0.10185	9.818
21	4.034	0.1987	50.423	0.01983	0.09983	10.017
22	5.437	0.1839	55.457	0.01803	0.09803	10.201
23	5.871	0.1703	60.893	0.01642	0.09642	10.371
24	6.341	0.1577	66.765	0.01498	0.09498	10.529
25	6.848	0.1460	73.106	0.01368	0.09368	10.675
26	7.396	0.1352	79.954	0.01251	0.09251	10.810
27	7.988	0.1252	87.351	0.01145	0.09145	10.935
28	8.627	0.1159	95.339	0.01049	0.09049	11.051
29	9.317	0.1073	103.966	0.00962	0.08962	11.158
30	10.063	0.0994	113.283	0.00883	0.08883	11.258
35	14.785	0.0676	172.317	0.00580	0.08580	11.655
40	21.725	0.0460	259.057	0.00386	0.08386	11.925
45	31.920	0.0313	386.506	0.00259	0.08259	12.108
50	46.902	0.0213	573.770	0.00174	0.08174	12.233
55	68.914	0.0145	848.923	0.00118	0.08118	12.319
60	101.257	0.0099	1253.213	0.00080	0.08080	12.377
65	148.780	0.0067	1847.248	0.00054	0.08054	12.416
70	218.606	0.0046	2720.080	0.00037	0.08037	12.443
75	321.205	0.0031	4002.557	0.00025	0.08025	12.461
80	471.955	0.0021	5886.935	0.00017	0.08017	12.474
85	693.456	0.0014	8655.706	0.00012	0.08012	12.482
90	1018.915	0.0010	12723.939	0.00008	0.08008	12.488
95	1497.121	0.0007	18701.507	0.00005	0.08005	12.492
100	2199.761	0.0005	27484.516	0.00004	0.08004	12.494

Period N	Single sum compound amount (F/P,i,N) $(1 + i)^N$	Single sum present worth (P/F,i,N) $\dfrac{1}{(1 + i)^N}$	Uniform series compound amount (F/A,i,N) $\dfrac{(1 + i)^N - 1}{i}$	Sinking fund (A/F,i,N) $\dfrac{i}{(1 + i)^N - 1}$	Capital recovery (A/P,i,N) $\dfrac{i(1 + i)^N}{(1 + i)^N - 1}$	Uniform series present worth (P/A,i,N) $\dfrac{(1 + i)^N - 1}{i(1 + i)^N}$
1	1.100	0.9091	1.000	1.00000	1.10000	0.909
2	1.210	0.8264	2.100	0.47619	0.57619	1.736
3	1.331	0.7513	3.310	0.30211	0.40211	2.487
4	1.464	0.6830	4.641	0.21547	0.31547	3.170
5	1.611	0.6209	6.105	0.16380	0.26380	3.791
6	1.772	0.5645	7.716	0.12961	0.22961	4.355
7	1.949	0.5132	9.487	0.10541	0.20541	4.868
8	2.144	0.4665	11.436	0.08744	0.18744	5.335
9	2.358	0.4241	13.579	0.07364	0.17364	5.759
10	2.594	0.3855	15.937	0.06275	0.16275	6.144
11	2.853	0.3505	18.531	0.05396	0.15396	6.495
12	3.138	0.3186	21.384	0.04676	0.14676	6.814
13	3.452	0.2897	24.523	0.04078	0.14078	7.103
14	3.797	0.2633	27.975	0.03575	0.13575	7.367
15	4.177	0.2394	31.772	0.03147	0.13147	7.606
16	4.595	0.2176	35.950	0.02782	0.12782	7.824
17	5.054	0.1978	40.545	0.02466	0.12466	8.022
18	5.560	0.1799	45.599	0.02193	0.12193	8.201
19	6.116	0.1635	51.159	0.01955	0.11955	8.365
20	6.727	0.1486	57.275	0.01746	0.11746	8.514
21	7.400	0.1351	64.002	0.01562	0.11562	8.649
22	8.140	0.1228	71.403	0.01401	0.11401	8.772
23	8.954	0.1117	79.543	0.01257	0.11257	8.883
24	9.850	0.1015	88.497	0.01130	0.11130	8.985
25	10.835	0.0923	98.347	0.01017	0.11017	9.077
26	11.918	0.0839	109.182	0.00916	0.10916	9.161
27	13.110	0.0763	121.100	0.00826	0.10826	9.237
28	14.421	0.0693	134.210	0.00745	0.10745	9.307
29	15.863	0.0630	148.631	0.00673	0.10673	9.370
30	17.449	0.0573	164.494	0.00608	0.10608	9.427
35	28.102	0.0356	271.024	0.00369	0.10369	9.644
40	45.259	0.0221	442.593	0.00226	0.10226	9.779
45	72.890	0.0137	718.905	0.00139	0.10139	9.863
50	117.391	0.0085	1163.909	0.00086	0.10086	9.915
55	189.059	0.0053	1880.591	0.00053	0.10053	9.947
60	304.482	0.0033	3034.816	0.00033	0.10033	9.967
65	490.371	0.0020	4893.707	0.00020	0.10020	9.980
70	789.747	0.0013	7887.470	0.00013	0.10013	9.987
75	1271.895	0.0008	12708.954	0.00008	0.10008	9.992
80	2048.400	0.0005	20474.002	0.00005	0.10005	9.995
85	3298.969	0.0003	32979.690	0.00003	0.10003	9.997
90	5313.023	0.0002	53120.226	0.00002	0.10002	9.998
95	8556.676	0.0001	85556.760	0.00001	0.10001	9.999

Period N	Single sum compound amount (F/P,i,N) $(1 + i)^N$	Single sum present worth (P/F,i,N) $\dfrac{1}{(1 + i)^N}$	Uniform series compound amount (F/A,i,N) $\dfrac{(1 + i)^N - 1}{i}$	Sinking fund (A/F,i,N) $\dfrac{i}{(1 + i)^N - 1}$	Capital recovery (A/P,i,N) $\dfrac{i(1 + i)^N}{(1 + i)^N - 1}$	Uniform series present worth (P/A,i,N) $\dfrac{(1 + i)^N - 1}{i(1 + i)^N}$
1	1.120	0.8929	1.000	1.00000	1.12000	0.893
2	1.254	0.7972	2.120	0.47170	0.59170	1.690
3	1.405	0.7118	3.374	0.29635	0.41635	2.402
4	1.574	0.6355	4.779	0.20923	0.32923	3.037
5	1.762	0.5674	6.353	0.15741	0.27741	3.605
6	1.974	0.5066	8.115	0.12323	0.24323	4.111
7	2.211	0.4523	10.089	0.09912	0.21912	4.564
8	2.476	0.4039	12.300	0.08130	0.20130	4.968
9	2.773	0.3606	14.776	0.06768	0.18768	5.328
10	3.106	0.3220	17.549	0.05698	0.17698	5.650
11	3.479	0.2875	20.655	0.04842	0.16842	5.938
12	3.896	0.2567	24.133	0.04144	0.16144	6.194
13	4.363	0.2292	28.029	0.03568	0.15568	6.424
14	4.887	0.2046	32.393	0.03087	0.15087	6.628
15	5.474	0.1827	37.280	0.02682	0.14682	6.811
16	6.130	0.1631	42.753	0.02339	0.14339	6.974
17	6.866	0.1456	48.884	0.02046	0.14046	7.120
18	7.690	0.1300	55.750	0.01794	0.13794	7.250
19	8.613	0.1161	63.440	0.01576	0.13576	7.366
20	9.646	0.1037	72.052	0.01388	0.13388	7.469
21	10.804	0.0926	81.699	0.01224	0.13224	7.562
22	12.100	0.0826	92.503	0.01081	0.13081	7.645
23	13.552	0.0738	104.603	0.00956	0.12956	7.718
24	15.179	0.0659	118.155	0.00846	0.12846	7.784
25	17.000	0.0588	133.334	0.00750	0.12750	7.843
26	19.040	0.0525	150.334	0.00665	0.12665	7.896
27	21.325	0.0469	169.374	0.00590	0.12590	7.943
28	23.884	0.0419	190.699	0.00524	0.12524	7.984
29	26.750	0.0374	214.583	0.00466	0.12466	8.022
30	29.960	0.0334	241.333	0.00414	0.12414	8.055
35	52.800	0.0189	431.663	0.00232	0.12232	8.176
40	93.051	0.0107	767.091	0.00130	0.12130	8.244
45	163.988	0.0061	1358.230	0.00074	0.12074	8.283
50	289.002	0.0035	2400.018	0.00042	0.12042	8.304
55	509.321	0.0020	4236.005	0.00024	0.12024	8.317
60	897.597	0.0011	7471.641	0.00013	0.12013	8.324
65	1581.872	0.0006	13173.937	0.00008	0.12008	8.328
70	2787.800	0.0004	23223.332	0.00004	0.12004	8.330
75	4913.056	0.0002	40933.799	0.00002	0.12002	8.332
80	8658.483	0.0001	72145.692	0.00001	0.12001	8.332

Period N	Single sum compound amount $(F/P,i,N)$ $(1 + i)^N$	Single sum present worth $(P/F,i,N)$ $\dfrac{1}{(1 + i)^N}$	Uniform series compound amount $(F/A,i,N)$ $\dfrac{(1 + i)^N - 1}{i}$	Sinking fund $(A/F,i,N)$ $\dfrac{i}{(1 + i)^N - 1}$	Capital recovery $(A/P,i,N)$ $\dfrac{i(1 + i)^N}{(1 + i)^N - 1}$	Uniform series present worth $(P/A,i,N)$ $\dfrac{(1 + i)^N - 1}{i(1 + i)^N}$
1	1.150	0.8696	1.000	1.00000	1.15000	0.870
2	1.322	0.7561	2.150	0.46512	0.61512	1.626
3	1.521	0.6575	3.472	0.28798	0.43798	2.283
4	1.749	0.5718	4.993	0.20027	0.35027	2.855
5	2.011	0.4972	6.472	0.14832	0.29832	3.352
6	2.313	0.4323	8.754	0.11424	0.26424	3.784
7	2.660	0.3759	11.067	0.09036	0.24036	4.160
8	3.059	0.3269	13.727	0.07285	0.22285	4.487
9	3.518	0.2843	16.786	0.05957	0.20957	4.772
10	4.046	0.2472	20.304	0.04925	0.19925	5.019
11	4.652	0.2149	24.349	0.04107	0.19107	5.234
12	5.350	0.1869	29.002	0.03448	0.18448	5.421
13	6.153	0.1625	34.352	0.02911	0.17911	5.583
14	7.076	0.1413	40.505	0.02469	0.17469	5.724
15	8.137	0.1229	47.580	0.02102	0.17102	5.847
16	9.358	0.1069	55.717	0.01795	0.16795	5.954
17	10.761	0.0929	65.075	0.01537	0.16537	6.047
18	12.375	0.0808	75.836	0.01319	0.16319	6.128
19	14.232	0.0703	88.212	0.01134	0.16134	6.198
20	16.367	0.0611	102.444	0.00976	0.15976	6.259
21	18.822	0.0531	118.810	0.00842	0.15842	6.312
22	21.645	0.0462	137.632	0.00727	0.15727	6.359
23	24.891	0.0402	159.276	0.00628	0.15628	6.399
24	28.625	0.0349	184.168	0.00543	0.15543	6.434
25	32.919	0.0304	212.793	0.00470	0.15470	6.464
26	37.857	0.0264	245.712	0.00407	0.15407	6.491
27	43.535	0.0230	283.569	0.00353	0.15353	6.514
28	50.066	0.0200	327.104	0.00306	0.15306	6.534
29	57.575	0.0174	377.170	0.00265	0.15265	6.551
30	66.212	0.0151	434.745	0.00230	0.15230	6.566
35	133.176	0.0075	881.170	0.00113	0.15113	6.617
40	267.864	0.0037	1779.090	0.00056	0.15056	6.642
45	538.769	0.0019	3585.128	0.00028	0.15028	6.654
50	1083.657	0.0009	7217.716	0.00014	0.15014	6.661
55	2179.622	0.0005	14524.148	0.00007	0.15007	6.664
60	4383.999	0.0002	29219.992	0.00003	0.15003	6.665
65	8817.787	0.0001	58778.583	0.00002	0.15002	6.666

Period N	Single sum compound amount (F/P,i,N) $(1 + i)^N$	Single sum present worth (P/F,i,N) $\dfrac{1}{(1 + i)^N}$	Uniform series compound amount (F/A,i,N) $\dfrac{(1 + i)^N - 1}{i}$	Sinking fund (A/F,i,N) $\dfrac{i}{(1 + i)^N - 1}$	Capital recovery (A/P,i,N) $\dfrac{i(1 + i)^N}{(1 + i)^N - 1}$	Uniform series present worth (P/A,i,N) $\dfrac{(1 + i)^N - 1}{i(1 + i)^N}$
1	1.200	0.8333	1.000	1.00000	1.20000	0.833
2	1.440	0.6944	2.200	0.45455	0.65455	1.528
3	1.728	0.5787	3.640	0.27473	0.47473	2.106
4	2.074	0.4823	5.368	0.18629	0.38629	2.589
5	2.488	0.4019	7.442	0.13438	0.33438	2.991
6	2.986	0.3349	9.930	0.10071	0.30071	3.326
7	3.583	0.2791	12.916	0.07742	0.27742	3.605
8	4.300	0.2326	16.499	0.06061	0.26061	3.837
9	5.160	0.1938	20.799	0.04808	0.24808	4.031
10	6.192	0.1615	25.959	0.03852	0.23852	4.192
11	7.430	0.1346	32.150	0.03110	0.23110	4.327
12	8.916	0.1122	39.581	0.02526	0.22526	4.439
13	10.699	0.0935	48.497	0.02062	0.22062	4.533
14	12.839	0.0779	59.196	0.01689	0.21689	4.611
15	15.407	0.0649	72.035	0.01388	0.21388	4.675
16	18.488	0.0541	87.442	0.01144	0.21144	4.730
17	22.186	0.0451	105.931	0.00944	0.20944	4.775
18	26.623	0.0376	128.117	0.00781	0.20781	4.812
19	31.948	0.0313	154.740	0.00646	0.20646	4.843
20	38.338	0.0261	186.688	0.00536	0.20536	4.870
21	46.005	0.0217	225.026	0.00444	0.20444	4.891
22	55.206	0.0181	271.031	0.00369	0.20369	4.909
23	66.247	0.0151	326.237	0.00307	0.20307	4.925
24	79.497	0.0126	392.484	0.00255	0.20255	4.937
25	95.396	0.0105	171.981	0.00212	0.20212	4.948
26	114.475	0.0087	567.377	0.00176	0.20176	4.956
27	137.371	0.0073	681.853	0.00147	0.20147	4.964
28	164.845	0.0061	819.223	0.00122	0.20122	4.970
29	197.814	0.0051	984.068	0.00102	0.20102	4.975
30	237.376	0.0042	1181.882	0.00085	0.20085	4.979
35	590.668	0.0017	2948.341	0.00034	0.20034	4.992
40	1469.772	0.0007	7343.858	0.00014	0.20014	4.997
45	3657.262	0.0003	18281.310	0.00005	0.20005	4.999
50	9100.438	0.0001	45497.191	0.00002	0.20002	4.999

Table A-A-13

25% INTEREST FACTORS

Period N	Single sum compound amount (F/P,i,N) $(1 + i)^N$	Single sum present worth (P/F,i,N) $\dfrac{1}{(1+i)^N}$	Uniform series compound amount (F/A,i,N) $\dfrac{(1+i)^N - 1}{i}$	Sinking fund (A/F,i,N) $\dfrac{i}{(1+i)^N - 1}$	Capital recovery (A/P,i,N) $\dfrac{i(1+i)^N}{(1+i)^N - 1}$	Uniform series present worth (P/A,i,N) $\dfrac{(1+i)^N - 1}{i(1+i)^N}$
1	1.250	0.8000	1.000	1.00000	1.25000	0.800
2	1.562	0.6400	2.250	0.44444	0.69444	1.440
3	1.953	0.5120	3.812	0.26230	0.51230	1.952
4	2.441	0.4096	5.766	0.17344	0.42344	2.362
5	3.052	0.3277	8.207	0.12185	0.37185	2.689
6	3.815	0.2621	11.259	0.08882	0.33882	2.951
7	4.768	0.2097	15.073	0.06634	0.31634	3.161
8	5.960	0.1678	19.842	0.05040	0.30040	3.329
9	7.451	0.1342	25.802	0.03876	0.28876	3.463
10	9.313	0.1074	33.253	0.03007	0.28007	3.571
11	11.642	0.0859	42.566	0.02349	0.27349	3.656
12	14.552	0.0687	54.208	0.01845	0.26845	3.725
13	18.190	0.0550	68.760	0.01454	0.26454	3.780
14	22.737	0.0440	86.949	0.01150	0.26150	3.824
15	28.422	0.0352	109.687	0.00912	0.25912	3.859
16	35.527	0.0281	138.109	0.00724	0.25724	3.887
17	44.409	0.0225	173.636	0.00576	0.25576	3.910
18	55.511	0.0180	218.045	0.00459	0.25459	3.928
19	69.389	0.0144	273.556	0.00366	0.25366	3.942
20	86.736	0.0115	342.945	0.00292	0.25292	3.954
21	108.420	0.0092	429.681	0.00233	0.25233	3.963
22	135.525	0.0074	538.101	0.00186	0.25186	3.970
23	169.407	0.0059	673.626	0.00148	0.25148	3.976
24	211.758	0.0047	843.033	0.00119	0.25119	3.981
25	264.698	0.0038	1054.791	0.00095	0.25095	3.985
26	330.872	0.0030	1319.489	0.00076	0.25076	3.988
27	413.590	0.0024	1650.361	0.00061	0.25061	3.990
28	516.988	0.0019	2063.952	0.00048	0.25048	3.992
29	646.235	0.0015	2580.939	0.00039	0.25039	3.994
30	807.794	0.0012	3227.174	0.00031	0.25031	3.995
35	2465.190	0.0004	9856.761	0.00010	0.25010	3.998
40	7523.164	0.0001	30088.655	0.00003	0.25003	3.999

Period N	Single sum compound amount (F/P,i,N) $(1 + i)^N$	Single sum present worth (P/F,i,N) $\dfrac{1}{(1 + i)^N}$	Uniform series compound amount (F/A,i,N) $\dfrac{(1 + i)^N - 1}{i}$	Sinking fund (A/F,i,N) $\dfrac{i}{(1 + i)^N - 1}$	Capital recovery (A/P,i,N) $\dfrac{i(1 + i)^N}{(1 + i)^N - 1}$	Uniform series present worth (P/A,i,N) $\dfrac{(1 + i)^N - 1}{i(1 + i)^N}$
1	1.300	0.7692	1.000	1.00000	1.30000	0.769
2	1.690	0.5917	2.300	0.43478	0.73478	1.361
3	2.197	0.4552	3.990	0.25063	0.55063	1.816
4	2.856	0.3501	6.187	0.16163	0.46163	2.166
5	3.713	0.2693	9.043	0.11058	0.41058	2.436
6	4.827	0.2072	12.756	0.07839	0.37839	2.643
7	6.275	0.1594	17.583	0.05687	0.35687	2.802
8	8.157	0.1226	23.858	0.04192	0.34192	2.925
9	10.604	0.0943	32.015	0.03124	0.33124	3.019
10	13.786	0.0725	42.619	0.02346	0.32346	3.092
11	17.922	0.0558	56.405	0.01773	0.31773	3.147
12	23.298	0.0429	74.327	0.01345	0.31345	3.190
13	30.288	0.0330	97.625	0.01024	0.31024	3.223
14	39.374	0.0254	127.913	0.00782	0.30782	3.249
15	51.186	0.0195	167.286	0.00598	0.30598	3.268
16	66.542	0.0150	218.472	0.00458	0.30458	3.283
17	86.504	0.0116	285.014	0.00351	0.30351	3.295
18	112.455	0.0089	371.518	0.00269	0.30269	3.304
19	146.192	0.0068	483.973	0.00207	0.30207	3.311
20	190.050	0.0053	630.165	0.00159	0.30159	3.316
21	247.065	0.0040	820.215	0.00122	0.30122	3.320
22	321.184	0.0031	1067.280	0.00094	0.30094	3.323
23	417.539	0.0024	1388.464	0.00072	0.30072	3.325
24	542.801	0.0018	1806.003	0.00055	0.30055	3.327
25	705.641	0.0014	2348.803	0.00043	0.30043	3.329
26	917.333	0.0011	3054.444	0.00033	0.30033	3.330
27	1192.533	0.0008	3971.778	0.00025	0.30025	3.331
28	1550.293	0.0006	5164.311	0.00019	0.30019	3.331
29	2015.381	0.0005	6714.604	0.00015	0.30015	3.332
30	2619.996	0.0004	8729.985	0.00011	0.30011	3.332
35	9727.860	0.0001	32422.868	0.00003	0.30003	3.333

Table A-A-15

40% INTEREST FACTORS

Period N	Single sum compound amount $(F/P,i,N)$ $(1 + i)^N$	Single sum present worth $(P/F,i,N)$ $\dfrac{1}{(1 + i)^N}$	Uniform series compound amount $(F/A,i,N)$ $\dfrac{(1 + i)^N - 1}{i}$	Sinking fund $(A/F,i,N)$ $\dfrac{i}{(1 + i)^N - 1}$	Capital recovery $(A/P,i,N)$ $\dfrac{i(1 + i)^N}{(1 + i)^N - 1}$	Uniform series present worth $(P/A,i,N)$ $\dfrac{(1 + i)^N - 1}{i(1 + i)^N}$
1	1.400	0.7143	1.000	1.00000	1.40000	0.714
2	1.960	0.5102	2.400	0.41667	0.81667	1.224
3	2.744	0.3644	4.360	0.22936	0.62936	1.589
4	3.842	0.2603	7.104	0.14077	0.54077	1.849
5	5.378	0.1859	10.946	0.09136	0.49136	2.035
6	7.530	0.1328	16.324	0.06126	0.46126	2.168
7	10.541	0.0949	23.853	0.04192	0.44192	2.263
8	14.758	0.0678	34.395	0.02907	0.42907	2.331
9	20.661	0.0484	49.153	0.02034	0.42034	2.379
10	28.925	0.0346	69.814	0.01432	0.41432	2.414
11	40.496	0.0247	98.739	0.01013	0.41013	2.438
12	56.694	0.0176	139.235	0.00718	0.40718	2.456
13	79.371	0.0126	195.929	0.00510	0.40510	2.469
14	111.120	0.0090	275.300	0.00363	0.40363	2.478
15	155.568	0.0064	386.420	0.00259	0.40259	2.484
16	217.795	0.0046	541.988	0.00185	0.40185	2.489
17	304.913	0.0033	759.784	0.00132	0.40132	2.492
18	426.879	0.0023	1064.697	0.00094	0.40094	2.494
19	597.630	0.0017	1491.576	0.00067	0.40067	2.496
20	836.683	0.0012	2089.206	0.00048	0.40048	2.497
21	1171.356	0.0009	2925.889	0.00034	0.40034	2.498
22	1639.898	0.0006	4097.245	0.00024	0.40024	2.498
23	2295.857	0.0004	5737.142	0.00017	0.40017	2.499
24	3214.200	0.0003	8032.999	0.00012	0.40012	2.499
25	4499.880	3.0002	11247.199	0.00009	0.40009	2.499
26	6299.831	0.0002	15747.079	0.00006	0.40006	2.500
27	8819.764	0.0001	22046.910	0.00005	0.40005	2.500

Period N	Single sum compound amount (F/P,i,N) $(1 + i)^N$	Single sum present worth (P/F,i,N) $\dfrac{1}{(1 + i)^N}$	Uniform series compound amount (F/A,i,N) $\dfrac{(1 + i)^N - 1}{i}$	Sinking fund (A/F,i,N) $\dfrac{i}{(1 + i)^N - 1}$	Capital recovery (A/P,i,N) $\dfrac{i(1 + i)^N}{(1 + i)^N - 1}$	Uniform series present worth (P/A,i,N) $\dfrac{(1 + i)^N - 1}{i(1 + i)^N}$
1	1.500	0.6667	1.000	1.00000	1.50000	0.667
2	2.250	0.4444	2.500	0.40000	0.90000	1.111
3	3.375	0.2963	4.750	0.21053	0.71053	1.407
4	5.062	0.1975	8.125	0.12308	0.62308	1.605
5	7.594	0.1317	13.188	0.07583	0.57583	1.737
6	11.391	0.0878	20.781	0.04812	0.54812	1.824
7	17.086	0.0585	32.172	0.03108	0.53108	1.883
8	25.629	0.0390	49.258	0.02030	0.52030	1.922
9	38.443	0.0260	74.887	0.01335	0.51335	1.948
10	57.665	0.0173	113.330	0.00882	0.50882	1.965
11	86.498	0.0116	170.995	0.00585	0.50585	1.977
12	129.746	0.0077	257.493	0.00388	0.50388	1.985
13	194.620	0.0051	387.239	0.00258	0.50258	1.990
14	291.929	0.0034	581.859	0.00172	0.50172	1.993
15	437.894	0.0023	873.788	0.00114	0.50114	1.995
16	656.841	0.0015	1311.682	0.00076	0.50076	1.997
17	985.261	0.0010	1968.523	0.00051	0.50051	1.998
18	1477.892	0.0007	2953.784	0.00034	0.50034	1.999
19	2216.838	0.0005	4431.676	0.00023	0.50023	1.999
20	3325.257	0.0003	6648.513	0.00015	0.50015	1.999
21	4987.885	0.0002	9973.770	0.00010	0.50010	2.000
22	7481.828	0.0001	14961.655	0.00007	0.50007	2.000

Table A-A-17

ARITHMETIC GRADIENT CONVERSION FACTORS (TO UNIFORM SERIES)

$$(A/G, i, N) = \left[\frac{1}{i} - \frac{N}{(1+i)^N - 1}\right]$$

					Interest rate i						
N	2%	4%	6%	8%	10%	15%	20%	25%	30%	40%	50%
1	0.00	0.00	0.00	0.00	0.00	0.00	0.00	0.00	0.00	0.00	0.00
2	0.50	0.49	0.49	0.48	0.48	0.47	0.45	0.44	0.43	0.42	0.40
3	0.99	0.97	0.96	0.95	0.94	0.91	0.88	0.85	0.83	0.78	0.74
4	1.48	1.45	1.43	1.40	1.38	1.33	1.27	1.22	1.18	1.09	1.02
5	1.96	1.92	1.88	1.85	1.81	1.72	1.64	1.56	1.49	1.36	1.24
6	2.44	2.39	2.33	2.28	2.22	2.10	1.98	1.87	1.77	1.58	1.42
7	2.92	2.84	2.77	2.69	2.62	2.45	2.29	2.14	2.01	1.77	1.56
8	3.40	3.29	3.20	3.10	3.00	2.78	2.58	2.39	2.22	1.92	1.68
9	3.87	3.74	3.61	3.49	3.37	3.09	2.84	2.60	2.40	2.04	1.76
10	4.34	4.18	4.02	3.87	3.73	3.38	3.07	2.80	2.55	2.14	1.82
11	4.80	4.61	4.42	4.24	4.06	3.65	3.29	2.97	2.68	2.22	1.87
12	5.26	5.03	4.81	4.60	4.39	3.91	3.48	3.11	2.80	2.28	1.91
13	5.72	5.45	5.19	4.94	4.70	4.14	3.66	3.24	2.89	2.33	1.93
14	6.18	5.87	5.56	5.27	5.00	4.36	3.82	3.36	2.97	2.37	1.95
15	6.63	6.27	5.93	5.59	5.28	4.56	3.96	3.45	3.03	2.40	1.97
16	7.08	6.67	6.28	5.90	5.55	4.75	4.09	3.54	3.09	2.43	1.98
17	7.53	7.07	6.62	6.20	5.81	4.93	4.20	3.61	3.13	2.44	1.98
18	7.97	7.45	6.96	6.49	6.05	5.08	4.30	3.67	3.17	2.46	1.99
19	8.41	7.83	7.29	6.77	6.29	5.23	4.39	3.72	3.20	2.47	1.99
20	8.84	8.21	7.61	7.04	6.51	5.37	4.46	3.77	3.23	2.48	1.99
21	9.28	8.58	7.92	7.29	6.72	5.49	4.53	3.80	3.25	2.48	2.00
22	9.71	8.94	8.22	7.54	6.92	5.60	4.59	3.84	3.26	2.49	2.00
23	10.13	9.30	8.51	7.78	7.11	5.70	4.65	3.86	3.28	2.49	
24	10.55	9.65	8.80	8.01	7.29	5.80	4.69	3.89	3.29	2.49	
25	10.97	9.99	9.07	8.23	7.46	5.88	4.74	3.91	3.30	2.49	
26	11.39	10.33	9.34	8.44	7.62	5.96	4.77	3.92	3.30	2.50	
27	11.80	10.66	9.60	8.64	7.77	6.03	4.80	3.93	3.31	2.50	
28	12.21	10.99	9.86	8.83	7.91	6.10	4.83	3.95	3.32		
29	12.62	11.31	10.10	9.01	8.05	6.15	4.85	3.96	3.32		
30	13.02	11.63	10.34	9.19	8.18	6.21	4.87	3.96	3.32		
35	15.00	13.12	11.43	9.96	8.71	6.40	4.94	3.99	3.33		
40	16.89	14.48	12.36	10.57	9.10	6.52	4.97	4.00			
45	18.70	15.70	13.14	11.04	9.37	6.58	4.99				
50	20.44	16.81	13.80	11.41	9.57	6.62	4.99				

Table of Random Numbers*

48867	33971	29678	13151	56644	49193	93469	43252	14006	47173
32267	69746	00113	51336	36551	56310	85793	53453	09744	64346
27345	03196	33877	35032	98054	48358	21788	98862	67491	42221
55753	05256	51557	90419	40716	64589	90398	37070	78318	02918
93124	50675	04507	44001	06365	77897	84566	99600	67985	49133
98658	86583	97433	10733	80495	62709	61357	66903	76730	79355
68216	94830	41248	50712	46878	87317	80545	31484	03195	14755
17901	30815	78360	78260	67866	42304	07293	61290	61301	04815
88124	21868	14942	25893	72695	56231	18918	72534	86737	77792
83464	36749	22336	50443	83576	19238	91730	39507	22717	94719
91310	99003	25704	55581	00729	22024	61319	66162	20933	67713
32739	38352	91256	77744	75080	01492	90984	63090	53087	41301
07751	66724	03290	56386	06070	67105	64219	48192	70478	84722
55228	64156	90480	97774	08055	04435	26999	42039	16589	06757
89013	51781	81116	24383	95569	97247	44437	36293	29967	16088
51828	81819	81038	89146	39192	89470	76331	56420	14527	34828
59783	85454	93327	06078	64924	07271	77563	92710	42183	12380
80267	47103	90556	16128	41490	07996	78454	47929	81586	67024
82919	44210	61607	93001	26314	26865	26714	43793	94937	28439
77019	77417	19466	14967	75521	49967	74065	09746	27881	01070
66225	61832	06242	40093	40800	76849	29929	18988	10888	40344
98534	12777	84601	56336	00034	85939	32438	09549	01855	40550
63175	70789	51345	43723	06995	11186	38615	56646	54320	39632
92362	73011	09115	78303	38901	58107	95366	17226	74626	78208
61831	44794	65079	97130	94289	73502	04857	68855	47045	06309
42502	01646	88493	48207	01283	16474	08864	68322	92454	19287
89733	86230	04903	55015	11811	98185	32014	84761	80926	14509
01336	66633	26015	66768	24846	00321	73118	15802	13549	41335
72623	56083	65799	88934	87274	19417	84897	90877	76472	52145
74004	68388	04090	35239	49379	04456	07642	68642	01026	43810
09388	54633	27684	47117	67583	42496	20703	68579	65883	10729
51771	92019	39791	60400	08585	60680	28841	09921	00520	73135
69796	30304	79836	20631	10743	00246	24979	35707	75283	39211
98417	33403	63448	90462	91645	24919	73609	26663	09380	30515
56150	18324	43011	02660	86574	86097	49399	21249	90380	94375
76199	75692	09063	72999	94672	69128	39046	15379	98450	09159
74978	98693	21433	34676	97603	48534	59205	66265	03561	83075
85769	92530	04407	53725	96963	19395	16193	51018	70333	12094
63819	65669	38960	74631	39650	39419	93707	61365	46302	26134
18892	43143	19619	43200	49613	50904	73502	19519	11667	53294
32855	17190	61587	80411	22827	38852	51952	47785	34952	93574
29435	96277	53583	92804	05027	19736	54918	66396	96547	00351
36211	67263	82064	41624	49826	17566	02476	79368	28831	02805
73514	00176	41638	01420	31850	41380	11643	06787	09011	88924
90895	93099	27850	29423	98693	71762	39928	35268	59359	20674
69719	90656	62186	50435	77015	29661	94698	56057	04388	33381
94982	81453	87162	28248	37921	21143	62673	81224	38972	92988
84136	04221	72790	04719	34914	95609	88695	60180	58790	12802
58515	80581	88442	65727	72121	40481	06001	13159	55324	93591
20681	59164	75797	08928	68381	12616	97487	84803	92457	88847

*Reproduced with permission from the Rand Corporation, *A Million Random Numbers*. (New York: The Free Press, 1955).

Table of Random Normal Deviates*

1.102	− .944	.401	.226	1.396	−1.030	−1.723	− .368	2.170	.393
.148	−1.140	.492	−1.210	− .998	.573	.893	− .855	−2.209	− .267
2.372	1.353	− .900	− .554	− .343	.470	−1.033	−1.026	2.172	.195
− .145	.466	.854	− .282	−1.504	.431	− .060	.952	− .343	.735
.104	.732	.604	− .016	− .266	1.372	− .925	−1.594	−2.004	1.925
1.419	−1.853	− .347	.155	−1.078	.623	− .024	.498	.466	.049
.069	− .411	− .661	− .037	.703	.532	− .177	.395	− .278	.240
.797	.488	−1.070	− .721	−1.412	− .976	−1.953	− .206	1.848	.632
− .393	− .351	.222	.557	−1.094	1.403	.173	− .113	.806	.939
− .874	−1.336	.523	.848	.304	− .202	−1.279	.501	.396	.859
.125	−1.170	− .192	1.387	2.291	− .959	.090	1.031	.180	−1.389
−1.091	− .649	− .514	− .232	−1.198	.822	.240	.951	−1.736	.270
2.304	.481	− .987	−1.222	.549	−1.056	.277	− .919	.148	1.517
− .961	2.057	− .546	− .896	.165	− .343	.696	.628	− .929	− .965
− .783	.854	− .139	1.087	.515	− .876	− .448	.485	.589	− .804
.487	.557	.327	1.280	−1.731	− .339	.295	− .724	.720	.331
− .299	.979	− .924	− .649	.574	1.407	− .292	− .775	− .511	.026
1.831	− .937	−1.321	−1.734	1.677	−1.393	−1.187	− .079	− .181	− .844
.243	.466	−1.330	1.078	−1.102	1.123	− .421	− .674	2.951	− .743
−2.181	−1.854	−1.059	− .478	−1.119	.272	− .800	.841	− .061	2.261
.154	− .333	1.011	−1.565	1.261	.776	1.130	1.552	− .563	.558
−1.065	1.610	.463	.062	− .086	.021	1.633	1.788	.480	2.824
1.083	− .760	− .012	.183	.155	.676	−1.315	.067	.213	2.380
.615	− .594	− .028	− .506	− .054	3.173	.817	.210	1.699	1.950
.178	− .500	1.100	1.613	1.048	2.323	− .174	− .033	2.220	− .661
− .507	−1.273	.596	.690	−1.724	−1.689	.163	− .199	− .450	.244
.362	− .588	−1.386	.072	.778	− .591	.365	.465	2.472	1.049
.775	1.546	.217	−1.012	.778	.246	1.055	1.071	.447	− .585
.818	.561	−1.024	2.105	− .868	.060	− .385	1.089	.017	.873
.014	.240	− .632	− .225	− .844	.448	1.651	1.423	.425	.252
−1.236	−1.045	−1.628	.687	.983	− .840	−1.835	−1.864	1.327	− .408
− .567	−1.161	.010	− .853	.111	1.145	1.015	.056	.141	1.471
.278	−1.783	.170	− .358	.705	− .054	1.098	.707	− .585	− .305
− .959	− .497	.688	− .268	−1.431	− .791	− .727	.958	.237	.092
1.249	.037	.497	.579	− .227	.860	.349	2.355	2.184	−1.744
− .915	− .164	−1.166	1.529	.008	.636	−1.080	− .688	2.444	−1.316
.132	2.809	−1.918	−1.083	− .642	− .179	.339	.637	.063	− .079
− .156	−1.664	1.140	.295	1.086	−2.546	− .002	− .672	.205	− .039
.538	−1.143	− .390	.165	− .160	.457	−1.307	.273	− .670	− .988
.027	− .057	.742	− .149	− .801	1.702	− .346	− .053	.892	−1.181
.023	.423	1.051	− .831	− .325	− .795	−1.129	− .287	.172	− .793
− .196	−1.457	1.060	.557	− .190	− .891	− .768	.282	−1.432	− .447
.133	.577	− .332	−1.932	.220	.189	−1.521	.896	− .781	− .899
.020	− .217	− .856	.605	.072	.520	1.222	− .181	− .266	−1.222
1.405	1.065	1.350	1.353	−2.289	−1.003	.375	1.621	−1.126	.937
.178	−1.237	− .520	− .603	−1.615	− .358	.605	− .407	−2.579	−1.811
−1.438	.104	−1.821	− .390	− .630	1.294	1.470	.991	− .355	−1.285
1.768	− .175	− .450	.915	− .221	− .019	1.864	.038	.058	1.212
.099	1.076	2.348	−1.550	.458	.147	−1.223	.994	−1.657	1.264
.951	.252	−1.261	− .963	.221	− .036	− .395	.252	−1.379	1.885

*Reproduced with permission from the Rand Corporation, *A Million Random Numbers*. (New York: The Free Press, 1955).

Unit Normal Loss Integral (UNLI)*

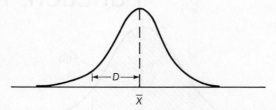

D	.00	.01	.02	.03	.04	.05	.06	.07	.08	.09
.0	.3989	.3940	.3890	.3841	.3793	.3744	.3697	.3649	.3602	.3556
.1	.3509	.3464	.3418	.3373	.3328	.3284	.3240	.3197	.3154	.3111
.2	.3069	.3027	.2986	.2944	'2904	.2863	.2824	.2784	.2745	.2706
.3	.2668	.2630	.2592	.2555	.2518	.2481	.2445	.2409	.2374	.2339
.4	.2304	.2270	.2236	.2203	.2169	.2137	.2104	.2072	.2040	.2009
.5	.1978	.1947	.1917	.1887	.1857	.1828	.1799	.1771	.1742	.1714
.6	.1687	.1659	.1633	.1606	.1580	.1554	.1528	.1503	.1478	.1453
.7	.1429	.1405	.1381	.1358	.1334	.1312	.1289	.1267	.1245	.1223
.8	.1202	.1181	.1160	.1140	.1120	.1100	.1080	.1061	.1042	.1023
.9	.1004	.09860	.09680	.09503	.09328	.09156	.08986	.08819	.08654	.08491
1.0	.08332	.08174	.08019	.07866	.07716	.07568	.07422	.07279	.07138	.06999
1.1	.06682	.06727	.06595	.06465	.06336	.06210	.06086	.05964	.05844	.05726
1.2	.05610	.05496	.05384	.05274	.05165	.05059	.04954	.04851	.04750	.04650
1.3	.04553	.04457	.04363	.04270	.04179	.04090	.04002	.03916	.03831	.03748
1.4	.03667	.03587	.03508	.03431	.03356	.03281	.03208	.03137	.03067	.02998
1.5	.02931	.02865	.02800	.02736	.02674	.02612	.02552	.02494	.02436	.02380
1.6	.02324	.02270	.02217	.02165	.02114	.02064	.02015	.01967	.01920	.01874
1.7	.01829	.01785	.01742	.01699	.01658	.01617	.01578	.01539	.01501	.01464
1.8	.01428	.01392	.01357	.01323	.01290	.01257	.01226	.01195	.01164	.01134
1.9	.01105	.01077	.01049	.01022	$.0^2 9957$	$.0^2 9698$	$.0^2 9445$	$.0^2 9198$	$.0^2 8957$	$.0^2 8721$
2.0	$.0^2 8491$	$.0^2 8266$	$.0^2 8046$	$.0^2 7832$	$.0^2 7623$	$.0^2 7418$	$.0^2 7219$	$.0^2 7024$	$.0^2 6835$	$.0^2 6649$
2.1	$.0^2 6468$	$.0^2 6292$	$.0^2 6120$	$.0^2 5952$	$.0^2 5788$	$.0^2 5628$	$.0^2 5472$	$.0^2 5320$	$.0^2 5172$	$.0^2 5028$
2.2	$.0^2 4887$	$.0^2 4750$	$.0^2 4616$	$.0^2 4486$	$.0^2 4358$	$.0^2 4235$	$.0^2 4114$	$.0^2 3996$	$.0^2 3882$	$.0^2 3770$
2.3	$.0^2 3662$	$.0^2 3556$	$.0^2 3453$	$.0^2 3352$	$.0^2 3255$	$.0^2 3159$	$.0^2 3067$	$.0^2 2977$	$.0^2 2889$	$.0^2 2804$
2.4	$.0^2 2720$	$.0^2 2640$	$.0^2 2561$	$.0^2 2484$	$.0^2 2410$	$.0^2 2337$	$.0^2 2267$	$.0^2 2199$	$.0^2 2132$	$.0^2 2067$
2.5	$.0^2 2005$	$.0^2 1943$	$.0^2 1883$	$.0^2 1826$	$.0^2 1769$	$.0^2 1715$	$.0^2 1662$	$.0^2 1610$	$.0^2 1560$	$.0^2 1511$
3.0	$.0^3 3822$	$.0^3 3689$	$.0^3 3560$	$.0^3 3436$	$.0^3 3316$	$.0^3 3199$	$.0^3 3087$	$.0^3 2978$	$.0^3 2873$	$.0^3 2711$
3.5	$.0^5 5848$	$.0^5 5620$	$.0^5 5400$	$.0^5 5188$	$.0^4 4984$	$.0^4 4788$	$.0^4 4599$	$.0^4 4417$	$.0^4 4242$	$.0^4 4073$
4.0	$.0^5 7145$	$.0^5 6835$	$.0^5 6538$	$.0^5 6253$	$.0^5 5980$	$.0^5 5718$	$.0^5 5468$	$.0^5 5227$	$.0^5 4997$	$.0^5 4777$

*Reprinted from R. Schlaifer, *Probability and Statistics for Business Decisions* (New York: McGraw-Hill Book Company, 1959) by permission of the publisher.

Key: Exponents after 0 means number of 0's before significant digits. For example, UNLI at D of 2.51 = $.0^2 1943$ = .001943

The Standardized Normal Distribution Function, * *F(S)*

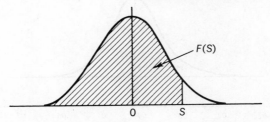

s	0.00	0.01	0.02	0.03	0.04	0.05	0.06	0.07	0.08	0.09
0.0	0.5000	0.5040	0.5080	0.5120	0.5160	0.5199	0.5239	0.5279	0.5319	0.5359
0.1	0.5398	0.5438	0.5478	0.5517	0.5557	0.5596	0.5636	0.5675	0.5714	0.5753
0.2	0.5793	0.5832	0.5871	0.5910	0.5948	0.5987	0.6026	0.6064	0.6103	0.6141
0.3	0.6179	0.6217	0.6255	0.6293	0.6331	0.6368	0.6406	0.6443	0.6480	0.6517
0.4	0.6554	0.6591	0.6628	0.6664	0.6700	0.6736	0.6772	0.6808	0.6844	0.6879
0.5	0.6915	0.6950	0.6985	0.7019	0.7054	0.7088	0.7123	0.7157	0.7190	0.7224
0.6	0.7257	0.7291	0.7324	0.7357	0.7389	0.7422	0.7454	0.7486	0.7517	0.7549
0.7	0.7580	0.7611	0.7642	0.7673	0.7703	0.7734	0.7764	0.7794	0.7823	0.7852
0.8	0.7881	0.7910	0.7939	0.7967	0.7995	0.8023	0.8051	0.8078	0.8106	0.8133
0.9	0.8159	0.8186	0.8212	0.8238	0.8264	0.8289	0.8315	0.8340	0.8365	0.8389
1.0	0.8413	0.8438	0.8461	0.8485	0.8508	0.8531	0.8554	0.8577	0.8599	0.8621
1.1	0.8643	0.8665	0.8686	0.8708	0.8729	0.8749	0.8770	0.8790	0.8810	0.8830
1.2	0.8849	0.8869	0.8888	0.8907	0.8925	0.8944	0.8962	0.8980	0.8997	0.90147
1.3	0.90320	0.90490	0.90658	0.90824	0.90988	0.91149	0.91309	0.91466	0.91621	0.91774
1.4	0.91924	0.92073	0.92220	0.92364	0.92507	0.92647	0.92785	0.92922	0.93056	0.93189
1.5	0.93319	0.93448	0.93574	0.93699	0.93822	0.93943	0.94062	0.94179	0.94295	0.94408
1.6	0.94520	0.94630	0.94738	0.94845	0.94950	0.95053	0.95154	0.95254	0.95352	0.95449
1.7	0.95543	0.95637	0.95728	0.95818	0.95907	0.95994	0.96080	0.96164	0.96246	0.96327
1.8	0.96407	0.96485	0.96562	0.96638	0.96712	0.96784	0.96856	0.96926	0.96995	0.97062
1.9	0.97128	0.97193	0.97257	0.97320	0.97381	0.97441	0.97500	0.97558	0.97615	0.97670
2.0	0.97725	0.97778	0.97831	0.97882	0.97932	0.97982	0.98030	0.98077	0.98124	0.98169
2.1	0.98214	0.98257	0.98300	0.98341	0.98382	0.98422	0.98461	0.98500	0.98537	0.98574
2.2	0.98610	0.98645	0.98679	0.98713	0.98745	0.98778	0.98809	0.98840	0.98870	0.98899
2.3	0.98928	0.98956	0.98983	0.9^20097	0.9^20358	0.9^20613	0.9^20863	0.9^21106	0.9^21344	0.9^21576
2.4	0.9^21802	0.9^22024	0.9^22240	0.9^22451	0.9^22656	0.9^22857	0.9^23053	0.9^23244	0.9^23431	0.9^23613
2.5	0.9^23790	0.9^23963	0.9^24132	0.9^24297	0.9^24457	0.9^24614	0.9^24766	0.9^24915	0.9^25060	0.9^25201
3.0	0.9^28650	0.9^28649	0.9^28736	0.9^28777	0.9^28817	0.9^28856	0.9^28893	0.9^28930	0.9^28965	0.9^28999
3.5	0.9^37674	0.9^37759	0.9^37842	0.9^37922	0.9^37999	0.9^38074	0.9^38146	0.9^38215	0.9^38282	0.9^38347
4.0	0.9^46833	0.9^46964	0.9^47090	0.9^47211	0.9^47327	0.9^47439	0.9^47546	0.9^47649	0.9^47748	0.9^47843

For example: $F(2.41) = 0.9^22024 = 0.992024$

*Reprinted from A. Hald, *Statistical Tables and Formulas* (New York: John Wiley & Sons, Inc., 1952), by permission of the publisher.

Glossary of Commonly Used Symbols

Mathematical Operations

$E(\ )$ Expected value of ( ). Also, mean of ( ).

$V(\ )$ Variance of ( ).

$P(\ )$ Probability of ( ).

$\sigma(\ )$ Standard deviation of ( ). Also, $\sqrt{V(\ )}$.

$U(\ )$ Utility of ( ).

Σ Summation.

∂ Partial derivative.

Economic Analysis Methods and Costs

A.W.   Annual worth method.

A.C.   Annual cost method.

P.W.   Present worth method.

R.R.   Rate-of-return method.

C.R.   Capital recovery cost (annual cost of depreciation plus interest on investment).

Compound Interest Symbols (Reference: Table 2-1)

i Effective interest rate per interest period.

N Number of compounding periods.

P Present sum of money (present worth). The equivalent worth of one or more cash flows at a relative point in time called the present.

F Future sum of money (future worth). The equivalent worth of one or more cash flows at a relative point in time called the future.

A End-of-period cash flows (or equivalent end-of-period values) in a uniform series continuing for a specified number of periods.

G Uniform period-by-period increase or decrease in cash flows or amounts (the arithmetic gradient).

Discrete Compounding Interest Factors (Reference: Table 2-1)

$(F/P, i\%, N)$ Single sum compound amount factor.

$(P/F, i\%, N)$ Single sum present worth factor.

$(P/A, i\%, N)$ Uniform series present worth factor.

$(A/P, i\%, N)$ Capital recovery factor.

$(F/A, i\%, N)$ Uniform series compound amount factor.

$(A/F, i\%, N)$ Sinking fund factor.

$(A/G, i\%, N)$ Arithmetic gradient conversion factors (to uniform series).

Bibliography

Part I—Texts

DeGarmo, E. Paul, *Engineering Economy*. New York: The Macmillan Company, 1967.

Engineering Economy. Second Edition. New York: American Telephone and Telegraph Company, Engineering Department, 1963.

Fleischer, G. A., *Capital Allocation Theory*. New York: Appleton-Century-Crofts, 1969.

Grant, E. L., and W. G. Ireson, *Principles of Engineering Economy*. Fourth Edition, Revised Printing. New York: The Ronald Press Company, 1964.

Jeynes, Paul H., *Profitability and Economic Choice*. Ames, Iowa: The Iowa State University Press, 1968.

Roscoe, E. S., *Project Economy*. Homewood, Ill.: Richard D. Irwin, Inc., 1960.

Smith, G. A., *Engineering Economy*. Ames, Iowa: The Iowa State University Press, 1968.

Taylor, G. A., *Managerial and Engineering Economy*. Princeton, N.J.: D. Van Nostrand Co., Inc., 1964.

Thuesen, H. G., and W. J. Fabrycky, *Engineering Economy*. Third Edition. Englewood Cliffs, N.J.: Prentice-Hall, Inc., 1964.

417

Part II—Texts

Archer, S. H., and C. A. D'Ambrosio, *The Theory of Business Finance: A Book of Readings*. New York: The Macmillan Company 1967.

Barges, Alexander, *The Effect of Capital Structure on the Cost of Capital*. Englewood Cliffs, N.J.: Prentice-Hall, Inc., 1963.

Barish, N. N., *Economic Analysis for Engineering and Managerial Decision Making*. New York: McGraw-Hill Book Company, 1962.

Beranek, William, *Analysis for Financial Decisions*. Homewood, Ill.: Richard D. Irwin, Inc., 1963.

Bierman. H. J., et al, *Quantitative Analysis for Business Decisions*. Homewood, Ill.: Richard D. Irwin, Inc., 1965.

Bierman, Harold, Jr., and Seymour Smidt, *The Capital Budgeting Decision*. Second Edition. New York: The Macmillan Company, 1966.

Blackwell, David, and M. A. Gershick, *Theory of Games and Statistical Decisions*. New York: John Wiley & Sons, Inc., 1954.

Bowman, Mary Jean, *Expectations, Uncertainty, and Business Behavior*. New York: Social Science Research Council, 1958.

Carr, Charles R., and Charles W. Howe, *Quantitative Decision Procedures in Management and Economics*. New York: McGraw-Hill Book Company, 1964.

Chernoff, Herman, and Lincoln E. Moses, *Elementary Decision Theory*. New York: John Wiley & Sons, Inc., 1959.

Cohen, Jerome B., and Edward D. Zinbarg, *Investment Analysis and Portfolio Management*. Homewood, Ill.: Richard D. Irwin, Inc., 1967.

Egerton, R. A. D., *Investment Decisions Under Uncertainty*. Liverpool, England: Liverpool University Press, 1960.

English, J. M., *Cost Effectiveness: Economic Evaluation of Engineered Systems*. New York: John Wiley & Sons, Inc., 1968.

Farrar, Donald Eugene, *The Investment Decision Under Uncertainty*. Reprint of Ph. D. Dissertation, Harvard University, 1961. Englewood Cliffs, N.J.: Prentice-Hall, Inc., 1962.

Fellner, W., *Probability and Profit*. Homewood, Ill.: Richard D. Irwin, Inc., 1965.

Fishburn, Peter C., *Decision and Value Theory*. New York: John Wiley & Sons, Inc., 1964.

Fredrikson, E. B., *Frontiers of Investment Analysis*. Scranton, Pa.: International Textbook Co., 1965.

Grayson, C. J., Jr., *Decisions Under Uncertainty*. Boston, Mass.: Harvard Business School Press, 1960.

Haavelino, Trygve, *A Study in the Theory of Investment*. Chicago: The Chicago Press, 1960.

Hackney, John W., *Control and Management of Capital Projects*. New York: John Wiley & Sons, Inc., 1965.

Hanssman, F., *Operations Research Techniques for Capital Investment*. New York: John Wiley & Sons, Inc., 1968.

Haynes, W. W., *Managerial Economics: Analysis and Cases*. Revised Edition. Austin, Texas: Business Publications, Inc., 1969.

Hester, Donald D., and James Tobin. *Risk Aversion and Portfolio Choice*. Cowles Monograph 19. New York: John Wiley & Sons, Inc., 1967.

House, William C., *Sensitivity Analyses in Making Capital Investment Decisions*. Research Monograph No. 3. New York: National Association of Accountants, 1968.

Istvan, Donald F., *Capital-Expenditure Decisions: How They Are Made in Large Corporations*. Indiana Business Report No. 33. Bloomington, Ind.: Indiana University Press, 1961.

Kaufman, G., *Statistical Decisions and Related Techniques in Oil and Gas Exploration*. Ph. D. Dissertation, Harvard University, 1961.

Kempster, John H., *Financial Analysis to Guide Capital Expenditures*. New York: National Association of Accountants, 1967.

Lasser, J. K., *Your Income Tax*. New York: Simon and Schuster, Inc. (see latest edition).

Luce, R. D., and H. Raiffa, *Games and Decisions*. New York: John Wiley & Sons, Inc., 1957.

Markowitz, Harry M., *Portfolio Selection: Efficient Diversification of Investments*. New York: John Wiley & Sons, Inc., 1959.

Massé, Pierre, *Optimal Investment Decisions: Rules for Action and Criteria for Choice*. Englewood Cliffs, N.J.: Prentice-Hall, Inc., 1962.

Meier, R. C., W. T. Newell, and L. Pazer, *Simulation in Business and Economics*. Englewood Cliffs, N.J.: Prentice-Hall, Inc., 1969.

Merrett, A. J., and A. Sykes, *The Finance and Analysis of Capital Projects*. New York: John Wiley & Sons, Inc., 1963.

Mock, E. J., *Financial Decision Making*. Scranton, Pa.: International Textbook Co., 1967.

Morris, William T., *The Analysis of Management Decisions*. Homewood, Ill.: Richard D. Irwin, Inc., 1964.

Pessemier, E. A., *New-Product Decisions: An Analytical Approach*. New York: McGraw-Hill Book Company, 1966.

Peters, W. S., and G. W. Summers, *Statistical Analysis for Business Decisions*. Englewood Cliffs, N. J.: Prentice-Hall, Inc., 1968.

Peterson, D. E., *A Quantitative Framework for Financial Management*. Homewood, Ill.: Richard D. Irwin, Inc., 1969.

Pflomm, Norman E., *Managing Capital Expenditures*. Studies in Business Policy No. 107. New York: National Industrial Conference Board, 1963.

Quirin, G. D., *The Capital Expenditure Decision*. Homewood, Ill.: Richard D. Irwin, Inc., 1967.

Rakowski, M., *Efficiency of Investment in a Socialist Economy*. New York: Pergamon Press, 1966.

Reisman, Arnold, *Engineering Economics: A Unified Approach*. New York: Reinhold Publishing Corp., 1969.

Riggs, J. L., *Economic Decision Models for Managers and Engineers*. New York: McGraw-Hill Book Company, 1967.

Robichek, A. A., and S. C. Myers, *Optimal Financing Decisions*. Englewood Cliffs, N.J.: Prentice-Hall, Inc., 1965.

Schlaifer, Robert, *Analysis of Decisions Under Uncertainty, Vol. I*. New York: McGraw-Hill Book Company, 1967.

Schlaifer, Robert, *Probability and Statistics for Business Decisions*. New York: McGraw-Hill Book Company, 1959.

Schweyer, Herbert E., *Analytical Models for Managerial and Engineering Economics*. New York: Reinhold Publishing Corp., 1964.

Schackle, George L. S., *Uncertainty in Economics*. London: Cambridge University Press, 1955.

Solomon, Ezra, *The Management of Corporate Capital*. New York: The Free Press, 1959.

Solomon, Ezra, *The Theory of Financial Management*. New York: Columbia University Press, 1963.

Spencer, M. H., *Managerial Economics*. Third Edition. Homewood, Ill.: Richard D. Irwin, Inc., 1968.

Terborgh, G., *Business Investment Management*. Washington: Machinery and Allied Products Institute, 1967.

U.S. Treasury Department, *Your Federal Income Tax: 1970 Edition for Individuals*. IRS Publication No. 17 (revised annually).

———, *Tax Guide . . . for Small Businesses* (Individuals, Corporations, Partnerships). IRS Publication No. 334 (revised annually).

———, *Depreciation, Investment Credit, Amortization, Depletion*. IRS Publication No. 5050, December, 1965.

———, *Depreciation Guidelines and Rules: Revenue Procedure 62-21*. IRS Publication No. 456 (see latest edition).

———, *Tables for Applying Revenue Procedure 62-21*. IRS Publication No. 457, August, 1962.

_____, *Regulations Relating to Depreciation: Treasury Decision No. 6182*, Part I of Title 26 (1954), Code of Federal Regulations. IRS Publication No. 311 (see latest edition).

Van Horne, James C., *Financial Management and Policy*. Englewood Cliffs, N.J.: Prentice-Hall, Inc., 1968.

Walter, J. E., *The Investment Process*. Boston: Graduate School of Business, Harvard University, 1962.

Weingartner, H. Martin, *Mathematical Programming and the Analysis of Capital Budgeting Problems*. Chicago: Markham Publishing Co., 1967.

Part II—Articles

Angell, W., "Uncertainty, Likelihoods, and Investment Decisions," *Quarterly Journal of Economics*, Vol. 74, No. 1, February 1960, 1–28.

Barber, B. M., "The Use of Probability Multipliers in Replacement Analysis," *Engineering Economist*, Vol. 4, No. 1, Fall 1958.

Bennion, Edward G., "Capital Budgeting and Game Theory," *Harvard Business Review*, Vol. 34, No. 6, November–December 1956, 123.

Bernoulli, Daniel (1700–1782), "Exposition of a New Theory on the Measurement of Risk," English translation by Louise Sommer, *Econometrica*, Vol. 22, 1954, 23–26.

Boulding, K. E., "Ethics of Rational Decision," *Management Science*, Vol. 12, No. 6, February 1966.

Brennan, J. F., "On the Optimum Mean Life of Physical Plants," *Journal of Industrial Engineering*, Vol. 16, No. 6, November–December 1965.

Caplin, Mortimer M., and Robert A. Klayman, "Depreciation—1965 Model," *The Journal of Accountancy*, Vol. 119, No. 4, April 1965, 34–42.

"The Capital Expenditure Control Program, a Summary of Practice," Accounting Practice Report No. 7, *N.A.A. Bulletin*, Vol. 40, March 1959, Section 3.

Cord, J., "A Method for Allocating Funds to Investment Projects When Returns Are Subject to Uncertainty," *Management Science*, Vol. 10, No. 2, January 1964.

Cramer, Robert H., and Barnard E. Smith, "Decision Models for the Selection of Research Projects," *Engineering Economist*, Vol. 9, No. 2, Winter 1964.

Dean, Burton V., "Replacement Theory," *Progress in Operations Research*, Vol. 1, edited by R. L. Ackoff. New York: John Wiley & Sons, Inc., 1961.

Dreyfus, Stuart E., "A Generalized Equipment Replacement Study," *Journal of the Society for Industrial and Applied Mathematics*, Vol. 8, No. 3, September 1960, 425–435.

Eisen, M., and M. Leibowitz, "Replacement of Randomly Deteriorating Equipment," *Management Science*, Vol. 9, No. 2, January 1963, 268–276.

Elmaghraby, Salah E., "Probabilistic Considerations in Equipment Replacement Studies," *Engineering Economist*, Vol. 4, No. 1, Summer 1958.

English, J. Morley, "A Discount Function for Comparing Economic Alternatives," *Journal of Industrial Engineering*, Vol. 16, No. 2, March–April 1965.

_____, "Economic Comparison of Projects Incorporating a Utility Criterion in the Rate of Return," *Engineering Economist*, Vol. 10, No. 2, Winter 1965.

_____, "New Approaches to Economic Comparison for Engineering Projects," *Journal of Industrial Engineering*, Vol. 12, No. 6, November–December 1961, 375–378.

Fishburn, P. L., "Decision Under Uncertainty: An Introductory Exposition," *Journal of Industrial Engineering*, Vol. 17, No. 7, July 1960, 341–353.

Fisher, James L., "A Class of Stochastic Investment Problems," *Operations Research*, Vol. 9, No. 1, January–February 1961, 53–65.

Fleischer, G. A., "A Technique for Determination of Project Priority When Considering Irreducibles," *Engineering Economist*, Vol. 11, No. 2, Winter 1966.

Freund, R. J., "The Introduction of Risk Into a Programming Model," *Econometrica*, Vol. 24, July 1956.

Green, P. E., "Risk Attitudes and Chemical Investment Decisions," *Chemical Engineering Progress*, Vol. 59, No. 1, January 1963, 35.

Hart, A. G., "Risk, Uncertainty, and the Unprofitability of Compounding Probabilities," *Studies in Mathematical Economics and Econometrics.* Chicago: University of Chicago Press, 1942, 110–118.

Harris, Lawrence, "A Decision-Theoretic Approach on Deciding When a Sophisticated Forecasting Technique Is Needed," *Management Science*, Vol. 13, No. 2, October 1966.

Heebink, David W., "Isoquants and Investment Decisions," *Engineering Economist*, Part I, Vol. 7, No. 4, Summer 1962; Part II, Vol. 8, No. 1, Fall 1962.

Herschleifer, Jack, "The Bayesian Approach to Statistical Decision: an Exposition," *The Journal of Business*, Vol. 24, No. 4, October 1961.

Hertz, David B., "Risk Analysis in Capital Investments," *Harvard Business Review*, Vol. 42, No. 1, January–February 1964.

Hetrick, James C., "Mathematical Models in Capital Budgeting," *Harvard Business Review*, Vol. 39, No. 1, January–February 1961.

Hillier, Frederick S., "The Derivation of Probabilistic Information for the Evaluation of Risky Investments," *Management Science*, Vol. 9, No. 3, April 1963.

_____, "Supplement to 'The Derivation of Probabilistic Information for the Evaluation of Risky Investments,'" *Management Science*, Vol. 11, No. 3, January 1965.

_____, "The Evaluation of Risky Interrelated Investments," Technical Report No. 73, Department of Statistics, Stanford University, July 24, 1964.

Isaacs, Herbert H., "Sensitivity of Decisions to Probability Estimation Errors," *Operations Research*, Vol. 11, 1963, 536–552.

Kaufman, Gordon M., "Sequential Investment Analysis Under Uncertainty," *Journal of Business*, Vol. 36, No. 1, January 1963, 39–64.

Latane, Henry A., "Criteria for Choice Among Risky Ventures: The Problem of Rational Decision Making," *Journal of Political Economy*, Vol. 67, No. 2, April 1959.

Lintner, J., "The Cost of Capital and Optimal Financing of Corporate Growth," *Journal of Finance*, Vol. 18, No. 2, May 1963, 292–310.

_____, "The Valuation of Risk Assets and the Selection of Risky Investments in Stock Portfolios and Capital Budgets," *Review of Economics and Statistics*, Vol. 47, No. 1, February 1965, 13–37.

Magee, John F., "Decision Trees for Decision Making," *Harvard Business Review*, Vol. 42, No. 4, July–August 1964.

_____, "How to Use Decision Trees in Capital Investment," *Harvard Business Review*, Vol. 42, No. 5, September–October 1964.

Miller, M. H., and F. Modigliani, "Dividend Policy, Growth and the Valuation of Shares," *Journal of Business*, Vol. 34, No. 4, October 1961, 411–433.

_____, "The Cost of Capital, Corporation Finance and the Theory of Investment," *American Economic Review*, Vol. 48, No. 3, June 1958, 261–297.

Naik, M. D., and K. P. Nair, "Multistage Replacement Strategies," *Journal of the Operations Research Society of America*, Vol. 13, No. 2, March–April 1965, 279–290.

Naslund, Bertil, and Andrew Whinston, "A Model of Multi-Period Investment Under Uncertainty," *Management Science*, Vol. 8, No. 2, January 1962, 184–200.

Norton, John H., "The Role of Subjective Probability in Evaluating New Project Ventures," *Chemical Engineering Progress Symposium Series*, Vol. 59, No. 42, 1963.

Radnor, Michael, "A Critical Evaluation of the Field of Engineering Economy," *Journal of Industrial Engineering*, Vol. 15, No. 3, May–June 1964.

Reisman, A., "Capital Budgeting for Interrelated Projects," *Journal of Industrial Engineering*, Vol. 16, No. 1, January–February 1965.

Reisman, A., and E. S. Buffa, "A General Model for Investment Policy," *Management Science*, Vol. 8, No. 3, April 1962, 304–310.

Roberts, Harry V., "The New Business Statistics," *Journal of Business*, Vol. 33, January 1960.

Sharpe, W., "A Simplified Model for Portfolio Analysis," *Management Science*, Vol. 9, No. 2, January 1963, 277–293.

Smith, G. W., "Decreasing Utility for Money and Optimal Corporate Debt Ratios," *Engineering Economist*, Vol. 13, No. 2, Winter 1968.

Swalm, R. O., "Capital Expenditure Analysis—A Bibliography," *Engineering Economist*, Vol. 13, No. 2, Winter 1968.

_____, "Utility Theory—Insights Into Risk-Taking," *Harvard Business Review*, Vol. 44, No. 6, November–December 1966.

Teichroew, Robichek, and Montalbano, "Mathematical Analysis of Rates of Return Under Uncertainty," *Management Science*, Vol. 11, No. 3, January 1965, 395–404.

Terry, Herbert, "Comparative Evaluation of Performance Using Multiple Criteria," *Management Science*, Vol. 9, No. 3, 1963.

Thompson, W. W., Jr., "Some Mathematical Models for Evaluating Investment Strategies," *Journal of Industrial Engineering*, Vol. 17, No. 2, February 1966.

Van Horne, J., "Capital Budgeting Decisions Involving Combinations of Risky Investments," *Management Science*, Vol. 13, No. 10, October 1966.

Walker, Ross, G., "The Judgment Factor in Investment Decisions," *Harvard Business Review*, March–April 1961.

Weinwurm, Ernest H., "Measuring Uncertainty in Managerial Decision Making," *Management International*, Vol. 3, No. 3/4, 1963.

White, James McDonald, "Some Comments on Decision Theory Under Uncertainty and Minimax," *Engineering Economist*, Vol. 8, No. 4, Summer 1963.

Wilson, Charles Z., "Budgeting Appliance Saturation Studies: A Cost of Uncertainty Approach," *Management International*, Vol. 4, No. 2, 1964.

Winfrey, Robley, "Statistical Analysis of Industrial Property Retirements," Bulletin 125, Engineering Experiment Station, Iowa State College, 1936.

Index